Communicating In A Crisis

A guide for management

Communicating In A Crisis

A guide for management

Rene A. Henry

Author of *You'd Better Have A Hose
If You Want to Put Out the Fire*

Gollywobbler Productions

LIBRARY OF CONGRESS CATALOGING-IN-PUBLICATION DATA

Henry, Rene A. (1933-
Communicating In A Crisis: A guide for management
Rene A. Henry – 1st ed.
          p.   cm.
          Includes biographical references and index

      1. Crisis communications. 2. Crisis management. 3. Public relations.
      4. Risk communications. 5. Public Affairs 6. Customer service.
      7. Reputation management. I. Title

Library of Congress Control Number: 2008928463

ISBN # Hardcover: 978-0-9674535-1-4
          Paperback: 978-0-9674535-2-1

© 2008, Rene A. Henry

Gollywobbler Productions
Seattle, Washington

First Edition, 2008

10 9 8 7 6 5 4 3 2 1

Printed in the U.S.A. on acid-free paper meeting NISO standards for permanency of paper for printed materials.

Cover design by Jack Cullimore
Jack Cullimore Graphic Design, Ilwaco, Washington

Other Books by Rene A. Henry

Offsides! Fred Wyant's Provocative Look Inside the National Football League,
Gollywobbler Productions and Xlibris, 2001

You'd Better Have A Hose If You Want To Put Out the Fire,
Gollywobbler Productions, 2001

Bears Handbook – Stories, Stats and Stuff About Baylor University Football,
co-author with Mike Bishop, Midwest Sports Publishing, 1996

Marketing Public Relations – the HOWs that make it work!,
Iowa State University Press, hardcover 1995, paperback 2000

MIUS and You – The Developer Looks At A New Utility Concept,
co-author with Joseph J. Honick and Richard O'Neill,
U.S. Department of Housing & Urban Development, 1980

How To Profitably Buy & Sell Land, John Wiley & Sons, 1977

Special Thanks

The author wishes to specially thank the following for their assistance with this book –

Clive E. C. Banfield, KSJ, St. Thomas, U.S. Virgin Islands

Jay W. Bell, marketing and communications consultant, Forestville, California

Jonathan Bernstein, president, Bernstein Crisis Management, Sierra Madre, California

Pat Boyle, emergency planner, U.S. Environmental Protection Agency, Philadelphia, Pennsylvania and former senior director of communications for the American Red Cross Southeastern Pennsylvania Chapter

Jack Cullimore, Jack Cullimore Graphic Design, Ilwaco, Washington

Hon. Cari Dominguez, former chair, Equal Employment Opportunity Commission and former assistant secretary of labor, Gaithersburg, Maryland

Michael Fineman, president, Fineman PR, San Francisco, California

Elise Friedbauer, Esq., Seattle, Washington

Deborah Gardner, CMP, speaker and president, Compete Better Now! LLC, Phoenix, Arizona

Joseph J. Honick, president, GMA International, Bainbridge Island, Washington

Anne Sceia Klein, president, Anne Klein Communications Group, Marlton, New Jersey

Tower Kountze, government relations advisor, Husch Blackwell Sanders, Omaha, Nebraska

Anastasia Kostoff Mann, chairman and CEO, Corniche Travel Group, West Hollywood, California

John Martin Meek, president and CEO, HMI, Inc., Green Valley, Arizona

Mary Miner, Edmonds, Washington

Professor Ken Mizrach, Seton Hall University, South Orange, New Jersey

John Myer, Esq., Seattle, Washington

Jack O'Dwyer, J.R. O'Dwyer Company and www.odwyerpr.com, New York, New York

C. Robert Paul, Jr., retired vice president public relations emeritus, U.S. Olympic Committee, Bayside, New York

Rich Perelman, president, Perelman, Pioneer & Company, Los Angeles; former vice president-Press Operations, Los Angeles Olympic Organizing Committee for the Games of the XXIII Olympiad (Los Angeles 1984)

Harvey P. Posert, former vice president of public and industry relations, Robert Mondavi Winery, St. Helena, California

Stephen M. Reed, associate vice president for external relations, office of the president, California State University, Monterey Bay, California

Catherine Ritzinger, Seattle, Washington

Gene Ritzinger, Seattle, Washington

Joan Ritzinger, Seattle, Washington

Joan Short, president of WorldWide Golf & Travel, Inc., Newport Beach, California

Dr. Melvin L. Sharpe, APR, Fellow PRSA, professor emeritus, Ball State University and former chair PRSA Educators Academy and College of Fellows, Muncie, Indiana

Jude Sotherlund, former deputy assistant secretary of labor, author and corporate consultant, Merritt Island, Florida

Lawrence Teller, senior advisor, U.S. Environmental Protection Agency, Philadelphia, Pennsylvania

John Vondras, former vice president AT&T Wireless, managing director AT&T Indonesia, and managing director Belize Telecom, Scottsdale, Arizona

John J. Walsh, Esq., senior counsel, Carter Ledyard & Milburn LLP, New York, New York

TABLE OF CONTENTS

1   A Crisis Can Strike Anytime, Anyplace, Anywhere 5

2   The Crisis Team and the Plan 31

3   Managing the Crisis 51

4   Who Said "Silence Is Golden"? 63

5   Stupid Is As Stupid Does 81

6   You Can Fight Back and Win 105

7   Do the Right Thing – Be Responsible and Win Public Support 127

8   Crises On Land, In the Air and on the Seas 151

9   Workplace Crises – Murder, Violence, Harassment and Discrimination 181

10   Even the Government Makes Mistakes 199

11   Foul! Is This Anyway to Play the Game? 213

12   Institutional Arrogance in the Ivory Tower 243

13   The Aggie Pigs and President Bush 263

14   The Importance of Customer Service 283

15   Closing the Book After an Incident 301

INTRODUCTION

From almost the day I began a career in public relations, I have had to deal with crises. There were no books to read, or guidelines to follow, and the communications strategy basically came down to using good, common sense and street-smarts. During the 1990s, I often wrote and spoke on crisis management and communications and I would give the audience prepared hand-outs with guidelines, tips and tactics. I decided that there was a need for a book on this subject, so in 2000, I authored *You'd Better Have A Hose If You Want to Put Out the Fire*. Since then a score of books have been published on this subject. But crises continue, and the people responsible for managing and communicating them, obviously are not buying, borrowing, or reading the books available to help them.

I wrote *Communicating In A Crisis* for the senior people in management who most likely will be part of the crisis response team and held accountable in a crisis – the CEO; executive vice president; general counsel; heads of public relations/public affairs/corporate communications, human resources, manufacturing/production, sales and marketing, and security. This book also will give entry and mid-level communications professionals an overview, and how-to approach to crises. It will serve as a checklist and reminder for senior practitioners.

As did my first book, *Communicating In A Crisis* should serve as a textbook for faculty to use with students, and as a resource not only for corporate executives, but also officials of other types of organizations including nonprofit, higher education institutions, trade associations, government at all levels, and NGOs.

The interaction between the public relations professional and the lawyer is very important to understand. A number of examples are included throughout this book, especially in Chapter 4, "Who Said Silence Is Golden?" I believe that if senior executives and attorneys had a better understanding of media relations and crisis communications, many crises could be contained as only a regrettable incident. To paraphrase the Spanish philosopher George Santayana, we need to anticipate the future by learning from the past.

I believe this, or any book on crisis communications, should also be required reading for students graduating from law school or business school, so they will at least have exposure to the subject before it becomes reality. However, Timothy Sullivan, the retired president of The College of William & Mary and former dean of its law school, once reminded me, "Lawyers make very little money preventing crises, and a lot of money resolving them." I had suggested to him a seminar on this subject for graduating law school students ready to take the bar exam and begin practice.

Whether or not it is this book, there should be at least one book on crisis management and communications in the library of every law firm, law school, business school and journalism-public relations school in the country, and only an arm's reach away from the CEO of a company or nonprofit organization, and the president or chancellor of a college or university.

Unfortunately, many management officials believe they are immune to crises. As a result, they do not have a crisis team or plan in place, and are either unprepared or underprepared to deal with a crisis. The public relations firm Burson-Marsteller surveyed the CEOs of a number of major corporations following the 9/11 terror attack and found that 81 percent of the companies reported that their existing crisis plans were inadequate, and only 63% had made an effort to re-evaluate their existing plans.

When Fred Thompson, a senior public relations executive reviewed my first book, he wrote: "This book is the closest thing to business preservation insurance that you will find. Keep it with all the other emergency numbers and manuals you rely on, because sooner or later, you're going to need it."

A new addition to this book is a summary check list at the end of each chapter. Faculty can use this as a review with students. Professionals can refer to the checklist for discussion in meetings with a crisis team, or during internal roundtables or workshops at any organization.

All of the anecdotes and case histories in the book reinforce the basic principles of managing and communicating in a crisis. Every case history presents a lesson to be learned. There are specific crises related to the travel and tourism industry in Chapter 8, the workplace in Chapter 9, governments in Chapter 10, sports in Chapter 11, and higher education in Chapter 12. All are relative to crises that can happen in any business or industry or nonprofit. A number of crises cited in this book could have been avoided with proper customer service. Chapter 14 is devoted to customer service.

Every company, organization and institution is vulnerable to five generic crises that are outlined in Chapter 1. Additionally, each is vulnerable to crises specific to its business, product, or service. Chapter 1 also outlines 10 ways to prevent situations from becoming crises, and how to manage and communicate during a crisis.

In my 50-year career as a public relations counselor, I have been involved in crises faced by many different types of organizations. Among these were the largest owner and producer of California redwood lumber at a time when environmentalists advocated taking private timber lands for a national park; a large university where I headed university relations and advised the president and was a member of his executive cabinet; California agriculture interests during the time Cesar Chavez was organizing the United Farm Workers labor movement; and a telecommunications and media company operating in five countries where, as vice president, I directed its public relations activities. I have also owned and operated my own counseling firm, worked for both profit and nonprofit organizations, and the federal government. I have experienced crises involving product recalls, dealing with unions, government relations, and sports issues. Some of my experiences are documented in this book as case histories.

I have always practiced the philosophy of being proactive and aggressive. This includes fighting back when maligned. In media relations, where ethics and integrity matter, I believe there should be no time limit in righting a wrong. Chapter 6 has an example of how the *Columbia Journalism Review* did the right things five years after calling the head of a company a "world-class, phone-sex operator."

Crisis management and communications is no mystery, and it is not magic. It's simply basic, down-to-earth common sense, and being practical. Anticipation and preparation are critical, and an experienced, professional team must respond.

Communicating in times of crises encompasses all of the broad techniques of public relations, public affairs, corporate communications, and media relations. With the litigious nature of society today, there is no excuse for any organization not being prepared, and not having an action plan in place. However, even the best laid plans may not prevent a crisis. But being prepared as completely as possible with a plan and team in place certainly should make it much easier for all concerned to respond to any emergency.

RENE A. HENRY, September 2008

CHAPTER 1

A CRISIS CAN STRIKE ANYTIME, ANYPLACE, ANYWHERE

Exxon Valdez. Bhopal. Three-Mile Island. ValuJet. Watergate. Tylenol. TWA 800. Texaco. Monicagate. Pepsi. Waco. "Mad Cow" disease. E-coli. Atlanta's Olympic Park.

When I wrote *You'd Better Have A Hose If You Want to Put Out the Fire* in 2000, my first book on crisis management and communications, I knew that people throughout the world would immediately recognize these as major crises. In less than a decade, there is a new list of immediately recognized crises: 9/11. Katrina. Columbine. The D.C. sniper. Virginia Tech. Subprime mortgages. Enron. Minneapolis Interstate bridge collapse. Ford and Bridgestone/Firestone. Tainted and poisoned toothpaste and pet food. WorldCom. Recall of toys made in China. Add to this list scores of major crises in collegiate and professional sports. And every decade there will be scores of more crises to add to the list.

We have always had crises, and we always will have crises. Many crises are inevitable and will happen regardless of any measures taken to prevent them. How a company, organization, institution or individual responds to a crisis is critical to its public image and reputation and sometimes even survival.

What Is A Crisis?

Webster has a number of definitions for *crisis* ranging from the "turning point for better or worse in an acute disease or fever" and "an emotionally significant event or radical change of status in a person's life to an unstable or critical time or state of affairs in which a decisive change is impending, especially one with the distinct possibility of a highly undesirable outcome."[1]

Depending on how it is handled, a crisis can certainly make an executive sick or lead to a change of employment. The goal of a good incident manager is to contain the crisis and get closure as quickly as possible. The ultimate cost of a crisis is determined by the way it is managed and communicated, and could determine the future profitability and success of an organization.

Risk Management and Communications/Crisis Management and Communications

Risk management identifies a hazard and anticipates the risk to public safety, such as the release of toxic chemicals or an explosion. Risk managers also assess a company's potential financial and property loss in a crisis or national disaster, like a hurricane or tornado. It is no surprise that risk management is tied closely to insurance for the organization.

Crisis management is how a crisis is managed and hopefully avoided. Crisis communications is a critical element of crisis management, and determines how the story is told to the public at large, internal publics, and the media. Crisis communications also informs how the public to communications to before, during and after a crisis. Crisis management, crisis communications and risk management are all closely related. Often people will use risk communications interchangeably with crisis communications.

The rules that a professional communicator follows are virtually the same after a serious incident happens, and is ready to become, or already is, a crisis. Crisis communications is all-encompassing and anticipates and includes all hazards and risk.

Two Chinese symbols make up the word for crisis: *challenge* and *opportunity*.[2] In fact, the Chinese say there is an opportunity inherent in every crisis.[3] Public relations professionals who are practitioners in crisis management and communications should look at both the challenge and the opportunity in every crisis. Crisis communicators must consider what they can do to produce positive results.

Anyone Is Vulnerable

Any CEO who believes he or she is immune from a crisis is the most vulnerable. No one is immune from natural disasters and even terrorist attacks. Business and government, however, do not have a monopoly on crises. A list of crisis prone organizations would include higher education, sports, local public school districts, the entertainment industry, church and religious organizations, non-profit associations and virtually every field of endeavor.

Unfortunately, too many companies and organizations are either unprepared or underprepared for a crisis, or the CEO and senior management are in denial, saying, "It can't happen to me or my company."

The worst possible crisis is when someone dies. Even more catastrophic is if someone dies after using a company's product. In 1971, a man died after from botulism after eating a can of Bon Vivant vichyssoise soup, which was regarded as one of the leading gourmet soups on the market. The company recalled 6,444 cans of soup made in the same batch, but the U.S. Food and Drug Administration extended the ban to all Bon Vivant products and ordered the company shut down. Only five cans of soup were found contaminated with botulin toxin. But, the recall ended all public confidence in the company's products, and Bon Vivant filed for bankruptcy within a month. The company couldn't survive the crisis, and went out of business.[4]

Johnson & Johnson faced a similar crisis when people died after an outside party tainted Tylenol, but the company took a positive, aggressive approach to resolving the problem. While the airlines have had a multitude of problems in recent years, nothing impacts an airline harder than the crash of one of its planes.

Resolve the Crisis Before It Becomes Material For Television Or A Movie

The objective of crisis communications is to close the problem and resolve the conflict as quickly as possible. While some crises are unavoidable, others are exacerbated because of the way the problem is mishandled. There is no excuse for the discourtesy of not returning a telephone call or not taking the time to listen to a customer complaint. Customer service plays a very important role in crisis management as you will read in Chapter 14.

No CEO, director, senior manager, employee, shareholder or customer wants to see negative headlines and stories repeated time and again in newspapers, magazines, and on television and talk radio, and be reminded of mistakes management made in not getting quick closure on an incident.

A continuing crisis generally will follow, with editorials, op/eds, letters-to-the-editor, satirical political cartoons and comments on Internet blogs. Depending on the type of crisis, chances are that it will be written into a joke, monologue or skit for *Saturday Night Live*, Jay Leno, David Letterman, Conan O'Brien, *The Daily Show* with Jon Stewart, and Jimmy Kimmel. If political in any way, it may be further exploited by television's Mark Russell and political cartoonists on the editorial and op/ed pages of leading newspapers.

Gary Trudeau, creator of the "Doonesbury" comic strip that is syndicated internationally, took Nike to task for its manufacturing overseas, for exploitive labor practices and domestic marketing practices. Millions of daily newspaper readers throughout the world saw Nike satirized for several months. Jokes and other uncontrollable gossip and rumors will flourish – especially on the Internet with its myriad of blogs, bulletin boards and chat boards.

There is always the probability the crisis could become a television movie-of-the-week or a feature film, either in a true sense or one where the incident is fictionalized for legal purposes. In the case of a film, the crisis will be replayed for as many as seven-to-10 years and longer – first in movie theaters, then followed by cassette sales, re-run in theaters, television, foreign distribution, primary cable networks and then secondary cable networks.

Crisis can also become the story line in a popular television drama series or a sitcom. Within weeks after an incident, or crisis, there is a remarkable similarity between what happened and how a screenwriter has portrayed it on *Boston Legal,* any of the *Law & Order* or *CSI* programs, *Gray's Anatomy, Shark* or other popular television series. Then there are re-runs on cable, and many other popular series that were once aired in Primetime remind people of past crises.

A best-selling book, *A Civil Action*, and a film based on that book, again made public a 1980 environmental lawsuit against W. R. Grace. Although neither proven in court nor supported by scientific research, the lawsuit alleged that Grace and Beatrice Foods had contaminated municipal wells and drinking water, sickening the residents of Woburn, Massachusetts. The Disney/Touchstone film, was released in December 1998, nearly 20 years after the crisis, with a $25 million promotional budget. While Grace management said it had taken significant steps to improve its environmental policies and programs during the previous 10 years, it felt the movie painted an inaccurate and misleading picture of the company.[5]

However, it wasn't long before Grace was back in the news again. The U.S. Environmental Protection Agency determined that vermiculite ore mined at the former Grace mine in Libby, Montana was contaminated with asbestos. Grace's Zonolite insulation for attics was made from vermiculite and installed in some 35 million homes across the U.S.

By early 2002, Libby residents were asking the EPA to declare a health emergency that would allow EPA to remove the Zonolite attic insulation from homes in the area. A story that December in the *St. Louis Post-Dispatch* reported that in April 2002, Christine Todd Whitman, former governor of New Jersey and then administrator of EPA, was ready to warn the public of asbestos in Grace's Zonolite insulation, but the White House Office of Management and Budget quashed the announcement.[6] On April 10, 2002, William M. Corcoran, vice president of Grace, said that the insulation releases only small amounts of dust over a long period of time. However, unrelated or related killing the story might be, in December 2001, Halliburton, the company where Vice President Dick Cheney once served as CEO, faced nearly $125 million in asbestos-related liabilities after losing three lawsuits, and investors were selling the stock.

Lawsuits were filed by mining employees as well as homeowners who owned the contaminated insulation. Any possible resolution was further delayed in November 2003 by U.S. District Court Judge Judith Fitzgerald in Pittsburgh.[7] In September 2005, Grace sent letters to 700 of 870 Libby area residents enrolled in the company's medical plan, telling them they either no longer have an asbestos-related disease or may not be as sick as they thought they were. The first letter told them that a review by medical experts indicated they had no asbestos-related condition and the second letter acknowledged the presence of an asbestos-related "condition" or "illness." The letters immediately prompted a groundswell of opposition and frustration from asbestos patients whose benefits were being reduced.[8]

It was three years later before Judge Fitzgerald ruled that asbestos found in the Zonolite attic insulation "does not pose an unreasonable risk of harm" and denied the plaintiff's motion for a ruling on the claims. She said that evidence has established the risk of exposure is "less than that of dying in a bicycle accident, drowning or from food poisoning."[9]

In an unrelated case, the state of New Jersey alleged that two former Grace executives had lied when they claimed asbestos contamination at the company's Hamilton Township plant had been cleaned up in conformance with state regulations when it was closed in 1995.[10] Following the release of the Disney movie *A Civil Action*, how believable would Grace's reputation be in defending the vermiculite and asbestos charges in a court of public opinion?

Pacific Gas and Electric Company, the energy giant known as PG&E, was singled out in the movie *Erin Brockovich* which dramatizes the true story of Erin Brockovich's fight against PG&E. Her investigation discovered a systematic cover-up of the industrial poisoning (Hexavalent chromium) of the water supply in the town of Hinkley, California that threatened the health of the entire community. In the movie, released in 2000, she found that PG&E was responsible for the extensive illnesses diagnosed among residents of Hinkley and she fought to bring the company to justice. The film's tagline is: "She brought a small town to its feet and a huge company to its knees." Julia Roberts won the Academy Award's Oscar for best actress playing Brockovich. The film has been shown around the world in theaters and on television and is regularly replayed on cable channels.[11]

When the movie *The Incident* was released, Brown & Williamson and all tobacco companies suffered another public setback about corporate honesty and integrity.

Two California public utilities took action by anticipating how public sentiment could be turned against them if Arthur Hailey's *Overload* were made into a movie or television mini-series as was *Hotel, Wheels, Moneychangers* and his other novels. In the first chapter of *Overload*, an elderly couple is found frozen to death in their Chicago home after the utility company cut off service. In the 1970s, knowing Hailey's book soon would be published and later made into a movie, Pacific Lighting and Southern California Gas Co. formed a media company that produced several successful feature films, television documentaries and movies of the week. It had a good track record and the ownership of the company was not well known. The media company acquired all of the movie and TV rights to *Overload,* promptly shelved it, and then disbanded the company. This is truly anticipating a crisis and taking preventive steps to protect image and reputation.

Five Generic Crises

Almost every company, organization and institution is vulnerable to five generic crises. These should be included in any crisis management and communications plans.

1. Terrorism

While there had been terrorist attacks throughout the world for decades, Americans were awakened on 9/11 to the cold fact that it can happen in the U.S. The Department of Homeland Security regularly points out the vulnerability of the U.S. to another terrorist attack. There are numerous websites available with information that should be considered in developing any crisis plan. Organizations and experts that advise on terrorism and counterterrorism note that targets could be facilities that could cause an explosion or release biological, chemical, radioactive and other hazardous materials and the need to protect water and food supplies and computer networks.

However, all terrorist attacks in this category are not necessarily from Al-Qaeda or the Taliban. There are other violent dissident groups. Pacifist environmentalists climb and chain themselves in tall trees they do not want cut down. However, some eco-terrorism extremists are violent and have sabotaged operations of timber companies and even imbedded objects in trees that could seriously injure a logger doing his or her job. Some anti-development activists have actually set fire to model homes in new housing developments to protest building while others have torched gas-guzzling SUVs in the parking lots of automobile dealers.

Research laboratories and colleges and universities are susceptible to animal-loving extremists who have destroyed years of work by releasing animals and destroying and trashing files.

This form of terrorism is done to intimidate governments or civilians and is described by the FBI and law enforcement agencies as "eco-terrorism" or "eco-sabotage" because it is directed at things, property and machines. The organizations in the U.S. most commonly labeled as "eco-terrorists" are the Animal Liberation Front (ALF), Earth Liberation Front (ELF) and sometimes Earth First! In 2001, the FBI named ELF as "one of the most active extremist elements in the U.S." and a "terrorist threat."[12]

Companies with executives based in foreign countries also need to be concerned about kidnapping and extortion of the executive or members of their family.

2. Acts of Mother Nature

During the past 40 years, earthquakes, floods, hurricanes, landslides, tidal waves, tornadoes, volcanic eruptions, cyclones, wildfires, severe winter storms and other natural disasters have killed more people that the wars in the Iraq, Afghanistan and Vietnam. These catastrophes have killed some three million people, affected the lives of more than two billion others, and caused incalculable suffering and personal and property loss. Some of nature's most violent disasters strike quickly with little or no warning.

Natural disasters have tripled during the past decade and the number of people affected has risen. More than two million people died from natural disasters during the 1970s, and 800,000 during the 1990s.[13]

The December 26, 2004 Indian Ocean tsunami brought waves as high as 100 feet devastating the shores of Indonesia, Sri Lanka, India and Thailand. The October 2005 Kashmir earthquake in Pakistan killed some 75,000 people. May 2008 brought disasters to Myanmar and China. On May 2, Cyclone Nargis pummeled

Myanmar, formerly known as Burma, and killing more than 80,000 people and more than 56,000 still missing.

Just 10 days later, on May 12, an earthquake with a magnitude of 7.9 struck the Sichuan province of China killing more than 75,000, injuring more than 245,000, and leaving 4.8 million people homeless. Tens of thousands are still missing. It was the worst earthquake to hit China since the 1976 Tangshan disaster that killed 240,000 people. And between August 13 and September 26, 2004, Hurricanes Charley, Frances, Ivan and Jeanne ripped their way through Florida, causing more than $20 billion in damage. On August 28, 2005, Katrina tore past New Orleans and into the Gulf Coast, causing $81.2 billion in damage, becoming the worst natural disaster in U.S. history.[14]

There is no way to prevent Mother Nature from releasing her forces. However, both a logistics management plan and a communications plan need to be in place for potentially serious weather events. The Federal Emergency Management Agency (FEMA) has guidelines for different types of natural disasters, hazards and emergencies. Various types of disasters are outlined with recommendations what to do before, during and after the disaster. Crisis team planners should determine disaster risks prevalent for the location of their company's operations, and then go to the FEMA website for further background information and suggestions.[15]

3. Sexual Harassment and Discrimination

Sexual harassment and discrimination incidents are magnets for media coverage and one of the fastest-growing crisis categories affecting organizations today. Regardless how hard a company tries – how many seminars, workshops, education classes and discussion groups it holds – this still is a potential crises. If it happens, it is extremely embarrassing and often very expensive to the leadership.

Recent Supreme Court decisions and guidelines from the Equal Employment Opportunity Commission have made it clear to employers that training must be provided to all employees on how to prevent sexual harassment and other forms of workplace harassment and discrimination. Every preventive effort must be taken to avoid this crisis.

When I was looking for my first job after graduating from college and hoped to work on "Madison Avenue" in New York, I saw ads in *The New York Times* for jobs which I qualified for that had a bold face line at the bottom, "Ivy Only." If I answered the ad with a letter and my résumé there was never a response.

When I tried to drop off a résumé in person or schedule an appointment with someone in human resources, the receptionist behind a desk with a bronze "Ivy Only" plaque politely refused it. In those days, most of the major advertising and public relations agencies and publishing firms would only consider someone who had a degree from an Ivy League university. Women also had to come from their Ivy counterparts including Vassar, Mt. Holyoke, Smith and Wellesley, and were considered only for secretarial and receptionist positions, but only after they had graduated from a business school and could type.

Before the Civil Rights Act of 1964 (also referred to as Title VII) outlawed employment discrimination for race, color, religion, sex and national origin, the Age Discrimination In Employment Act of 1967 and the Americans With Disabilities Act of 1990, discrimination was blatant and pervasive. "Today, discrimination has become more subtle and thus more difficult to prove," says Naomi Churchill Earp, chair of the EEOC. "The graying of the workforce and the increased gender and ethnic diversity of the workforce also present new challenges and opportunities for employees, employers and the Commission."[16]

In 1995, the EEOC received more than 15,000 complaints of sexual harassment, double that of 1991.[17] In 2006, the EEOC received 75,768 charges of discrimination from the private sector and 7,802 from the federal sector.[18]

4. Violence in the Workplace

According to the Occupational Safety and Health Administration of the U.S. Department of Labor, two million assaults and threats of violence occur at work in the U.S. every year. Nothing can guarantee that an employee will not become a victim of workplace violence, but employers must take every step possible to reduce the odds.

The National Crime Victimization Survey reports that this included 396,000 aggravated assaults, 84,000 robberies and 1,000 homicides. A substantial number of employees have reported being bullied or harassed on the job, in addition to the assaults and threats.

"Going Postal" was the phrase used to describe violence in the workplace after 40 postal employees were killed by fellow workers in 15 shootings between 1986 and 1999.[19] But since then, postal workers have had more concern over anthrax and bioterrorism than guns. In October 2001, two workers at the Brentwood facility in Washington, D.C. died of anthrax symptoms and two more were diagnosed with the disease.[20] Within weeks, traces of anthrax were subsequently found in post offices in Wallingford, Connecticut and Princeton, N.J.[21] Just two years later, 11 neighborhood post offices and facilities were closed in the Washington, D.C. area because of possible anthrax contamination.[22]

According to former Postmaster General Marvin Runyon, murder is the No. 1 cause of death for women in the workplace.[23] In 97.5 percent of the cases, men with an average age of 36, were responsible for workplace murders. Firearms were used in 81 percent of the cases. And in one-fourth of the incidents, the person responsible committed suicide.[24]

5. Environmental Pollution

Ever since Rachel Carson wrote *Silent Spring* in 1962, people have become increasing conscious of the world in which we live. Who could ever argue against wanting clean air, clean water, clean soil or against having a safe and healthy place in which to live, work and play? However, it was nearly a decade after Carson's book was published that the first Earth Day was held on April 22, 1970, to further stimulate the green movement in the United States.

Even after it was announced that former Vice President Al Gore was awarded the 2007 Nobel Peace Prize, critics challenged him and scientists for their stand on global warming. Gore shared his prize with the Intergovernmental Panel on Climate Change, a United Nations network of some 2,000 scientists around the world. The Norwegian Committee praised both "for their efforts to build up and disseminate greater knowledge about man-made climate change."[25] Earlier in 2007, Gore won an Oscar from the Academy of Motion Picture Arts and Sciences for his documentary film about climate change, "An Inconvenient Truth."

No one wants to be labeled a polluter today, and with all of the green movements underway, any error will be immediately known to the public. Pollution also can be expensive when not complying with regulations results in fines by oversight agencies. Exxon to date has paid $3.5 billion in cleanup costs, government settlements, fines and compensation for its 1989 oil spill in Valdez, Alaska. It is fighting an additional $2.5 billion in punitive fines, and no value can be placed on how it has damaged the company's image to be responsible for the watershed pollution event of a generation.[26]

After a year-long federal lawsuit, American Electric Power of Columbus, Ohio, agreed to pay $4.6 billion to reduce chemical emissions that cause acid rain that has killed trees and fish and eaten away at national landmarks in the Northeast. The company was fined an additional $75 million in civil penalties and cleanup costs, and the total settlement is the largest single environmental enforcement in history. The settlement will save $32 billion a year in health costs for Americans, according to Granta Nakayama of the U.S. Environmental Protection Agency. "Less air pollution from power plants means fewer cases of asthma and other respiratory illness," he said.[27] It was not the first time AEP had been fined by the government. It had to pay $500,000 in 1998 for a number of violations at its Donald C. Cook nuclear plant in Bridgeman, Michigan. "We have acknowledged our responsibility to address the issues cited, fix them completely, and ensure this never happens again," said Robert Powers, AEP senior vice president.[28]

In October 2007, DuPont was found guilty of wanton, willful and reckless conduct, and ordered to pay $196.2 million in punitive damages to residents living near its former zinc-smelting plant in the small community of Spelter, West Virginia. The residents claimed that the company lied to them for decades about health threats from pollution. The total cost to DuPont amounts to nearly $400 million when combined with previous verdicts from earlier phases of the trial. "The verdict should tell state environmental regulators and executives of DuPont that it's not acceptable to put profits ahead of the health and safety and the environment of West Virginia," said Mike Papantonio, attorney for the plaintiffs.[29]

In May 1997, John Browne, then chief executive of British Petroleum PLC, broke ranks with other oil and gas executives when he said he believes the possibility of climate change cannot be discounted and should be acted upon. He announced plans for BP to invest $20 million to become one of the world's leading solar companies.[30] The tagline "beyond petroleum" was introduced while he headed BP. In 2001 he was named Lord Browne of Madingley by British Prime Minister Tony Blair.

The green image Browne wanted for BP was quickly tarnished by a March 23, 2005 explosion at a BP refinery in Texas City, Texas that killed 15 people and injured more than 170. A year later, BP spilled 201,000 gallons of crude oil into Alaska's Prudhoe Bay. In February 2004 a scheme to inflate the price of propane by buying massive quantities of the gas resulted in the Justice Department's charging four traders with 20 counts of mail and wire fraud and commodities violations. In 2007 BP agreed to pay $373 million to settle criminal and civil charges for overcharging propane consumers by millions of dollars and ignoring environmental warnings that led to the deadly-explosion and largest crude oil spill on Alaska's North Slope.[31] .

One company created a new crisis for itself when environmental group Greenpeace said it had a leaked copy of the company's crisis management plan. According to Greenpeace, the company's crisis plan recommended labeling environmental critics as "terrorists," threatened to sue "unalterably green" journalists, and dispatched "independent scientists" on media tours to counteract bad news for the industry.

The company failed to anticipate the worst of worst-case scenarios – that some conscientious person would obtain the plan and leak it," said Shelley Stewart of Greenpeace. "Lying is a growth industry," she said regarding the public relations firm that prepared the plan. The organization used the leaked copy to mount its own public relations campaign and supposedly made copies of the plan available to the public, creating a crisis that was not anticipated.[32]

Corporate American Created Greed Crises in the 1990s

Corporate America introduced a new type of crisis during the 1990s that was generated totally by greed. One of the biggest crisis newsmakers was the collapse of Enron. Kenneth Lay, CEO and chairman, and Jeffrey Skilling, who became CEO, were guilty of fraud and conspiracy. Lay, who once was one of Houston's most respected power brokers and philanthropists, died July 5, 2006 and his conviction was vacated. Skilling was sentenced to 24 years and four months in prison. Andrew Fastow, former chief financial officer, was sentenced to seven years in prison. In all, there were 34 criminal defendants from the company's senior management.[33]

Dennis Kozlowski, former CEO of Tyco International, and Mark Swartz, former chief financial officer, were found guilty of stealing $600 million from the company to fund extravagant lifestyles. Both were sentenced September 19, 2005 to 8-1/3 years to 25 years in prison, fined and ordered to pay restitution.[34]

Two telecom executives also were sent to jail. Bernard Ebbers, founder and former CEO of WorldCom, was convicted of fraud and conspiracy in 2005 in what was the largest accounting scandal at the time in the U.S. He was sentenced to 25 years in prison.[35] Joe Nacchio, former head of Qwest, was forced to resign during a multi-billion dollar accounting scandal. He was sentenced to six years in prison for illegally selling $52 million in stock while not telling his investors that Qwest faced serious financial risks.[36]

John Rigas, the founder and CEO of Adelphia Communications and his son, Timothy, former chief financial officer, were convicted of conspiracy, bank fraud and 15 charges of securities fraud. John Rigas at age 80 was sentenced to 15 years in prison. His son was sentenced to 20 years. The family had run the company for more than 50 years and investors lost billions when the company collapsed.[37]

Samuel D. Waksal, former CEO of ImClone Systems, was sentenced to 87 months in jail and fined $3 million for charges of insider trading and fraud. He tried to sell his stock in the company after hearing that the company's application for a cancer drug Erbitux was going to be rejected by the U.S. Food and Drug Administration.[38] He shared this information with his friend, Martha Stewart, who then was convicted of a felony other than inside trading, sentenced to prison and fined. Ironically, just eight months later the FDA approved Erbitux for treatment of colorectal cancer.[39]

Fraud, conspiracy and stealing by CEOs and corporate leaders cannot be anticipated with a communications plan in place. The professional responsible for public relations in the company will have to be sufficiently experienced and use his best judgment in knowing how to tell the story.

Business and Industry Related Crises

In addition to the five generic crises, each business and industry will have crises specific to its products or services. It doesn't take a Ph.D. or even an M.B.A. to know that if you are in the oil business and have storage tanks or tankers transporting oil across oceans and rivers, that the single biggest crisis could be an oil spill. Or if you are in the food or restaurant business, you want to worry about E-coli bacteria, salmonella or other forms of contamination. An airline will need plans in place for a terrorist attack or hijacking, a crash, weather and delays. A chemical company needs to know what to do in the event of an explosion, a fire, a leak of oil or a chemical into a lake, river or other public area. Colleges and universities are vulnerable to a multitude of crises from violence and attacks on students and faculty to athletic scandals.

A hotel operator will want to protect against a fire, food poisoning, or an attack on a guest. Banks need to consider robbery and shootings and embezzlement. Hospital management will be concerned with deaths, an outbreak of infection, a stolen baby, food poisoning or a fire. If you operate an amusement park, you worry about someone being injured or killed on a ride. There is a risk associated with every product or service.

Cruise lines have had a number of crises in recent years including mysterious deaths, people falling overboard, food poisoning and outbreaks of Norovirus and other viral and infectious diseases. Utility companies including telephone, electric, gas, cable television and Internet providers need to be prepared to deal with interruption of service to customers.

Almost every year there seems to be a recall by an automobile or truck manufacturer for one reason or another. Toy manufacturers have had their share of recalls when a product is not considered safe for children.

Every company, organization and institution needs to take an in-depth look at its manufacturing and sales processes, its products and services, and anticipate any possible specifically-related crisis.

How to Prevent Situations From Becoming Crises

There are 10 steps a company, organization or institution needs to take or have in place to hopefully prevent a crisis, quickly close the crisis, or to meet the crisis as a challenge and create a positive opportunity.

1. Anticipate and Have A Plan

This will be discussed in more detail in the Chapter 2. Anticipate every possible crisis and "what if ..." every possible incident and scenario. Organize a crisis management and communications team, and then create a detailed plan to communicate and be in a position to control the message to the media and all publics.

2. Respond Immediately

When a crisis strikes, respond immediately. Have the spokesperson prepared and ready to go. Follow the steps outlined in the crisis communications plan and put the team into action. The first few hours are most important in establishing credibility and building public trust and believability. Do not stonewall. Be responsive to the media and inform the people who need to be kept informed, especially employees, shareholders, vendors and customers.

Eliminate "no comment" from your vocabulary. One way or the other, the media will get information, but it may be inaccurate and the sources unreliable. In a crisis, perception is stronger than reality and emotion stronger than fact. When those responsible do not communicate, the crisis still gets played out in the media and possibly even later in court.

The communications plan should "what if..." all potential situations, and in many cases a news release can already be prepared for media distribution. For example, if a crisis team believes the company may be a target for a labor strike, a news release can be prepared, approved by all concerned and put on the shelf for future use. One former client faced a situation where the two top officers traveled frequently, and might not be reachable for a quick response to the media. Having a pre-approved news release would allow the company to quickly respond until the top executive could be reached.

If there is potential of litigation, either as a plaintiff or defendant, have detailed fact sheets and background materials prepared and ready to release to the media when needed.

Use the company's website as one of the important information vehicles and have someone assigned to keep it constantly updated.

3. Do Not Overtalk

Just the opposite of stonewalling, do not overtalk or release information without having all of the facts. Never speculate on what may or may not be happening. Be sure to analyze each situation for its newsworthiness. Some information may not warrant media attention. Former White House Press Secretary Marlin Fitzwater said: "You don't have to explain what you don't say."[40]

You don't have to answer every question. Just because a question is asked doesn't mean you have to answer, but you should have some kind of response. In any crisis, there are questions that you simply cannot or should not answer. Hypothetical questions, proprietary questions and speculative questions should be politely turned away. The spokesperson needs to be trained and reminded that he cannot be expected to know the answer to every question asked. But never withhold information that should be disclosed.[41]

4. Always Tell the Truth

Never lie or deceive the media or public with misinformation. Sir Winston Churchill once said: "A lie gets halfway around the world before the truth has a chance to get its pants on."[42] It is all right to say "I don't know" if you don't have the facts. The media and public will respect you for that, and know that you are telling the truth. Never speculate. Colin Powell said it is best to get facts out as soon as possible, even when new facts contradict the old. "Untidy truth is better than smooth lies that unravel in the end anyway," he wrote in his book, *My American Journey.*[43]

According to a survey conducted by the Porter/Novelli public relations firm, 95 percent of people are more offended about a company lying about the crisis than the crisis itself. Even worse, 57 percent polled believe that companies either withhold negative information or lie.[44]

However, if you are in a crisis in a political campaign in the State of Washington, the state's Supreme Court, in a 5-4 decision, declared that lying is not unconstitutional, or, put another way, it's just fine.[45]

5. Accept Responsibility

If there is a problem, admit it. Be accountable and accept responsibility. There is an old Belizean Creole proverb, *bad ting neba gat owner*, which literally means bad things never have owners. Everybody disclaims responsibility when things go wrong.

Today almost no one wants to be responsible or held accountable for their actions. Fingers are always pointed at someone else. Real life situations all too often mirror a cartoon by Bill Kean, creator of the comic strip "The Family Circus." In one cartoon, all of the balloons have the children saying "not me" in response to a "who is responsible?" question.

Today's leaders in government and business and even the media have fueled a rising tide of public distrust and skepticism. The sooner a company accepts responsibility for its actions, the stronger is its credibility with the general public and the media. In any crisis situation, the faster a company, organization, institution or individual tells a public it is responsible and accountable, the faster it will be able to manage communications and have its message believed or even better, closure on the incident and crisis.

Stanley O'Neal, CEO of Merrill Lynch, had the conviction to say he made a mistake because of the firm's involvement in the subprime mortgage game. "Some errors of judgment were made," O'Neal said as Merrill Lynch posted its first quarterly loss in six years and wrote down $7.9 billion on subprime securities, resulting in a $2.3 billion net loss and a reduced credit rating for the company. He accepted responsibility and admitted it, but also lost his job.[46]

In October 2004, Citigroup had banking problems in Japan because of ethical violations and lax controls that may have led to money laundering. Charles Prince, chairman and CEO, flew to Tokyo and with Douglas Peterson, CEO of Citibank Japan, confronted what happened by publicly apologizing and making amends, Japanese-style. A photograph of the two men bowing deeply, bent forward from the waist and heads lowered, was transmitted around the world. Prince then fired three top executive responsible for the violations.[47] Just three years later, Prince resigned as head of Citigroup in the wake of a $6.5 billion third quarter writedown and an estimated additional $8 to $11 billion in losses because of sharp declines in the value of subprime-related securities.[48]

In research done by *IR Magazine,* some 5,000 Wall Street security analysts surveyed rated Citigroup as the worst communicator and JPMorgan Chase as the best during the subprime mortgage crisis. Analysts said Citigroup was the least effective in disclosing its exposure. "There was a feeling that they didn't know the full extent or were attempting to soft-pedal it," said Neil Stewart, the magazine's executive editor.[49]

Ronald J. Alsop, staff reporter for *The Wall Street Journal,* believes doing the right thing, no matter how painful, is especially important in a crisis. In his book, *The 18 Immutable Laws of Corporate Reputation,* he cites how Johnson & Johnson did the right and trustworthy thing in 1982 in responding to Tylenol poisoning with its product recall. He compares this with how Roman Catholic bishops covered up incidents of sexual abuse by priests and put the church's reputation above the interests of its parishioners. "Cover-ups almost never work. Why? Because today almost anyone can disseminate information quickly and widely on the Internet, where it can be seen by millions of people," writes Alsop. "In addition, the Internet is a key source of story ideas for many mainstream news reporters and editors."[50]

A company's liability issues may need to be resolved with the attorneys involved but winning in the court of public opinion, in the long run, is far more important that winning a decision in court. Never go into a denial mode. The media and the public will believe a spokesperson who accepts responsibility, and this is one way to build public trust.

6. Select the Right Spokesperson

Determine in advance who will speak for the company in the event of a crisis. More than likely there will be several individuals who are the only ones authorized to speak for the organization during a crisis. Have one individual designated as the primary spokesperson and another as the backup. Additionally the company should have individuals who can serve as technical experts or advisors, such as a financial expert, engineer, or someone who can speak about a highly technical subject.

Too often the wrong person speaks publicly, and others, because of an "ego syndrome" just want to get in front of a camera. The names of those who are authorized to speak needs to be communicated to all so they understand that requests for comment by the media or anyone else must be directed to an authorized spokesperson.

Always remember that the media will seek out anyone for a soundbite, so there must be a policy in the crisis plan and everyone made aware of it regarding the official voice of the company or institution.

It is important that the person be believable. This doesn't mean being slick or polished. He must be someone the public will trust to tell the truth. All spokespersons must be professionally trained and completely prepared for the media. If time permits, there should be a rehearsal before any media interviews to review all anticipated questions.

"The CEO should be one of the spokespersons, but not necessarily the primary spokesperson," says Jonathan Bernstein, of Bernstein Crisis Management, a national consultancy on crisis management headquartered in Southern California. "The fact is that some chief executives are brilliant business people, but not very effective in-person communicators."[51]

Public opinion has shown that lawyers are not the most trusted of spokespersons and especially outside consulting attorneys. It is best to get the CEO or one of the most senior executives in front of the media as soon as possible.

7. Stop Rumors and Correct Misinformation

A no-response is almost the same as implied consent. When something incorrect is printed or said, immediate action should be taken to point out the error and ask for a correction. Otherwise, the media involved will only assume that what was written or said is correct. One publication could print a damaging story with incorrect information. Another publication could assume the information was correct and refer to it in a followup article. When repeated over and over, fiction and errors become fact.

In a matter of seconds, the Internet can spread misinformation or rumors around the world. This is why it is so important to have open lines of communication with all employees, customers, vendors, shareholders and friends. You want to control your message as best as you possibly can but you can't control what others say. The media will seek out anyone with any connection to the company or organization for information and a quote. Be sure that all authorized spokespersons have correct and current information.

Just as there are clipping services that read newspapers and magazines for any mention of a company or organization, and services that monitor radio and television programs, there are monitoring services that can be retained that regularly check the Internet for information. Adversaries, disgruntled employees and former employees, and whistleblowers can leak confidential information, misinformation or outright lies that are republished on Internet websites, message boards or blogs, and eventually find their way into mainstream media.

Ronald J. Alsop believes companies must protect their corporate reputation by refuting any harmful rumor that is picking up momentum on the Internet. "Ignoring the spread of a detrimental rumor is dangerous in the extreme," he writes. "The correct strategic response is to neutralize the attack with a factual response." He cites Coca-Cola as one company which is a frequent target of many rumors, and which publishes denials and refutations on its own website, while others, including Nike, develop a separate websites devoted exclusively to refuting rumors.[52]

The electronic age has created entirely new problems for crisis managers and attorneys. "Thanks to modern technology, all a person needs to extract and use misinformation from a false, archived article is a PC, Google, and a disposition to work someone else's old material into an article on the theory that if Big Media reported it five years ago without repercussions, it must be true," says John J. Walsh, senior counsel of Carter Ledyard and Milburn, New York.[53] In most jurisdictions, after one year, statutes of limitation expire on libel and defamation claims against a publication.

Walsh notes that a media crisis based on an article or broadcast can occur without warning, and often can be precipitated by a whistleblower and a quick decision by the media to go public. He says the injured party can ask for a correction, a retraction or an apology. A correction by the publisher tells the public that a mistake was made and provides the correct facts. A retraction advises the public that specific statements are withdrawn, usually accompanied by an apology or at least a statement of regret.[54]

I consider Walsh one of the finest First Amendment attorneys in the country today, and if a company, organization, institution or individual is facing a crisis, I would want him involved at the first hint of a negative media story. Working in concert with public relations counsel, I would have him visibly lead the response effort directed at media editors and senior management. A call or letter from Walsh often can get a proposed story dropped or substantially and favorably altered.

Sometimes the information you release could be wrong, and this must be corrected. During the Persian Gulf Desert Storm operation, Colin Powell had an argument with General Norman Schwarzkopf regarding television comments that four Scud missile sites had been taken out when, in fact, air reconnaissance photos showed that the targets were fuel trucks. A CNN camera crew shot film of the destroyed trucks and contradicted Schwarzkopf. Powell told his general to admit the error. "Protect your credibility, it's a precious asset," said Powell. "It is better to admit a mistake than be caught in one."[55]

8. Show Compassion and Remorse

It is not against the law to show compassion, sympathy, passion and remorse for victims and their families and friends. This often is when the public relations counsel and lawyers disagree. The public relations professional wants to win in the court of public opinion, and the lawyers are concerned about potential liability and losing in a court of law.

"Expressing sorrow or concern publicly in the wake of a tragic event is understandable. It is also critical," says Jeff Braun, founder and president of Crucial Communications Group, LLC, a Houston, Texas-based firm specializing in crisis and emergency response communications training and support. "Empathy or caring is a key component of credibility. And establishing credibility must be the overriding goal of any communication. If your audience does not see you as a credible source, you won't get your message across or be able to address people's concerns. Empathy and caring accounts for half of a person's credibility and is assessed in the first 30 seconds. You have to convince the listener that you are credible, believable, trustworthy, and even likeable."

Compare what Braun recommends with how San Diego State University responded when a student opened fire in a classroom and shot and killed three faculty members who didn't agree with his thesis. When the university refused to comment, the media interviewed a maintenance worker and two people who had been in the classroom when the shooting began.[56] The university missed an opportunity not only to tell its story, but to express remorse and show compassion for the loss of three members of its family as well as their families and friends.

9. Build Your Reputation Before A Crisis

Never take any chance of losing your credibility with the media and public. That is why it is so very important to establish your reputation before a crisis and have credibility in the bank. Build relationships with the media so they know you are telling the truth in the face of challenges from adversaries.

According to Harris Interactive, a company's reputation is often overlooked as a component of business growth. In today's market, consumer trust is at an all-time low.[57] Following the series of high-profile scandals that have irreversibly changed the corporate landscape, Hill & Knowlton believes the need to establish trust and confidence is more recognized than ever.[58]

The degree to which a company will get the public to believe its story will depend on the company's reputation before a crisis. Magazines will publish lists of "most admired companies" or "best companies to work for." But this doesn't always translate into winning public trust if the public relations department and the people who are in contact with the media have not established their reputation and credibility with the media.

But Americans today also are less trusting of the news media. Of 1,100 individuals surveyed, 42 percent responded that the media are not credible in general, and that television news, newspapers and magazines all were less credible than five years earlier. Only eight percent considered the government, and two percent considered political parties, to be believable sources of information.[59]

Scores of books have been written and are available on the subject of corporate reputation.

10. Listen

During a crisis, it is important to listen to what the public and adversaries are saying and to be sure that they, and the media, understand what you are saying. Listening is essential to communicating, negotiating, resolving conflicts and even avoiding crises. You have to be an active listener to anticipate the actions of others. However, listening is hard work. For some people, it is very difficult, but it can be learned. Listening is truly an admirable and enviable art for those who listen well.

From our earliest development years, we all are taught how to speak, read and write. No one is there to teach us how to listen. Stephen R. Covey ranks listening as one of his 7 *Habits of Highly Effective People*. "Seek first to understand, then to be understood," he says. "Most people don't listen with the intent to understand; they listen with the intent to reply. They're either speaking or preparing to speak."[60]

"The ability to listen to others is essential," says Harvard University's Dr. Lawrence Susskind, conflict resolution guru and author of *Dealing With an Angry Public*. "When high-ranking spokespersons or executives are being assaulted by those who are fearful, anxious, and angry, they must put aside their own feelings and defensiveness so they can listen carefully to what people have to say.

"Good leaders, effective in times of crisis, must be as keyed into their audience's interests as their own," Susskind adds. "You will not be able to acknowledge the concerns of others if you cannot hear them. Listening must be active. This means reiterating what has been heard to be sure the message has been received."[61]

In any conflict or negotiation, you must be an active listener. Focus on the speaker and your adversaries, take notes, ask questions, and make eye contact so they know you are listening. Communication must be two ways. Communicate your expectations clearly, accurately, timely and honestly. According to Covey, words represent only 10 percent of communication. The sounds we make and our inflection represents 30 percent, and our body language another 60 percent.

Remember that the less you say, the more someone else will be able to re-member what you say. It is just as important for someone listening to you to fully understand your message as it is for you to understand what they are saying. Saul Alinsky, who wrote the bible on nonviolent disruption, *Rules for Radicals*, says it best: "If you try to get your ideas across to others without paying attention to what they have to say, you can forget about the whole thing."[62]

Summary Checklist

- A crisis can strike anytime, anywhere.
- No company, organization, institution or individual is immune from a crisis.
- Get closure and resolve the crisis as quickly as possible.
- The five generic crises: 1) terrorism; 2) acts of nature; 3) sexual harassment and discrimination; 4) violence in the workplace; and 5) environmental pol-lution.
- Other crises: corporate greed; business and industry related.
- How to prevent situations from becoming crises:
    1. Anticipate and have a plan.
    2. Respond immediately.
    3. Do not overtalk.
    4. Always tell the truth.
    5. Accept responsibility.
    6. Select the right spokesperson.
    7. Stop rumors and correct misinformation.
    8. Show compassion and remorse.

9. Build your reputation before a crisis.

10. Listen.

Endnotes

[1] *Merriam-Webster's Collegiate Dictionary*, Tenth Edition, Merriam-Webster, Incorporated, Springfield, Mass., 1993, pg. 275.

[2] Council for Advancement and Support of Education, promotional flyer for "Crisis Management" seminar March 10-11, 1994, Atlanta, Ga., pg. 2.

[3] Raymond J. O'Rourke, "Learning from Crisis: When the Dust Settles," *The Public Relations Strategist*, Public Relations Society of America, Summer 1997, pg. 35.

[4] Wikipedia and Raymond J. O'Rourke, "Learning From Crisis: When the Dust Settles," *The Strategist,* Public Relations Society of America, Summer 1997, pg. 35.

[5] International Conference of the Public Relations Society of America, Boston, Mass., Oct. 19, 1998, presentation by Katherine Tynberg, president, The Tynberg Group, Inc., and Mark Stoler, assistant vice president for health and Jane McGuineness, director of corporate communications, W. R. Grace.

[6] Andrew Schneider, *St. Louis Post Dispatch*, Dec. 27, 2002 and Paul Peters, *Boise Weekly*, Aug. 15, 2007.

[7] Karen Dorn Steele, *The Spokesman-Review,* Boise, Idaho, Nov. 25, 2003.

[8] Lynette Hintze and Brent Shrum, *The Daily Inter Lake*, Kalispell, Mont., Sept. 25, 2005.

[9] Lynette Hintze, *Daily Inter Lake*, Kalispell, Mont., Dec. 19, 2006.

[10] Rita Cicero, staff writer, *Environmental Litigation Reporter*, Vol. 25, Issue 23, June 16, 2005.

[11] Wikipedia.

[12] Wikipedia.

[13] Ilan Noy, Department of Economics, University of Hawaii at Manoa, "The Macroeconomic Consequences of Disasters," Working Paper No. 07-7, February 2007.

[14] Associated Press August 27, 2006 and Wikipedia.

[15] Federal Emergency Management Agency, www.fema.gov/hazard/index.

[16] "A Message from the Chair," Annual Report of the U.S. Equal Employment Opportunity Commission, 2006.

[17] Michael Meyer, "School for Scandal – How to handle sexual-harassment charges," *Newsweek*, May 20, 1996, pg. 44.

[18] Annual Report of the U.S. Equal Employment Opportunity Commission, 2006.

[19] Lenny Savino, *The Philadelphia Inquirer*, Sept. 1, 2000, pg. A3.

[20] Laura Meckler, Associated Press, October 22, 2001.

[21] Associated Press, October 27, 2001 and December 2, 2001.

[22] CIDRAP News, November 7, 2003.

[23] *The New York Times*, Associated Press dispatch, December 18, 1994.

[24] Ibid.

[25] Walter Gibbs and Sarah Lyall, "Gore Shares Peace Prize for Climate Change Work," *The New York Times*, October 12, 2007.

[26] Lara Jakes Jordan, Associated Press, October 9, 2007.

[27] Lara Jakes Jordan, *op. cit.*, and MSNBC.com, October 9, 2007.

[28] Knight-Ridder/Tribune Business News, October 16, 1998.

[29] Vicki Smith, Associates Press, *The Herald-Dispatch*, Huntington, W. Va., October 19, 2007.

[30] Martha M. Hamilton, "Energizing Solar Power," *The Washington Post*, august 26, 1997, pg. D1.

[31] Lara Jakes Jordan, The Associated Press, October 26, 2007.

[32] Jonathan Bernstein, "Bleach Company's Crisis-Management Plan Leaked to Greenpeace," *Media Insider*, PR Newswire, September 15, 2000.

[33] *Houston Chronicle*, www.chron.com/news/specials/enron.

[34] CBS News, www.cbsnews.com/stories.

[35] Wikipedia.

[36] Sandy Shore, Associated Press, July 27, 2007.

[37] MSNBC, Associated Press, July 8, 2004.

[38] Matthew Harper, *Forbes*, June 10, 2003.

[39] ACS News Center, American Cancer Society, February 13, 2004.

[40] Judy A. Smith, "Learning from Crisis: In the Heat of Battle," *The Strategist*, Public Relations Society of America.

[41] Fraser P. Seitel, "Crisis Management 'To Don't' List," Part II, *O'Dwyer's PR Daily*, May 16, 2001.

[42] Quotations Site by Danielle Hollister, www.bellaonline.com.

[43] Colin Powell with Joseph E. Persico, *My American Dream*, Ballantine Books, 1996, pg. 285.

[44] *Public Relations Journal*, September 1993.

[45] Joseph Honick, "Restore Dignity To Political Debate," www.odwyerpr.com, October 11, 2007.

[46] Matthew Goldstein, "Why Merrill Got Burned So Badly," *Business Week*, November 5, 2007.

[47] Lorelei Albanese, "Burson-Marsteller Study Finds Boardroom Lacks Communications Skills," *Caribbean Business*, July 7, 2005, pg. 34.

[48] Tomoeh Murakamitse, "Citigroup chief quits," *The Washington Post,* November 5, 2007.

[49] "Survey: Citigroup Is Worst Sub-Prime Communicator," odwyerpr.com, March 28, 2008.

[50] Ronald J. Alsop, *The 18 Immutable Laws of Corporate Reputation,* Wall Street Journal Books, The Free Press, Simon & Schuster, Inc., 2004.

[51] Jonathan Bernstein, "The Ten Steps of Crisis Communications," Bernstein Crisis Management, www.bernsteincrisismanagementcom.com.

[52] Ronald J. Alsop, *op. cit.*

[53] John J. Walsh, "Fighting False Allegation," *GC New York*, March 14, 2005.

[54] Ibid.

[55] Colin Powell, *op. cit.*

[56] Matthew Fordahl, Associated Press, "Three slain on campus; alleged gunman was defending thesis," *Bryan-College Station Eagle*, Bryan, Texas, August 16, 1996, pg. A3.

[57] Annual RQ 2006, Harris Interactive.

[58] Hill & Knowlton, Inc., Corporate Resolution Watch, 2006.

[59] National Family Opinion Consumer and Mail Panel, *Jack O'Dwyer's Newsletter,* August 7, 1996, pg. 2.

[60] Stephen R. Covey, *7 Habits of Highly Effective People*, Fireside, Simon & Schuster, Inc., 1990.

[61] Lawrence Susskind and Patrick Field, *Dealing With An Angry Public*, The Free Press, Simon & Schuster, Inc., 1996.

[62] Saul D. Alinsky, *Rules for Radicals*, Vintage Books, Random House, 1971.

CHAPTER 2

THE CRISIS TEAM AND THE PLAN

Anticipate. Plan. Respond.

Unfortunately, too many CEOs are not prepared to deal with a crisis when it happens. The public relations firm Burson-Marsteller conducted a survey after September 11, 2001 and 81 percent of CEOs in the U.S. who responded said their existing crisis plans were inadequate. What was even more surprising was that only 63 percent of these CEOs had since re-evaluated their existing crisis plans.

The 9/11 terror attack on the World Trade Center should have sent a message to every chair, president and CEO of a company, organization or institution in world to immediately evaluate how prepared they were in the event of a crisis. This was followed by the anthrax scare, and some people were afraid to open their mail. Then the sniper attacked virtually paralyzed the metropolitan area around Washington, D.C.

We have been living in a different world since 9/11. After the attack, the public was frightened and scared. Rhetoric, mixed signals and contradictory statements were coming out of the White House, CIA, FBI, Department of Justice and other federal agencies, which only made things worse. Americans didn't know what or whom to believe, so they didn't trust any of the messages they were receiving.

By October 2002, U.S. consumer confidence fell to its lowest level in nearly nine years. The Conference Board, an independent economic research firm in New York, pegged the index at 79.4, its fifth straight monthly decline from an average reading of 90 expected by economists. It also was the biggest month-to-month decline since a 17-point drop from August to September 2001.[1]

The Consumer Confidence Index is defined as the degree of optimism on the sate of the U.S. economy that consumers express through their activities of savings and spending. It is based on 5,000 households and has been issued monthly since 1985 when it was indexed at 100.[2]

Even today, too many CEOs are unprepared for a crisis. Business schools training future corporate leaders not only do not offer courses on crisis management and communications, or suggest them when taught in another college and the same university, but do not have seminars or workshops for graduating seniors to better prepare them for the real world. The same is true in our law schools today. So much of crisis planning and communications is just pure common sense.

"If you don't prepare, you will take more damage," says Jonathan Bernstein of Bernstein Crisis Management. "When I look at existing crisis management plans, what I often find is a failure to address the many communications issues related to crisis/disaster response. Organizations do not understand that. Without adequate communications:[3]

* Operational response will break down.

* Stakeholders (internal and external) will not know what is happening and quickly be confused, angry, and negative.

* The organization will be perceived as inept, at best, and criminally negligent, at worst.

A survey of 251 marketing executives by *BtoB* magazine and Eric Mower and Associates, Syracuse, N.Y.-headquartered national advertising agency, reported that 53 percent said their company has undergone a crisis that resulted in negative media coverage or a decline in sales or profitability. However, 57 percent said their company has no crisis-response plan prepared!

Just half of the 43 percent of companies that say they do have a crisis plan said they have trained spokespersons. And 10 percent of these expressed concern whether they would be able to implement the plan that is in place. Of the companies that said they experienced crises, 23 percent said it took 3-12 months for the brand to recover from a crisis; 13 percent up to two years; and 18 percent said that they had not recovered even after two years.[4]

Of the companies that did have a crisis plan in place, 29 percent said the plan was sufficient to protect the brand, 26 percent said it protects the brand somewhat, and 20 percent reported the plan does not protect the brand at all. Layoffs, shutdowns and business foreclosures precipitated 56 percent of the crises, followed by operational or services failures (45 percent) legal or ethical problems (33 percent) and a negative word-of-mouth attack by someone wanting to damage the business (32 percent).

"If companies choose not to be prepared for a crisis, they and shareholders will pay the price, because crises have a way of twisting and turning until they do serious bottom-line damage," said Peter Kapcio, director of reputation management services and head of the crisis communications practice at Eric Mower and Associates. "In most cases, it's not the initial trigger of the crisis that causes the damage; it's what follows a botched response."[5]

The First Step - Organize the Team

The first step to getting a plan is to organize a crisis team. Then develop the crisis management plan and the crisis communications plan. The CEO should name the chair of the team. In most cases this should be the person in charge of public relations or corporate communications. However, some CEOs, especially in smaller companies, may wish to head the team.

The structure of a team will vary according to company, organization and institution but must have ownership and leadership from the very top and a commitment of involvement. In a publicly held company, the team could be composed of:

- Vice president of public relations.
- Vice president of human resources.
- The executive vice president or senior vice president appointee and representative of the CEO.
- General counsel and head of legal affairs.
- Senior officer in charge of international relations if the company has operations in foreign countries.
- Vice president of sales and marketing.
- The chief financial officer or head of investor relations.
- A technical officer who knows the manufacturing, operations and technology processes.
- A customer service manager.
- The chief of security depending.
- Outside public relations counsel to provide guidance and experience with other clients. This is especially important if the public relations executive does not have sufficient crisis communications experience, and also to provide an outside opinion in the event of a disagreement with legal counsel.

The fewer number of people on the team, the better. Each member of the team must be completely committed and understand the importance of participating in the planning and implementation of the plan. Each will be given specific responsibilities during a crisis. A non-public company would have virtually the same team composition without representation from investor relations.

In companies with multiple operations, such as a manufacturing or chemical company with plants in a number of cities, or an oil company with various refineries, each local operation must have a crisis management and communications plan which mirrors that of corporate headquarters. Also there will be a policy established as to who speaks for the company and who releases information to the public.

A Different Team Structure for Higher Education and Non-Profits

The structure of a team would change slightly at a college or university, but still include the CEO or his or her representative, the heads of public relations (or university relations, whatever the title might be), business services, student affairs, human resources, legal and security. Added to this list would be the provost, executive director of the alumni association, the heads of development and the faculty senate, and a representative of the student body. Again, it would be prudent to consider retaining experienced outside public relations counsel for guidance.

In a volunteer driven non-profit charitable institution, such as a 501(c)(3), the executive director or head of staff operations and the president or chair elected by the members would be members of the team. Included again would be heads of public relations, human relations, development and legal. Being an organization of volunteers, the team should consider adding one or more members of its board of directors or representatives of the rank-and-file membership.

The Team's Challenge

The chair of the team has the responsibility for keeping the team and the plan current, calling periodic meetings of the team, and making any changes in team members, as required. A team should meet at least two times a year and preferably three. All team members must attend all meetings when called. At least once a year, and perhaps twice, the CEO should meet with the team.

There should be backup members of the team, who play the role of understudy, and must be as fully prepared and capable of responding if a team member is out of town, sick or otherwise cannot do his or her job when needed.

If the organization does not have a crisis plan, the newly appointed chair should talk with his counterparts at other similar companies, organizations and institutions that do have a plan in place and ask to borrow a copy. This could serve as a blueprint for developing the plan. This should be done well before the first meeting of the team.

Everyone on the team should be given a small, billfold-size, plastic encased card that has all telephone numbers (direct dial office, home, cell, pager and any others) and e-mail of every member of the team as well as any other individuals who may need to be contacted in the event of a crisis.

The team also needs to provide leadership. According to Jonathan Bernstein of Bernstein Crisis Management, intra-organizational infighting is one of the leading causes of crises, and plays a major role in exacerbating crises that may otherwise have remained minor.[6]

Who Gets Called and When

The crisis plans needs to detail who gets called and when. Some crises, such as an explosion or violent attack in the workplace will require an emergency response. Others, such as a complaint filed with the Equal Employment Opportunity Commission for discrimination will allow a reasonable time to respond.

Every crisis plan should have a cascading notification system used to activate the communications plan. Cascading notification permits one individual to contact several other individuals who in turn contact several others. In a crisis, the first person contacted or made aware of the crisis will know whom to call and notify.

The calling tree will vary according to the type of crisis. The plan should detail what happens, for example, if there is an explosion at a chemical plant miles away from headquarters or a violent attack in a manufacturing facility. There will be an on-side coordinator at each facility.

Here is an example of how a calling tree and notifications should be prioritized:

1. Those who must implement and manage the communications response, either on-site or at headquarters.
2. Those who will be asked to respond publicly regarding the crisis.
3. Those who will support the communications response.
4. Those with a special need-to-know, such as senior management, a victim's family, off-site response agencies and government officials.
5. The news media and the general public.[7]

The local operating head of the plant should be the first person notified and then it should be spelled out in order of priority whom he will notify at headquarters. This might be the head of manufacturing or a division vice president, who in turn would call the CEO and public relations director. If the plant has a public relations person on staff, that individual needs to be called immediately. This person in turn will notify his or her counterpart at the corporate office, and form a plan of action to deal with the crisis and local and area media. Keeping local community leaders and elected officials informed is critical.

In the case of violence in the workplace, a terrorist attack or a suicide, generally security will be the first to know. The plan should detail whom security calls next. If the crisis is one where a complaint of harassment or discrimination has been filed with an oversight agency, human resources generally will be the first to know. The plan needs to spell out the next person to be notified. If litigation is involved, chances are the first person to know will be the general counsel.

The first calls made are to get the crisis team organized and ready to respond. Every member of the crisis team will have a list of people to call. Every member of the public relations staff will have a list of names to call. And everyone called by these individuals will have other names to call. A calling tree needs to be created and periodically checked, with all numbers kept current. After internal management has been notified and the plan is being followed, the media will be the first to be called.

After the initial response, other publics need to be informed. The plan should have a means of communicating with employees. In advance, an employee hot line should be ready to use in the event of an emergency. Other ways of communicating the employees can be done on an intranet website, available only to people so authorized by the company, e-mail, or a system to send recorded messages to all employees.

If the company is publicly held, then a plan is needed to communicate to shareholders. This can be done through those responsible for investor relations. The plan should determine other important publics which need to be notified including customers and suppliers, labor leaders, and government oversight and regulatory agencies.

Develop a matrix listing all of the publics to be kept informed on the left, and all of the various types of potential crises along the top. Then in each box, a priority number should be assigned, depending on how quickly that group needs to be informed of the crisis.

Have Materials Prepared and Ready to Distribute

When any crisis unfolds, press materials should already have been prepared in anticipation of the problem. Fact sheets on the company, its products or services, biographies on the key executives and spokespersons, maps and diagrams, and other basic information should be current and ready to be downloaded from a computer to a printer to a copy machine and back to an Internet web page. Photographs of executives, buildings, products and technical drawings also are important, and should be made available to the media and posted on the web page.

In many situations, the first news release should already be prepared as part of the plan so there can be an immediate response while looking into all of the facts. This should be anticipated, depending on the possible crisis, such as a union problem or potential serious weather problem. You want to be able to respond in the event the CEO or spokesperson may not be readily available, or if the CEO wants legal counsel to sign off on a news release. Any delay in a response can increase the crisis and only create distrust by the media and the general public. Where possible, plan on even two or three general news releases that can be prepared in advance, approved by all involved, and then held in a safe place in the event they are ever needed.

A news release prepared in advance may not always work and be prepared once the facts are gathered, to move very quickly. Legal counsel must understand this priority. A delayed response is a negative factor that increases proportionately from the time of the incident to the time of the public announcement.

The Briefing Book

An important document to have prepared and immediately brought up to date with all issues involved in the crisis is a comprehensive briefing book. This will be organized so the spokesperson or any member of the crisis team or public relations team can use it to answer questions from the media.

The book will be organized by issues with answers based on the organization's policies. Each issue should be concise and brief, and almost in the form of a soundbite. Where facts may be challenged, they should have supporting documentation and reference footnotes. Spokespersons at the U.S. State Department and other federal agencies regularly use briefing books in briefings and meetings with the media. A briefing book also insures that everyone is giving the media and the public the same answer. The briefing book should be considered a living document, and during the time of the crisis pages may need to be added or changed daily, even hourly.

There is no need to distribute any briefing book to anyone until there is a crisis. And then it should be quickly reviewed to be certain it is current.

Have VNRs Ready

If the company has a product that is vulnerable to tampering, have video news releases, B-roll and photographs prepared and ready to distribute to refute any false claim. In 1993, a couple in Tacoma, Washington reported a syringe in a can of Diet Pepsi. Seattle media reported the story, prompting the U.S. Food and Drug Administration to issue a five-state alert advising consumers to inspect Diet Pepsi. Two days later a woman in Cleveland, Ohio made the same claim. This situation quickly escalated to 52 claims in 23 states, with people saying they found a wood screw, bullet, cracked vial, broken sewing needle and other objects in Diet Pepsi cans. The story was then reported on network television news and the major wire services.

Pepsi's crisis team invited the camera crews for an on-site visit to see how Diet Pepsi was canned, and to rule out any possibility of sabotage. Video news releases, produced and distributed by satellite to local television stations across the country, were aired on 403 stations and seen by 187 million viewers. Craig Weatherup, the company's CEO for North America, appeared on every major television network with B-roll to show that any contamination was virtually impossible in plants. Media advisories were distributed twice a day.

"If you're going to conduct your trial in the media, you've got to do it with the tools they're used to working with," said Rebecca Maderia, vice president of public relations. While the FDA officials concentrated on finding the sources of reported contamination, Pepsi concentrated on letting the public know the safety and reliability of its packaging process. The scare ended in seven days and the FDA arrested 53 people in 20 states for lying about consumer product tampering. The crisis cost Pepsi $25 million in lost sales and another $10 million in marketing coupons. Within two months sales were back to normal, and Pepsi enjoyed a seven percent increase by year-end.[8]

Any company subject to product tampering should have B-roll ready to distribute and today it could be made into a VNR and also immediately linked to a website. Reaction time is critical because lost sales will be almost incalculable.

The Command Center

The location and size of the command center will vary according to the type of crisis. The command center should be a place where the media can assemble, have working space and be kept informed. This will be for the most serious of crises. For worst-case scenarios, estimate how many reporters would cover the event, and reserve a large enough room in corporate headquarters or in a nearby institution that would always be available. In the case of a non-emergency crisis, a room could be rented in a local hotel.

The command center should be designed to handle most crisis scenarios. Have areas for the public relations staff and crisis team to meet and work, complete with desks, phones, computers, copy machines, fax machines and office supplies. In addition to extra cell phones, it is advisable to have at least one satellite phone. Have tables and chairs where media can write and work with Internet access, telephone outlets and electrical power. Another area of the center should have a raised platform or stage with a lectern or podium to hold media briefings. Proper lighting needs to be available, as well as a sound system, preferably with a mult-box. There should be a large screen to project slides, video or Internet sites. Consider this for the command center:

- Office and headquarters for public relations staff.
- Conference meeting room for crisis team, staff or other needs.
- Adjacent room with copy machines, fax machines and office supplies.
- Large room for working press.
- Areas designated for television.
- Assembly area where media announcements and updates can be made, with stage or raised platform and sound system.
- A "green room" or prep room for executives or senior management to use before any press conference.

Everything needs to be detailed on floor plans so anyone in facilities can immediately set up all of the rooms on short notice, without having to locate people to get answers.

There needs to be space outside for television to park trucks and vans with satellite antennas. Inside there should be areas reserved where television and radio media can work. All media covering the event will need parking accommodations.

And once this is done, an alternate site should be selected for the command center including the possibility of using tents in an outside area.

Depending on the desired security of the location, special credentials can be prepared in advance for the media to control access to certain areas of the building or where media will be allowed. The credentials should be large, color-coded and with a lanyard so a journalist can hang his ID around his neck. Each credential should be numbered and logged by the public relations team. Chances are that time will not permit photographs to be taken and included as part of the credential. Consider having each credential bar-coded so it could be scanned with appropriate security devices to further control access to specific areas as well as identify the credential holder. Control is important and all legitimate media should be accommodated. All staff, members of the crisis team and selected other senior staff should be credentialed as well so they can be immediately identified by the security staff. The color code will determine who has access and where.

The Public Relations Media Team

Every member of the public relations team will have specific assignments. Define the tasks and assign them to the most qualified individuals. The head of the department should not have any specific responsibilities, and should be flexible to undertake any task if and when needed. The tasks could include:

- Notifying the media. The person responsible for this will be responsible for keeping the media list updated and current.
- Media relations, including credentialing, parking, special services.
- Distributing news releases directly by fax or e-mail or handout in the command center as well as possibly using PR Newswire or Business Wire.
- Updating and posting news and information on the website and intranet for internal communication. This individual will have a list of what to post on the website, including maps, photos, background information on the company and its products and services.
- Notifying senior management in headquarters and all operating companies internationally.
- Gathering information and monitoring all coverage of the events. Using an outside service for help should be considered.
- Notifying various publics as defined: employees, shareholders, local community leaders and officials, customers, vendors, etc.

• Liaison with public relations counterparts at other agencies, including local police and sheriff, elected officials (mayor, governor), hospitals, state and federal regulatory and oversight agencies (U.S. Environmental Protection Agency, U.S. Department of Transportation, and state counterparts).

Other Crisis Team Activities

Everyone involved will have an assignment. Human resources will be responsible for contacting and activating crisis intervention counselors and psychologists, caregivers, ambulance services and even mortuaries in the event of deaths. All those brought in for a crisis will be carefully screened before a crisis and understand their responsibilities during a crisis. Human resources, coordinating with the CEO, will be responsible for notifying next of kin in the event of a serious injury or death.

Human resources also should have lists and rosters of all people who would normally be working in each office in each building, and this should be broken down by time of day. At a university, the provost or registrar should have the names of all students in each class at any given time. Should there be a disaster, you need to know the names of the people who might normally be working at any given time and where.

Security will have established relationships with local law enforcement agencies and a plan that will coordinate all activities and events, including secured areas, parking areas and traffic flows and patterns.

If the company is publicly held, the head of investor relations will be responsible for notifying the shareholders (working with the public relations staff), institutional investors, investment banking houses, market makers who have sizeable holdings and key financial analysts. The chief financial officer should call the bankers and lenders to explain any possible financial significance of the events.

Liaison With Other Agencies

Depending on the crisis and product or service, chances are other agencies and organizations will be involved. These could range from state and federal regulatory or oversight agencies to local police, hospitals and even relief organizations.

The public relations staff needs to have relationships established with counterparts at these organizations, with an understanding of keeping everyone informed with any public statement. For example, should there be an explosion at a chemical plant, the company's public relations people should be prepared to work with the U.S. Environmental Protection Agency, the Department of Homeland Security and other agencies.

The ideal situation, and what would be considered best for all concerned, is to work together and coordinate what is said and made public. There should be one lead communicator speaking for all of the agencies. Chances are, because of the many egos involved this will not happen. Public relations representatives for each of the involved organizations need to talk to one another, and there should be a central place to meet and discuss communications and media relations strategies.

Because an organization may have oversight and regulatory power, do not let the agency public relations representatives dictate policy or bully you on what is to be released and when. You must protect the image of your company first and foremost. If you cannot agree on a news release or a federal or state agency wants to withhold release of the information, you must do what is in your best interests.

If any organization releases information that is incorrect, misleading or possibly damaging to your company or organization, it needs to be immediately refuted. Hopefully the originating organization will make the announcement, but if it does not, be prepared to go public with your side of the story.

Think Cellphones

If you think you can control the message and want to be open and transparent, remember almost everyone today has a cellphone. When people were held captive on airplanes stuck on tarmacs waiting to take off, they used cellphones not only to call friends and relatives, but the media. Many phones today have cameras and can transmit still and video images which can be posted on the Internet or aired on television.

In a building lockdown situation, assume that anyone in the building will be interviewed by the news media, so be straightforward and as accurate as possible with information.

"Today, most everyone with a cell phone has the ability to report a story, upload it to a website, and essentially broadcast it to the world, said Jeff L. Braun, founder and president of Crucial Communication Group, LLC in Houston, Texas.

The University of Arizona in Tucson learned the hard way in 2002 when there was a shooting in a building in its medical school. A disgruntled student went to the office of a professor and shot and killed her. He then walked into a classroom and shot another professor before killing himself. Peter Likens, president of the university, and his security team locked down the building and set up a command center at an intersection several blocks away.

Almost immediately students in the classroom who witnessed the tragic event were on their cellphones with friends. Television had the story even before Likens and his team had established their command center. Then, while Likens and the university communications team stonewalled about giving any information to the media, television reporters announced the identity of the gunman, showed video of his apartment, talked with his neighbors, and interviewed students who were in the classroom.

It was four hours after the incident before the university had any statement to make. By then, it was old news.

Understand Why People Get Angry

Consensus builders and dispute mediators Lawrence Susskind and Patrick Field write in their book, *Dealing With An Angry Public*, that there are many reasons for the public to be angry. "Business and government leaders have covered up mistakes, concealed evidence of potential risks, made misleading statements, and often lied. Indeed, our leaders have fueled a rising tide of public distrust of both business and government by behaving in these ways."[9]

Susskind, a professor at MIT and Harvard Law School, says there are three basic reasons the public gets angry:

1. Because they have been adversely affected by something a company, organization or institution has done.
2. Because they fear being adversely affected by something you are proposing to do.
3. Because they disagree in principle with something you stand for.

He says the traditional response is to prove the public has not been or will not be adversely affected by something you have done or plan to do, and that differences in values are downplayed.[10]

According to a survey conducted by Porter/Novelli public relations firm, in the heat of a crisis many people do not believe everything being told them even if it is the truth. The survey revealed that the public gets angry when a company refuses to accept blame or responsibility (75 percent); when they believe the crisis could have been avoided (72 percent); and when the company supplied incomplete or inaccurate information as a response to the problem.[11]

Opposition Research and Advocacy Research

In any plan, identify and know who will be opposing you and who are friends you can count on. The number of people who have access to this information should be extremely limited, and based on a need-to-know. When the research is done, it is best kept locked and secured until there is a crisis. However, as with the overall crisis plan, it needs to be reviewed periodically and kept current.

If you are in a dispute that could elevate to a crisis situation, opposition research is essential. This could involve employee/labor relations, community relations and where issues could become very political. Identify the key players. Obtain biographical information on your adversaries. Are they more likely to respond violently or non-violently? What strategies have they used in the past? Who are they? Who are the leaders? Who will most likely be the spokespersons? Review their speeches, books, papers and articles they have authored as well as public statements. Do you have quotes? Contradictory statements? What is their philosophy? Education? Job experience? Their qualifications to speak on issues involved?

Who are their media allies? What media will support them editorially? Determine what organizations and individuals can be expected to provide third-party support for your adversaries, complete with detailed information and biographies. Will celebrities be involved who can be expected to speak in their behalf.

What causes do they advocate? Do they have the facts? How do they "spin" the truth? If there are several organizations, what are they? What do they stand for? Who provides the funding? Is the organization legitimate or a front for another organization?

In meetings or negotiations can the individuals involved be trusted not to leak confidential information to the media? Are they effective in using the media? Will they be cooperative?

Document, footnote and reference the sources of all of your information. If you use controversial data, you probably will be challenged on its accuracy. Have this at your fingertips.

The more you know about your potential adversary, the better prepared you will be. You need to anticipate what your opponent may say or do, how or when he will take action, and what you can do to prevent being in a defensive posture. Anticipate how the public will react to issues. Focus-group research and public-opinion polls will help determine whether you can expect public support. You need to understand different points of view and identify various levels of understanding and misunderstanding. Will the public believe you? Will the media believe you?

A "must read" book in the library of anyone involved in crisis planning is Saul D. Alinsky's *Rules for Radicals*. The book was written in 1971 as a "how to" primer for students and dissenters. "All change means disorganization of the old and organization of the new," wrote Alinsky, who died in 1972. "When there is agreement, there is no issue; issues only arise when there is disagreement or controversy. An organizer must stir up dissatisfaction and discontent; provide a channel into which the people can angrily pour their frustrations."[12]

Alinsky's advice for organizers should be understood by all trying to resolve a crisis. He believes that the art of communication is the single most important quality for an organizer. "One can lack any of the qualities of an organizer - with one exception - and still be effective and successful. Communication with others takes place when they understand what you're trying to get across to them. If they don't understand, then you are not communicating, regardless of words, pictures, or anything else. People only understand things in terms of their experience, which means that you must get within their experience."

His advice on communication should be followed by any spokesperson. "Further, communications is a two-way process," Alinsky said. "If you try to get your ideas across to others without paying attention to what they have to say to you, you can forget about the whole thing."[13]

Once you have done this for the opposition, repeat the same information for your advocates and friends who will help you during a crisis, especially third-party endorsements or people who will write letters to the editor or commentaries and op/ed pieces for editorial sections of publications.

Prepare Spokespersons for the Media

It is essential that the team and spokesperson receive media relations training. Even the most proficient and articulate executives realize that they must be prepared before standing in front of the media, many of whom will be adversarial and even hostile. One course in media relations training is not always sufficient, and selected spokespersons should be retrained with refresher courses on an annual basis. A number of firms specialize in personalized media relations training and group sessions that can run from $1,000 to $10,000 a day. An untrained, novice spokesperson who does not get the message across can mean disaster for a company during a crisis.

Any person who may represent a company on radio, television or in public should be professionally trained. Most executives today in business, industry, associations, non-profit organizations and government at some time will be in front of a camera, a microphone, a reporter with a pen, notebook and tape recorder, or a public audience.

The spokesperson needs to be equally prepared to meet with a large group at a press conference or media briefing or handle a one-on-one interview. For face-to-face interviews, be as prepared as possible by watching the host or interviewer in action to get an idea of his or her style and technique. Is the person aggressive? Does the person interrupt and not let the guest always finish an answer? Is it a friendly and relaxed approach? If you are going to be on a panel or with other guests on a talk show, will any be adversaries? If so, have background information on your adversaries and competition. For newspaper and magazine reporters, review other articles they have written to get an idea of their style.

Veteran newsman Walter Cronkite says that the subject of the interview has more control over a news interview than the reporter. He wrote that in his book, citing a disagreement he had with Pierre Salinger when Salinger was White House Press Secretary for John F. Kennedy. Cronkite says that at any time during his interview, the president could inject a statement, whether the question was asked or not.[14] A CEO in an adversary position should remember this and be prepared to make an important point even if not asked the question.

Dan Rather learned this the hard way when he became hostile with then vice president George H. W. Bush during the 1988 presidential campaign. Roger Ailes was advising Bush, and insisted that the interview on CBS be live so nothing could be edited out. He also gave Bush an "out" to quickly bring an end to the interview. As it turned out, Rather concentrated on Bush's involvement in the Iran-Contra affair. When Rather pushed too hard, Bush asked Rather to back off, which he did not. Bush then said to Rather, "I came here to discuss my qualifications to be president and you are questioning me on only one subject. What if we judged you on the time you walked off the CBS set and left the network dark for five minutes." Rather then ended the interview.

For any interview, be candid and brief. If possible, have an "out" or question to ask the interviewer. The average soundbite is 7.2 seconds. Of all of your responses that is what most likely will be used on radio or television. Many newspapers and magazines also use only one or two soundbite-length quotes. Make your main point in 30 seconds or less or no more than about 120 words.

Keep the language simple. Avoid unfamiliar acronyms, jargon and technical terms that the public may not understand. If technical questions are anticipated and need an explanation, have someone available from your organization who can speak on the subject. Be simple and talk as if you want an eighth-grader to understand what you say. Do not overanswer or overqualify your answers.

During the rehearsal and pre-interview training, anticipate the questions that may be asked, and prepare and practice 30-second answers on subjects you expect to discuss. Know how to turn a tough question into a positive answer.

If the reporter is hostile, do not get argumentative or uncooperative. Be cool and remain in control. Always remember with absolute confidence that you know more about your company and the subject than the reporter.

If a question doesn't make sense, come up with an answer that does make sense. Just because a question is asked is no reason you have to answer it. You can always give the answer you want to make your point, and either talk around the question or lead into the issue you want to emphasize. Or you can ignore the question and give the answer you want, as Sen. Ted Kennedy did during an NBC *Today Show* interview with Bryant Gumble. Gumble wanted Kennedy to talk about recent personal problems stemming from an Easter holiday incident in Palm Beach that involved his nephew. Kennedy only wanted to make points about health care legislation, and he gave the answers he wanted to be on television with complete disregard for the questions asked by Gumble.[15]

Remember body language and facial expressions. Dr. Vincent T. Covello, founder of the Center for Risk Communication, says generally what you say counts for 75% of the message, and body language counts 25%. However, in high-concern situations, body language can represent 75% of the message and what you say only 25%.[16]

Go to the interview or press conference prepared with the one, two or three points that you want to make. Then have more than one way to make that point so your answers are not always the same, but you are making the same point.

Always stay in charge of the interview. Never allow yourself to be put in a defensive position. Never let another person put words in your mouth and if the interviewer makes a wrong assumption, correct it before answering the next question. If interrupted before a point is made, correct the error first before continuing. On ABC's *Primetime Live* with Sam Donaldson, Ted Koppel said that it is OK for a guest to tell the interviewer "it is none of your business" or "your question is out of line." He said that sometimes he, Dan Rather, and a number of other journalists get too personal or too far off-base in questioning a guest.[17]

If a television interview is taped, you don't have to rush to answer as you would on live television or radio. Continue to look directly into the camera, smile, and wait until you have the answer you want to give. This will be edited out because no news director is going to run 10, 15 or 30 seconds of you silently smiling into a camera. In a crisis situation, most media briefings and press conferences will be live.

If you are doing an interview with print media, either in a small group or one-on-one, be absolutely sure that the reporter understands what you have said and has quoted you correctly. Chances are the reporter will have a tape recorder as a backup, and it is all right for you to have one, as well as well as having your public relations head with you. If the reporter is not tape-recording the interview, speak slowly and deliberately so the reporter has correct information in his or her notes. Generally print interviews can be more casual, and this can pose a danger of being relaxed and caught off guard.

Publish the Manual

When the plan is prepared and all is done, organize everything in a three-ring binder and number each book. Many colleges and universities post their crisis communications plan on the Internet. Institutions heavily involved with laboratories doing research and those that use animals for research should limit distribution of the crisis manual. In most companies and organizations, the crisis book should be distributed only to the CEO, members of the crisis team and any others only on a need-to-know basis.

Security of the crisis manual is important because some information may be of value to adversaries. The head of the crisis team needs to control the distribution and should number each manual. The same is true for the briefing book which should be secured as well.

Summary Checklist

- Organize the crisis team.
- Create the crisis management and crisis communications plans.
- "What if?" all possible crises.
- Develop a calling tree and the order in which people get notified.
- Prepare materials ready for distribution to the media and others, including VNRs and a briefing book.

- Plan the command center with alternate location.
- Assign responsibilities for the public relations media team.
- Be ready to liaison with other agencies.
- Use cellphones to control the message and realize anyone with a cellphone beyond your control can contact the media.
- Understand why people get angry.
- Develop opposition research and advocacy research.
- Have the spokespersons prepared and ready.

Endnotes

[1] Mark Gongloff, staff writer, CNN/Money, October 29, 2002.

[2] Wikipedia.

[3] Jonathan Bernstein, "The 11 Steps of Crisis Communications," *Crisis Manager*, Bernstein Crisis Management, September 1, 2005.

[4] "Most B2B Marketers Have No Crisis Plan in Place," *Marketing Charts*, October 10, 2007 and *Media Buyer Planner*, October 11, 2007.

[5] Ibid.

[6] Jonathan Bernstein, "25 MORE Crisis Management Lessons Learned," *Crisis Manager*, January 2008.

[7] Andrew Stern, The Sunwest Group, Dallas, Texas, interview, April 1997.

[8] *Journal of the Interactive Media Lab,* College of Journalism and Communications, University of Florida, Gainesville, Fla., Fall 2002, and Roadside America.

[9] Lawrence Susskind and Patrick Field, *Dealing With An Angry Public*, The Free Press, a division of Simon & Schuster Inc., New York, N.Y., 1996, pg. 1.

[10] Lawrence Susskind, "Dealing With An Angry Public" seminar by the MIT-Harvard Public Disputes Program, November 13-14, 1997, Cambridge, Mass.

[11] *Public Relations Journal*, September 1993.

[12] Saul D. Alinsky, *Rules for Radicals*, Vintage Books, a division of Random House, New York, N.Y., 1971, pg. 117.

[13] Ibid.

[14] Walter Cronkite, *A Reporter's Life*, Alfred A. Knopf, New York, N.Y., 1996, pg. 24.

[15] "Today Show," NBC-TV, June 5, 1991.

[16] Dr.Vincent T. Covello, Health and Environmental Risk Communication Workshop, 1999.

[17] Ted Koppell, "Primetime Live," ABC-TV, May 29, 1996.

CHAPTER 3

MANAGING THE CRISIS

Being prepared is only part of the public relations and communications challenge during a crisis. How a company or organization responds when a crisis actually happens is the ultimate measure of success or failure.

Was the crisis plan effective? Was the right spokesperson chosen? Was the response timely? Was the response believable? As soon as possible after a crisis, it is important to bring the crisis team together for a meeting and critique of everything that happened.

You have to be flexible because every aspect of every crisis cannot always be anticipated, even with the best planning and "what if?" sessions. Members of the crisis team and their principal deputies need to be empowered to know they can act on their own. They must be entrepreneurial and know when to take the lead.

The rooms you had planned to use for the command center, for media briefings and for working press room may not be usable because of an explosion or fire. You should have planned for a backup facility, but is it available?

Communications is your key to coordination. But what if your telephone system, that provides not only your regular service, but your cellular phones, computers and fax machines, cannot be used? An Illinois Bell System fire knocked out phone service to tens of thousands of Chicago-area customers for weeks. A similar problem occurred in New York City several years earlier. In 1959, the U.S. Army Corps of Engineers projected that a high-tide hurricane affecting New York harbor would shut down phone service for a month or more in Manhattan. The communications plan for a catastrophic California earthquake anticipates that land-based telephone service will be disrupted during the first 24 to 36 hours of the emergency period.[1]

Radio is the communications mode of choice for emergency managers because it is portable, available and versatile. Battery-powered radios are not susceptible to downed wires, loss of power, damage to switching stations or inundated switchboards. How the communications system works depends on how it links to other essential parties – your own team, emergency response, fire, police and media.[2]

The First Minutes Are Critical

The late Robert J. Stone who was a senior executive at The Dilenschneider Group and Edelman Public Relations in New York, said that a response must come in the first 10-15 minutes of a crisis or credibility can be lost. This is why it is so important to have materials prepared in anticipation of a crisis. Following are his rules:

- Take charge or take it on the chin.
- Don't follow your first impulse to minimize the situation.
- Assume the worst so you will extend yourself to maximum effort.
- Don't wait for all the facts; full details won't be available early on.
- Head for the scene to assess damage.
- Be the source for bad news, not the victim of it.[3]

In a crisis, the CEO or top executive of the company or organization must be available, according to the late Ed Turner, former executive vice president of CNN. "With the technology we have today, people can be instantly available any place in the U.S. or the world. Have your most credible authority front and center. A 'no comment' is 'guilty' and dumb," said Turner, who ran the cable network from 1980-1998. "Credibility is all you have to offer. Build this trust over time." He also believed it is all right to say "I don't know" or "I can't talk about it."[4]

What you say, when you say it, and who says it are critical. Preferably the CEO should be the spokesperson. You do not want the organization's attorney as a spokesperson, and under no circumstances should any outside lawyer speak for you. Be sure a competent, experienced professional is in charge of media relations during a crisis. This is no time for novices or amateurs. Sometimes over-anxious, well-meaning people start talking before thinking.

"Don't duck the press in the hope that we will leave you alone," said Margo Slade, assistant national editor of *The New York Times*. She said companies in crisis tend to treat reporters as though they are "armed and dangerous."[5] "The job of reporters is to get the story. They'll do that with or without your cooperation," says John DeFrancesco, former Chicago public relations counselor. "The risk of being uncooperative, however, is that the story can be based on hearsay, rumor and misinformation from outside sources. Such a story can be damaging to your company and its reputation. Conversely, when informed in a timely, honest manner, reporters will tend to write the facts, and the attention to the crisis in the press can subside quickly.[6]

"If the first time you're speaking to a reporter who covers your business is when there is a crisis or negative news event, then the reporter's worst instincts are bound to take over," says Andrew Gilman, president of CommCore Consulting Group. "One of the best ways to prepare for the inevitable is to get to know your media," he said, speaking at the National Law Firm Marketing Association. "If the reporters know you, your products, and your personal credibility, you may get the benefit of judgments in articles and news stories."[7]

Manage the Release of Information, Be In Control

Hopefully with the "what if" process, the crisis has been anticipated and an approved news release already prepared. It should be on its way to the media minutes after all the facts have been evaluated and confirmed. If not, the spokesperson needs to be immediately briefed and a statement made as soon as possible. Once you have all of the facts, disclose them.

You want to manage the release of information and stay in control. You want the media to depend on you for the story and updates. This will happen only if reporters and editors know they can trust, believe and depend on you. The last thing you want is for the media to interview adversaries, seek out uninformed sources, get random cellphone calls or follow up on unfounded rumors.

The media center is the operations or command and control hub where communications to the media should take place and will be detailed in the crisis plan. Backup command centers should be considered in the event of a natural disaster, or for any reason the primary center could not be used. Be sure to plan for parking and access for television remote trucks, as well as convenient parking for all journalists.

Optional entries and exits are important. They can be secured so spokespersons making announcements can leave without being trapped.

When the media center is established, let the media know when you are going to make announcements. Tell them what you know, distribute background information and fact sheets, and set a time for the next announcement within a stated period of time (such as within the next 45 to 90 minutes). Come back on time and with answers to questions they have asked. As long as you keep giving the media updated reports, and at the times you specified, they will be less likely to leave the center and seek out others who offer a discordant message that conflicts with what you want communicated.

Take advantage of all communications tools you have at your disposal. Internet. Intranet. Streaming video. Satellite. The Internet and Intranet provide a means to quickly and distribute information broadly. Compressed video is an inexpensive way to link to media sources if you are based in a remote location. One-on-one or simultaneous media interviews can be conducted using this inexpensive but non-broadcast-quality system. Consider using a satellite facility, if one is available, for periodic updates at broadcast quality.

The basic principles always apply – be honest, tell the truth, never lie, do not mislead, tell it quickly, do not stonewall, show compassion, don't hide behind a "no comment," be on the record with all statements, and don't give the media a chance to speculate or get comments from unreliable sources. If there is some information you cannot disclose, such as withholding a name until a family member has been notified, let the media know the reason. If you just don't have the answer to a question, say, "I don't know," and let the media know you will seek to get the answer. If information can be made clearer to the media by the use of charts, graphs, maps, and drawings, use them wherever possible.

Expect Disagreement With Lawyers

A policy difference can be expected between the public relations counselor and the attorney over whether or not to accept responsibility for the crisis, or even publicly apologize and say "I'm sorry." Psychologists say that "I'm sorry" ranks just behind "please help me" as the most powerful of appeals. Attorneys may fear this opens the door for lawsuits, but many can be mitigated by winning public favor.

Where victims are killed or injured or their property devastated, it is not against the law to show humility or compassion, or express sympathy for the victims and to their families. As much as 50 percent of an organization's credibility can be lost by displaying a lack of caring. Take the advice of Will Rogers who said: "People want to know that you care, before hearing about what you know."

What is said, and when it is said may polarize the public relations counselors and the attorneys. The CEO will have to decide whose recommendations will be accepted. The public relations counselor will be concerned with the image, reputation, credibility, trustworthiness and believability of the company. These are not areas of concern for a lawyer because few have had training or experience or even exposure to public relations or public affairs disciplines. The most important advice the attorney can give is whether or not what is being said is legal and not in violation of any law.

When MIT paid $6 million to settle a lawsuit brought against the university for negligence in the hazing death of an underclass student, President Charles Vest not only issued a public apology, but hugged the mother of the boy who died and said, "I hope this isn't too late." Columnist Brian McGrory writing in the *Boston Globe* praised Vest. "Yes, a public apology, as in an admission of wrongdoing, an expression of regret, some human words, all for the whole world to see," McGrory wrote. "Because of this, there are lawyers all over America wearing black armbands today. There are partners in white-shoe firms gathering in conference rooms in downtown skyscrapers at this very moment, so stricken they cannot enjoy their lavish catered lunches. There are law professors at the most prestigious schools burning through case files in a vain search for precedents."[8]

Most lawyers have little understanding of the media, and will want to move slowly and cautiously, delaying any announcement as long as possible. Some lawyers may even harbor a resentment of journalists.

According to Fraser P. Seitel, attorneys immediately presume the worst and believe, incorrectly, that all crises, whether personal or corporate, revolve around legal issues. "Legal repercussions are critical, of course," he says. "But so are public relations implications. In some crises, the latter clearly outweigh the former." Seitel also believes that it can be suicidal for a client, especially an innocent one, to hire an attorney rather than an experienced public relations professional to present the case to the public.[9]

"Lawyers are so afraid of possible litigation that they go out of their way to be dull, and then wonder why the other side gets all of the media attention in a crisis," says Pete Oppel, managing director of Fairchild/Oppel in Dallas. "The public can smell communication that sounds like it was driven by lawyers," says Larry Kamer, principal in GCI Kamer-Singer, San Francisco. "Crisis managers have to talk to each other. What can we say that puts the needs of consumer first?"[10]

One of the best examples of a CEO taking the advice of public relations counsel over legal counsel is what John Hall, CEO of Ashland Oil did in 1988. This is a classic example of doing the right thing and is detailed in Chapter 7. When one of the company's storage tanks collapsed and released one million gallons of diesel fuel into the Monongahela and Ohio Rivers near Pittsburgh, Hall took full responsibility for the accident, admitting actions that had clear legal implications, but that won public trust and support for Ashland Oil.

The Importance of Training Spokespersons

On December 3, 1984, a Union Carbide subsidiary pesticide plant in Bhopal, India, released 40 tons of methyl isocyanate gas that killed between 2,500 and 5,000 people. It was one of the world's worst industrial disasters. Warren Anderson, Union Carbide's chairman, rushed to Bhopal and told his colleagues at headquarters, "We can't show our concern about this tragedy by me staying in Danbury. [11]

However, three days after the incident, the media reported that the company had repeatedly refused to provide a detailed description of the system used to store and process the lethal gas. For all the good that Anderson wanted to do, here is how his director of Health, Safety and Environmental Affairs handled a press conference:[12]

Reporter: I think you've said the company was not liable for the Bhopal victims.

Director: I didn't say that.

Reporter: Does that mean you are liable?

Director: I didn't say that either.

Reporter: Then what did you say?

Director: Ask me another question.

You wonder who advised Charles Harper, chairman of R.J. Reynolds, before a company annual meeting. When he was asked about children and second-hand smoke, Harper responded by saying if children don't like to be in a smoky room that they will leave. When told that infants can't readily leave, he said, "At some point they will learn to crawl."[13]

And then there are the Internet lies and false accusations. In 1999 someone posted on the Internet a completely false interview between a female broadcaster from National Public Radio and a U.S. Army Lt. General Reinwald about teaching Boy Scouts how to use firearms. The fabricated interview ended when the mythical general profanely insulted the reporter. This piece of fiction reappeared in 2001, attributed to Marine Corps General Reinwald. By 2007 the fictitious Lt. General Reinwald became the real General Peter Cosgrove of Australia and an interview with the Australian Broadcasting Corporation. The interview is one of many that became a long standing Internet hoax.[14]

When not prepared, people make stupid comments every day. At the Astro-dome in Houston, House Majority Leader Tom Delay (R-Texas) stopped to talk with three young Katrina Hurricane evacuees from New Orleans and said, "Now tell me the truth boys, is this kind of fun?"[15] While testifying before Congress and asked to estimate the number of Iraqi insurgents, Defense Secretary Donald Rumsfeld responded, "I am not going to give you a number for it because it's not my business to do intelligent work."[16] Did televangelist Pat Robertson, founder of the Christian Broadcasting Network do the Christian thing when he called for the assassination of Venezuelan President Hugo Chavez? "You know, I don't know about this doctrine of assassination, but if he thinks we're trying to assassinate him, I think that we really ought to go ahead and do it. It's a whole lot cheaper than starting a war," Robertson said.[17]

The spokesperson must be clear and concise if you want the message to be understood. Truthfully position your organization and its message and give both the public and media credit for being able to understand what they are being told. Avoid what an English professor and non-practicing attorney at Rutgers University-Camden calls doublespeak. "The purpose of doublespeak is to *not* say something while pretending to do so," says William Lutz. He notes that the federal government is the worst offender but that corporate America is only a half-step behind. Following are some examples he gives:[18]

- Negative gain in test scores v. test scores dropped.
- Meaningful downturn in aggregate output v. recession.
- Normal payroll adjustments v. layoffs.
- Volume related production schedule adjustment v. closed down a production plant.
- Repositioned v. fired.

On-The-Record, Off-The-Record

What can be said "off-the-record" depends on whether or not you can trust the person to whom the information is being told to keep it confidential. The best practice is only to say or put in writing what would not embarrass you or not create a crisis if published in a newspaper or reported the next day on radio and television. Confidential sources aside, some reporters have been forced to reveal sources or go to jail if found in contempt by a judge. This has happened more frequently in recent years.

The best policy is to speak on-the-record all the time. If you are communicating with financial analysts on Wall Street, for example, you must always be on-the-record.

Here are four situations to guide how information is given to the media:

On-the-record – Everything that is said is for publication and may be directly attributed to the source or paraphrased.

Background – Information given to the journalist can be used directly as given and quoted directly but without a name being used. Sometimes the media will note "according to a high level individual," or cite a generic title.

Deep background – This is information given to the journalist to help prepare the story but no direct quotes can be used and not even indirect attribution. Generally deep background material will lead a journalist to other sources for quotes, such as Watergate's "Deep Throat."

Off-the-record – Absolutely no direct or indirect quote can be attributed to the source of the information or to a title, department or any other generic source. Again, this will help the reporter position the information.

Keep Employees Informed

It is critical to keep employees informed. You want to dispel any rumors. You also want all employees to have current, factual information. This can be done any number of ways with an Intranet, blast telephone messages that can be delivered to their home phones and cellphones, or by having a special 800 number that can be called with updated voice messages.

Employees will be asked questions by their family, friends and neighbors and even possibly the media. You cannot control their message and you certainly want it to be correct. Good investigative reporters also will contact employees and their families at their homes.

Surveys by author and counselor Tom Harris and Northwestern University-Edelman Public Relations Worldwide indicate that employee relations is now the number two priority as companies are practicing "inreach" before "outreach." Editors at *PR Reporter* also predict that the new direction of public relations will make this primary.[19] In a crisis situation, communicating to employees is extremely important.

Internal communications are especially critical when there is violence in the workplace, a terrorist attack or a hostage situation. You need to help your employees heal after such crises, and bring normalcy back to the workplace.

Burton St. John III, a public relations consultant for the U.S. Postal Service in St. Louis, notes that it is important to have psychological counselors with excellent people skills on the scene within 24 hours. The CEO or leader of the organization needs to make face-to-face contact with as many employees and victims as possible. During the second 24 hours, employees move from shock and denial to anger and anxiety. This can last for weeks or months. St. John believes it is important to cut red tape and move quickly. In the case of a fatality, he says, "Often the simple act of completing a memorial service will bring some closure."[20]

Decisions made during a crisis can impact relationships and trust for years to come, according to Don Sherry, manager of communications for Oklahoma Natural Gas in Oklahoma City. The company's headquarters are located less than a block from the site of the bombed Murrah Federal Building and employees physically felt the explosion. Because of damage to the building, offices were temporarily moved.[21]

Employee assistance program and counseling were given top priority. A decision to return to the downtown offices was delayed, and employees were allowed to stay longer at the temporary location. Supervisors were given wide latitude in granting leaves and vacations. Supervisors and employees were encouraged to respect others' feelings.[22]

All of the usual forms of communications were used – publications, e-mail, recorded news hotline. "The most important and effective," says Sherry, "was direct, one-on-one conversation and small group meetings. Our president spent a day meeting personally with as many employees as possible, conveying the company's concern and appreciation for work under the most trying of circumstances." Oklahoma Natural Gas supported the desire of many employees to contribute funds to aid victims by matching employee gifts and making a separate corporate contribution.

If the Information Is Public, Say So

On July 4, 1966, President Lyndon B. Johnson signed the Freedom of Information Act that went into effect the following year and applies only to federal agencies. However, all of the states and most of the territories have enacted similar laws to require disclosures by agencies of state and local governments. Many are combined with open- meetings legislation that requires government meetings to be open to the public. These laws also are described as open records or sunshine laws.

The Electronic Freedom of Information Act Amendment was signed by President Bill Clinton on October 2, 1996, broadening the legislation to include electronic technologies. The first such freedom of information legislation is thought to have been enacted by Sweden in 1766. Today more than 70 countries throughout the world have followed suit.

The person requesting a public document does not have to provide a reason for the request. The burden of proof falls on the agency being asked for the information. If extensive time is required to produce and copy the document, the government body is allowed to charge a fee for services at cost.

In most cases, the open records or FOIA officer will be in public relations or public affairs, not the legal department. Lawyers at Texas A&M University provoked *The Dallas Morning News* to sue the university. The newspaper claimed the university's attorneys were not forthright in producing requested public documents, misled and possibly even lied to investigative reporters, and did everything possible to circumvent the Texas Open Records Act.[23] The newspaper agreed to dismiss its lawsuit when Texas A&M adopted new procedures for all open records requests. The agreed-to order replaced the general counsel as the recipient of all open records requests and named the executive director of university relations, the university's top public relations officer, as the new responsible party.

Journalists often use FOIA to request information when they are involved in investigative reporting. One enterprising journalist decided to let the open records law do some of his research. A request by the journalist to Texas A&M was for copies of all FOIA requests by two investigative reporters from *The Dallas Morning News*. While the request could not be legally denied, because of open records laws, he knew exactly what information his competition was seeking, so he reduced the chance that he would miss a possible story opportunity. As a matter of professional courtesy, the university's public relations department told the two investigative reporters of their competitor's open records requests.

Contractors who bid on government contracts and lose to competitors often will request copies of the winning contracts.

Companies whose stock is publicly traded may not be governed by FOIA and open records legislation, but must comply with the Securities and Exchange Commission and Sarbanes-Oxley. In the wake of scandals at Enron, Tyco International and WorldCom, Sen. Paul Sarbanes (D-Maryland) and Congressman Michael G. Oxley (R-Ohio) enacted wide-ranging legislation that established new standards for all public company boards, management and public accounting firms. It was overwhelmingly approved 423-3 in the House of Representatives and 99-0 in the Senate.

During my professional career, I was responsible for FOIA at the U.S. Environmental Protection Agency and the U.S. Agency for International Development, as well as at Texas A&M University. Because of the volume of requests at EPA, I initiated a system of sending within 24 hours to anyone requesting information a reply postcard with request number assigned. At Texas A&M, most of the information requested by journalists could be provided by telephone without the need of completing a formal request form. I set a policy that virtually anything that touched our desks was public information. This action helped rebuild media trust in the university that was nearly destroyed by the lawyers.

When in doubt, err on the side of disclosure. Never hide or refuse to disclose information that is public, or it will only further exacerbate the crisis and create greater public distrust.

Summary Checklist

- Be flexible in managing the crisis and how you respond.
- The first minutes are critical and the team must be operational ready.
- Be in control and manage the message and release of information.
- Keep the media informed on a regular basis.
- Rely on basics of public relations.
- Resolve differences with lawyers but remember the story must be told.
- Where victims are involved show humility, compassion, remorse and sympathy.
- It is not against the law to say "I'm sorry" or to apologize.
- Remember the advice of Will Rogers: "People want to know that you care before they care about what you know."
- Understand being on-the-record and off-the-record when talking with media.
- Keep employees and all important publics informed.
- If the information is public, disclose it; never withhold or hide, and err on the side being right.

Endnotes

[1] Robert D. Vessey and Jose A. Aponte, "Needed: The Right Information at the Right Time," *Communication When It's Needed Most*, The Annenberg Washington Program in Communications Policy Studies of Northwestern University, 1989, pg. 9.

[2] Ibid.

[3] Meeting in Philadelphia with Robert J. Stone, November 7, 1996.

[4] Ed Turner, executive vice president, CNN, Atlanta, comments during "Media Relations: The Good, The Bad, The Ugly," conference of Public Relations Society of America, Nashville, Tenn., June 5, 1996.

[5] Ibid.

[6] "How To Handle Media In Time Of Crisis," *Newsline*, Summer 1997, DeFrancesco-Goodfriend Public Relations, Chicago, Ill., pg. 1.

[7] *Public Relations Tactics*, May 1997, pg. 4.

[8] Lawrence Susskind and Patrick Field, *Dealing With An Angry Public*, The Free Press, a division of Simon & Schuster Inc., New York, N.Y., 1996, pg. 9.

[9] Thomas J. Lueck, "Crisis management at Carbide," *The New York Times*, December 14, 1984, pg. D1.

[10] "Crisis PR," *PR Week*, October 30, 2000, pg. 15.

[11] "The Best of the Worst," *Public Relations Tactics*, February 1997, pg. 4.

[12] Fraser P. Seitel, "The Legalities Of Condit's PR," *Jack O'Dwyer's PR Daily*, July 10, 2001.

[13] *PR Reporter*, September 25, 2000, pg. 4.

[14] NPR Hoax E-mail, "The Reporter and General Reinwald," www.npr.org, November 7, 2007, and "Equipped Quip," www.snopes.com.

[15] *Houston Chronicle*, September 9, 2005.

[16] Dana Milbank, "Capitol Hill Journal," *The Washington Post*, February 16, 2005.

[17] Media Matters for America, August 22, 2005.

[18] Rosland Briggs, "Efforts of 'spin doctors' have professor spinning," *The Philadelphia Inquirer*, November 28, 1996, pg.D-1.

[19] "Progress: Studies Find Employee Relations Now Second Priority," *PR Reporter*, January 5, 1998, pg. 4.

[20] Burton St. John III, "Recovery Communications – Helping Your Employees Heal After Workplace Violence," *Public Relations Tactics*, May 1997, p. 1, 14, 27.

[21] "Think It Thru: Crisis Decisions Have Lasting Impact," *Channels*, July 1995, Exeter, N.H., pg. 1

[22] Ibid., pg. 2.

[23] *Dallas Morning News v. Texas A&M University, et al,* Cause No. 93-04440, 345th District Court, Travis County, Texas, September 10, 1993.

CHAPTER 4

WHO SAID "SILENCE IS GOLDEN"?

No one really knows who first said "Silence is golden," but more than likely it was an attorney. The lawyer-driven "no comment" could well have evolved from "silence is golden." Both of these phrases could be why the great wordsmith, William Shakespeare, wrote the following in Henry VI: "The first thing we do, let's kill all the lawyers."[24]

Actually "silence is golden" more recently comes from "speech is silvern, silence is golden" from Thomas Caryle's *Sartor Resartus*, where he translates a "Swiss inscription." This also is a common German proverb that has been traced back to the *Talmud* in ancient Babylonia.[2]

Then there is the case of Sir Thomas More. His silence so infuriated King Henry VII that he was beheaded on July 6, 1535. Sir Thomas refused to accept the King's claim to be the supreme head of the Church of England and said nothing in his defense.

The rules of good crisis communications have been outlined in the previous chapters but fundamentals and basics cannot be repeated enough – respond quickly, always tell the truth, never lie, and never say "no comment." It is all right to say "I don't know," but never deceive, never mislead, and be open and honest with the media and all of the audiences to whom the story must be communicated.

"'No comment' or 'no comment because it's in litigation' don't serve the organization's reputation, credibility, or market share very well and rarely protect it against future litigation, or reduce settlement costs," says James Lukaszewski, founder and president of The Lukaszewski Group, White Plains, N.Y. "In high profile cases, saying nothing may be the costliest single mistake."[3]

During a seminar sponsored by Edelman Public Relations Worldwide, panelists said a "no comment" implies guilt. James Fink of Opinion Research Corp.

said 40 percent of the people believe large companies accused of wrongdoing are guilty when they do not respond, and that jumps to more than 60 percent when the company refuses to talk about litigation.[4] Polls shows the public particularly distrusts business. A September 1998 poll found more than half of the people believe a company is guilty of something if it is being investigated by a government agency, and more than half believed companies are probably guilty when a lawsuit is filed against them.[5]

James Cox, senior vice president at Hill & Knowlton with some 30 years of litigation communication experience, said that companies are at risk if they follow legal counsel to avoid the media during a lawsuit. "Public relations has to be engaged early in the litigation process to protect the company's reputation from plaintiffs' attacks. Besides the damage to the company's reputation, there is the risk of losing the hearts and minds of future judges and jurors who will hear the case in court. The public relations team needs to field its own 'expert witnesses' as credible third parties to convince the media about the company's character and commitments. We have seen too many high-profile examples where a company's reputation, brand, business, and shareholder value is damaged by early litigation charges."[6]

Judy Smith, deputy White House press secretary to Marlin Fitzwater in the George Herbert Walker Bush Administration, says Fitzwater taught her that you don't have to explain what you don't say. Also an attorney, she says to avoid spokesperson babble. "If a question is asked and you don't know the answer, or if you are confronted with a rumor, be honest and be brief," she says. Here is one way she suggests to reply: "I don't have that answer yet, but I will get it for you." And when badgered she suggests you take a deep breath, be straight forward and say, "I don't know the answer but I'll find out."[7]

In an April 30, 1998 press conference, President William Clinton came up with creative ways to avoid saying "no comment" to 15 of 29 questions he was asked. Here are some examples: "I don't have anything to say about that." "I cannot comment on these matters because they are under seal." "I have nothing to add to my former answer." "I have been advised, and I think its good advice under the circumstances, but I just don't have anything else to add about that."[8]

"There are dozens of ways to say 'no comment' without saying 'no comment,'" says crisis counselor Jonathan Bernstein.

Don't Withhold Information

Do not withhold providing the media and public information that will come out eventually. It is better to volunteer information than have the media find out about it and make it public. Don't take the philosophy of Evillene, the Wicked Witch of the West in *The Wiz* who sang "Don't Nobody Bring Me No Bad News." Negative information has to be disclosed just as information that will positively benefit the company. The more information that can be disclosed early on will correlate to building trust and believability by the media and the public.

The late Meg Greenfield wrote in her *Newsweek* column how various political and presidential administrations contribute to their own misery even more than the press could ever hope to do. "The framework for the drama is created first by a series of dodges and feints and denials and plain falsehoods that set them up for exposure. They continue to let the truth out only under pressure, and in dribs and drabs, each time having to admit a little more, and also explain a lot more about their previous, now discredited assertions," she wrote. "This only creates an ever increasing and more attentive audience for the story."[9]

"Don't restrict access. It's like waving a red flag. It signals hiding something," says Tim Wheeler, environmental writer of *The Baltimore Sun*. "Reporters want to have access to people who know the issues. Attorneys are the worst. You must go over the lawyer's head to the top person. Attorneys want to control and even refuse to talk about documents that are public."[10]

During the Persian Gulf Desert Storm operation General Colin Powell had an argument with General Norman Schwarzkopf regarding comments on television that four Scud missile sites had been taken out, when in fact air reconnaissance photos showed that the targets were fuel trucks. A CNN camera crew filmed the destroyed trucks and contradicted Schwarzkopf. Powell told his general "protect your credibility – it's a precious asset." Powell's rule is that it is better to admit a mistake than be caught in one.[11]

Be Careful How You Answer

Ron Levy, president of Episodic Public Relations and a media expert, says that sometimes public relations professionals not only have the right, but the duty, not to answer a reporter's questions. In addition to sensing when not to comment, he believes that it is wise to remember what not to say. For example:

1. You don't know the answer. Don't say "I don't know" if you do know. Saying this is like adding, "but the possibility you raise is not so ridiculous or unlikely that I'm willing to deny it."

2. Don't say "I'll find out for you" if you've already found out, but would rather not say. An example would be saying "he's not in" if he really is. Saying "I don't know" or "I'll have to check" as an effort at evasion may bring you a string of questions that make you seem increasingly ridiculous and make your organization seem decreasingly credible.

   Once it is clear to a reporter that you're going to keep saying "I don't know" or "I'll have to check," you can be asked "Isn't is a fact that your CEO is known to have done a series of increasingly wicked deeds, including misdemeanors and even felonies?" Your management may be outraged, if you report not knowing, or are unable to say whether a senior officer is well known throughout the organization as being a secretary-chaser, a foot-tapper in men's rooms, an expense account abuser or a chicken plucker.

3. Management may prefer that the answer come from someone more expert than you.

4. You have reason to believe your answer will be twisted.

5. Management has told you not to answer until you clear it with the lawyers. Even if you are under such orders, you may be able to get legal clearance to protect your organization if the need arises – "I haven't cleared a statement on that through legal, but speaking just for myself, not the organization, that sounds absolutely ridiculous!" That same kind of "speaking for myself" statement enables you to say, when a lawsuit has been announced but your people haven't received the paper, not "we can't comment yet until we read the papers" (innocent people, when accused, tend to deny promptly) but "I can't wait to comment on that which I'll do after we get the papers." One way, you sound like the organization is maybe guilty but cautious; the second way, like the organization is innocent and eager to reply and maybe it's the accuser who's guilty of unfounded and ridiculous claims.

6. Answering would be unlawful, perhaps as "selective disclosure" telling a material fact to some investors before others.

7. The inquiry is not for business information but for personal secrets.

Levy says that saying "he's not in" if your CEO or the individual in question is in, may create the peril that cameras will be able to catch him sneaking out the back door, or show his car in his parking space in the organization's parking lot, or be broadcast before amusing segments in which others in your organization are shown saying "He just left two minutes ago;" "I don't think he came in today;" "I think he's in Europe;" "Who's he, I'm new here;" or even, "I won't comment because I know anything I say can be held against us."

It might seem safe enough to say "I'll have to check the records" but that may bring a question of what records you'll check – and be evidence that there ARE records – and if there's an inquiry by a prosecutor or a Congressional committee, the records you've acknowledged may be subpoenaed.

He points out another big problem that comes from falsely saying one of these things is that it makes you a liar, a fact which if uncovered may embarrass the organization and cause it to fire you, even if you lied in the hope of protecting the organization. The announcement may be: "He's no longer with our company and we have zero tolerance for mis-statements." It can kill a whole career.

If you realize you've started to say something false and don't want to admit that right away, don't just keep going, figuring there's no way to turn back. "Thou shalt not covet thy neighbor's wife" is an admirable rule but if you find that you do covet her, at least don't do anything about it that could make things worse. So interrupt yourself, if you've started saying something you regret, and say something like "I want to hold off on this for the moment." The wife you save may be your neighbor's, the saved reputation may be your organizations, and the neck you save may be your own.

Never settle for a non-answer to an accusatory question, or an answer that sounds damaging, if you can go ahead and state the positive opposite. For example, is the company causing increased consumer prices? "Actually, the company is helping to hold down prices in four ways," and then go ahead and name them. "Is the company causing a safety peril? "The company is promoting safety in six ways" which you promptly describe. A high proportion of charges against a company are that it is charging too much or causing a safety peril or that someone in the company has done something horrible. You can almost surely clear in advance a statement on what the company is doing vigorously to hold *down* prices, *promote* safety, and deter or detect early any behavior that's out of line.

Very importantly, Levy says to avoid quantifying the peril. Saying that "some degree of danger is unavoidable in manufacturing" sounds like an admission of guilt. So it's better to say "the company uses three kinds of experts and seven measures to maximize safety," and then tell what they are.

Just as sports fans distinguish between our team and the visiting team or even the opposing team, the media and public tend to judge quickly when there's a controversy which is the good guy and the bad guy. If you are able to cite a long string of good deeds your company is doing (and it's a list that already exists, if you get a statement on what good causes your company gives to) you may rally support from the groups you've helped and from the general public.

"We each tend to see goodness in one who helps the old lady across the street," says Levy. "But be sure it's an old lady, not thy neighbor's wife."[12]

Perhaps Rumsfeld Should Have Been Silent

If silence indeed would be golden, perhaps it should have been practiced by Donald Rumsfeld. A toy company manufactured a 12 inch tall "Rummy" doll that speaks 28 different statements from historic press conferences. Some examples:

- "There are known knowns, there are things we know that we know. There are known unknowns, that is to say there are things that we now know we don't now. But there are also unknown unknowns, there are things we do not know we don't know, and each year we discover a few more of those unknown unknowns."
- "I would not say the future is necessarily less predicable than the past. I think the past was not predicable when it started."
- "Needless to say the President is correct. Whatever it was he said."
- "Well, um, you know, something's neither good nor bad but thinking makes it so, I suppose, as Shakespeare said."
- "Learn to say 'I don't know.' If used when appropriate, it will be often."
- "I believe what I said yesterday. I don't know what I said, but I know what I think, and I assume that's what I said."
- "If I know the answer, I'll tell you the answer, and if I don't, I'll just respond, cleverly."
- "Oh, Lord, I didn't mean to say anything quotable."

In addition to the Rummy doll there are others including Presidents Clinton, Reagan and both Bushes.[13] Yogi Berra would be proud!

Lawyers Are Often the Problem

Anyone practicing crisis communications has heard someone say, "If you lose in the court of public opinion, it doesn't matter what happens in the court of law." In a crisis, the ultimate objective should be to win in both the court of public opinion and the court of law.

Attorneys are responsible for protecting the company's legal position while the public relations counselor is responsible for protecting the company's image and reputation. And there will be conflicts. New York developer Douglas Durst was besieged by bad press for weeks after scaffolding collapsed at his Times Square Condé Nast construction site. He said from the beginning there was tension between his public relations counsel, who advocated immediate assistance to the thousands of displaced workers and residents, and the lawyers, who advised caution. The lawyers won. Durst lost.[14]

Harold Suckenik, a lawyer long active in public relations, says lawyers should never head public relations for a company or organization. "Lawyers normally operate in an adversarial milieu and are used to addressing small audiences, such as a judge or 12 jurors, as compared to audiences that may number in the millions," he says. "Lawyers are also used to working very slowly. They believe that the longer things take, the better – people forget things, move, die, give up, etc. Media, however, travel at blinding speed."[15]

Law schools don't prepare their graduates to enter the legal world knowledgeable about media relations, crisis management or public relations. Even a half-day seminar for graduating seniors would be better than no exposure at all. This creates serious problems during crisis situations when an attorney will want to stonewall the media and all public disclosure, while the public relations and crisis communications professional will want immediate and full disclosure. One must wonder if a course isn't given for attorneys to be suspicious of journalists. Attorneys are almost unanimous in their belief that an apology is completely out of the question because it could open the door for law suits. "Law schools don't teach crisis management and communications because lawyers make very little money preventing crises, but make a lot of money resolving them" says Timothy J. Sullivan, former president of The College of William & Mary and former dean of its law school. Business schools also need to educate their students on this subject.[16]

Crisis communications may get help if former U.S. District Judge Stanley Sporkin in Washington, D.C. has his way. He believes it is time for a university to create an institute of crisis management to teach business people how to handle corporate emergencies. Judge Sporkin has lectured on this subject for a decade and told *The Washington Post* that a "vast majority of crises are avoidable." He discussed developing an academic program with Paul Brest, dean of the Stanford University Law School, which already has merged crisis management training into its executive education programs and in-house counsel seminars.[17]

An attorney was the recipient of the first Muzzle Award given by Intel's former chairman and CEO, Andrew Grove. The award, a leather dog muzzle mounted on a wooden plaque, is given after a company official makes a foolish remark. The first Muzzle was given in the early 1980s after general counsel Roger Borovoy was quoted as saying: "Negotiating with the Japanese is like negotiating with the Devil."[18] In this case, perhaps silence would have been golden.

Sometimes one has to wonder whether or not *The Madwoman of Chaillot* by Jean Giraudoux was required or optional reading in law school. The author wrote: "You're an attorney. It's your duty to lie, conceal and distort everything ...."[19]

Jim Carey and Al Franken Will Love This

I'm sure Jim Carey, star of *Liar Liar*, and Al Franken author of *Lies and the Lying Liars Who Tell Them*, would love to meet the five justices of the Supreme Court of the State of Washington who said it is OK to lie!

In its 5-4 decision, the sharply divided justices ruled that the First Amendment even protects political campaign lies and struck down as unconstitutional a law barring political candidates from deliberately making false and even malicious statements about their opponents. The case was brought after a former state senate candidate was fined for making false statements about her opponent in a campaign flyer.

"There can be no doubt that false personal attacks are too common in political campaigns with wide-ranging detrimental consequences," said Justice James J. Johnson, writing the majority opinion. "However, government censorship is not a constitutionally permitted remedy." The four dissenting justices warn that the ruling is an invitation for lies and deceit in political campaigns.

Stewart Jay, a professor of constitutional law at the University of Washington, says the court is saying it shouldn't be in the business of regulating political speech. "The court has decided that it's just too dangerous to give the state the ability to decide when speech is true or false," he says.

This ruling bucks a trend by more than a dozen states that passed similar laws, and deviates from a 1991 U.S. Sixth Circuit Court of appeals decision that upheld a similar statute in Ohio.

The five justices who say it is all right to lie are: Gerry L. Alexander, chief justice; Charles W. Johnson, associate chief justice, and justices James M. Johnson, Susan Owens, and Richard B. Sanders. Dissenting were justices Bobbe J. Bridge, Tom Chambers, Mary E. Fairhurst, and Barbara Madsen. After their appointment expires, Washington State Supreme Court Justices must run for re-election, like all other political candidates. After the court's decision, how will the public know whether a candidate is telling the truth or lying?[20]

A Second Time Around For Washington

In 1998, the Washington Supreme Court by the same 5-4 split vote struck down a law enacted in 1984 that banned false political advertising. Then Justice Richard Sanders wrote the majority opinion and said: "The law chills political speech and assumes the people of this state are too ignorant or disinterested to investigate, learn, and determine for themselves the truth of falsity in political debate."[21]

In response to this decision, famed radio commentator Paul Harvey reported that the court decreed that it is legally permissible for a politician to lie. "We all knew that they often do it, but we didn't expect that they would be given a court's OK to do it," he said.[22]

Ethics, Lying A Universal Problem

Regrettably, telling lies is on the increase. The Ethics Resource Center reports there has been little if any meaningful reduction in unethical behavior in U.S. companies even six years after high-profile corporate scandals. Its survey 2007 of 2,000 employees at both publicly-held and private companies showed that conflicts of interest, abusive behavior and lying pose the most severe ethics risks today. Nearly 25 percent of employees lie today compared with 19 percent in 2005.

The businesses where people most likely will not tell the truth were hospitality and food, and arts, entertainment and recreation, both 34 percent. "Despite new regulation, and significant efforts to reduce misconduct and increase reporting when it does occur, the ethics risk landscape in American business is as treacherous as it was before implementation of the Sarbanes-Oxley Act of 2002," said Dr. Patricia Harned, president of Ethics Resource. "Since Enron, businesses are focusing more on compliance with the law than on building cultures where lying isn't tolerated."[23]

Don't Always Blame the Lawyers

During any crisis, leadership and the final decision for what course of action is to be followed rests with the CEO, so don't necessarily blame the attorneys during crisis situations. More often than not, the communications professional and the lawyer will disagree on how aggressive to be, how much can be told to the media and the public, and when it can be told.

A lot depends on the culture of the institution. Nonprofit organizations tend to be more conservative because of a volunteer, outside, board of directors. Most cannot respond quickly when a consensus of the board is needed in a crisis situation. The board's chairperson will probably want the final decision to be that of the attorney rather than the public relations communicator.

In the military, rank may have its privilege, but it creates problems in crisis situations. A lieutenant or captain may be very reluctant to tell a general what should be done or give the best advice. Also flag officers may be overly cautious in taking advice from a junior officer, even if the officer has had professional training in the communications field.

The same is true at all levels of government. Attorneys are more likely to be more adamant in their demands about what can and cannot be said and will always opt for silence. Senior executives in government are more likely to heed the advice of their legal counsel than their public relations practitioner. However, the farther one travels from the D.C. Beltway, the greater the influence of the professional communicator. Governors and mayors, in crisis situations, are more likely to take advice from their public relations counsel, press officer or pollster than their lawyer.

Keep Communications Privileged

Public relations counselor Jim Lukaszewski cautions attorneys and public relations practitioners to be aware that the attorney-client privilege protects certain confidential communication only between lawyer and client, from discovery in civil, criminal, or administrative proceedings. He says the Work Product Doctrine protects from discovery (although not absolutely) materials prepared or collected by an attorney in preparation for or in anticipation of litigation.

"Under the Work Product Doctrine, public relations work that, in an attorney's opinion, should be protected from discovery must be 'prepared, developed, or collected at the direction of an attorney in preparation for or in anticipation of possible litigation,'" he continues. "The doctrine includes materials prepared by investigators, consultants, accountants, engineers, etc., who are 'acting under an attorney's direction.'" He notes that obviously you must consult an attorney for specific guidance and warns that waiver of the doctrine can easily occur. "Virtually any unauthorized disclosure of information to parties without specific direction or authorization by counsel waives protection," Lukaszewski says.[24]

A Collaborative Effort

Relationships between the legal and public relations counselors need to be more collaborative believes Kathy R. Fitzpatrick, professor of public relations in the School of Communications at Quinnipiac University, Hamden, Connecticut. "Both serve the institution and it can't be an oil and water team," she says.[25]

Fitzpatrick, who is an attorney with a bachelor's degree in journalism, sees a trend with public relations associated with litigation to force defendants to settle before going to court. "In a court of law you are concerned with a closed universe – the judge and jury; the rules of procedure and law, and a legal vocabulary," she says. "In the court of public opinion you have to deal with the general public and target audiences and constituents. Litigation public relations is not an attempt to interfere with due process. It may be an attempt to influence resolution of conflict and should be a pro-active effort to maintain the positive reputation of the client company.

"The plaintiff's typical strategy is to be aggressive with the following objectives: to counteract defendant's advantage (David v. Goliath) and gain public sympathy; to bring public attention to an issue; to force a favorable settlement; to invite class action participation; to embarrass and discredit the defendant; and to pre-empt impending suits by another party," she says.[26]

Fitzpatrick says a defendant can have three typical strategies: defensive, with a "no comment" approach; responsive and end up scrambling; or proactive by defining the situation and managing the issues and process. She outlines the following objectives for defendants:

- to preserve the client company's credibility;
- to counteract negative publicity resulting from public charges;
- to make the company's viewpoint heard;
- to ensure balanced media coverage;
- to diffuse a hostile environment;

- to aid public understanding of the charges and judicial process;
- and, to take advantage of increased media attention and enhance the organization's visibility and reputation among important constituents.

Boards of Directors Also Can Be Problems

A well-intentioned board of directors that wants to micromanage can create a crisis. A classic case is that of William Aramony who was president of United Way of America. During his 22 years as head of the organization that serves 2,100 autonomous United Way locals, he increased annual receipts from $787 million to more than $3 billion and was responsible for an agreement with the National Football League that involved player participation and network advertising exposure.

When media began to inquire about Aramony's extravagant lifestyle and travel expenses, including flying the Concorde and purchases by United Way spin-off companies of condominiums in New York City and Coral Gables, Florida, the board not only vetoed a preemptive media approach, but closed off the public relations department to reporters. Anthony DeCristofaro, then vice president of corporate communications, and Sunshine Janda Overkamp, vice president for membership, marketing and communications, both wanted to go public with the scandal. "The media looked to others within the organization for details. The building became a sieve of information," said DeCristofaro. "The result was an experience you can't buy and probably don't want to."

Just days before his resignation, United Way's executive committee gave Aramony a unanimous vote of confidence. During a one-hour teleconference on February 28, 1992, he announced his resignation to his staff of 275 and to 90 local chapters. Dr. LaSalle D. Leffall, Jr., chair of the board's executive committee, who two years later was elected President of the American College of Surgeons, praised Aramony for his "decades of service" and said his committee "has reaffirmed its vote of confidence in him and his work." Some United Way executives in the field expressed anger at the board's limited response to critical press coverage and had already called for Aramony to step down. Other local chapters were withholding dues payments until they got satisfactory explanations about Aramony's expenses and management practices.

In 1995, Aramony was convicted on 25 counts, including conspiracy to defraud, mail fraud, wire fraud, transportation of fraudulently acquired property, engaging in unlawful monetary transactions, and aiding in the filing of false tax returns.

During the three-week trial, prosecutors portrayed him as a corrupt womanizer who spent hundreds of thousands of dollars of the charity's money to finance flings with young women, including sex in the back of limousines rented with the charity's funds. He also took trips to London, Paris, Las Vegas and Egypt and defrauded United Way of an estimated $1.2 million. District Judge Claude Hilton gave him seven of the eight years he faced under federal sentencing guidelines.

Even today "the frequently asked questions" or FAQ pages of many local United Way websites, which didn't exist when the story became public, have disclosures about Aramony to distance the local chapters from what happened at the national office.[27]

Sometimes Even the News Media Won't Comment

Any newspaper, magazine, radio or television reporter expects you to respond and do so immediately. Unfortunately, members of the media do not respond themselves the way they expect everyone else to respond. And, you have little recourse to let the world know their actions.

Reporters, producers, publishers and others in the news media don't always set a good example for people they want to interview. Alan Hirsch, president of G+A Communications, New York, collects articles when the news media say ""no comment" or avoid comment. Here are several from his collection:[28]

"*New York Post* editor Ken Chandler and *Post* publisher Martin Singerman didn't return repeated calls. Sports editor Greg Gallo said through a secretary that he was unavailable," - *Newsday*, December 13, 1996.

"Both father (Arthur O. Sulzberger) and son (Arthur Sulzberger, Jr.) [*The New York* Times] couldn't be reached for comment." - *The Wall Street Journal.*

"A spokeswoman for Channel 2 said Carey (general manager) could not be reached for comment." - *Newsday*

Today, media companies are very careful about disclosing news involving sister companies. If NBC is doing a story about General Electric, the announcer will mention that GE is the parent company of the network. The same for ABC and Disney.

However, sometimes media companies have suppressed stories that might hurt them. Richard Bressler, Time Warner's chief financial officer, asked journalist Steven Brill to kill a profile of William Baer, a Federal Trade Commission official, scheduled to appear in a Brill newsletter. Brill was the founder of *Court TV, The American Lawyer* and several smaller legal and business publications owned by Time Warner. Peter Haje, Time Warner's general counsel, asked Brill to kill a story in *The American Lawyer* about the Scientology litigation because it criticized reporting in *Time* magazine. Another company attorney asked him not to cover a case in Court TV involving a Warner music company.[29]

No Response = Implied Consent

Frank Swoboda of *The Washington Post* believes that a "no comment" is better than lying to a reporter. "Lie once and you are a liar forever," he says.[30] Former White House press secretary Mike McCurry said he got into trouble because he made a conscious choice not to ask President Clinton about his relationship with Monica Lewinsky. "I didn't seek the truth about Monica," he says. Yet he maintained his personal integrity by sticking to one important standard: "I cannot compound or further any lie."[31]

Never miss an opportunity to tell the public a positive story. However the attack may come – a newspaper editorial, a comment on a talk radio show, an erroneous remark made by a television reporter or even a letter to the editor or a posting on an Internet blog – look at the negative as being an opportunity to not only to correct an error or misunderstanding, but to say even more.

No response can even be worse than "no comment." That is why it is so important to have a crisis plan in place so the opportunity to tell a positive story will not be lost. It all comes down to anticipation, preparation/planning and response.

In February 2008 the board of visitors of The College of William & Mary decided not to renew the contract of Gene R. Nichol who had served nearly three years as president. Michael K. Powell, the former commissioner of the Federal Communications Commission, and an attorney, spoke for the board as its rector and sent an e-mail out to all alumni, students, faculty and friends that said: "... this decision was not in any way based on ideology or any single public controversy. ... Many policies championed by President Nichol are fully embraced by the board." When informed, Nichol, a former law school dean, announced he was resigning immediately and would not wait until his term expired on June 30. He then sent an e-mail letter to the same people saying he was the victim of a "relentless, frequently untruthful and vicious campaign" and that the board offered him substantial economic incentives not to characterize his termination as a fight over ideology or make any other statement without their approval. A crisis exploded.

Journalists who called the college's office of university relations asking to speak with Powell were given his contact number. Unfortunately, the local and national news media had almost all negative stories about the crisis with reports ranging from it being a cultural war over religion, First Amendment rights, and constitutional law to pressure from conservatives and members of the state legislature, and alumni threatening to cancel multimillion dollar gifts. Internet blogs were filled with statements both pro and con.

Powell's followup was to post a second statement and a Q&A on the regent's section of the college's website. Then the board spent a day on campus meeting with students, faculty, staff and anyone who wanted to meet with them to try and restore order. Because of the crisis, the college's image and reputation suffered its worst black eye since it was founded in 1693.

Before and after the campus meetings, Powell did meet with important local media. However, the college stayed in its responsive, rather than proactive mode, and did not pursue one-on-one interviews or editorial board meetings with national media. It also did not send any subsequent news releases to the media to further tell the board's reasons for its decision. Powell did not direct any messages to the general public throughout Virginia to win support for the tax supported college. His effort program was basically directed to internal audiences.

Anyone who e-mailed Powell for further clarification got the same generic 50-word response, regardless of the question asked. In fact, the author, who sent letters and e-mails to Powell on a completely different subject several times over the preceding 15 weeks, without even an acknowledgment, got the same 50-word reply e-mail when again asking for an answer.[32]

Powell, who is a William & Mary alumnus, could have taken advantage of the crisis to tell a very positive story about the college. He didn't. He should have looked to his father, Colin Powell, for the way the general communicates, whether or not it is a crisis situation. Powell's own gate guardians, Michael J. Fox, secretary to the board of visitors, and Sandra J. Wilms, administrative assistant, obviously never read the e-mails to him and both ignored e-mails sent to them for information. Since 1985, the presidents of William & Mary have been former law school deans. The attitude and philosophy of lawyers regarding crisis communications for more than 20 years could have so permeated the institution's culture that no one today knows how to respond.

Remember, not responding is the same as giving implied consent, that you agree with what was said or written, or you do not refute what was said or written. In effect, you agree. You never want this to happen. Perhaps Shakespeare was right and obviously Sir Thomas More was wrong.

Summary Checklist

- Always respond. Silence is not golden. You might not be beheaded like Sir Thomas More, but you could be looking for a new job.
- Never, never, ever tell the media "no comment."
- Anticipate, plan/prepare and respond.
- Remember a no response can often be worse than a "no comment."
- Never withhold information that eventually will become public.
- The quicker you get out all of the facts, the quicker you can get closure on the crisis.
- Treat the disclosure of bad news the same as you would good news.
- Be careful how you answer. Don't let your response get taken out of context.
- Expect there to be problems with lawyers regarding what can be said and when. Lawyers have no training in crisis management or communications.
- Five Supreme Court Justices in the State of Washington say it is OK for politicians to lie.
- Ethics and lying have become a universal problem.
- Don't always blame the lawyers if something goes wrong.
- Keep communications between lawyers and public relations practitioners privileged.
- Collaborate with the attorneys.
- Stand up to boards of directors who can sometimes be problems.
- Don't expect the media to respond the way they demand you to respond.
- Remember that in every crisis there is a positive opportunity.

Endnotes

[1] William Shakespeare, *Henry VI*, part II, act IV, scene II.

[2] Bergen Evans, *Dictionary of Quotations*, Delacourte Press, New York, N.Y., 1968, pg. 631.5.

[3] James E. Lukaszewski with Douglas A. Cooper, "You're Courting Disaster ... Without A Litigation Communications Strategy," *Executive Action*, The Lukaszewski Group, White Plains, N.Y., April/May/June 1992.

[4] *Jack O'Dwyer's Newsletter*, November 13, 1995, pg. 7.

[5] *Public Relations Reporter*, January 4, 1999, pg. 6.

[6] E-mail, James Cox, November 26, 2007.

[7] Judy A. Smith, "Learning from Crisis: In the Heat of the Battle," *Public Relations Strategist*, pg. 33.

[8] *Jack O'Dwyer's Newsletter*, January 24, 1996, pg. 3.

[9] Meg Greenfield, "The Last Word," *Newsweek*, December 2, 1996, pg. 100.

[10] Tim Wheeler, environmental writer, *The Baltimore Sun*, during meeting of environmental communicators, Baltimore, Md., June 12, 1997.

[11] Colin Powell with Joseph E. Persico,, *My American Dream,* Ballantine Books, 1996, pg. 285.

[12] E-mail, Ron Levy, Episodic Public Relations, December 5, 2007.

[13] Al Kamen, "A holiday gift that keeps on talking," *The Washington Post*, November 24, 2007; www.politicalhumor.about.com; www.slate.com.

[14] "After the Fall," *Public Relations Tactics*, October 1998, pg. 1.

[15] *Jack O'Dwyer's Newsletter, January 24, 1996, pg. 3.*

[16] *Letter to the author from Timothy J. Sullivan, Esq., July 1, 2004*

[17] *Jack O'Dwyer's Newsletter*, September 11, 1996, pg.9.

[18] Stephen C. Rafe, APR, "How To Say 'No Comment,'" *Public Relations Tactics, October 1998.*

[19] *The International Thesaurus of Quotations,* compiled by Rhoda Thomas Tripp, Thomas Y. Crowell Company, New York, N.Y., 1970, pg. 525.34.

[20] Rickert v. Public Disclosure Commission, Docket No. 77769-1, Supreme Court of the State of Washington, October 4, 2007; Austin Jenkins, Oregon Public Broadcasting, October 4, 2007; Eric Firkel, Paper Chase, University of Pittsburgh School of Law, October 7, 2007.

[21] Hunter T. George, Associates Press, June 11, 1998.

[22] Ohio Bible Fellowship, Bucyrus, Ohio.

[23] "Ethics Risk Landscape Just As Treacherous," 2007 National Business Ethics Survey, Ethics Resource Center, Arlington, Va., November 28, 2007; Aili McConnon, "An Uptick In Untruths," *Business Week*, December 17, 2007.

[24] Letter of September 4, 1997 to the author from James E. Lukaszewski, The Lukaszewski Group Inc., White Plains, N.Y.

[25] Kathy R. Fitzpatrick, "The Newest PR Discipline Managing Legally Driven Issues," conference of the Public Relations Society of America, Nashville, Tenn., November 11, 1997, and e-mail to the author, December 4, 2007.

[26] Ibid.

[27] Matthew Sinclair, "William Aramony Is Back On The Streets," *The NonProfit Times*, March 1, 2002; Michael Duffy, "Resignation Charity Begins At Home," *Time*, June 24, 2001; Charles E. Shepard, "United Way Head Resigns Over Spending Habits," *The Wash-*

ington Post, February 28, 1992; *Public Relations News.*

[28] *Jack O'Dwyer's Newsletter, May 21, 1997, pg. 7.*

[29] *Jonathan Alter, "The Dog That Barked," Newsweek, July 21, 1997, pg. 53.*

[30] *"Honest Is Best Policy In A Crisis," Jack O'Dwyer's Newsletter*, June 30, 1999, pg. 2.

[31] "McCurry on McCurry," *Ragan's Media Relations Report*, June 1, 1999, pg. 3.

[32] Susan Kinzle, "William and Mary President Resigns," *The Washington* Post, February 13, 2008; "Presidential Ouster at William & Mary," insidehighered.com, February 13, 2008; *David* G. Savage, "Where religion, ideology and the Web cross," *The Los Angeles* Times, February 17, 2008; Marc Fisher, "College Got What It Signed Up For," *The Washington Post*, February 17, 2008; Editorial, "William and Mary: What not to learn from a president's departure," *The Washington Post*, February 18, 2008; Associated Press, "Gene Nichol resigns college presidency," *Rocky Mountain News*, Denver, Colorado, February 18, 2008. Shawn Day, "Vandalism targets William and Mary officials," *The Daily Press*, Newport News, Virginia, February 18, 2008; William & Mary websites, www.wm.edu/bov and www.wm.edu/news, and e-mails between the author and Michael Connolly and Brian Whitson, William & Mary office of university relations, March 2008.

CHAPTER 5

STUPID IS AS STUPID DOES*
*with thanks to Forrest Gump

People do stupid things. Really stupid things. And, when they do, they often create crises or they make crises even worse.

Many crises are inevitable and will happen regardless. However, using plain common sense is the best possible approach to preventing many crises.

Case histories and anecdotes in this chapter will serve as examples both of what not to do, and practices that professionals have used to resolve crises.

Think Twice About Suing When A Celebrity Is Involved

The Texas cattlemen should have thought twice before taking on Oprah Winfrey. They sued the most popular woman on television. Not only was there no win in the court of law, they lost in the court of public opinion. Everything negative about beef was talked about again and again during the trial, which became an international event for Amarillo, a city of 150,000 in the northwest Texas Panhandle.

What created all of the controversy was the April 16, 1996 *Oprah* show. This aired shortly after British officials announced that mad-cow disease had been linked to the deaths of 20 people in Britain who ate infected beef. Appearing on her show was Howard Lyman, a Montana cattle rancher turned vegetarian activist who said that feeding animal parts to cattle was a common practice that could spread mad cow disease, or bovine spongiform encephalopathy (BSE), to humans. Mad cow disease destroys the brain and forced the slaughter of 1.5 million cows in Britain.[1]

Winfrey also had as a guest, Gary Weber, an animal expert from the National Cattlemen's Beef Association. Lyman compared the disease to AIDS. After he supplied more details, Winfrey said: "Now doesn't that concern you all a little bit right here, hearing that?" The studio audience responded with cheers. "It has stopped me cold from eating another hamburger," she continued, "I'm stopped."

After the broadcast aired, cattle prices, which already had been falling, dropped to near 10-year lows. Ninety minutes after the show aired in Chicago, cattle prices had fallen $1.50 a pound, testified Tim Brennan, a futures trader and member of the Chicago Mercantile Exchange. Brennan said a colleague tipped him to the show's topic moments after it went on the air and he hastily placed a "sell" order. Winfrey's attorney suggested it was the traders themselves who caused the biggest cattle market plunge in a decade and not his client.[2]

Hollywood descended on Amarillo as Winfrey moved the production of her show there during the trial. Texans Patrick Swayze, Clint Black and his wife, Lisa Hartman were among her first guests. Bumper stickers expressed the emotion of the townspeople: "Amarillo Loves Oprah" and "The Only Mad Cow in America Is Oprah." As popular as her show was, only seven of the 58 people in the jury pool had ever seen it.[3]

Enforcing All Rules Could Backfire

Marina Baktis and Vanessa Chekroun, co-founders of Mutts & Moms, a Pasadena, California dog rescue shelter, probably got far more publicity for their nonprofit organization than they would have liked after taking on Ellen DeGeneres. At the center of the crisis was a little black Brussels Griffon mixed terrier named Iggy. DeGeneres spent $3,000 to have Iggy neutered and trained to be nice with her three cats and gave an additional $400 to Mutts & Moms. But the dog didn't adapt.

DeGeneres and her partner, Portia de Rossi, had a similar problem with another dog they adopted from the animal adoption agency and they returned it for Iggy. When Iggy didn't work out, they gave him to Cheryl Marks, her hairdresser, for her husband and 11- and 12-year-old daughters to enjoy.

When Baktis said DeGeneres had violated an agreement with her agency by giving Iggy to another family, she went to the Marks' home and took back the dog. "I never intended to do anything but place the dog in a loving home," a tearful DeGeneres told her television viewing audience. "Seven million dogs are euthanized each year, and this should be about rescuing the dogs. I made a big mistake, and never wanted the family or the dog to suffer."

According to Keith Fink, the attorney representing Baktis and Chekroun, the contract says the dog must be returned to the rescue group if the owners decide not to keep it. "Ellen is no lover of Iggy," Fink said. "The people who are the animal lovers, who have given their life for dogs, are my clients."

The animal-loving public was outraged at Mutts & Moms, which was besieged with e-mails and threats because many local animal shelters have benefited from DeGeneres' support. She frequently makes appearances at benefits for various rescues, and when she has a scheduling conflict, she often provides funding and other support.

"I feel everyone has made huge mistakes – Ellen has publicly admitted she made a mistake and was in violation of a contract, and Marina could have handled the situation more sensibly," said Jo Forman, a former costume supervisor for *Frasier* and founder of the Bill Foundation, a dog-rescue group based in Beverly Hills.

"This is what gives rescue groups a bad name," said Marc Rosen, a producer at Rosen-Obst Productions and chairman of Operation Doggy Drop. "Ellen is a beacon of support for animal adoptions, now they are souring her against that endeavor."

Ed Boks, general manager of the Los Angeles Department of Animal Services, said "This seems like an extraordinary situation. I don't think they're [Mutts & Moms] acting in the animal's best interests.

I wonder if anyone thought to ask Iggy where he wanted to live.[4]

Since the incident, DeGeneres and Richard Thompson, the former owner of Meow Mix, have teamed up to rebuild animal shelters across the U.S.[5]

Hollywood or Science?

Steve Shapiro, associate chairman of the physics department at Brookhaven National Laboratory, blames Christie Brinkley for shutting down the facility.

In 1999, Brinkley went to Washington, D.C. to meet with Bill Richardson when he was Secretary of Energy, to coerce him into shutting down this nuclear facility. Brookhaven was located on top of one of only four single-source freshwater springs in the U.S. This one extended the length of Long Island. She pointed out that it had been more than two years since the public learned that Brookhaven had been leaking radioactive water into the ground unnoticed for more than a decade.

Brinkley, along with actor Alec Baldwin and many other celebrities and media elite, is a member of STAR, acronym for Standing for Truth Against Radiation. Richardson was concerned about closing one of the country's most productive scientific labs but if he did not, the political fallout could pose significant problems for both him and the Clinton Administration.

The supermodel outlined in detail a scenario that would unfold if Brookhaven was not mothballed, including further groundwater contamination and potential worker exposure to cancer-causing substances. She also reminded Richardson that if he did not acquiesce, his political ambitions could be seriously comprised.

Richardson insisted that Brookhaven was closed for budget reasons and not politics. "I was impressed with Christie Brinkley's commitment, professionalism and sincerity," he said.

Shapiro disagrees. "Christie had a great deal of influence in the decision," he said. "Models have more to say about the fate of Brookhaven than a Nobel Prize-winning scientist. This is scary."[6]

Cupcakes for Paris

Los Angeles County Sheriff Lee Baca was widely criticized when he sent Paris Hilton home with Mrs. Beasley's Gourmet Cupcakes after she had served only three days of her 45-day sentence for violation of her probation for alcohol-related reckless driving. Baca said he had reassigned Hilton to home confinement because of her "severe medical problems." Steve Lopez of *The Los Angeles Times* noted that [releasing Paris] was big of [Baca], but [Los Angeles County Jail] is filled with people who have serious physical and mental problems. How many of them get sent home with cupcakes? The problem, according to RadarOnline.com may be the Sheriff's "close ties to the Hollywood community."[7] One late-night comedian suggested that if the judge was seeking justice, he would have sentenced Paris to 45 days in a Hilton hotel room.

Can You Trust Your Doctor's Recommendation?

If you're getting a replacement hip or knee, maybe you should ask your doctor if he is being paid by the manufacturer of the replacement part, and if so, how much and for what. The U.S. Department of Justice alleged that consulting fees paid to physicians by five device manufacturers violated federal anti-kickback laws. As part of the settlement, Zimmer Holdings, Stryker, Johnson & Johnson subsidiary DePuy Orthopaedics, Biomet, and Smith & Nephew post consultant lists on their websites. With the exception of Stryker, the firms paid settlements ranging from $26.9 to $169.5 million.

Zimmer Holdings' Internet site has 14 pages showing it paid 771 doctors, hospitals and medical associations more than $86 million for a variety of consultant services. The Warsaw, Indiana firm manufactures artificial hips and knees.

The American Academy of Orthopaedic Surgeons recommends that its members tell any patient if they are being paid by the manufacturer of a replacement knee or hip. Some device makers compensated physicians for heavy usage of products comparable to paying royalties. Other companies rewarded physicians for perfectly legitimate inventions and procedures.

The Mayo Clinic in Rochester, Minnesota disclosed that 22 of its physicians received $3.9 million in 2007 from three companies with the majority of the money going to six doctors for royalties on products they invented. Other prestigious hospitals also are becoming more transparent for their patients.[8]

Bridgestone/Firestone and Ford – Too Little, Too Late

The 2000 Ford-Firestone crisis is an excellent case history from which to learn basic rules of crisis communications. The crisis led to the federal investigation of some 100 deaths, more than 300 incidents involving Ford Explorers with Firestone tires and the recall of 6.5 million Firestone tires.

A great deal has been written on this debacle, and there are pages of opinions, recommendations, theories and blame posted on the Internet. Was the cause in the design? Or manufacturing? Or tire pressure? "Anyone who believes Ford and Firestone doesn't know what's causing this lives in a fantasy world," said Tab Turner, a Little Rock, Arkansas lawyer who is handling 20 lawsuits against Ford and Firestone.[9]

Some basic rules that could have been followed:

- *Show compassion.* Because there were deaths, both companies could have began by showing empathy and remorse and saying, "I'm sorry."

- *Select the right spokesperson.* Was Jacques Nasser, the CEO of Ford, the best spokesperson? Ford gained more public support when William Clay "Bill" Ford, Jr., the company's chairman and great-grandson of both Henry Ford and Harvey Firestone, took over as the official spokesperson with the media and in Ford's television commercials.

- *Don't stonewall or hold back information.* Management at Firestone, owned since 1988 by Japan's Bridgestone, stonewalled the media which could have been the result of a cultural difference in dealing with public problems. The company's first spokesperson was an executive vice president when CEO Masatoshi Ono should have been out front. From the beginning, Ono should have said, "I'm sorry" and "we will fix the problem."

- *Don't overtalk.* "Firestone spent too much time talking about what it believed was the cause of the tire shredding," says Richard Nicolazzo of Nicolazzo & Associates, Boston, Massachusetts strategic communications counseling firm. "Rhetoric about 'under-inflation,' 'improper maintenance,' and 'hot road conditions' did little to calm the driving public. By emphasizing these points, Firestone was blaming the victim," he adds. "Ultimately, the reason they recalled the tires was because there appeared to be a quality control problem. It would have been better to say 'whatever is wrong, we will make sure every customer is taken care of.'"[10]

- *Coordinate with others involved.* The two companies should have collaborated early and coordinated their crisis- response efforts rather than blame each other. Nasser said Ford didn't know there was a defect with the tires "until we virtually pried the claims from Firestone's hands and analyzed it."

- *Do not delay in accepting responsibility.* Not until he appeared at a Congressional hearing did Bridgestone's Ono accept responsibility. "We accept full and personal responsibility," he told members of Congress regarding the recall of 6.5 million tires, mostly on Ford Explorers. However, he added that a design defect that was causing tread to peel away at high speeds and the company's party line by executives was to blame consumers for improperly maintaining their tires.

- *Be sure facts are documented.* During a third round of Congressional hearings, John Lampe, Firestone executive vice president, said "Running an overloaded Explorer at low tire pressure, particularly in hot climates, appears to be a serious part of the problem we are now facing." Ford had been recommending a lower tire pressure than Firestone for the tires involved.

- *Don't blame the consumer.* While the finger-pointing at Ford may have helped Firestone in a court of law, it did not in the court of public opinion.

- *Always tell the truth, never lie and get the facts out as quickly as possible.* Bridgestone/Firestone failed to do this in sworn testimony and public statements. Executives said that the company wasn't aware of potentially fatal tread-separation problems until July 2000. During the Congressional hearings, an investigation by the National Highway Traffic Safety Administration probe that began in May linked Firestone tires to at least 101 deaths in the U.S. and internal documents indicated that the company knew of tire trouble in 1994. In 1997, Bridgestone/Firestone began receiving many complaints about tire failure but never notified Ford. Congress had company reports from 1998, 1999 and 2000 that showed tread peeling from tires and one of the types involved in the recall.

In 1998, because of a growing number of claims involving Firestone tires on Ford Explorers, State Farm Insurance alerted the federal government. Rollover tests were performed and Ford was told about instability problems. Ford then got reports of tread separations in Saudi Arabia and later asked Firestone to investigate problems in Venezuela. Firestone reported back that nothing was wrong. Labor unrest can lead to crisis problems. In July 2000 Firestone discovered that more than half of the tires manufactured at its Decatur, Illinois plant between 1994 and1996 had tread separation. The company settled a worker's strike there in 1996.

In Japan, the value of Bridgestone's stock fell by $10 billion before slightly recovering. The company said the recall would cost $350 million but it was expected to increase substantially before the end of the recall. North America accounts for 40 percent of the company's sales.

The National Transportation Safety Agency linked more than 119 deaths and 500 injuries to Firestone tires used on the Ford Explorer. It also said it had received 3,500 complaints about accidents, principally Ford Explorer rollovers with Firestone tires.

Fleishman-Hillard, Firestone's public relations agency, resigned the account Labor Day weekend when the company refused to take its advice and be more aggressive with its communications.[11] "When there are significant cultural differences between the foreign owners of a company and the natives of the country in which they're doing business, those owners must be willing to defer crisis communications strategy and decisions to those who best understand the culture(s) in which they are communicating," says Jonathan Bernstein of Bernstein Crisis Management. This could have been one critical reason for Bridgestone's response.[12]

The Bridgestone crisis along with public relations blunders by Mitsubishi Motors Corp. and other major Japanese companies prompted the Tokyo Chamber of commerce and Industry in mid-July 2000 to print 1,000 copies of a book on how to effectively deal with the media during a crisis. The copies sold out in one day and another 42,000 were printed. Japan's leading economic daily, *Nihon Keizai Shimbun*, editorialized that Ford had done an effective public relations campaign and blamed the tires for the problems, "Bridgestone's silence strategy failed in that it only bred mistrust in consumers and investors," said Glen Fukushima, president of Arthur D. Little consulting firm in Japan. "Public relations is not considered all that important in Japan."[13]

Two Wrongs Don't Make A Right, Even for The Donald

Soon after Donald Trump agreed to apologize to the St. Regis Mohawk Indians for trying to block the tribal council's plans for a casino in the Catskills, he announced plans to build a Mohawk Indian-run casino on Manhattan's West Side. Trump spent $118,000 to finance a media campaign by The New York Institute for Law and Society that accused the Mohawks of "habitual violence and illegality."

In addition to a $250,000 fine paid to New York's Temporary State Commission on Lobbying, Trump spent another $50,000 for an ad campaign in upstate New York to apologize and avoid a public hearing before the commission.

It was not clear if "The Donald" was announcing a serious move or trying to regroup after being identified as the instigator of ads which the St. Regis Tribal Council called "racist." Gaming analysts also noted that Trump feared that any new casino in the Catskills could impact his holdings in Atlantic City.[14]

New Business Campaign "Bombs" Out

Why would anyone, especially a law firm, send a fake hand grenade paperweight through the mail? But this is what Quinn Emanuel Urquhart, Oliver & Hedges, LLP, did with a "Business is War" marketing campaign. Michael Fineman wondered what were they thinking as this action made his PR Blunders of the Year.

The company, which says its 375 lawyers makes it the country's largest business litigation firm, targeted technology companies for new business with some 600 grenades sent by priority mail. "Our marketing consultant told us this is Silicon Valley, they're youthful, kind of aggressive, edgy, and so this is an effective promotion to do," Steve Madison, a senior partner told the *San Francisco Chronicle*.

One recipient and a Sunnyvale, California recycling plant, which found a discarded grenade, called the local bomb squad. Another ended up with the U.S. Postal Service, and Inspector Linda Joe said this was not the first time mailed promotional devices have created problems. She said while she felt the mailing violated common sense it would be hard to prove that any laws were violated or that the law firm and its marketing consultant intended any harm.

The law firm said the promotion was cleared in advance with postal officials.

It fired its marketing consultant, offered to pay for the time spent by the bomb squad, contacted all recipients with an offer to send couriers to round up the fake grenades.[15]

If Not Grenades, Why Not Eggs?

Executives and personalities at Philadelphia radio station WMMR-FM ended up with egg on their faces after a ridiculous promotion asking listeners to mail raw eggs to the station in a letter-size envelope. To further compound the crisis, no one at the station even realized that the contest would coincide with the April 15 income-tax-return deadline.

Local postal authorities unwittingly participated in the crisis by faxing the radio station the postal regulations for mailing perishable items. The regulations served as contest rules, and the first person to successfully mail an unblemished and properly packaged egg in a #10 envelope would win $1,000.

Local post offices weren't amused as workers found raw eggs oozing over other mail, including tax returns. "If an egg got into our high-tech equipment, it could be very costly to repair," said Paul Smith of the U.S. Postal Service in Philadelphia. "We would never do this again," said Sam Milkman, the station's program director. "It was a lack of foresight on our part." WMMR apologized on air hourly to all postal workers.

Potato Chips or French Fries?

In 2005, Bill Lockyer, California's attorney general, filed suit to force top makers of potato chips and French fires to warn consumers about an (allegedly) potential cancer-causing chemical found in the popular snacks. Specifically named as defendants were McDonald's Corp., Wendy's International Inc., PepsiCo's Frito-Lay Inc. and Procter & Gamble Co.

According to Jonathan Bernstein of Bernstein Crisis Management, the lawsuit charges the companies with violating a 1986 state law requiring companies to provide warnings before exposing people to known carcinogens or reproductive toxins – in this case, a substance called "acrylamide."

"In 2002, scientists found potatoes and other starch foods cooked at high temperatures contained low levels of acrylamide," says Bernstein. "But (as always) other studies have discounted the potential toxicity or acrylamide to humans. The FDA, to date, has said that 'high doses of acrylamide can cause cancer in laboratory animals, although it is not clear whether it causes cancer in humans at the much lower levels found in food.' "However, the companies named really weren't in a high-threat position and any of them could have made statements about their commitments to consumer safety and other calming messages. Instead, Procter & Gamble spokeswoman Kay Puryear made this statement to CNN: 'Acrylamide is available whether those foods are prepared in a restaurant, at home or by the packaged goods industry,' she said. 'We stand behind, and absolutely think, our products are as safe as ever.' The first sentence is not in the least reassuring," says Bernstein, "and in the second, you will note that she does not say, 'Our products are safe.'"

Here are lessons Bernstein recommends for crisis managers:[16]

- If you don't say it, they can't print it.

- When there are allegations that raise consumer fears, messages of reassurance should be the first thing said by defendant companies.

- Remember that the Internet ensures that your mis-statements will be around the haunt you for a lon-n-n-ng time. And it will preserve your wise comments as well.

This Crisis Is Its Own Novel

Judith Regan, who had her own publishing imprint at HarperCollins called Regan Books, filed a $100 million defamation lawsuit in November 2007 against Rupert Murdoch's media conglomerate, News Corp., alleging she was asked by company officials to lie to federal investigators to protect the presidential bid of Rudolph Giuliani. Regan said News Corp.'s political agenda was to protect Giuliani's campaign related to the controversies involving Bernard Kerik, his former police commissioner, whom the former mayor promoted to head Home Security for the city.

Regan had confided to company executives as early as 2001 that she had an affair with Kerik, whose book, *The Lost Son*, she published soon after the 9/11 attacks. In December 2004, George W. Bush nominated Kerik to be Secretary of Homeland Security, and a week later Bush withdrew the nomination, explaining that Kerik had employed an illegal immigrant as a nanny. Regan says in her lawsuit that a News Corp. executive advised her to lie and withhold information from investigators concerning Kerik.

In November 2005, New Jersey officials said Kerik abused his position as New York City correction commissioner in the late 1990s by accepting tens of thousands of dollars from a construction company that had long standing ties to organized crime. In 2006, Kerik pleaded guilty to two unrelated ethics violations after an investigation by the Bronx District Attorney's office, and he was ordered to pay $221,000. A year later, federal prosecutors asked a grand jury to indict him on 16 charges, including tax, mail and wire fraud, corruption, conspiracy and lying to the Internal Revenue Service.

Regan also charged that company officials orchestrated a "smear campaign" to discredit her in 2006 after she promoted a memoir by O.J. Simpson, *If I Did It, Here's How It Happened*. She is often a favorite of New York gossip columnists because of her in-your-face personality, and an episode of *Law & Order* was based on her hypothetical murder.[17]

Martha, Don't Trademark Our Town

Katonah, New York is one of three small unincorporated hamlets in the town of Bedford in Westchester County, an hour drive from New York City. It has 12,438 residents and the average house sells for $912,000. Martha Stewart bought a 152-acre estate on the edge of town near the former home of John Jay, first Chief Justice of the U.S. Supreme Court.

It is a charming village with shops that include Katonah Yarn and Katonah Architectural Hardware, and many of the small businesses, where Stewart and her staff shop. People were concerned when she wanted to trademark a furniture line named Katonah. "To the people of Katonah, it is like identity theft," said Lydia Landesberg, president of the Katonah Village Improvement Society.

The townspeople told the U.S. Patent and Trademark Office they feared a Stewart trademark could prevent some local stores from using the name of their own village. Stewart's lawyers, who noted that no one protested Philadelphia cream cheese, withdrew the trademark application in all categories except furniture, pillows, mirrors and chair pads.[18]

Charities Under Fire For Not Giving Back

The University of Washington Medical Center was the main sponsor and sole benefactor of the annual Seattle Marathon, but in 2007 it received just one percent of more than $1 million in revenues raised by the race organizers. Signs, banners and the public address announcer told more than 11,000 runners that their efforts were to "to benefit UW Medical Center Patient & Family Housing Fund." The same information was posted on the marathon's website.

Compare this with the 2007 Portland (Oregon) Marathon, which donated $200,000, to charity and the annual Susan G. Komen Race for the Cure 5K fun run which raised $1.8 million with 84 percent going directly to breast cancer screening, treatment, education and research.

When the low payout of the Seattle Marathon was made public, many people were outraged, and the spokespersons fumbled for excuses. "Only money given in addition to race fees goes to the UW Medical Center Patient & Family Housing Fund," said Tina Mankowski, UW Medicine spokeswoman, when she apologized to runners who mistakenly believed that part of their race fee would go to charity. We weren't looking for $12,000 back. We were really looking for an opportunity to talk to the public about organ donation." The university also paid the race organizers $125,000 to help put on the race.

"The sole purpose of the marathon is to be the area's best running and walking event," said John Kokes, president of the Seattle Marathon Association. "The marathon exists as an athletic event, not a fundraising event."

"We chose to become a lead sponsor for the event to promote public understanding and awareness for organ donation," says Dr. Mark A. Emmert, president of the University of Washington. "This was accomplished through the stories included in materials prepared by the Marathon Association, as well as by participation of more than 200 transplant patients and their supporters who either walked or ran the marathon. Team Transplant helped spread the word that organ donation works, while encouraging the community to sign donor cards.

"As a regional transplant center, UW Medical Center can perform these life saving surgeries only when donor organs are available. Sadly, the number of individuals electing to become donors has steadily declined," Dr. Emmert added. The UW program also assists families with housing needs while they are awaiting organ transplants. He noted that the registration forms clearly indicated that supporting the housing fund was voluntary and optional, and that a contribution was separate from the registration fee.[19]

"We don't do the event to make a lot of money," said Louise Long, race director, whose firm was paid $162,000. Four board members resigned when Long did not answer their questions regarding finances and conflicts of interest. There has not been an audit of finances in 37 years.

"Shame. Shame on organizers for misleading not only the public but the people they purport to be helping, all the while jacking up entry fees and making sure they got paid," wrote *Seattle Times* columnist Nicole Brodeur.[20]

In February 2008 the university cancelled its title sponsorship of the marathon but said it would continue to contribute some money, medical care and water for the runner.

Better Not Mess With Da Coach

When football great Mike Ditka learned that his Hall of Fame Assistance Trust Fund had given only a small amount of money to needy former NFL players, he decided to dissolve the charity he had founded in 2004. In three years it had raised $1.3 million and reportedly distributed only $57,000 to former players. Ditka said the trust actually had given away $159,000.

A former coach of the Chicago Bears, "Coach of the Year" multiple times and honored in both the college and pro football Halls of Fame, Ditka said the fund's balance of more than $600,000 would be divided equally between Misericordia, a residential facility for developmentally disabled youth, and Gridiron Greats Assistance Fund, another fund that helps former professional football players in need.[21]

Televangelists Should Watch Out for the Senator

Senator Charles Grassley (R-Iowa) of the Senate Finance Committee sent a 42-page questionnaire to leaders of many religious charities. One was Joyce Meyer, who has even been criticized by other pastors for her elaborate lifestyle and office fixtures that include a $23,000 chest of drawers. Her estimated annual income was reported to be $124 million.

Another was Creflo Dollar, a former football player turned pastor who has two homes and two Rolls Royces, and gave a gift of $500,000 to Kenneth Copeland. The senator wants Copeland, a protégé of Oral Roberts, to answer why he pays no taxes and whether use of his ministries' jet for flights to Hawaii and Fiji qualified as business trips.[22]

In October 2007, Richard Roberts, televangelist and son of Oral Roberts, was named as a defendant in a lawsuit alleging improper use of Oral Roberts University funds for political and personal purposes, along with the improper use of university resources. He resigned as president of the university. and still hosts a religious television show and conducts international evangelistic crusades.

Two Sides To Every Story

When toys made in China were recalled by manufacturers, American consumers blamed Chinese companies. I was in China in August and September 2007 when this was making headlines. The Chinese felt they were being unfairly blamed and criticized. One political cartoon showed an oversized, bloated Uncle Sam with dollar bills coming out of pockets sitting on two tiny Chinese workers – one worker was labeled "reduce costs," and the other "faster production time."

On August 14 Mattel recalled more than nine million toys made in China citing possible problems with lead paint and magnets that could be swallowed. Just days earlier America's largest toymaker had recalled 1.5 million toys from a different Chinese supplier because of lead paint.

Reports from CNN International and the BBC from Singapore and Hong Kong and English-language newspapers blamed U.S. manufacturers for demanding the lowest possible production costs, for design flaws, and for not having supervisors or inspectors on site. This was not reported by the media in the U.S. Some foreign journalists cited problems American consumers are having with repeated recalls of U.S. produced ground beef, spinach and other food products contaminated with e-coli, and suggested that this be put in perspective with the toy recalls.

Proactive public relations techniques are new to the Chinese, and they have not undertaken aggressive campaigns to tell their story globally on most subjects. "If you can see it, you'll believe it" is old Chinese saying, and people need to understand that there are two sides to most stories.

Unlike most toymakers, Mattel actually owns and runs some of its own factories in China. This may be the reason just a month after the recalls why the toy giant met with, and apologized to, officials of the Chinese government. The apology was made one week in advance of a trip to China by Mattel's chief executive, Robert Eckert, to personally inspect new manufacturing safeguards.

The U.S. media buried well into the apology story Eckert's statement that the recall of 17 million doll accessories and cars had nothing to do with manufacturing, but with Mattel's design of magnets. Compounding the problem is the fact that political candidates are often very uninformed by young and inexperienced staff. On the campaign trail in New Hampshire, Democratic presidential candidate Senator Barak Obama of Illinois said that since 80 percent of all toys were being imported from China, he would ban all toys made in China, and he specifically cited small magnets as hazards. Chinese officials acknowledged some problems but insisted media has hyped the issue. The writer of the story also did not do his homework.[23]

The toy industry is a multi-billion dollar business in China. To protect its interests, the government has closed some 800 manufacturers, and has 200,000 inspectors checking all kinds of plants and manufacturers, including pharmaceuticals and farming.[24]

Changing the Public's Perception

Five major crises in the chemical industry prompted a five-year, $50 million advertising campaign to reverse the decline in public opinion of the industry. Polls showed that only Big Tobacco was held in lower regard. It even changed its name from the Chemical Manufacturers Association to the American Chemistry Council. Here are the tragic crises that changed the industry:

- *Hoffman-LaRoche, 1976, Seveso, Italy.* An explosion at a Swiss-owned factory released a cloud of dioxin that killed pets and farm animals and poisoned nearby land. Although no people died, subsequent tests revealed the highest levels of dioxin ever found in humans.

- *Hooker Chemical and Plastics, 1978-80, Love Canal near Niagara Falls, N.Y.* Almost 1,000 families were evacuated in 1980 when it was discovered their homes were built on a decades-old dumping ground for 20,000 tons of industrial waste. This led to the creation of EPA's Superfund.

- *Peroleos Mexicanos (Pemex), 1984, San Juan Ixhuatepec, Mexico.* Multiple explosions ripped through a storage facility resulting in an inferno that leveled 20 blocks of a Mexico City suburb and killed at least 500 people. It was the worst industrial accident in Mexico, which has one of the highest chemical-accident rates in the world.

- *Union Carbide, 1984, Bhopal, India.* A highly toxic compound used to make pesticides leaked and killed at least 3,000 people, and made another 75,000 sick. The company blamed sabotage. The accident was a major factor in the development in the U.S. for emergency response plans for chemical facilities and community right-to-know laws.

- *Phillips Petroleum, 1989, Pasadena, Texas.* Leaking gases at a refinery ignited, triggering a series of explosions that killed 23 people and injured more than 120. An investigation revealed that there was no backup system to protect against leaks. This led to new safety guidelines by the Occupational Safety and Health Administration for petrochemical plants.

The chemical industry believes its efforts have worked. "Members of the American Chemistry Council are among the most safety-conscious companies in the world," says Phil Cogan, director of external relations for the Chemical Safety and Hazard Investigation Board, a federal agency whose members are appointed by the President of the U.S.

Others, however, see a wide gulf between industry rhetoric and reality. "The same old accidents occur time and time again," says Irv Rosenthal, a member of the Chemical Safety Board. The Board also says the significance of chemical mishaps in the U.S. is not their size but frequency.

Environmental groups also have strong opinions. "Companies continue to take positions in state legislatures that undermine the regulatory process and deny the public's right to know," says Ross Vincent, chairman of the Sierra Club's Environmental Quality Strategy Team and a member of the American Chemistry Council's Public Advisory Panel.

Federal law requires chemical companies to inform local communities what it is making and storing. "If they do commit to communications, they are inexperienced at selecting the right people," says Carol Forrest, an Illinois consultant who helps chemical companies. She recalls one company spokesperson who claims she didn't really need to understand environmental regulations, and wouldn't discuss accident prevention measures because that would confirm that accidents might occur. "This attitude is beyond stupid," says Forrest.[25]

She Giveth and She Taketh Away $38 Million

Less than a year after Washington, D.C. businesswoman Catherine R. Reynolds gave $38 million to the Smithsonian Institution, she withdrew her gift. Reynolds' donation was planned to create a 10,000-square-foot hall of individual achievement at the National Museum of American History.

"Never in our wildest dreams did we anticipate that the notion of inspiring young people by telling the stories of prominent Americans from all disciplines would be so controversial," she wrote Lawrence M. Small, Secretary of the Smithsonian. "Apparently the basic philosophy of the power of the individual to make a difference is the antithesis of many within the Smithsonian bureaucracy."

Museum curators questioned whether her close involvement in the development of a museum presentation would put fund-raising ahead of scholarly integrity. They attacked the planned emphasis on famous individuals instead of focusing on demographic groups or ordinary Americans.

Reynolds' vision was to feature the life stories of prominent Americans who were Nobel laureates, Medal of Honor recipients, self-made entrepreneurs and civil rights leaders. The Smithsonian was concerned about any connection of the exhibit to the American Academy of Achievement, an organization run by her husband, Wayne Reynolds, that annually brings together dozens of superachievers with hundreds of high school students.[26]

Some Classic Blunders

Since 1994, Michael Fineman, president of Fineman PR in San Francisco, has been publishing his list of the top PR blunders of the year, all of which are in the crisis category. If a company didn't get sufficient public exposure the first time around for its crisis, being on Fineman's list, which is widely published, will insure it gets recognized time and again. In 2003, *Time* magazine ranked his list #2 of the 10 best "10 Best Lists."

Fineman publishes his annual PR Blunders List as a reminder of how critical public relations is to businesses and organizations. His selections are limited to Americans, American companies or incidents that happened in the U.S. Selections are limited to avoidable acts or omissions that cause adverse publicity; and image damage done to self, company, society, or others and was widely reported during the year. During his 20-year career, he has helped numerous clients with crises ranging from product recalls and food safety to labor disagreements and college campus safety. Following are some of his classics:

Got Beer? PETA's milk mistake. (2000) Milk is up there with motherhood and apple pie, but the People for the Ethical Treatment of Animals thought college students should be imbibing beer instead. PETA's reasoning was that milk promotes cruelty to cows, and its campaign targeted college kids on the Internet and in brochures. It included a free keychain that doubled as a bottle opener. Not surprisingly, the campaign was deemed irresponsible. "Alcohol is the No. 1 drug problem for our youth," Millie Webb, president of Mothers Against Drug Driving told *USA Today*. PETA's phones and website were besieged by complaints, and the campaign, along with the group's image, fell flat.

Rush to Judgment. Not all PR gaffes (2006) revolve around a racist theme – the ailing and disabled were popular, if ill-advised, targets as well. Rush Limbaugh stated that Michael J. Fox's involuntary Parkinson's-induced spasms on a commercial that endorsed stem cell research were "purely an act." Predictably, this incredibly insensitive comment caused an avalanche of support for Fox, including, according to *Time*, "a woman whose 17-second video in support of Fox drew 200,000 views" on YouTube.com. What was the upshot for Limbaugh?

Not only did reaction against the statement help lose his beloved GOP a Missouri Senate seat, but it could help lose them the entire U.S. Senate. And the stem cell initiative passed.

Pat Robertson's Diplomacy. Televangelist Pat Robertson made the list in 2005 for making un-Christian comments suggesting that the U.S. "take out" Hugo Chavez, president of oil-rich Venezuela, and again in 2006 for saying Israeli Prime Minister Ariel Sharon's severe stroke was his divine punishment for "dividing God's land."

Philip Morris Can't Keep Bad Judgment "In Czech." In 2002, *The Wall Street Journal* reported that a Philip Morris study, commissioned in the Czech Republic, found that smoking deaths saved the Czech government $147 million annually, or $1,227 per person in social welfare expenses such as health-care costs. The report characterized the savings as "positive effect" of cigarette consumption. Reaction was predictably negative, prompting full-page ads from anti-smoking groups, showing a cadaver's foot with a toe tag that read "$1,227." Philip Morris belatedly issued an apology and acknowledged its mistake, saying that no one benefits from smoking-related diseases, but the PR damage had already been done.

Grasso's Big Compensation, Poor Communication. Richard Grasso's $140 million compensation package was a vestige of the bullish 1990s, but couldn't stand up to the media scrutiny of the bearish 2000s. Grasso, chairman of the New York Stock Exchange, made several PR blunders after his package was disclosed in 2003. "Mr. Grasso badly misread the growing anger over his pay and the harm it has caused the exchange. He also erred in listening to high-profile supporters, including former Mayor Rudolph Giuliani, who urged him to tough it out," *The Wall Street Journal* observed. *USA Today* opined on Grasso's mistakes of stonewalling the press, while minimizing the payday fuss: "Instead of defusing what turned into a major crisis, Grasso and his communications team ended up making it worse. The handling of the scandal may end up in a PR textbook on how not to handle a crisis." While Grasso lost in the court of public opinion, he went his own way and kept the $140 million.

How Fineman PR Helped the Odwalla Recall

An excellent example of the right way to handle a crisis in the first 48 hours is the way Fineman Associates PR dealt with Odwalla, Inc. On October 30, 1996, Odwalla, the largest fresh-juice brand in the western U.S. was notified by health officials in Seattle that its apple juice had been linked epidemiologically to an outbreak of e-coli poisoning. Most of the cases involved children, several of whom had contracted the very serious Hemolytic Uremic Syndrome. Unfortunately, one child died, and after investigation, the U.S. Food & Drug Administration conclusively linked the outbreak to Odwalla's juices.

Odwalla immediately issued a voluntary recall of all apple juice-containing products. The following days the company recalled all products that had been processed on the same line as the apple juice products. The media gave the story top coverage from the start of the crisis.

According to Michael Fineman, the crisis created many perils for the public company, any one of which could have meant ruin. "In one day, the company's stock value dropped by one-third, a $31 million loss," he said. "It faced the rejection of its entire product line by both consumer and retailers. It faced lawsuits from consumers affected by the poisoning. It faced further losses of capital and value of its stock.

"It faced the prospect of having to pasteurize its products, which would cause it to lose its major taste differentiation from larger, conventional competitors. It faced the loss of brand equity and its corporate image as purveyor of health-giving, blessed-by-nature products. Worst of all," he added, "it faced the terrible and demoralizing fact that its products were causing serious injury to consumers, for whom the company's mission was to create health and pleasure."

The strategy of the crisis communications program was planned as follows:

- Efficient and effective communication of the recall of Odwalla customers;
- Communication of the company's humane concerns for those who were struck ill;
- Maintenance of Odwalla's previously excellent reputation with customers, consumer, business partners and the financial community by demonstrating responsible handling of the crisis;
- Protection of the corporate image and brand equity of wholesome, flavorful, quality products;
- Minimal speculation about the facts of the case and about the company's long-range viability;
- Preparation for various scenarios the crisis could pose in the near term, including a decision to pasteurize Odwalla products.

In consultation with The Evans Group in Seattle, Fineman Associates counseled its client on the best actions to take and the best ways to communicate with its key audiences. Key elements of the resulting strategy were:

1. Be an active "partner" with the FDA and other health officials in tracking down the cause and eliminating consumer risk;
2. Regarding consumers affected by e-coli, be a responsible, concerned neighbor rather than a legal adversary;
3. Communicate new information candidly and regularly with the media in a timely manner, without speculating and assigning blame;
4. Disclose information about safety procedures currently in place;
5. Express willingness to change procedures to improve safety while maintaining quality;
6. Lead industry in discovering and implementing solutions;
7. Consolidate and conduct all media communications from Odwalla headquarters in Half Moon Bay, California, rather than at its plant near Fresno.

The agency expressed concerns and took responsibility for anyone harmed, participated in teleconferences with the FDA and Washington State health officials, scheduled daily press briefings and sent out news releases instructing consumers on the recall, return for refunds and e-coli poisoning symptoms,. The plant manager was given a short statement to advise the press, and was media-trained. B-roll video of the plant production process was satellite-fed nationally.

Client spokespersons were monitored and critiqued. A comprehensive contingency public relations action plan was created for every possible combination of events that could occur in the future.

Market research conducted in November showed that 94 percent of consumers in affected areas had heard about the crisis. Of those, 97 percent felt that Odwalla had the right response. More than half reported that they felt more favorable toward Odwalla than they had prior to the crisis. The stock, which fell from $18 per share to $9 at its lowest point, rebounded to $13 and began to climb.

Daily news analysis showed that the media was unanimous in its early praise for Odwalla's management of the situation; the company was positioned as being both caring and responsible; consumers were quoted saying they perceived the situation as an unfortunate tragedy for everyone, including Odwalla, as opposed to a catastrophe caused by the company; and the stories which followed reflected the tone initially set forth in the strategic plan. Following the first 48 hours of the crisis, the extra personnel needed to implement the remainder of the plan were provided by Edelman Public Relations Worldwide.[27]

Summary Checklist

- Review all case histories and relate to similarities with your company, organization or client.
- In each case history there are basic principles that were or were not followed. Keep these in mind in reading and reviewing each.
- Be careful if your crisis involves taking on a celebrity.
- Use the case histories for group discussion and continued professional development including ways crises could have been better handled or avoided.

Endnotes

[1] Sue Anne Presley, "Testing A New Brand of Libel Law," *The Washington Post*, January 17, 1998, pg. A1; Bob Janis, Reuters, "Cattlemen trembling as Oprah trial nears;" *The Palm Beach (Florida) Post*, January 18, 1998, pgs. 1F-3F; Martin Babineck, "Lawyer says Winfrey incited her audience against beef," *The Philadelphia Inquirer*, January 22, 1998, pg. A2; Shaheena Ahmad and Marissa Melton, "Oprah takes the bull by the horns," *U.S. News & World Report*, January 26, 1998, pg. 15; and Chip Brown, associated Press, "Winfrey says she sought balance," *The Philadelphia Inquirer*, February 5, 1998, pg. A9.

[2] Mark Babineck, Associated Press,"Oprah's lawyer goes after the livestock trader," *Philadelphia Tribune*, February 13, 1998, pg. 5A.

[3] Mark Babineck, Associated Press, "Lawyer says Winfrey incited her audience against beef," *The Philadelphia Inquirer*, January 22, 1998, pg. 2; Babineck, "In Texas, full house for Oprah," *The Philadelphia Inquirer,* January 24, 1998, pg. 1A; and Kerry Curry, Reuters, "In Texas, Oprah Winfrey greets fans during jury selection," *The Philadelphia Inquirer,* January 21, 1998, pg. A12.

[4] Carla Hall, Deborah Netburn and Gina Piccalo, *The Los Angeles Times* and latimes. com, October 18, 2007.

[5] "Celebrity Roundup," *Time*, December 24, 2007.

[6] "She's A Super Model Citizen," *George*, August 2000.

[7] Michael Fineman, Fineman PR, news release, December 11, 2007.

[8] Arlene Weintraub, "Is the Hip Bone Connected to A Fee?," *Business Week*, December 3. 2007.

[9] Lawrence Ulrich, *Detroit Free Press*, September 27, 2000.

[10] Richard Nicolazzo, "PR Pro Says Ford & Firestone Blew Tire Recall," *O'Dwyer's PR Daily*, August 15, 2000.

[11] Keith Naughton and Mark Hosenball, "Ford vs. Firestone," *Newsweek*, September 18, 2000; "Lessons of a Blowout," *PRWeek*, October 9, 2000; Lloyd N. Newman, "Lessons from Bridgestone/Firestone," *Business & Economic Review*, January-March 2001; James R. Healey, "Documents imply Firestone knew of tire trouble in '94," *USA Today*, October 4, 2000.

[12] Jonathan Bernstein, "25 MORE Crisis Management Lessons Learned," *Crisis Manager*, January 2008.

[13] Miki Tanikawa, *New York Times Service*, "How to Control a Crisis? Japanese Discover PR," *International Herald Tribune*, September 28, 2000.

[14] Jim Adams, "Trump will help Indians takes back Manhattan Island," *Indian Country Today*, September 20, 2000; Knight Ridder News Services, October 23, 2000.

[15] Matthew B. Stannard, "Marketing Firm's Mailing Of Gag Grenades Bombs, Lawyers' consultants fired after scares," *San Francisco Chronicle*, September 21, 2000, and Michael Fineman, Fineman Associates Public Relations news release, December 28, 2000.

[16] Jonathan Bernstein, "You Still Want French Fries With That?," *Crisis Manager*, September 1, 2005.

[17] William K. Rashbaum, "Kerik Is Accused of Abusing Post as City Official," *The New York Times*, November 16, 2005 and ""U.S. Will Ask a Grand Jury to Indict Kerik," *The New York Times*, November 8, 2007; *The Los Angeles Times* and Associated Press news services, "Regan: I was asked to protect Giuliani, *The Seattle Times*, November 15, 2007.

[18] Barbara Kiviat, "Óne Community's fight over its good name," *Time*, November 19, 2007; Wikipedia.

[19] Letter of December 19 to the author from Dr. Mark A. Emmert, president of the University of Washington.

[20] Nick Perry, "Marathon: Just 1% of money goes to charity," *Seattle Times*, November 26, 2007 and "UW apologizes to marathoners over charity tiff," *Seattle Times*, November 27, 2007; Nicole Brodeur, "Marathon Has Image To Fix, Fast," *Seattle Times*, November 27, 2007; John Kokes, "Community should be proud of its well-organized marathon," *Seattle Times*, December 6, 2007; Nick Perry and Jonathan Martin, "Clashes could cost marathon its top sponsor," *Seattle Times*, December 19, 2007, pg. A1.

[21] Associated Press, *Minneapolis Star-Tribune*, December 11, 2007.

[22] David Van Biema, "Going After the Money Ministries," *Time*, November 26, 2007.

[23] Campaign Digest, "Obama: I would ban all toys from China," *The Seattle Times*, December 20, 2007, pg. A8.

[24] Renee Montagne and Adam Davidson, "Mattel Recalls 9 Million Toys Made In China," National Public Radio, August 14, 2007; Mark Trumbull, "Chinese Toy Recalls Show Need For Stringent Quality Control," *The Christian Science Monitor*, August 16, 2007;

Abigail Goldman, "Mattel apologizes to China," *The Los Angeles Times*, September 22, 2007; Barry Petersen, "Keeping An Eye On Chinese Toymakers," CBS Evening News, December 18, 2007.

[25] James S. Boune, "Leaks, spills and PR pills," *PR Week*, July 24, 2000.

[26] *Los Angeles Times* and *Washington Post* News Services, "Fed-up patron cancels most of $38 million gift to Smithsonian," *Tucson Citizen*, February 6, 2002, pg. 5A.

[27] Case history study, Fineman PR corporate brochure.

CHAPTER 6

YOU CAN FIGHT BACK AND WIN

If you are wrongfully attacked, fight back. If your image or reputation has been unfairly damaged, correct the story. Even worse, if sales and revenues are threatened or have been impacted, a quick turn around is critical. Sometimes you can be guilty by association and need to separate your company or organization from others. Be sure you pick your battles carefully and you have a well-planned campaign.

When a lawsuit is filed against the media it generally is for libel. Libel law places a heavy burden of proof on the plaintiff – the company that believes it has been wronged – which makes it difficult for the prosecutor. Also many jury awards are reduced or thrown out on appeal.

The Associated Press defines libel as injury to reputation. Words, pictures or cartoons that expose a person to public hatred, shame, disgrace or ridicule, or induce an ill opinion of a person are libelous.[1] The State of California has a more detailed definition: "Libel is a false and unprivileged publication by writing, printing, picture, effigy, or other fixed representation to the eye, which exposes any person to hatred, contempt, ridicule, or obloquy, or which causes him to be shunned or avoided, or which has a tendency to injure him in his occupation."[2]

Black's Law Dictionary defines libel in its most general sense as "any publication that is injurious to the reputation of another." This can include defamation expressed by print, writing, pictures or signs. A number of cases are cited further elaborating on the definition of libel. States can define defamation of a private person so long as they do not impose liability without fault.[3]

The case of *N.Y. Times v. Sullivan* is cited because under the First Amendment, there can be no presumption of malice or bad faith consistent with freedom of the press if the plaintiff is a public figure. Malice must prove that the defendant published material either knowing it to be false or recklessly without regard as to whether it is true or false. Prior to this decision in 1964, which went to the U.S. Supreme Court, media comment on the conduct of public officials or public figures was free from liability for libel only in certain limited circumstances, usually difficult to prove during a trial. Facts had to be substantially true. This shifted the responsibility to the plaintiff to prove actual malice and that the material was false.[4]

Ethics and Libel

The first line in the Code of Ethics of the Society of Professional Journalists is: "The Society of Professional Journalists believes the duty of journalists is to serve the truth." Section III, Ethics, says: Journalists must be free of obligation to any interest other than the public's right to know the truth." And under Section IV, Accuracy and Objectivity, paragraph 1 is: "Truth is our ultimate goal," and paragraph 3, "There is no excuse for inaccuracies or lack of thoroughness."

Pointing out that libel is injury to reputation, the Associated Press in Chapter 2 of its Libel Manual writes, "There is only one complete and unconditional defense to a civil action for libel: that the facts stated are PROVABLY TRUE. (Note well that word, PROVABLY.) Quoting someone correctly is not enough. The important thing is to be able to satisfy a jury that the libelous statement is substantially correct."[5]

When a reporter considers that the information in hand is *probably* true and not *provably* true there is a problem. This is what leads to litigation. A 52-page report by the Libel Defense Resource Center found that between July 1994 and June 1996 that on appeal, defendants were successful in reversing the verdicts in nearly half of the cases and also succeeding in having the awards reduced. The study showed that 12 of 25 appeals were reversed outright. It also confirmed that libel defendants were far more successful appealing cases involving public plaintiffs than in appeals involving private plaintiffs. This compared to 43 percent, or 64 of 149 cases where liability was reversed from plaintiffs' verdicts between 1984 and 1986.[6]

However, companies and individuals have sued the media and won. While the size of punitive damage awards is increasing, the number of media cases going to trial is low. There were fewer trials in 1996 than the average per year in the 1980s.[7] General Motors took on NBC because it felt that the network's *Dateline NBC* news magazine program used misinformation and rigged tests to show that a line of its pickup trucks were unsafe. In its filmed "tests," NBC used explosives to dramatize the supposed lack of safety of GM trucks.[8]

Supermarket chain Food Lion was awarded $5.5 million from Capital Cities-ABC when a jury found the methods *PrimeTime Live* used to gather the story were the same as fraud, trespassing and breach of loyalty.[9] The amount was subsequently reduced to $315,000.[10]

A small Houston firm that sold mortgage-backed securities, MMAR Group, Inc., went out of business shortly after *The Wall Street Journal* depicted it as a freewheeling operation that overpriced its products and deceived the Louisiana pension fund, its top customer.[11] A seven-person federal jury found that the October 21, 1993 story by reporter Laura Jereski libeled the firm and awarded a record $222.7 million in damages, nearly four times the next biggest libel award.[12] Of this amount, $200,020,000 was for punitive damages.[13]

Nearly four years later, Houston Federal Judge Ewing Werlein, Jr. eliminated $200 million in punitive damages but let stand actual damages of $22.7 million against Dow Jones and $20,000 in punitive damages personally against writer Jereski. If affirmed by the courts this would be the largest ever allowed to stand. Floyd Abrams, an attorney who has represented major news organizations in First Amendment legal battles, said he was not surprised that the court reduced the amount. "Had this judgment remained in effect, it would have chilled all reporting by all newspapers," he said.[14]

Former U.S. Senator Alan K. Simpson (R-Wyoming), who prides himself on having a reputation of being a fierce media critic, says: "America's media elite have become lazy, complacent, sloppy, self-serving, self-aggrandizing, cynical and arrogant beyond measure. We live in a society in which journalistic ethics – commitment to fairness, respect for privacy, even simple human compassion – all seem to take a seat way in the back of the bus.[15]

Simpson said in high school journalism he was taught about the five Ws – who, what, where, when and why. He says today "maybe we need to use the five Cs because the professional today is more interested in conflict, controversy and cleverness than it is in clarity." He writes that the fifth C is for coiffure and how television newspeople must always have their hair carefully coiffed.

Sometimes an apology from the media with some financial settlement will be a victory for a company. Philip Morris sued ABC News for $10 million. It was settled with an apology and payment of $15 million for legal work. In its letter of apology, ABC continued to maintain that the "principal focus of the reports was whether cigarette companies use the reconstituted tobacco process to control the levels of nicotine in cigarettes in order to keep people smoking." The ABC statement also noted that Philip Morris "categorically denies it does so."[16]

Jane Kirtley, head of the Reporters Committee for Freedom of the Press, told *USA Today* that the settlement "sends the message that corporate America can use a libel suit to discourage investigative reporting." In contrast, Richard Funess, president of Manning, Selvage & Lee/Americas, said "the networks must look long and hard at this incident ... tabloid journalism has crept into TV ... the networks must be more careful in their quest for ratings."[17]

In the 1980s, Alta Dena Dairy, a family-owned California dairy, was the country's largest producer of certified raw milk. It was always under attack by bureaucrats to pasteurize all of its dairy products. After being talked out of suing *The Los Angeles Times*, the dairy took on a county and state bureaucracy by mounting an aggressive, proactive marketing communications campaign and ended up getting favorable media support and rewinning its customers.

Food Lion - Not Libel But Investigative Methods

The issue between Food Lion and ABC was not over libel, but over the way *Prime-Time Live* obtained the story that it aired November 5, 1992. The accuracy of the story was not an issue in the litigation. The report, narrated by Diane Sawyer, accused the supermarket chain of selling rat-gnawed cheese, expired meat and old ham and fish washed in bleach to stop the smell. Food Lion asked for $52.5 million to $1.9 billion in punitive damages. The jury deliberated six days before agreeing on $5.5 million to the company and $47,750 to its employees. The jury foreman said: "The media has a right to bring the news, but they have to watch what they do."[18]

PrimeTime Live producers Lynn Dale and Susan Barnett got jobs as food handlers and infiltrated several stores to expose alleged wrongdoings by using tiny cameras and microphones hidden in their clothes and wigs. The show interviewed seven current and former Food Lion employees who talked about unsanitary handling practices. The company said the story was deceptive and the broadcast was staged and misleadingly edited.[19]

The court reduced the award to $315,000 and refused Food Lion's request that ABC pays its legal fees. ABC attorney Nat Lewin said large penalties should not be imposed on the media for being deceptive to get a story unless it results in bodily harm. "Making false representations in order to get into position to see, report or photograph what has been concealed has been an integral part of investigative journalism for centuries," Lewin said.[20] Attorneys for the supermarket chain argued that what ABC wanted was "tantamount to a license to cheat, lie and trespass with blanket protection of the U.S. Constitution."[21]

First Amendment attorneys, professional associations representing media interests and television executives expressed concern over the decision. Roone Arledge, president of ABC News, noted that the punitive damages were 4,000 times the amount of compensatory damages. "If large corporations were allowed to stop hard-hitting investigative journalism, the American people would be the losers," he said.[22] Andrew Heyward, president of CBS News, said "There is a public disenchantment to a degree with exploitative journalism and some of the backlash has spilled onto legitimate investigative reports."[23]

Speaking to a group at the National Press Club in Washington, D.C., ABC's Sam Donaldson said he was still using hidden cameras for a story. He added that ABC lost the case because the jury found the network trespassed when its employees lied to get Food Lion jobs.[24]

Public Figures Are Especially Vulnerable

A March 2, 1976 story in the *National Enquirer* brought action from Carol Burnett. The publication wrote: "In a Washington restaurant, a boisterous Carol Burnett had a loud argument with another diner, Henry Kissinger. Then she traipsed around the place offering everyone a bite of her dessert. But Carol really raised eyebrows when she accidentally knocked a glass of wine over one diner and starting giggling instead of apologizing. The guy wasn't amused and 'accidentally' spilled a glass of water over Carol's dress."[25]

Burnett's attorneys demanded a correction or retraction. On April 6, the newspaper published this: "An item in this column on March 2 erroneously reported that Carol Burnett had an argument with Henry Kissinger at a Washington restaurant and became boisterous, disturbing other guests. We understand these events did not occur and we are sorry for any embarrassment our report may have caused Miss Burnett."

On April 8 she filed suit. What came out in the trial was that Burnett, her television producer husband Joe Hamilton and three friends were dining in Washington where she was invited to perform at the White House. During dinner she had two or three glasses of wine but was not inebriated. She talked with a young couple at a table next to hers. When curiosity was expressed about her dessert, apparently a chocolate soufflé, she gave the couple small amounts of it on plates they had passed to her table. A family behind her table offered to exchange some of their baked Alaska for a portion of the soufflé, and they as well were accommodated.

When she and her party were leaving, a friend introduced her to Henry Kissinger. After a brief conversation, they left the restaurant. There was no "row" or argument. The conversation was not loud or boisterous. Burnett never "traipsed around the place offering everyone a bite of her dessert," nor was any wine or water spilled and no "giggling instead of apologizing."

In 1981 a jury awarded Burnett $1.6 million with $300,000 in compensatory damages and $1.3 million in punitive damages. The judge reduced the judgment to $50,000 compensatory and $750,000 punitive for a total of $800,000. An appeals court reduced the punitive damages for the *National Enquirer* to $150,000 for a total settlement of $200,000. The court held that $750,000 was not justified since it constituted approximately 35 percent of Burnette's net worth and nearly 50 percent of her net income for the period under consideration. With regard to compensatory damages, the court held that the item at issue was libelous on its face, concluding its message carried the implication that Miss Burnett's actions were the result of some objectionable state of inebriation. As a result she was required to show the court only those general damages arising from her loss of reputation, shame, mortification and injured feelings.[26]

Tiger's Wife Hits Winning Stroke

Elin Nordegren Woods, wife of golfing great Tiger Woods, was awarded $183,250 and an apology from *The Dubliner*, an Irish magazine that published an abusive article and a faked nude photo of her.

The article appeared in the magazine's September 2006 issue and angered Tiger on the first day of Ryder Cup competition in Ireland, which the U.S. lost to Europe. Trevor White, publisher of *The Dubliner* conceded that the article was "cheap, tasteless, deliberately offensive and was also completely untrue." He also said the photograph was not of Ms. Woods.

The publication's headline described her as "Ryder Cup filth" and claimed she "can be found in a variety of sweaty poses on porn sites across the Web." The article also insulted the wives of golfers Chad Campbell, David Toms and Jim Furyk, who did not sue.

Ms. Woods, who was a former swimsuit model, said the money would be donated to cancer-support charities in memory of Heather Clarke, the late wife of British golfer Darren Clarke.[27]

Know When and When Not To Fight Back

McDonald's should have thought twice before spending $16.4 million to win $98,198 in damages against two British vegetarian activists in the longest court battle in the United Kingdom.[28] The 314-day trial in 1994 had 28 pretrial hearings, 130 witnesses, 40,000 pages of documents and an 800-page ruling from Justice Roger Bell. Former mailman Dave Morris and bar worker Helen Steel had called McDonald's "a multinational corporate menace that abused animals, workers and the environment, and promoted an unhealthy diet." The activists claimed victory because they brought to public and media attention the company's business practices. Justice Bell said McDonald's was "culpably responsible for animal cruelty and ran ad campaigns that exploit impressionable children."[29]

Morris and Steel distributed pamphlets in the late 1980s entitled "What's wrong with McDonald's? Everything they don't want you to know." Paul Preston, McDonald's top executive in the U.K., said he was "broadly satisfied," but puzzled by the judge's comments on animal cruelty. "My responsibility is to protect our reputation and that's exactly what we've done."[30] The court found that some of the charges, such as "mistreatment of chickens," was true, but that the company does not destroy rain forests, poison its customers nor discriminate against employees.[31]

In an editorial, *The Washington Post* wrote: "If slanging McDonald's in print were grounds for an action of libel in this country, we can think of whole academic disciplines that would be forced to shut up shop, not to mention nutritionists and those folks who keep describing all your favorite foods as containing 'the equivalent of six Big Macs' in calories or fat." The editorial noted a great difference between American free-speech guarantees and the kind of constraints inherent in British libel law in which corporations can sue individuals for defamation. Believing a statement to be true is no defense against libel if a judge rules it was false.[32]

The New York Times wrote: "McLibel a nadir in McDonald's PR history" and a "Pyrrhic victory."[33] "The PR equivalent of food poisoning," was what *USA Today* wrote.[34] "The family-friendly multinational that squashes free speech," was how *Newsweek* described the trial.[35]

McDonald's was particularly castigated by the media in the U.K. The *Financial Times* accused the company of failing to understand British culture. "McDonald's is guilty of completely misunderstanding one time-honoured British tradition – an acceptance of harmless eccentrics. Steel and Morris, with their oddball ideas, are much more a part of Britain than McDonald's. Their successors will still be ranting and raving on Britain's high streets long after the last McDonald's Golden Arch has been dismantled."[36]

Following the trial, the activists immediately began mass distribution of the same leaflets but in even greater numbers. While thousands of publications are being distributed around Britain, the information also has been placed on the Internet.[37]

Taking On the *Columbia Journalism Review*

The Columbia Journalism Review says it is recognized throughout the world as "America's premiere media monitor – a watchdog of the press in all its forms, from newspapers and magazines to radio, television, and cable to the wire services and the Web." The magazine was founded in 1961 under the auspices of Columbia University's Graduate School of Journalism.[38]

This distinguished publication has set exceptionally high standards for itself. For years, my image of the *CJR* and Columbia's Journalism School was the epitome of ethics and integrity in journalism. That is why I expected the ultimate in cooperation from its editors when I contacted them in 2003 to correct two extremely damaging articles it published in 1998.

In 1986 when he was only 27 years old, Jeffrey Prosser launched his company when he bought the Virgin Islands Telephone Company (Vitelco) from ITT for $86.5 million. A young Certified Public Accountant from Omaha, Nebraska, he was looked on as an outsider by many in the Virgin Islands. Prosser built Vitelco into Innovative Communication Corporation, a provider of local, long distance and cellular telephone, Internet access, cable television and television with offices in the U.S. and British Virgin Islands, Guadeloupe, Martinique, Saint-Martin, Sint-Maarten, France and Belize.

When he bought the *Virgin Island Daily News* from Gannett Company, Inc. in 1997, Prosser incurred the wrath of several journalists which led to not one, but two damaging articles in *CJR*. In the January/February 1998 article headlined "Gannett's Sellout in Paradise," writer Mark Hunter refers to Jeffrey Prosser as "... a world-class phone-sex operator" and a captioned photograph read: "Jeffrey Prosser ... makes much of his money from a phone-sex business."[39] *CJR* took another swipe at him and his companies with a defaming story in its May/June 1998 edition.[40]

Prosser's advisors talked him out of taking libel action against *CJR* or to even ask the publication to correct a number of errors. So, the story and the "phone-sex" label proliferated. Less than two years later, *The Wall Street Journal* did a page one story about him and the "phone-sex" label was in a bold face sub-headline.[41] Again, his lawyers and public relations advisors talked him out of any recourse. While not mentioned with a byline or as a contributor, one of the *CJR* authors now was an editor with *The Wall Street Journal*.

In January 2003, I came out of retirement to be vice president of public relations for Prosser's Innovative Communication Corporation and one of my first tasks was to correct the "phone sex" allegations.

Errors, Misinformation and Accusations Proliferate with the Internet

During the time of the publication of the three articles and my joining Innovative, the Internet virtually exploded with growth. There were numerous references to Jeffrey Prosser as a "world-class phone-sex operator" and other damaging misinformation on a number of websites complete with archives and search engines.

As I was developing an aggressive public relations campaign to build a positive image of Prosser and Innovative, almost monthly I had to explain the accusations made against him.

In early May 2003 I placed a telephone call to Michael Hoyt, *CJR*'s executive editor. I e-mailed him on May 29 when he hadn't returned my call. With no response by early July, I had the late Robert J. Stone, a long time friend and senior executive with The Dilenschneider Group, New York, our public relations agency, call Hoyt.

I then took one of my single most important actions and retained John J. Walsh, senior counsel of the New York law firm of Carter Ledyard & Milburn LLP. Walsh has a most impressive record in libel and defamation cases and is considered one of the country's most prominent First Amendment attorneys. His first project was to do extensive investigative research into the articles, taking them apart not only paragraph by paragraph, but word by word. His 10-page "white paper" of November 11, 2003, refuted all of the most damaging accusations made by the reporters. From the day Walsh signed off on his "white paper," I excerpted references on a regular basis with all public and media contacts.

I continued trying to arrange a meeting with *CJR*'s Hoyt. I wrote him a three-page letter on July 21 following up on Stone's conversation with him and expressed my appreciation for his willingness to consider a new story about *The Virgin Islands Daily News* under Prosser's ownership. A July 28 letter followed with a story about awards won by the newspaper. I expressed disappointment to Hoyt in an August 18 letter that he had not responded to my recent letters, phone calls and e-mails.

After March 24, 2004, I became more aggressive in trying to arrange a meeting with Hoyt and *CJR*. After being invited by the Prime Minister of Belize to buy the national telephone company, Prosser and the government announced what was the biggest business transaction in the country's history. Within hours Belize talk show hosts were fielding questions about "Who is this Yankee Doodle phone-sex operator who is buying our telephone company?" Responsible journalists listened to me. I excerpted appropriate pages from Walsh's "white paper" to fax to them with his biography.

Once I had things under control in Belize, I talked with Hoyt on April 5, 2004 and sent attachments of the many awards won by the newspaper during Prosser's ownership. Included were profiles of the editors and the members of Innovative's board of directors. I suggested a meeting with the executive editor as well as a prominent board member, Richard N. Goodwin, author, Oscar-winner and former advisor to President John F. Kennedy, and his wife, author and presidential historian Doris Kearns Goodwin.

This was followed by an April 14 letter and April 19 e-mail suggesting dates for meetings. With time running short when several of us would be in New York, I called Hoyt again but this time was directed to a member of his editorial staff, Brent Cunningham. He said he was completely familiar with all of my correspondence and documented material and curtly responded: "I see no reason whatsoever for any meeting, much less to even consider doing a story."

Refuting the *CJR*'s Accusations

During a May 4 telephone conversation, Hoyt asked me to again detail everything in writing for him which I did in a May 27 letter.

Here is how I responded to any reference to Jeffrey Prosser as a phone-sex operator: "Describing Mr. Prosser as "world class phone-sex operator" at best can be called a major misunderstanding of a segment of the business of virtually every domestic and international telephone carrier worldwide – so-called 'audiotext' traffic, which included 'adult' content provided to individuals using telephone service as the medium. Guyana Telephone & Telegraph (GT&T), which provided local and long distance service in and out of the former British colony, was just one small participant.

"By the time *CJR*'s January/February 1998 article was published, not only was it clear that Mr. Prosser would no longer be associated with GT&T and its revenue sources, but any attempt by *CJR*'s reporters and editors to understand the world-wide telephone industry's carriage of adult-content audiotext traffic would have reveled that Mr. Prosser was not a 'phone-sex operator' as that term, if it has any communicative value, is appropriate only to describe the adult content providers, not the carriers, whose wires or satellite transmission facilities move that content electronically from point to point.

"I hope that the relevance of all this to *CJR*'s classification of Jeffrey Prosser as a "world-class phone-sex operator" is apparent. The term is both incorrect and extremely damaging. In recent years, both Mr. Prosser and Innovative Communication have spent an inordinate amount of time answering questions prompted by the retrieval of that term from *CJR*'s electronic archive in diligence searches and clarifying GT&T's role as a *carrier only.*

"Internet searches by companies or governments with which Innovative seeks to do business invariably turn up these 'phone-sex' mischaracterizations. The two words convey to readers that Mr. Prosser is engaged in an unworthy, sleazy business and therefore, must be an unworthy, sleazy man."

"The same then could be said of the officers and owners of virtually every communications, media, and cable company in the United States and the rest of the world. Mr. Hunter's story makes no effort to explain the difference between the businesses of content carriers, such as telephone companies (like GT&T), cable companies, Internet service providers and Internet portals, and the content provided by others they are required and paid to carry. In similar fashion, cable service operators are carriers of adult programming (defined by the U. S. Supreme Court as protected speech because it is not pornography and thus must be made available to adults).

"Mr. Hunter's article suggests that Mr. Prosser's early success in business and the foundation of his wealth have been built on his participation in a disreputable business – phone sex. Yet AT&T, MCI, Verizon, Bell South, Qwest and the other long distance carriers in the U.S. and the world and all the local or regional telephone carriers in the U.S. do the same business in the same way. All the major cable operators – Cox, Comcast, Adelphia, Liberty and News Corp., and Internet service providers and portals including AOL/Time Warner, Google and Yahoo all provide their customers with access to the same type of content, and derive revenue from it as did GT&T. The same is true of the operators of Hilton, Marriott, Sheraton and most, if not all of the world's leading hotels and resorts.

"Moreover, under the applicable regulations, GT&T could not have refused to provide carriage any more than other carriers such as AT&T could. There was a long distance carrier such as AT&T or MCI on every one of these calls.

"Publicly held companies are required to break out certain categories of revenues if they exceed a certain percent of total gross revenues. This is what GT&T did in disclosing its audiotext revenue. Major U.S.-based telecoms do not break-out audiotext income because, while the total audiotext revenues most likely are considerably greater than the total revenues of GT&T, they did not represent a significant percent of overall revenues. For example the audiotext revenues of Verizon in the Dominican Republic alone were much greater than total revenues of GT&T in Guyana. The same is true for audiotext income of Cable & Wireless when it was in Hong Kong. Neither had to show specific dollar figures for audio-text income.

"We believe this should have been explained to your readers. If *CJR* labels Mr. Prosser as a "phone-sex" operator, you would have to do so with Rupert Murdoch, Michael Eisner and presidents and CEOs of scores of other companies.

"The question remains: What should be done about it?

The Validity of the *CJR* Sources

My letter challenged the sources used by Hunter and Richter. "We believe that both of your reporters were misled by biased and vocal enemies in the U.S. Virgin Islands community with clear motivations to injure Mr. Prosser by damaging his reputation. We strongly suspect that these adversaries were instrumental in persuading *CJR* and/or Mr. Hunter to criticize Gannett's decision to sell to Prosser – a decision which would look like even more of a "sell out" if the new owner could be portrayed as a sleazy "phone-sex operator."

"His winning bid for the Virgin Islands Telephone Company frustrated the plans of clients of a prominent Virgin Islands law firm who may have wanted to acquire Vitelco. By 1997-98, the law firm was representing Prosser's former partner, Cornelius Prior, who had retained GT&T and its audiotext revenue in his portfolio, in fruitless claims charging securities law violations.

"Another adversary, Virgin Islands attorney Lee Rohn, has sued Prosser or his businesses more than 20 times in the last five years, mostly to no effect. Her pedigree as a lawyer is marked by one disciplinary action after another. She is presently facing a criminal prosecution for drug trafficking after trying to board a plane with a concealed and undeclared quantity of marijuana (*Government v. Rohn*, Territorial Court Criminal No. 113/2003 St. Croix Division). She has been criticized by the Virgin Islands Attorney General and courts for violations of ethical rules.

"On May 28, 2003, *The St. Thomas Source* and *The St. Croix Source,* issued a correction of an article written by David S. North that accused an Innovative company of making payments to Kenneth Mapp while he was lieutenant governor in the Roy Schneider (former governor) administration. In its correction, *The Source* wrote: "... the article should have attributed the statement to Attorney Lee Rohn, who has taken sworn depositions from the three witnesses. However, none of the witnesses testified or told attorney Rohn that Kenneth Mapp was paid by ICC or any of its subsidiaries while employed as lieutenant governor of the Virgin Islands.

"We believe that these adversaries are the principle, and probably the exclusive, source for the unfounded tales and implications about Mr. Prosser and his companies. 'Consider the source' is an aphorism that could have originated in journalism. Whether it did or not, I suggest that the motivations of Mr. Prosser's Virgin Islands critics fall under its principle, a principle applied every day in newsrooms around the world."

Refuting the Writers and *CJR* Again

Both Messrs. Hunter and Richter would lead their readers to believe that the only reason Prosser bought *The Daily News* was to cease constant negative attacks on him.

My letter continued: "In no way has Mr. Prosser or anyone in management ever suggested much less tried to influence what has been reported on the news side. Mr. Richter quoted the former editor, Mike Middlesworth as follows: 'If you buy a newspaper you're entitled to have it reflect your view.' Any views of Mr. Prosser have only been on the editorial page.

"... The expressed fear in 1998 that the independence of *The Daily News* would be co-opted by Mr. Prosser or his business interests clearly has not been realized. The paper has remained a vigorous, independent voice reporting on matters of public concern to the people of the Virgin Islands .... In fact, [it] has flourished under the ownership of Jeffrey J. Prosser."

The paper has won numerous awards for reporting and public service and has become the most honored small circulation newspaper in the U.S.

Still No Response

The detailed letter to Hoyt drew no response. E-mails and letters continued in July and August of 2004 and still Hoyt would not meet. The frustration with *CJR* was discussed with Tower Kountze, a government affairs special at Blackwell Sanders Peper Martin, a law firm working for Innovative. Kountze offered to call contacts he had at Columbia University to see if they would intervene and make a meeting happen.

The university officials did not want to have it appear that they were getting involved in editorial policy with *CJR* and declined to help. On December 27, 2005 Kountze wrote Hoyt and noted how long a meeting had been sought to resolve issues surrounding the two stories. One paragraph was: "Respectfully, we ask that you or your superiors from *Columbia Journalism Review* or Columbia University meet with Mr. Henry. When his letter also went ignored, Kountze wrote Hoyt again on January 20, 2006 and expressed his own frustration. Included with his letter was a complete package of all letters and e-mails sent to Hoyt. The response, nearly seven weeks later, and some three years after Rene Henry's first contact with Hoyt, came from Howard A. Jacobson, deputy general counsel for Columbia University, who asked that all future communications be directed to him.

This letter was answered by Steven M. Kupka, a partner in the Blackwell Sanders firm, telling Jacobson that the only reason for the correspondence was to facilitate a meeting with *CJR*.

Enter John Walsh

At this point, I again involved John Walsh who wrote Jacobson on March 24, 2006. Some key points made in the letter by Walsh include:

"Thinking that the negative effects of being falsely characterized in an academic publication written for the journalism profession would be transitory and brief, Mr. Prosser did not reckon with the future capacity of the *CJR* article, fueled by the explosive growth of electronic archives and Internet search engines, to place this mistake, highly pejorative characterization continuously before researchers seeking information about him or his business operations. Because of that understandable inability to foresee this effect of the new Information Age, no demand for a retraction or correction was made and no lawsuit filed. As a result, the mischaracterization of Mr. Prosser has been kept as fresh as if it had been published last week, playing into the hands of competitors and adversaries who misuse it to their advantage, and badly misinforming the merely diligent seeking business information.

" … the remedy for a person in Mr. Prosser's position is not likely to be found in litigation. We recognize the effect of the short statutes of limitations provided in defamation law. We believe, however that there is a remedy for this situation, one long recognized in journalism, and that is the appropriateness (some might say obligation) of correcting errors made in reporting to the public, regardless of whether the error occurred days or years before. This remedy is particularly appropriate when the error can be shown to have severely damaging effects on a person or his business years after the initial publication.

"We believe that the serious consequences of uncorrected and constantly republished damaging error exemplified by Mr. Prosser's case are an emerging and emergent problem of the electronic Information Age which should engage the serious attention of those responsible for editing *CJR*, arguably journalism's most distinguished publication. In fact, we have hoped and continued to hope that Columbia University, headed by President Lee Bollinger, a well known and highly respected First Amendment scholar and writer, could, through its School of Journalism and possibly its Law School, play a leading role in considering the societal issues Mr. Prosser's situation presents and working with us to propose a solution or solutions. In fact, I would go so far as to hope that President Bollinger, as a First Amendment scholar and legal theorist, could be induced to contribute constructive thinking to the issue of how our society should deal with this problem of persistent, damaging republication of error."

Walsh proposed a meeting between all parties involved and asked that Bollinger be made aware of all issues.

A Suggested Resolution

Jacobson replied April 10 to Walsh saying *CJR* "is willing to consider" attaching a letter to the editor up to 750 words on the *CJR* website where the two articles appear and to include a brief statement in front of the two articles referring to the letter to the editor, and that *CJR* would reserve the right to edit any such letter.

In the first sentence of his April 24 reply, Walsh expressed "extreme disappointment" since "it implicitly indicates that there will be no meeting with *CJR* senior management or university level representatives, the question your letter presents is why an academic institution devoted to the maintenance of the highest principles of journalism would decline or meet with persons who desire to present facts which will demonstrate the incorrectness, unfairness and damaging aspects of the two articles in question, and also consider the development of an appropriate remedy to mitigate the harm that has been done already by the articles and eliminate or limit future injury.

"Mr. Henry has been working as a professional in the field of public relations for corporate, academic and governmental institutions for more than 50 years and tells me that in that span of time he has never been refused a meeting by any journalism organization to discuss facts in the context of a claim of serious error."

Walsh then outlined his points regarding the suggested letter to the editor and its length and content including there will be no rejoinder or commentary on the letter by *CJR*, and that if print copies of the magazine are in any libraries that the letter be inserted in the editions and their presence noted on the contents page by a sticker. He also again reiterated the importance of a meeting and the involvement of Lee Bollinger.

The Rebuttal Letter

The proposed letter was sent to Columbia on June 5 and acknowledged by Jacobson on June 15. I decided that a third party should sign the letter, not Jeffrey Prosser, nor I as head of public relations. The signer was Sir Ronald Sanders, a member of the Innovative board of directors, a long time friend of Prosser and an internationally renowned diplomat, journalist, author, and speaker.

In the first draft, the university and *CJR* took out any references that this was the first time in 50 years any media refused to meet with Rene Henry, that meetings had been requested time and again over a three-year period, and even wanted to delete the "Sir" title bestowed on Sanders by Queen Elizabeth. Correspondence exchanged in July and August and it was not until September 5 that Jacobson said Columbia approved the final version. It was several weeks later before the letter was posted on *CJR's* website. Following is the letter:

Letter to the editor
UNFAIR ARTICLES

I began my career as a broadcast journalist with the BBC and worked as a broadcaster in several countries of the Caribbean before becoming a diplomat and then a business executive. I was president of the Caribbean Broadcasting

Union and served on the first board of directors of the Caribbean News Agency, which is widely regarded as an independent and objective news organization. I have served on the executive board of UNESCO and held senior ambassadorial appointments in London and with the World Trade Organization. I am a member of the board of directors of Innovative Communication Corporation (ICC), which is owned by Jeffrey J. Prosser, a man I have known for over fifteen years.

I am surprised that, twice in six months, the *Columbia Journalism Review* published extremely damaging, incorrect, defamatory articles about Mr. Prosser and ICC. The two articles are in the January/February and May/June 1998 issues.

To label Mr. Prosser a "world class phone-sex operator" in the first article was entirely wrong. Neither Mr. Prosser nor ICC has ever operated phone-sex companies. The description, "phone sex operator," if it has any communicative value, is appropriate only to describe the adult content provider and not the carriers who transmit the content from point to point. No telephone company — not even ones that have very deep pockets and operate internationally — can dictate the content of messages sent over its system. The Guyana Telephone & Telegraph Company, of which Mr. Prosser was a shareholder and chairman, operated no differently than any other telephone company when "phone sex" material was carried over its system. AT&T, Bell South, Verizon, Sprint, Cingular — all carry telephone messages by voice and data that originate with subscribers, some of whose business is "phone sex," and just as these telephone companies and their shareholders are not phone sex operators, neither was Mr. Prosser.

When the defamatory articles were published in 1998, the Internet was in its infancy. No one had any idea that business competitors could use this medium indefinitely against Mr. Prosser and ICC. Adversaries have hired firms to repeatedly access the *CJR* articles so whenever anyone searches for information about Mr. Prosser and his company, the "phone sex" reference is always at or near the top of the list.

These articles completely overshadow the positive and constructive contribution that Mr. Prosser and ICC have made to economic and social development in several countries through the operations of state-of-the-art telecommunications services.

The articles also lead readers to believe that Mr. Prosser bought the *Virgin Islands Daily News* from Gannett to silence his critics and suggested he would ruin the newspaper. In fact, under his ownership, this newspaper has won the prestigious Silver Gavel from the American Bar Association and numerous awards and honors from organizations including the Associated Press Managing Editors, American Society of Newspaper Editors, and the Society of Professional Journalists. Mr. Prosser is scrupulous in his non-interference in the paper's editorial policy and operations.

I write a weekly commentary that is syndicated on Internet news Web sites and in newspapers across the Caribbean, including *The Daily News*. Neither Mr. Prosser nor the editor of *The Daily News* has ever attempted to direct or restrict my writings. The Prosser-owned *Daily News* keeps the people of the Virgin Islands fully informed about events in their territory, the U.S. mainland, neighboring countries, and the wider world. In doing so, very high journalistic standards of accuracy and objectivity are applied.

It is well known that Mr. Prosser and his wife are actively involved in their local communities, are generous benefactors, and created the Prosser-ICC Foundation, which gives more than $1 million a year to local organizations in the Virgin Islands. These are facts that are easily established and that *CJR*, in the interest of its own reputation, should disclose to its readers who, at any time, can read the existing articles on its Web site that damage Mr. Prosser.

Sir Ronald Michael Sanders, KCMG

London

Dangers of the Electronic Age

Regardless how hard you try, the Internet will further exacerbate any crisis. On January 25 in a page one story, *Roll Call*, which bills itself as "The Newspaper of Capitol Hill," had a headline: "Blunt's good friends are in the phone sex industry." Prosser had made a political contribution to Rep. Roy Blunt (R-Missouri) who was a frontrunner to replace Tom DeLay as House Majority Leader. The story reported: "Jeffrey Prosser, dubbed by the *Columbia Journalism Review* in a 1998 story 'a world-class phone-sex operator,' gave $5,000 to Blunt's Rely On Your Beliefs fund in 2005. ..."

When political campaigns geared up in September and October before the November 2006 elections, anyone to whom Jeffrey Prosser had donated was targeted for a smear campaign. News releases were widely distributed in a number of states, the false information posted on web sites and blogs, and hours and hours of time were spent seeking corrections, few of which were forthcoming.

Reporters from several major newspapers in states where candidates had been falsely accused because of the *CJR* articles, incorrectly assumed that because it was written by the *Columbia Journalism Review* it had to be correct.

You can fight back and win!

Summary Checklist

- When wronged, fight back.
- Don't delay taking action. For maximum leverage, take advantage of libel and defamation laws whenever possible.
- If the media values its ethics and integrity, there should not be a time limit on righting a wrong.
- Remember in the State of Washington, the state's Supreme Court has ruled it is all right for a politician and candidate running for election to lie.
- Get the most professional and experienced help possible. No price can be placed on the value of image or reputation.
- Document all contact with the media – e-mails, faxes, letters and phone calls placed and received.
- Be persistent and use all sources to open lines of communication. Don't be stonewalled by media.
- Litigation is not always the answer. Review the case histories of the Texas Cattleman v. Oprah and McDonald's v. British Veggies.
- High profile individuals are always potential targets for misinformation and false accusations.

Endnotes

[1] Norman Goldstein, *The Associated Press Stylebook and Libel Manual*, Addison-Wesley Publishing Company, Reading, Massachusetts, 1994. pg. 168.

[2] Civil Code, State of California, §45

[3] *Black's Law Dictionary,* sixth edition, West Publishing Co., St. Paul, Minnesota, 1990, pg. 915.

[4] Ibid. *New York Times v. Sullivan*, 375 U.S. 254, 84 S.Ct. 710, II L.Ed.2nd 686 (1964).

[5] *The Associated Press Stylebook and Libel Manual*, op. cit., pg. 283.

[6] Libel Defense Resource Center, news release, August 21, 1996, New York, N. Y.

[7] Ibid.

[8] *Jack O'Dwyer's Newsletter*, August 30, 1995, pg. 1.

[9] Estes Thompson Associated Press, *The Philadelphia Inquirer*, January 23, 1997, pg. 2.

[10] Associated Press, *The Philadelphia Inquirer,* August 30, 1997, pg. A3.

[11] *Time,* "More Bad News for Dow Jones," March 31, 1997, pg. 64.

[12] Larry Robinson, "One Heck of a Whupping," *Newsweek*, March 31, 1997, pg. 54

[13] Libel Defense Resource Center, *op.cit.*

[14] Rick Gladstone, Associated Press, "Judge overrules $200 million punitive award in libel case," *The Philadelphia Inquirer*, May 24, 1997, pg. 6.

[15] Alan K. Simpson, *Right in the Old Gazoo*, William Morrow and Company, Inc., New York, N.Y., 1997, pgs. 6-8.

[16] *Jack O'Dwyer's Newsletter*, August 30, 1995, pg. 7.

[17] Ibid.

[18] Estes Thompson, Associate Press, *op.cit.*

[19] Ginia Bellafante, "Hide and Go Sue," *Time*, January 13, 1997.

[20] Associated Press, "ABC: Award slashes in Food Lion case," *The Philadelphia Inquirer,* August 30, 1997, pg. A3.

[21] Ibid.

[22] Estes Thompson, Associated Press, *op.cit.*

[23] Ginia Bellafante, *Time, op.cit.*

[24] "ABC-TV Still Using Hidden Camera," *Jack O'Dwyer's Newsletter*, May 1, 1997, pg. 1.

[25] *California Appellate Reports*, 3rd series, 144, 1983, Appendix California Supplement, Bancroft-Whitney Co., San Francisco, pg. 991.

[26] Ibid.

[27] Associated Press and Reuters news services, "Magazine owes Woods' wife money, apology," *The Seattle Times*, November 9, 2007.

[28] "McLibel," *U.S. News & World Report*, June 30, 1997, pg. 48.

[29] Dirk Beveridge, Associated Press, "McDonald's purees British vegetarians in a libel case, but is vilified," *The Philadelphia Inquirer,* June 20, 1997, pg. A11.

[30] Ibid.

[31] "McDonald's Wins Suit; Leaflets Continue," *Jack O'Dwyer's Newsletter*, June 25, 1997, pg. 7.

[32] "Libel and the Big Burgers," editorial, *The Washington Post*, June 23, 1997, pg. A18.

[33] *The New York Times*, editorial page, June 20, 1997.

[34] *USA Today,* June 20, 1997.

[35] "Phyrric McVictory," *Newsweek,* June 30, 1997.

[36] *Jack O'Dwyer's Newsletter*, July 9, 1997, pg. 7.

[37] Dirk Beveridge, Associated Press, *op.cit.*

[38] "Who We Are," www.cjr.org.

[39] Mark Hunter, "Gannett's Sellout in Paradise," *Columbia Journalism Review,* January/February 1998.

[40] Konstantin Richter, "Sellout Revisited," *Columbia Journalism Review,* May/June 1998.

[41] Michael Allen and Mitchell Pacelle, "Island Empire: A Guy From Nebraska Hits It Big in St. Croix But Triggers a Backlash," *The Wall Street Journal*, February 1, 2000, pg. 1.

CHAPTER 7

DO THE RIGHT THING - TAKE RESPONSIBILITY AND WIN PUBLIC SUPPORT

You never want to experience a crisis, especially on a holiday weekend. But this is what happened when on New Year's weekend 1988, when Ashland, Inc. had its first major oil pollution accident in its 64-year history.

Saturday afternoon, January 2, at its facility 15 miles southeast of Pittsburgh, a storage tank collapsed releasing a 30-foot tidal wave of four million gallons of diesel fuel. Approximately 700,000 gallons of fuel spilled into the Monongahela River and threatened the drinking water of communities in Pennsylvania, Ohio and West Virginia.

What followed was a textbook procedure for handling crises. Ashland did the right thing and set an example for other companies. CEO and chairman John R. Hall put concern for the public above legal considerations and won support from the public, the media, employees, stockholders, environmentalists, and even regulatory agencies. Before the week ended, he sent a $210,000 check to Allegheny County.

Saturday, January 2, 1988 - Day 1

5:02 p.m. - While being filled, a storage tank collapsed at Ashland's terminal in West Elizabeth, Pennsylvania. Nearly four million gallons of fuel burst from the ruptured tank, slammed into another tank releasing 20,000 gallons more of gasoline, surged over containment dikes, and onto adjacent properties. The terminal's dike was large enough to hold the entire contents, but ruptured so suddenly that it sent a wave of oil over the embankment. It was later discovered that the oil had found its way to a storm drain, located on adjacent property, that emptied into the Monongahela River.[1]

5:21 p.m. - Ashland officials notified all emergency response organizations.

5:30 p.m. - Pittsburgh Public Safety Director Glenn Cannon began calling out emergency personnel and city Public Works Department.

8:30 p.m. - A county Specialized Intervention Team found additional leakage and diesel fuel in storm sewers.

9:00 p.m. - Five-inch hoses inflated with air were stretched across the Monongahela downstream from the spill to a lock eight miles downstream.

10:00-11:00 p.m. - The Special Intervention Team found damage to another storage tank and to pipes connected to a tank filled with gasoline. Ashland began to empty gasoline from that tank into a barge.[2]

11:00 p.m. - Ashland established its command post at the spill site.

Midnight - About 1,200 nearby residents were evacuated as a precaution since diesel fuel was in the river and the sewage system. Water intake valves on the river were closed, and 50,000 people faced potential water shortages. The Coast Guard halted all river traffic from the site to the point in Pittsburgh where the Monongahela meets the Allegheny River to form the Ohio River. Adjacent rail lines and highways were temporarily closed. Darkness and below-freezing winter weather added to the already difficult situation.[3]

Sunday, January 3 - Day 2

3:00 a.m. - Hazardous materials units 20 miles downstream attempted to contain the spill. Additional teams arrived during the morning and afternoon.

7:45 a.m. - Western Pennsylvania Water Co., a utility that serves 750,000 customers, closed one of its two water pumping stations. Officials pleaded with the public to conserve water.[4]

Morning - Hall rushed to his office as soon as he was called. With his president, Charles J. Luellen, he talked with colleagues at the accident site and elsewhere. He then isolated himself from distractions and had subordinates handle all outside queries. Later than day, he called Pennsylvania Governor Robert P. Casey and told him Ashland intended to clean up the mess as fast as it could.[5] Dan Lacy, vice president of corporate communications, recommended against a press release. "When a situation is evolving so rapidly, a release isn't good enough."[6]

Noon - Some 1,200 residents returned home. Governor Casey put the National Guard on alert to deliver emergency drinking water to hospitals and residents.

Afternoon - Media descended on the scene. The first of what became twice-a-day press conferences was held. The Coast Guard reported that 700,000 gallons flowed into the river and the rest was contained near the tank. "Our first priority will be the cleanup effort and that will take some time." said Ashland's Lacy.[7]

Monday, January 4 - Day 3

6:30 a.m. - When Hall arrived at work he thought everything was under control.[8] By mid-morning, he found things were not. Calls from public officials, reporters, local water companies and members of Ashland's own emergency management team revealed discrepancies about the facts. Reporters initially were told the tank was new and the company had a permit to construct it. Hall then learned his people spoke too soon – the tank was reconstructed from 40-year-old steel and a written permit had not been issued. He was further concerned when he learned that the tank had been tested with an alternate, rather than the prescribed test. He let his management know he was frustrated and that he wanted the right information.[9]

Early afternoon - The oil spill, 6 to 11 inches thick, was now 47 miles downstream headed toward Wheeling, West Virginia.[10] The temperature dropped overnight making cleanup even more difficult, but helped congeal the fuel which was beneficial for fish and wildlife.[11] Governor Casey ordered $2 million in state funds for the cleanup. Ashland was paying for the emergency hazard teams. A series of navigational locks and dams, only three miles from the terminal, churned the oil and water, causing it to emulsify and sink below the recovery booms. Officials feared this would contaminate submerged water intake pipes and treatment facilities. Water shortages forced some schools to close.[12]

As company engineers and government regulators began their investigations, questions were asked about why the tank collapsed. The 40-year-old tank was moved from Cleveland, Ohio to West Elizabeth. The metal was tested and its structural integrity passed all inspections. However, the Allegheny County Fire Marshal, Martin Jacobs, said his office had not issued a construction permit for it to be rebuilt. An Ashland spokesman said a permit was issued in 1986, but Jacobs may not have been notified because of its age.[13]

Late afternoon - The situation worsened from an environmental crisis to a public health and safety problem because of available water. Hall wanted to make a public statement but his lawyers cautioned he should carefully consider admitting any mistakes because of liability. Hall felt he had to be candid, and called for a press conference the following day in Pittsburgh.[14]

Tuesday, January 5 - Day 4

Flying to Pittsburgh, Hall rehearsed for the press conference with his advisers asking anticipated questions: "How long will it take to clean up the spill?" and "How much will it cost?" Hall stopped first at the spill site and commended tired workers for their work.[15]

Dozens of reporters confronted him as he began the media event thanking everyone who participated in the clean-up activity. He apologized to the people of the Pittsburgh area for the incident. "The company expects to pay the costs of the clean-up and reimburse the government agencies for reasonable expenses," he said.[16]

Hall admitted that the company did not have written building permits and did not follow standard steps to test the tank.[17] "In hindsight I might question the use of 40-year-old steel," he said. "We did not follow our normal refinery procedures in testing the tank after it was completed. I wish our people had pursued the application process [with Fire Marshal Martin Jacobs] more diligently." At first, the company said the tank was new.[18] Hall believed that the best thing to do was to tell everything he knew. "If we made mistakes, we have to stand up and admit them."[19]

In his remarks, Hall said: "I want to assure you that Ashland is a responsible corporate citizen. We have operated successfully in the oil refining business for 64 years, and maintain high safety standards at all of our operations, including 23 terminals similar to the one at Floreffe. We also have been responsive to community concerns where our operations are located. We intend to maintain that tradition and stick with the job until the cleanup is complete."

Ashland got praise from an attorney for the U.S. Environmental Protection Agency. "... [Ashland] is assuming ... all costs associated with the spill. The company has gone beyond what the EPA could do by providing additional water supplies to towns downriver. Federal regulations prevent EPA from providing alternative water supplies in case of a spill," he said.[20]

Wednesday, January 6 - Day 5

Hall cancelled business trips and stayed in Pittsburgh to meet with political leaders, editorial boards of local newspapers, and telephoned governors of Ohio and West Virginia.[21] Ohio Governor Richard Celeste declared a state of emergency for river communities preparing to close water intake pipes. The oil slick was now 17 miles long, 18 feet deep and 67 miles from Pittsburgh.[22]

Water service was partially restored to 23,000 people in the Pittsburgh suburbs of Robinson Township and North Fayette. Conditions were expected to be normal by the weekend.[23]

In a *USA Today*, Gerald Meyers, former chairman of American Motors Corporation, and professor of crisis management at Carnegie-Mellon University, said: "It looks as if they are dealing professionally with a bad situation. Ashland is following the rule carved in marble in (public relations) offices: Get the bad news out, and get it out fast." Ashland's Lacy said the company was following a crisis management practice that has been used for years. "Our attitude is to be candid and respond rapidly," he said.[24] The company subsequently decided that its previous practice lacked enough detail and developed a master plan based on its oil spill experience.

Ashland's efforts were not enough, however, to stop lawsuits. Four suburban Pittsburgh residents sued Ashland alleging "corporate maliciousness and negligence" that disrupted water service. They sought up to $10,000 each in compensatory and punitive damages and to make it a class-action suit.[25]

Thursday, January 7 - Day 6

Hall stayed in Pittsburgh. People began filling swimming pools with water. The oil slick was now 115 miles from the accident. Pipes were stretched across the river hooking up with communities that draw water from wells. As cities closed water intakes from the Ohio River while the fuel passed, others upstream resumed service.[26] Clean-up crews continued to work 24 hours a day operating floating booms in the Ohio and Monongahela Rivers.[27] Various observers attributed the collapse of the storage tank to cold weather, bad welds, poor testing, and brittle steel. All predicted that the initial crack would be traced to a weld.[28]

Friday, January 8 - Day 7

Ashland gave Allegheny County a $210,000 check. "In my memory, this is the first time payment has ever been made so expeditiously. It's just a new experience for us," said Tom Foerster, chairman of the county Board of Commissioners. "... [the payment] demonstrates the good will and good faith of the Ashland Oil Company to do whatever they can possibly to restore all of us to our pre-spill conditions."[29]

The national press and media in cities along the Ohio River praised Hall and Ashland for the way the crisis was being handled. Gerald Meyers said: "The lawyers are turning over in the classrooms at Yale and Harvard. Apologizing, that's an admission of guilt. The alternative is to stonewall and be accused of one of three things - ignorance, indifference or, worst of all, guilt. ... Honesty during a crisis is in vogue in management these days. ... Ashland is to be congratulated on how well they're executing it."[30]

"Hall was certainly honest about it. ... probably not too smart about it in a strictly legal sense," said Bruce Lazier, oil industry analyst for Prescott, Ball & Turben, New York. "I hope it doesn't cost them. The only real negative is why give up an admission that you screwed up? But I think Hall's admission is right."[31]

Following a helicopter tour of the damage, W. Tom Wiseman, mayor of Defiance, Ohio, a city of 20,000 downstream from the spill, credited Ashland for its openness. "They did not express concern about their liability," he said. "They came right out and said 'We want you to know we want this thing resolved, and we want to work with you.'"[32]

Headlines were positive with wire service stories:

"Ashland chief's honesty wins praise" - *The Cincinnati Enquirer*[33]

"Public, at least, likes Hall's honest, regret; lawyers another matter" - *The Herald Dispatch*, Huntington, West Virginia.[34]

"Ashland getting praise for candor" - *Louisville Courier-Journal*[35]

"For Ashland's Hall, honesty was the best policy" - *Akron Beacon-Journal*[36]

In an editorial, *The Pittsburgh Post-Gazette* wrote: "But the record must show that Ashland immediately notified the proper authorities so that containment efforts could begin quickly. Also, John Hall, Ashland's chief executive officer, forthrightly assumed the blame on behalf of the company and apologized to all harmed or inconvenienced by the spill. There was no ducking and bobbing about responsibilities over the spill itself. Furthermore, Mr. Hall has said the company will fully reimburse governments and agencies for the costs of the cleanup. He said Ashland will make donations to the Red Cross, the Salvation Army and volunteer fire departments as compensation for their outlays."[37]

The editorial writers for *The Herald-Dispatch* in Huntington, West Virginia reminded its readers of the severity of the spill and the thousands of people being impacted, yet wrote: "Still, we can't help but say 'well done' to John Hall, Ashland's no-nonsense chairman and CEO who told reporters and photographers at a Tuesday press conference that the firm accepted full responsibility for what happened. The polls show most Americans have scant regard for Big Business. And a big factor in that widespread public mistrust is that too many real-life businessmen come off looking every bit as shifty as television's J.R. Ewing. Not John

Hall. ... [his] unusual candor has gone a long way toward making the best of a bad situation."[38]

Following the news conference, Hall met with the editorial board at the *Pittsburgh Post-Gazette,* and then appeared on local television and radio. *Post-Gazette* staff writer Jim Gallagher added, "That kind of openness can give ulcers to corporate lawyers."[39] He wrote by getting quickly on stage, Hall personally showed his concern. "What they're trying to do is win in the court of public opinion," he added.[40]

Saturday, January 9 - Day 8

As the spill continued to move down river, Ashland president Charles Luellen called on the Wheeling, W. Va. emergency operations center and apologized to the people. "One reason we are here today is to see what more we can do," he said. As the spill passed Steubenville, Ohio, the city resumed water treatment. Wheeling businesses were closed and depended on mobile water tanks from the West Virginia National Guard.[41]

Sunday, January 10 - Day 9

Ice and cold weather slowed the slick's movement to one-half mile an hour as it virtually parked alongside Wheeling. The city's elaborate emergency plan all but collapsed as residents used too much water, and pumps failed on barges delivering water to the city's filtration plant. Sistersville, a town of 2,000 downriver from Wheeling, stockpiled water in swimming pools, moved portable tanks to the hospital and nursing homes, and loaded five 20,000 gallon rail cars for firefighters. Barge traffic and ice continued to hamper cleanup efforts.[42]

Monday, January 11 - Day 10

Mandatory water restrictions were lifted in Pennsylvania's Allegheny, Washington and Beaver counties. The lieutenant governor credited "outstanding cooperation by all residents and business" for making it possible to officially end the water crisis in Western Pennsylvania.[43] Cities and industries along the river were told to stay alert for the smell of diesel fuel near their intakes. The first 20 miles of the 40-mile long slick is under the water surface. Then there is a visible sheen on the water for another 20 miles.[44]

The media continued to praise Hall. "Ashland Oil and John R. Hall, are to be congratulated on their honesty and willingness to accept the blame for the January 2 fuel spill near Pittsburgh," wrote *The Ironton Tribune*.[45] WTVN Radio in Columbus, Ohio editorialized, "Credit where credit's due. ... The company promised to pay for cleanup efforts. ... many companies' first reaction would have been to stonewall in the face of such an incident. Ashland's open and honest approach should help the oil and chemical industries come to some conclusions about how to avoid a repeat performance."[46]

Tuesday, January 12 - Day 11

Ashland's Roger Schrum told reporters that the company was paying expenses daily, was continuing to coordinate cleanup efforts with EPA, Coast Guard and Pennsylvania Department of Environmental Resources and that it had hired the Battelle Institute to investigate the accident.[47]

Wednesday, January 13 - Day 12

Hall said he would open a Pittsburgh office Thursday to coordinate activities with various agencies, monitor environmental assessments and handle claims. Also, a firm experienced in handling oil spill claims would process claims from businesses and individuals. The company had spent more than $2 million to protect drinking water supplies that depend on the Ohio and Monongahela rivers.[48]

Thursday, January 14 - Day 13

The spill gained speed as it entered dams and locks, but then stagnated again on the river.[49]

Friday, January 15 - Day 14

Officials in EPA's mid-Atlantic regional office in Philadelphia termed "inadequate" Ashland's spill prevention plan. "The plan appears to be more of a general plan useful at any of Ashland's facilities," said Janet Viniski. "It doesn't contain enough specifics." During an EPA briefing on Capitol Hill, Senate staff members were told that an estimated 830,000 people would be affected, mostly due to depleted water supplies.[50]

Week #3 (January 16-22)

Stories appeared in *Business Week* and *Newsweek*. The *Louisville Courier-Journal* wrote that Ashland Oil "may well emerge with a better public image than before the disaster." The story added that the firm "went by the book" in implementing its crisis communications procedures as the news was passed from the tank farm workers up through the corporate hierarchy.[51]

On Wednesday, January 20 the company awarded $250,000 to the University of Pittsburgh's Center for Hazardous Materials Research for a year-long study to include a public information and education program on issues related to the spill's impact.[52] The company also opened a toll-free 800 claims line.[53]

While public relations professionals praised Ashland for its response, lawyers began advertising for customers to sue the company. City officials along the Ohio River praised Ashland for its cooperation during the crisis.[54] Law firms in Illinois and Pennsylvania advertised for victims to contact lawyers to see if they have a legal claim. "The response has not been overwhelming," said Pittsburgh attorney Paul M. Goltz. He said he was hired by a Wheeling hotel seeking $4,000 for expenses incurred in hiring experts to monitor how much drinking water was being used during the crisis, and by a woman who missed a day of work when she was sick because of contaminated water.[55]

The litigious activity prompted this letter to the editor:

'Nasty' attitude – "The recent water problem brought to light many nasty sides of Pittsburghers that I hope the national news did not pick up on. Before Ashland Oil gave $210,000 to begin payment for some of the services, many Pittsburghers and companies made a beeline for their lawyers. The people of Pittsburgh were inconvenienced, but I do not see a need for this get-rich attitude that some have. I feel that Ashland Oil Co. may have made a few mistakes, and that it will have enough problems with the government agencies, and that the people of Pittsburgh should make the best with what they have." - Ila Boyd, North Side[56]

Week #4 (January 23-29)

Allen Seiz, vice president of O'Donnell & Associates, Inc., a Pittsburgh consulting engineering firm, told a Pennsylvania State Senate committee that the tank "very likely" ruptured because the steel became too brittle as a result of the cold weather.[57]

Cincinnati shut off its water intake valves at 10 p.m. on Saturday (January 23) four hours before the spill was expected to arrive. The river supplies drinking water for about 850,000 people, but the city had enough water in reserve for it to remain closed for up to five days. The spill was expected to pass the city in two days.[58]

Testifying before a U.S. House of Representatives committee, Richard N. Wright, director for the Center for Building Technology of the National Bureau of Standards, said: "A crack opened the tank. It probably split the whole height of the tank in something like one-ten-thousandth of a second. It was hardly a leak. ... Good design, materials, inspection and testing prevent such fractures."[59]

A November 17, 1986 memo by Progress Services Inc. of Monroeville, Pennsylvania said X-rays showed that 22 of 39 welds on the tank were defective. This was strongly disputed by Larry Skinner, president of Skinner Tank Co. of Yale, Oklahoma. His company took down and rebuilt the tank. Skinner said that his company had no reason to ignore such defects because "it would have taken us about half an hour and cost about $300 extra to fix that many welds." The Progress Services memo, which Ashland immediately gave to investigative agencies, was not written until a month after the welding was finished, raising questions about whether there was an unresolved dispute between the firm and Ashland on the welding job. Copies also were given to Battelle Laboratories.[60]

Hall said he and his senior management were not aware of the information until Friday, January 22. He also noted that the faulty welds were not in the area of the tank where the steel wall cracked and issued this statement: "Based on a preliminary review (of the documents), it appears that Ashland's normal practices regarding weld inspections were not followed. In addition, a number of the old welds may have been defective." The company reassigned three employees who were involved in moving the tank from Cleveland to the Pittsburgh area.[61]

As Congressional hearings continued, Tom Luken (D-Ohio) said he was "aghast" that EPA had relinquished its public responsibilities by allowing Ashland to control the cleanup. He was challenged by James Seif, EPA's regional administrator, who said EPA was ready to take control anytime Ashland appeared ready to shirk its responsibility. Seif said he determined that Ashland had the resources and desire to clean up the spill and used the same contractors EPA would have hired.[62]

Week #5 (January 30-February 5)

In a January 27 news release, Hall said some employees might have known about defective welds more than a year before the tank collapse.[63] Later that week, at the annual shareholders' meeting, he said some questionable decisions were made by employees who built the tank. He said the company would inspect all 1,000 of its tanks.[64] The company took a 635,000-gallon rebuilt tank out of service in Evansville, Indiana for testing.[65]

Hall told a Senate committee: "We're embarrassed by this incident. However, we are proud of the valiant efforts our employees made to try to contain and clean up the spill and to help municipalities with water supplies. We've already paid $4 million to clean up the slick and provide drinking water for the 800,000 people."[66]

Continued rain and the series of locks and dams on the Ohio River helped move the spill along to Owensboro, Kentucky. Ashland announced it would begin a second stage cleanup on the Monongahela and Ohio rivers over the next three months under the review of the EPA.[67] Ashland stopped using a 3.3 million-gallon storage tank, also at Floreffe when it discovered flaws in certain welded seams.[68]

Week #6 (February 6-12)

Heavy rains increased the water and current in the Ohio River and the oil slick dissipated out of existence. "We lost it after it left Evansville, Indiana," said Jeanne Ison of the Ohio River Valley Water Sanitation Commission in Cincinnati. "It's so diluted we can't track it anymore."[69]

The U.S. attorney's office in Pittsburgh, conducting a criminal investigation into the spill, subpoenaed Ashland's records relating to the collapse of the collapsed tank.[70] The Pennsylvania Attorney General began one of at least a dozen separate investigations and studies.[71]

Week #7 (February 13-19)

The river cities began submitting bills to for reimbursement. Cincinnati officials said they would bill $386,000, more than half of it for overtime pay for water works personnel. "Ashland Oil so far has been very cooperative and has been prompt in paying bills submitted to it," said Cincinnati City Manager Scott Johnson. The City of Ashland submitted expenses of $19,944.[72]

Pennsylvania State Senator D. Michael Fisher (R-Allegheny) accused Ashland Oil of trying to "stonewall" his committee's investigation of the spill. Company vice president Philip Block said he could not answer many of the committee members' questions but agreed to supply written answers within a few weeks. "At this time, we do not have all of the facts," he said.[73]

Hall received positive comments from a U.S. Senate committee. "We commend you for coming here and making these statements. It's tough to 'fess up' like you have," Sen. Frank Lautenberg (D-N.J.) told him. Sen. John Chaffee (R-R.I.) agreed. "You have given us a candid statement, including some of your failings. That's unusual."[74]

Week #8 (February 20-26)

Water samples taken by the West Virginia Department of Environmental Resources and the Ohio River Valley Sanitation Commission revealed that one or more industries took advantage of the accident to dump their own chemicals in the river. There are 83 industrial discharge points along the 87 miles of the Ohio River from Pittsburgh to Wheeling. Edgar Berkey, then executive vice president of the University of Pittsburgh's Center for Hazardous Materials Research, said, "What these misdirected and misguided industrial people dumped are chemicals and materials far more harmful, far more biologically active, than the diesel fuel. They dumped dirty solvents because getting rid of them properly is expensive."[75] EPA's regional office in Philadelphia conducted a criminal investigation. "We received reports during the first two weeks after the spill that clandestine dumping had occurred," said EPA's Thomas Voltaggio.[76] Editorial writers in river cities blasted the polluters, who may escape any punishment, for dumping chemical wastes.[77]

The *Pittsburgh Post-Gazette* wrote there could have been better coordination between agencies when the accident happened. Columnist David Guo noted the first message from the National Response Center was logged at 5:30 p.m. with "Sketchy rept (sic) of 100,000 diesel spill. Sloreffe (sic)." Chief Warrant Officer Joe B. Lindsey of the Coast Guard surmised that Sloreffe was probably Floreffe. When he called Ashland at 5:33, 5:43 and 6:05 p.m., there was no answer since Ashland had shut off all power lines, and the tank collapse knocked out phone lines. He got only an answering service at 6:16 p.m. at the Pennsylvania Department of Environmental Resources. At 6:20, 50 minutes after the alert from Washington, he got his first on-the-scene report from an Ashland towboat operator. Communications breakdowns are an inevitable part of emergency response. Reporter Guo felt many gaps were too long and too common and created significant delays. The legislative hearings said both the Coast Guard and EPA were at fault. The Pittsburgh public safety director said his men waited at least six hours for a floating boom barrier to contain oil. In total, there were only about a half dozen telephones at the four command posts. Each group focused on one piece of a four-part crisis. The city was handling the leading edge of the spill; the Coast Guard containment upstream; the county dealt with the gasoline leak and potential explosion; and local volunteers, who knew the area, were running the evacuation.[78]

March 1988

Ashland reported that it was being examined by 55 government agencies and may face criminal charges, innumerable studies by public officials, academics and private companies.[79] EPA continued its investigation into hazardous chemicals dumped into the rivers following the oil spill, with no suspect.[80]

The company continued to receive praise. In the *Pittsburgh Post-Gazette*, lieutenant governor Mark Singel wrote: "Litigation is a fact of life, and it is likely that Ashland Oil will be in court for years. Ashland taught us, however, how a company *should* respond to an obvious error and its aftermath. Official and early statements from the company expressed more than regret – they assumed responsibility."[81] Singel also cited Ashland's public relations efforts having press liaisons always available and regular briefings held for updates and question-and-answer sessions. "This active press operation accomplished three things: It freed operations personnel from interruption; it kept the media and the public apprised of new developments and community water bulletins; and it reassured everyone that progress was being made," he wrote.[82]

A story in *Investor's Daily* quoted Lacy saying, "There was never any question of whether we would tell the truth. The question was when."[83]

May 1988

A study by Battelle Institute, the world's largest private independent research organization, reported the failure was caused by a "brittle steel fracture, emanating from a dime-size flaw in the tank's bottom course steel plate. ... Brittle steel fractures have been documented in older steel construction, resulting from a combination of stress and cold temperatures. ... Welding of the steel plates during both its initial construction and reconstruction resulted in embrittlement of the steel surrounding the flaw. These factors, combined with cold temperatures and the stress placed on the tank as it was being filled near capacity created the conditions required for brittle fracture."[84] The Battelle report also noted:[85]

* The flaw was in the steel since its manufacture and prior to its original installation on or about 1940.

* X-rays of the welds indicated that certain old welds did not meet current standards but tests indicated the old welds were stronger than the steel plate.

* Had a full hydrostatic test been performed the tank could have 1) withstood the test; 2) developed a slow leak; or 3) failed catastrophically.

Hall said that while the old steel used was in excellent condition, it did not meet industry standards, and that all future tank construction will be done in full compliance with the material, welding, and testing specifications of API 650.[86]

July 1988

Ashland signed a consent decree with the U.S. government agreeing to pay for the cleanup, reimburse the government $680,000 in expenses, and treat ground water for the next 30 years to be sure it is free of pollutants.[87]

September 1988

A federal grand jury in Pittsburgh indicted Ashland on two misdemeanor violations of the Clean Water Act and the Refuse Act. The Justice Department said the counts were the most stringent that could be brought against the company and that the government was continuing its inquiry to see if any individual employees violated the law. The U.S. Justice Department estimated cleanup and environmental costs at $12 to $15 million.[88]

Ashland officials expressed displeasure with Justice Department's decision to press criminal charges, pointing out its own efforts "to mitigate the spill's impact" and "the fact that the company quickly accepted responsibility for the incident." The company said it had spent $11.4 million already on the cleanup and that criminal provisions of the environmental protection statues are used only in instances of deliberate pollution.[89] The company cited three other large chemical spills in the Midwest, none of which resulted in criminal charges. "This will impair, rather than promote, environmental compliance." said the company.[90]

October 1988

The company pleaded not guilty and asked for a jury trial on criminal negligence charges.[91]

Ashland Oil accused Allegheny County authorities of perjury and obstruction of justice in the investigation that led to criminal charges. A civil subpoena produced a May 19, 1986 memo signed by Chief Inspector Charles Kelly of the Allegheny County Fire Marshal's office and addressed to his supervisor, Lt. Norman Smilnyak, in the county's Police Bureau.[92] Nearly 10 months after the spill, and steadfastly maintaining that Ashland erected the tank without obtaining county approval, implicit or otherwise, Deputy Fire Marshal Edward Babyak testified under oath in federal court that the company did have approval. Other county officials, Kelly and Fire Marshal Martin Jacobs testified under oath that no approval for construction of the tank had ever been given. Babyak suggested in his testimony that if there were a cover-up, it would involve a higher ranking official than Kelly or Jacobs. County Commissioner Chairman Tom Foerster ordered an internal probe by the county police bureau.[93]

In a speech at the Pittsburgh Press Club, Hall said the recent developments should raise questions about the thoroughness and objectivity of various investigations by state and federal authorities.[94]

Closing the Book

In a March 1991 speech to the Center for Corporate Response Ability, Hall summed up the financial impact on Ashland, noting the company paid some 4,300 claims to individuals at an average cost of less than $87 per claim. "... by February 1990, a little more than two years after the event, we reached an agreement to settle all outstanding issues for a maximum of $30 million, which included all previously paid claims and cleanup costs," he stated. "Nearly all of this was covered by insurance."[95]

Ashland's Crisis Steps

"We learned a lot of lessons from the spill," says Lacy. "When the tank collapsed, we didn't have a team and we didn't have a plan. We had to rely on our wits to get us through the crisis. We looked to the successful experience of other companies for guidance. Johnson & Johnson's handling of the Tylenol crisis taught us to show leadership, to stand up and be counted. To show concern. Take the heat. To do everything you can. And to do the right thing. "What that said to us was to get involved, to get in deep and to be a factor in the solution," he added. "So that's what we did. As a result, we've developed a recipe for crisis management." Here is Ashland's recipe for crisis management:[96]

1. Go to the site immediately.

2. Get first-hand information.

3. Marshal your resources and equipment to clean up the mess.

4. Contact governors and other local, state and federal officials who need to know and who need to answer questions from their constituents. It's better for you to call them before they call you.

5. Offer restitution to third parties.

6. Call in third parties – scientists and similar experts – for advice and independent analysis.

7. Meet the press. Go to the media, even if you don't have all the answers. Tell them what you know and what you don't know.

8. Listen to your media relations staff; they are your eyes and ears on public opinion. The questions being asked by the press are the same questions being asked by the public. Because of this, many times the media relations folks have a better handle on the seriousness of the situation than do the operating people. Because it is the *public* – rather than your own operating people – that decides how big the problem really is, in terms of public perception.

9. Stay on the job until the danger is gone, and the mess is cleaned up.

Using the Lesson Plan

Unfortunately for Ashland and Lacy, the company had a chance to apply the same techniques on September 16, 1990 when one of its tankers, the M.V. Jupiter, loaded with nearly two million gallons of gasoline, exploded and caught fire in the Saginaw River at Bay City, Michigan. Luellen, Lacy, Schrum and other officials were immediately on the scene to talk with emergency response personnel and the media. Ashland called in professionals to contain the fire, limit the environmental damage, determine the cause, and cleanup the mess.

As it turned out, a ship passing in the channel was going too fast and created a trough that pulled the Jupiter from its moorings, stretching the product hose unloading fuel. The captain of the passing ship refused to talk to the media. Local television editorials praised Ashland.

Take A Lesson From Ashland

Gerald Meyers wrote in *The Los Angeles Times* that Ashland Oil is a good role model to follow in a crisis.[97] Too bad Exxon USA didn't take that advice when in March 1989 its Exxon Valdez ran aground in Alaska's Prince William Harbor. As philosopher George Santayana wrote, in *The Life of Reason*, "Those who cannot remember the past are condemned to repeat it."[98]

Summary Checklist

- This case history is one of the best examples as well as a crisis communications classic of how a company did the right thing and won public trust and respect from the media.

- The crisis happened on a long holiday weekend but the crisis team was quickly assembled and responded.

- John Hall, spokesperson and CEO, may not have been the most articulate person, but he most important, he was believable and he was the top executive.

- Ashland sought to win more in a court of public opinion than a court of law.

- The company accepted responsibility.

- Ashland apologized and expressed regret.

- As the company got information it was released the media. It did not stonewall nor did it withhold information.

- It fully collaborated with state and federal regulatory and oversight agencies.

- When the company was falsely accused of erecting the tank without obtaining county approval, it fought back and won.

- Various local, state and federal agencies needed to communicate better among each other.

- The crisis cost Ashland a maximum of $30 million or $42.85 per gallon. The Exxon Valdez one year later, in March 1989, spilled 11 million gallons and the cost initially $2.9 billion, the per gallon cost was $263.63. And there is still litigation involving Exxon that could further increase the cost.

Endnotes

Information to document this case history was provided by news clippings and internal reports from Dan Lacy, vice president, corporate communications, Ashland Oil, Inc., Ashland, Kentucky, and a case study, "Ashland Oil Inc.: Trouble At Floreffe" by Anne K. Delenhunt, Harvard Business School, Boston, Mass., January 19, 1990.

[1] "Reassembled oil tank collapses, sending slick far downstream," *Engineering News Record*, January 14, 1988, pg. 12.

[2] "Spill on the Mon: A chronology," *Pittsburgh Post-Gazette*, January 4, 1988.

[3] Reuters, various news reports, January 3, 1988.

[4] Ibid.

[5] Clare Ansberry, "Oil Spill in the Midwest Provides Case Study in Crisis Management," *The Wall Street Journal*, January 8, 1988.

[6] Ibid.

[7] Associated Press, "AOI oil spill cleanup on at Pittsburgh," *The Daily Independent*, Ashland, Kentucky, January 4, 1988.

[8] Ibid.

[9] Ibid.

[10] Stephen Franklin, "Oil spill imperils water supply," *Chicago Tribune*, January 5, 1988, pg. 1.

[11] Wolfgang Saxon, "Monongahela Oil Spill Threatens Water Supplies in Pittsburgh Area," *The New York Times*, January 5, 1988, pg. B1.

[12] Ibid.

[13] Ibid.

[14] Clare Ansberry, *The Wall Street Journal*, *op.cit.*

[15] Ibid.

[16] John Hall, opening remarks of press conference, January 5, 1988, Pittsburgh.

[17] Ibid.

[18] David Guo and Bill Moushey, "Ashland concedes it never had permit for tank," *Pittsburgh Post-Gazette*, January 6, 1988, pg. 1; Bob Dvorchak, "Spilled fuel, search for cause spreading," *The Daily Independent*, Ashland, Kentucky, January 6, 1988, pg. 1; Associated Press, *The Plain Dealer*, Cleveland, Ohio, January 6, 1988, pg. A20; Catherine Chriss, "Chairman: Ashland lacked tank permits," *Lexington Herald-Leader*, Lexington, Kentucky, January 6, 1988, pg. 1A.

[19] Clare Ansberry, *The Wall Street Journal*, *op.cit.*

[20] Dow Jones Wire, January 6, 1988.

[21] Clare Ansberry, *The Wall Street Journal*, *op.cit.*

[22] Steve Kemme, "River cities cautious, not alarmed, over oil spill," *The Cincinnati Enquirer*, January 7, 1988, pg. 1A.

[23] Don Black, Gannett News Service, "Conditions to be normal by the weekend," *The Cincinnati Enquirer*, January 7, 1988, pg. A6.

[24] "Ashland Oil puts bad news behind," *USA Today*, January 7, 1988.

[25] Associated Press, "Suite by 4 charges negligence by AOI," *The Daily Independent*, Ashland, Kentucky, January 7, 1988, pg. A1.

[26] Michael Weisskopf, "Residents Fill Pools, Tubs as Spill Rolls On," *The Washington Post*, January 8, 1988, pg. 2.

[27] David E. Malloy, "Ashland Oil fully insured, will 'do whatever it takes,'" *The Herald-Dispatch*, Huntington, West Virginia, January 8, 1988, pg. A1.

[28] David Guo, "Weld, brittle steel suspected in spill," *Pittsburgh Post-Gazette*, January 8, 1988, pg. 1; Associated Press, National Wire, January 8, 1988.

[29] Mark Belko, "County gets Ashland's 1st check," *Pittsburgh Post-Gazette*, January 9, 1988.

[30] Earl Bohn, Associated Press, "What price honesty? Industry experts asses Hall's performance," *The Daily Independent*, Ashland, Kentucky, January 8, 1988.

[31] Ibid.

[32] Stephen Talbott, "Cooperation can limit spill liability," *The Plain Dealer*, Cleveland, Ohio, January 9, 1988, pg. B-6.

[33] Earl Bohn, Associated Press, "Ashland chief's honesty wins praise," *The Cincinnati Enquirer*, January 8, 1988, pg. B-8.

[34] Earl Bohn, Associated Press, "Public, at least, likes Hall's honest, regret; lawyers another matter," *The Herald-Dispatch,*, Huntington, West Virginia, January 8, 1988, pg. A3.

[35] Ben Z. Hersberg, "Ashland getting praise for candor," *Louisville Courier-Journal*, January 9, 1988.

[36] Associated Press, "For Ashland's Hall, honesty was the best policy," *Akron Beacon Journal*, Akron, Ohio, January 10, 1988, pg. E-4.

[37] "An overflow of good will," *Pittsburgh Post-Gazette*, January 8, 1988, editorial page.

[38] "Ashland doesn't try to duck the blame," *The Herald-Dispatch*, Huntington, West Virginia, January 8, 1988, editorial pages.

[39] Jim Gallagher, "Ashland scores high in public relations," *Pittsburgh Post-Gazette*, January 8, 1988.

[40] Ibid.

[41] Cass Peterson, "Best-Laid Plans Are Not Enough As Slick Arrives," *The Washington Post*, January 10, 1988.

[42] Rae Tyson, "Water is flowing again in oil's wake," *USA Today*, January 11, 1988; United Press International, "Sistersville next stop for spill," *The Charleston Gazette*, Charleston, West Virginia, January 11, 1988, pgs. A1, A12; Cass Peterson, "Wheeling Told To Save Water As Oil Lingers," *The Washington Post*, January 11, 1988; Associated Press, "Slick slowing down on trip downstream," *The Daily Independent*, Ashland, Kentucky, January 11, 1988, pg. A1.

[43] Andrew Sheehan, "Crisis is over," *Pittsburgh Post-Gazette*, January 12, 1998.

[44] Ibid.

[45] Opinion, "Ashland Oil cleanup sign of good neighbor," *The Ironton Tribune*, Ironton, Ohio, pg. A4.

[46] Editorial, WTVN Radio, Great American Television and Radio Company, Inc., Columbus, Ohio, January 12, 1988.

[47] "Ashland Oil Co. Says Insurance Covers Pennsylvania Oil Spill," *Report for Executives*, Bureau of National Affairs, Inc., Washington, D.C., January 13, 1988, pg. A-2.

[48] "Ready for claims," *The Herald-Dispatch*, Huntington, West Virginia, January 14, 1988, pg. B1; Associated Press, "AOI hires firm to help with claims," *The Daily Independent*, Ashland, Kentucky, January 14, 1988, pg. 15.

[49] Associated Press, "Lt. governor wants action on river spills," *The Cincinnati Enquirer*, January 15, 1988, pg. C2.

[50] Associated Press, "EPA: Oil Spill Plan Inadequate," national wire, January 15, 1988, 5:20 p.m.; "EPA Calls Ashland Anti-Spill Plan Inadequate," *The Washington Post*, January 16, 1988, pg. A-7.

[51] Robert B. Irvine, "Candor, quick action on spill may improve Ashland Oil's image," *The Courier-Journal*, Louisville, Kentucky, January 17, 1988, pg. E-1.

[52] "Pitt gets $250,000 to study spill," *The Pittsburgh Press*, January 21, 1988.

[53] *Lexington Herald-Leader*, Lexington, Kentucky, January 21, 1988, pg. B4.

[54] Tom Daykin and Jim Jordan, "The Big Spill: Ashland has to ride the waves," Business Monday, *Lexington Herald-Leader*, Lexington, Kentucky, January 18, 1988, pg. 1.

[55] Janice Bullard, "Lawyers Advertising For Oil Spill Claimants," *The Intelligencer*, Wheeling, West Virginia, January 19, 1998.

[56] Editorial Page, *The Pittsburgh Press*, January 19, 1988.

[57] Ralph Haurwitz, "Engineer says oil tank ruptured as its brittle steel broke in cold," *The Pittsburgh Press*, January 23, 1988, pg. A-5.

[58] John Eckberg, "Oil slick should slide right by," *The Cincinnati Enquirer*, January 24, 1988, pg. 1.

[59] Catherine Dressler, Associated Press, "Rare fracture caused oil tank to collapse, official says," *Lexington Herald-Leader*, Lexington, Kentucky, January 27, 1988, pg. B1.

[60] Mark Roth, "Builder claims no notice of bad tank welds," *Pittsburgh Post-Gazette*, January 28, 1998, pg. 1; "Paper says Ashland knew of risk to Monongahela," *The Christian Science Monitor*, January 28, 1988, pg. 2; Associated Press, "Tank's weld defects a surprise, Hall says," *The Daily Independent*, Ashland, Kentucky, January 28, 1988, pg. 1.

[61] Ibid.

[62] Jim Ross, "Congressman" EPA `too timid' in spill cleanup," *The Herald-Dispatch*, Huntington, West Virginia, January 27, 1998, pg. A1.

[63] Associated Press, "Faulty welds found a year before spill," *The Herald-Dispatch*, Huntington, West Virginia, January 28, 1988, pgs. A1-A2.

[64] "Ashland Targets Welds in Investigation of Fuel Spill," *The Oil Daily*, February 1.

[65] Associated Press, "Ashland takes fuel tank out of service for testing," *The Pittsburgh Press*, January 31, 1988, pg. 13.

[66] Reuter, "Ashland Pledges Thorough Cleanup Of Oil Spill," *Investor's Daily*, February 5, 1988.

[67] Associated Press, *The Daily Independent*, Ashland, Kentucky, February 2, 1988, pg. 11.

[68] "Ashland stops using tank at spill site," *Lexington Herald-Leader*, Lexington, Kentucky, February 5, 1988.

[69] Jim Ross, "ORSANCO loses track of slick," *The Herald-Dispatch*, Huntington, West Virginia, February 10, 1988.

[70] Reuters, "Ashland Oil records on spill subpoenaed," *Lexington Herald-Leader*, Lexington, Kentucky, February 8, 1988.

[71] Earl Bohn, Associated Press, "Slick disappearing, but spotlight remains bright on Ashland Oil," *The Sunday Independent,* Ashland, Kentucky, February 7, 1988, pg. 29.

[72] Associated Press, "River cities begin submitting cleanup statements to AOI," *The Daily Independent*, Ashland, Kentucky, February 19, 1997, pg. 13.

[73] Tara Bradley-Steck, Associated Press, "AOI `stonewalling' spill probe, panel told," *The Daily Independent*, Ashland, Kentucky, February 13, 1988, pg. A1, A14.

[74] Patrick Crow, "Ashland's redemption," Watching Washington, *Oil & Gas Journal*, February 15, 1988, pg. 29.

[75] Marylynne Pitz, "High levels of pollutants are found in Ohio River water," *Pittsburgh Post-Gazette*, February 22, 1988, pg. 6; Associated Press, "Dumped chemicals show up in river samples," *Sunday Gazette-Mail*, Charleston, West Virginia, February 21, 1988; Associated Press, "Some industries dumped chemicals in Ohio River after spill, official says," *The Sunday Independent*, Ashland, Kentucky, February 21, 1988, pg. 16; Associated Press, "Experts Say Plants Used Spill as Cover To Dump Pollutants," *The New York Times*, February 22, 1988; Associated Press, "Illegal Dumping Under Cover of Spill?," *The Washington Post*, February 22, 1988.

[76] Don Hopey, "EPA to investigate illegal pollutants in spill," *The Pittsburgh Press*, February 24, pg. 1; Associated Press, "EPA Gets Reports Of Illegal Dumping Into Ohio After Spill," *The New York Times*, February 25, 1988.

[77] "Worse than an oil spill," editorial, *The Pittsburgh Press*, February 23, 1988; "No sympathy for polluters," editorial, *The Daily Independent*, Ashland, Kentucky, February 25, 1988, pg. 14; "Sabotage on Ohio River," editorial, *Akron Beacon Journal*, Akron, Ohio, February 23, 1988, pg. A4; "Criminal polluters at work," editorial, *Lexington Herald-Leader*, Lexington, Kentucky, February 23, 1988, pg. A8.

[78] David Guo, "Vital hours were lost to poor coordination," *Pittsburgh Post-Gazette*, February 23, 1988.

[79] Thomas Easton, "Wake of massive spill stains Ashland Oil," *The Sun*, Baltimore, Maryland, March 20, 1988, pg. D-1.

[80] Don Hopey, "EPA still seeking chemicals reported in Ohio River," *The Pittsburgh Press*, March 11, 1988; Associated Press, "U.S. Rebuts Rumors of Poison Dumping," *The New York Times*, March 12, 1988, pg. 9.

[81] Mark S. Singel, "Good grades for crisis reaction," editorial pages, *Pittsburgh Post-Gazette*, March 4, 1988.

[82] Ibid.

[83] Art Hagoplan, "Executives Promote Honesty As Best Policy," *Investor's Daily*, March 2, 1988, pg. 1.

[84] "Ashland Releases Battelle Study On Diesel Storage Tank Collapse," news release by Roger Schrum, Ashland Oil, Inc. Communications Department, May 26, 1988.

[85] Ibid.

[86] Ibid.

[87] Ralph Haurwitz and Janet Williams, Scripps Howard News Service, "Prosecution mean to punish AOI, warn others, officials say," *The Daily Independent*, Ashland, Kentucky, September 17, 1988.

[88] Janet Williams and Ralph Haurwitz, "Ashland indicted in Mon diesel fuel spill," *The Pittsburgh Press*, September 15, 1988, pgs. A1, A6; Rick Wartzman, "Ashland Faces Criminal Counts From Fuel Spill," *The Wall Street Journal,* September 16, 1988, pg. 38; Reuters, "Ashland Indicted in Pa. Oil Spill," *New York Newsday*, September 16, 1988; Ruth Marcus, "Ashland Oil Is Indicted In Pennsylvania Oil Spill," *The Washington Post*, September 16, 1988; "Ashland indicted for Monongahela oil spill," *USA Today*, September 16, 1988; "Ashland Oil charged with criminal acts over spill," *Lexington Herald-Leader*, Lexington, Kentucky, September 16, 1988, pg. 3.

[89] Ibid.

[90] Ibid.

[91] "Firm Enters Innocent Plea On Environmental Charges," *The Wall Street Journal*, October 7, 1988, pg. C14; "Ashland Oil says it's not guilty of criminal negligence in spill," *The Herald-Dispatch*, Huntington, West Virginia, October 7, 1988, pg. C2; Associated Press, "Ashland Oil pleads not guilty in tank collapse," *Lexington Herald-Leader*, Lexington, Kentucky, October 7, 1988, pg. C17.

[92] "Ashland Oil Obtains Copy Of Approval for Fuel Tank," *The Wall Street Journal*, October 21, 1988, pg. A7; "Ashland accuses local investigators," *The Courier-Journal*, Louisville, Kentucky, October 21, 1988, pg. B3; David Guo, "Deputy fire marshal found key oil-tank memo," *Pittsburgh Post-Gazette*, October 22, 1988; Earl Bohn, Associated Press, "Ashland Oil finds proof in spill case," *The Herald-Dispatch*, Huntington, West Virginia, October 21, 1988, pg. A1; Editorial, "Ashland's new evidence," *The Pittsburgh Press*, October 22, 1988.

[93] Ibid.

[94] Ralph Haurwitz, "Ashland chairman questions quality of tank inquiries," *The Pittsburgh Press*, October 28, 1988.

[95] "Pittsburgh Oil Spill," remarked by John R. Hall, chairman and chief executive officer, Ashland Inc., to the Center for Corporate Response Ability, New York, N.Y., March 6, 1991.

[96] Dan Lacy, "Issues In Crisis Management, speech, Ashland Oil, Inc.

[97] Gerald C. Meyers, "Perrier's Crisis Management," *The Los Angeles Times*, February 25, 1990.

[98] John Bartlett, *Bartlett's Familiar Quotations*, 14th edition, 1968, Little, Brown and Company, Boston, pg. 867.

CHAPTER 8

CRISES ON LAND, IN THE AIR AND ON THE SEAS

Travel and tourism is one of the world's largest industries. It now accounts for US$3.3 trillion or more than 10 percent of the world's Gross Domestic Product. The industry is responsible for 230 million, or approximately 8 percent of all the jobs worldwide, and almost 9 percent of all capital investment. It expects growth of 4.3 percent during the next 10 years.[1]

The travel, tourism and hospitality industry has had some of the very best examples of how to deal with crises, as well as examples of the absolutely worst possible ways to deal with crises.

Airlines, cruise lines, hotels, tour operators, and others in the industry also have some of the best and worst customer service. Management that has ignored its customers, and through lack of leadership, provided poor customer service has been responsible for scores of crises and law suits.

Tourist destinations have suffered from natural disasters and the fury of Mother Nature. Resorts in Florida and along both the Gulf and East coasts of the U.S., and throughout the Caribbean, have been impacted numerous times by hurricanes and flooding. Tsunamis have hit Indonesia and Micronesia, and a devastating cyclone struck Myanmar (Burma). Other parts of the world have felt the violence of earthquakes and eruptions of volcanoes. The industry also needs to be prepared for acts of terrorism and civil and political unrest.

"We live in rapidly changing times where consumers are increasingly willing to claim their rights, lawyers are ever more litigious, and the media are ready and able to expose crises on a worldwide scale within minutes," says Peter de Jong, president and CEO of the Pacific Asia Travel Association. "An organization or destination in the midst of a crisis cannot fully control the behavior of people, lawyers, and the media; however, proper planning, adequate preparation, and effective management can help mitigate loss, and significantly reduce its impacts on all imaginable stakeholders."[2]

It's Not a Bird and It's Not Superman

The airline industry has had crisis after crisis, and more are just waiting to happen. Rather than resolving the problems and preventing the crises, the airlines could compile a multi-volume encyclopedia of excuses.

Customer service is missing from the vocabulary of almost every U.S. airline. Consumers are outraged and speaking out. Air rage and passengers out of control and fighting on planes in flight is alarming. Record numbers of flights are late both leaving and arriving, and it is getting worse every year. More passengers are being bumped off overbooked flights and more luggage, even that the airlines charged to check, is being lost. Few passengers can remember how airlines once prided themselves on service.

The U.S. has one of the oldest, aging fleet of planes in the world with much of the maintenance being outsourced to foreign countries with no federal oversight. Air traffic controllers complain of being overworked, understaffed and having to use antiquated technology. The most experienced and qualified are retiring, and no aggressive recruiting and training program is in place. The air traffic control system was developed in the 1950s and needs to be updated. Air traffic jumped 40 percent in the 10-year-period from 1995-2005.

Everyone connected with the business blames some one else, and no one accepts responsibility. The Federal Aviation Administration blames the airlines for jamming too many flights during the most popular travel times of the day at the larger and more congested airports. The anger, hostility, and frustration of airline employees get transferred to the customer. There are fewer employees working at counters, where airlines have replaced people with kiosks and machines.

The airlines first said 9/11 was the cause of all of their problem. Then they said it was because of rising fuel prices. But, problems started well before the price of oil went ballistic. Children flying alone have been lost. Airlines have lost elderly travelers with Alzheimer's. When airlines limited passengers to carry on baggage, they couldn't handle the increased number of checked bags and misplaced and lost them in record numbers.

Now the airlines like to blame the weather for their problems, and not because they have fewer planes in their fleets, fewer qualified pilots, smaller staffs, no backup planes or flight crews, and no plans for mechanical failures.

According to Robert Crandall, the CEO of American Airlines from 1985-1998, America's airline system has greatly deteriorated since Congress passed the Airline Deregulation Act of 1978. "Airline service, by any standard, has become unacceptable," he says. "Passenger complaints have skyrocketed. Airport congestion has become a staple of late-night comedy shows. Congress has not provided the money for a new air traffic control system based on global positioning that will reduce costs and traffic congestion." Until then, he believes flights at major airports need to be reduced.[3]

What Fliers Don't Know Won't Hurt Them

That was the attitude of NASA, which only after a year of stalling and under intense pressure from Congress, released an $11.3 million survey of airline pilots on safety. Between April 2001 and December 2004, Battelle Memorial Institute, a NASA contractor, interviewed 24,000 commercial airline and 5,000 general aviation pilots.

"It's hard for me to see any data here that the traveling public would care about or ought to care about," said Michael Griffin, NASA administrator. Earlier, a senior NASA official contradicted Griffin. Thomas S. Luedtke, associate administrator, said that revealing the findings could damage the public's confidence in airlines and affect airline profits.

A year before the report was released, Kate Hanni, co-founder of the Coalition for an Airline Passenger's Bill of Rights, discovered the airlines and the Department of Transportation were lying about tarmac delay statistics. "NASA has made it difficult to process and analyze the data, but already some interesting information has emerged," said Mark Mogel, vice president of research for the coalition. "The public will 'care' and 'ought' to be alarmed."

For 14 months, the Associated Press tried to obtain the survey from NASA under the Freedom of Information Act. "Release of the requested data, which are sensitive and safety-related, could materially affect the public confidence in, and the commercial welfare of, the air carriers and general aviation companies whose pilots participated in the survey," NASA's Luedtke wrote in his denial letter to AP. No airlines or pilots were identified in the survey.

"If the airlines aren't safe, I want to know about it," said Rep. Brad Miler (D-North Carolina), chairman of the House Science and Technology Investigations and Oversight committee. "I would rather not feel a false sense of security because they don't tell us." NASA directed its contractor, Battelle and all subcontractors, to return any project information and then purge it from their computers before October 30, 2007.

Hanni's research team at CAPBOR posted the first results of the survey on its website at www.flyersights.cm/downloads.html and included:

- Scores of aircraft inadvertently landed without tower clearance.

- Hundreds of reports of un-commanded in-flight movements of rudders, ailerons, spoilers, and high speed brakes, and hundreds more reports of engine fires and smoke, fumes or fires on flight decks and in passenger cabins.

- 1,290 instances of less than 500 feet of separation for airborne lanes, and thousands of instances where reserve fuel had to be used.

Officials involved in the survey said that they believe the unusually high response rate of 80 percent by pilots makes this survey more reliable than other reporting systems that rely on pilots to voluntarily report incidents.[4]

In April 2008, a whistle-blower again raised safety concerns at the FAA because the agency failed to stop falsifying controller error reports, even though it was made aware of the practice four years earlier. The Transportation Department's Inspector General found that Dallas air traffic controllers routinely and intentionally falsified reports involving planes that flew too close together, and blamed the pilots when the controllers created the safety problem.[5]

A Problem Well Before 9/11

Seldom have there been internal disagreements stronger than the one between the Department of Transportation's Inspector General, Mary Schiavo, and the Federal Aviation Administration. As the IG, her job was to investigate problems and see that they were fixed. She was an attorney, a former prosecutor, had a passion for aviation, and a licensed pilot when she was 18 years old.

Schiavo wrote in *Newsweek* that her office found serious deficiencies in airline inspections, parts and training, and in the air-traffic-control system. "Rather than checking every aircraft, many inspectors simply examine whatever plane happens by when they are on duty," she wrote. "I go out of my way to stay off commuter airlines. I have skipped conferences because I would not fly on marginal airlines. In recent years, small commuter planes have been more than twice as likely to be involved in an accident as the major carriers, and until this year the FAA allowed them to operate under significantly less stringent safety standards."[6]

Her recommendations and reports were largely refuted or ignored until the May 11, 1996 ValuJet crash in the Florida Everglades. The night following the crash, she went public with Ted Koppel on ABC's *Nightline* contradicting FAA administrator David Hinson who insisted the airline was "safe to fly." Schiavo disclosed FAA statistics that ValuJet's safety record was 14 times worse than other discount airlines, and added, "I would not fly ValuJet."[7]

No one "inside the beltway" could recall when an Inspector General went public with information so critical of a federal department. Government officials made television appearances and turned the spin doctors loose to reassure the public that discount airlines were safe to fly. Top DOT officials quickly shifted into a crisis mode. Secretary Frederico Peña reassured the public: "I have flown ValuJet. ValuJet is a safe airline, as is our entire aviation system. If ValuJet was unsafe, we would have grounded it."[8]

In her book, *Flying Blind, Flying Safe*, Schiavo writes that Peña "protected an airline just the way government had for decades." According to her, had it not been for an anonymous phone call, "FAA officials very likely would have continued with their charade." The field staff in Atlanta recommended in February that ValuJet be grounded. "They put it in writing. Someone quashed the memo."[9]

As FAA officials stonewalled Schiavo and the media and said they knew nothing about it, she found the critical memo written in official FAA jargon. "The memo, written three months before the crash, proved highly embarrassing to the FAA, and helped force the agency to re-evaluate its self-assured contention that ValuJet was a 'safe airline,'" she wrote. Following public outrage the FAA grounded ValuJet on June 17.[10]

Reverse Thrust, Reverse Spin for the FAA

The FAA backed off its spin. There were charges that Schiavo was "politically-motivated" since she served as Assistant Secretary of Labor in the Reagan Administration and was appointed Transportation IG by President George Herbert Walker Bush. In 1992, she found trouble in seven of the 10 FAA regions that 43 percent of the parts airlines purchased from suppliers were bogus, that engines were inspected only 52 percent of the time, and security was lacking at major airports since 40 percent of the time her staff passed inspections carrying fake bombs, guns, and knives.

According to Schiavo, Secretary Peña and FAA Administrator Hinson delayed releasing her report critical of security until after the 1996 Atlanta Olympic

Games. She claims it was sent to the National Security Adviser at the White House with a request that the document be classified.[11]

In a report on the crash, the National Transportation Safety Board criticized the FAA for not requiring fire suppression systems, and for inadequately overseeing the rapid growth of the low-budget airline. Nine years earlier, because of a 1988 fire, federal safety experts called for smoke detectors to be in cargo holds. However, the FAA bowed to industry pressure and rejected the recommendation.[12]

"Had the recommendation been implemented, it's only questionable whether the ValuJet accident would have happened at all," said Jim Hall, chairman of the safety board on *Meet the Press*. He noted that more than a year after the ValuJet crash, and nine years after the measure was first recommended, not one plane with a sealed cargo hold has been fitted with a fire detector and extinguisher.[13]

The FAA increased security at airports by requiring everyone to have a government-issued photo ID and be asked questions such as: "did you pack your own luggage?" and "has your luggage been in your possession at all times?" The agency has yet to implement a 1990 Congressional mandate with a three-year deadline to develop and install scanners that could screen for plastic explosives. There is a machine that can do the job called the CTX5000 SP made by InVision Technologies but the cost is $1 million. "The airlines don't want to do spend the money and the FAA won't force them," says an InVision spokesperson.[14]

Schiavo resigned on July 3, 1996. On September 24, 1997, ValuJet Airlines changed its name to AirTran Airlines.[15]

IG Recommendations for Customer Service

Calvin Scovel, the Transportation IG in 2007 for President George W. Bush, told a Congressional hearing that his office recommended federal regulators more aggressively oversee how airlines handle customer service.

Transportation Secretary Mary Peters supported the report, noting that the airlines agreed in 1999 to mitigate strandings and delays, and improve overall customer service at a time the industry was being criticized for poor performance. Eight years after the airlines said they would resolve the problems, Scovel's recommendations included:[16]

- Set time limits on tarmac delays and targets for reducing chronically delayed or canceled flights.
- Post statistics for on-time flight performance on websites.

- Customer service agents should be required to report a flight's on-time record to passengers when they call to book tickets.
- Large and medium-size airports should be required to establish ways to monitor and mitigate lengthy on-board delays.
- Establish a national task force of airlines, airport and regulators to create plans to deal with lengthy delays.

The Taxpayer Pays for Congress' Errors

Every time Congress decides to deregulate an industry it ends up costing the American taxpayer millions and billions of dollars. This happened with the savings and loan debacle in the 1980s. And with the energy and telephone industries.

Regardless of the political party in the White House, or who is controlling Congress, no one listens to the IGs, researchers, or the general public. The airlines spent millions of dollars lobbying Congress for deregulation. Sen. Howard Cannon (D-Nevada) introduced the Airline Deregulation Act which was signed into law by President Jimmy Carter on October 28, 1978. For passengers, shareholders, employees, and former employees, the industry has since been in a tailspin.

"It is amazing, but before deregulation, the American airline industry was quite healthy, safe and sound," said Anastasia Kostoff Mann, chairman/CEO of Corniche Travel Group, West Hollywood, California. "This perception is in contrast to statements in the Air Transport Association's Airline Handbook. When I need a good laugh, I read Chapter 2, which refers to airlines earnings as 'poor throughout the mid-70s, despite fare increases and capacity restraints.' It also says, 'Today's airline industry is radically different from what it was prior to 1978. Today it is a market-driven industry with customer demand determining the levels of service and price.'"[17]

"While the ATA may consider the industry's earnings 'poor' prior to deregulation, at least they had earnings," added Kostoff Mann. "The financial condition of the American-owned air carriers, with exception of Southwest, has been dismal since deregulation. Why? Because of the very same basic reasons which have caused the abysmal failure of each essential industry that our nation has deregulated – greed and stupid business practices.

"As an example, in 1994, the carriers joined hands in one of the greatest coincidences in business when they dropped travel agents. I say coincidence because each claimed not to have known what the competition was planning, to avoid anti-trust violations.

"The travel management companies, commonly known as travel agencies, had been paid up-front commissions averaging 10 percent to be the airlines' distribution arm for at least 85 percent of their product. This translated into booking, processing, producing and delivering their product – the actual airline ticket," Kostoff Mann continued. "Imagine a business where you could outsource the following all for a line item cost of only 10 percent, and this is just the short list:

1. Complete customer service for corporate and leisure travelers.
2. Product education, knowledge, and training.
3. All staffing and personnel requirements, including salaries, benefits, payroll taxes, increases, health insurance, and support offices, desks and equipment for the personnel.
4. Product packaging materials, ticket stock, ticket covers, invoices, envelopes, itinerary stock, etc.
5. Product delivery and pick-up, and re-delivery expenses.
6. All financial risks including invalid credit cards, bad debt, at 100 percent of the cost of the product.

"Over a period of several months, the airlines reduced travel agents' commissions ultimately to zero. What the travel agency community went through was horrific, and it was overnight. But it survived and like all survivors, the strongest and smartest companies made it. Our corporate and leisure travelers now pay for their transactions and know they are getting precise, excellent service.

"The airlines eliminated ticket offices and computerized with a system that favored their own products. Now they charge additional fees for tickets. They tried to buy corporate business and loyalty, offering large discounts, some as great as 50 percent, as one carrier tried to undercut the another, but it backfired.

"With mergers and more consolidation, there is less choice for the passenger. Today passengers have to pay for any and all bags they check, extra for an aisle seat, extra for a window seat, for a meal, or even a pillow. Imagine the immense cost to the airlines if they had to start servicing travelers again," said Kostoff Mann. "The only correct statement from the ATA handbook is indeed that the business is radically different today than it was prior to 1978."[18]

Under regulation, every effort was made to ensure that no airline ever went out of business. Congress was concerned following the troubles of the railroads and the bankruptcy of Penn Central that resulted in a massive taxpayer bailout.

However, since deregulation, many airlines today are only memories. Pan Am. TWA. Eastern. Braniff. National. Western. PSA. Piedmont. And, even no frills discounter People Express. During a 30-year period, 200 airlines have come and gone and investors and lenders have had to write off their losses.

Since 2001, the industry has laid off 165,000 employees. Pension funds for thousands of employees have gone south, impacting the Pension Benefit Guaranty Corp. Taxpayers will pay to replenish the assets.

"Our airlines, once world leaders, are now laggards in every category, including fleet age, service quality and international reputation," says Robert Crandall. "Consolidation will not resolve the woes of individual carriers, nor will it fix the nation's aviation problems. Mergers will not lower fuel prices. They will not increase economics of scale for already sizable major airlines. They will create very large costs related to consolidation. And they will anger airline employees.

"Given the recent concerns about aircraft safety, offshore maintenance of American aircraft should be prohibited," Crandall adds. "Maintenance performed in the U.S. is done under more demanding rules and a far higher level of FAA oversight than work done abroad."[19]

Legendary comedian Bob Newhart was a visionary when he recorded his 1960s monologue about the Grace L. Ferguson Airline & Storm Door Company.

Flying Mice

Even mice are flying these days. When an American Airlines Boeing 767 (tail N320) was brought to Kansas City for maintenance on May 1, 2006, workers said they found dead mice in the emergency oxygen masks, nests in air vents, live mice under the seats, and mice feces throughout the aircraft. A whistle blower gave a video to KSDK-TV and said between 900 and 1,000 mice could have been onboard.

Michelle F. Simmons in American Airlines customer relations said 17 live mice were found, and the number given the television station was greatly exaggerated. "There is nothing more important to us than the safety of our passengers and crew ... the safety of flight was never compromised on this aircraft. Nor was there a health danger associated with this aircraft," she wrote.

"We had to remove the seats and that's when everybody saw mice running around on the floor. One ran down the arm of a mechanic," said the whistle blower, a long-time American employee. He also said that when mice would get hungry, they ate insulation and chewed through wires. "If they shorted themselves and caused a fire, it would go though the cabin so fast we could have lost some lives," he added.

A log showed that on April 20 that N320 was at JFK in New York where mechanics noted a "mouse in the galley." The plane was put back in service and flew to Los Angeles. On April 23 there was another incident, but the plane kept flying until it was brought into Kansas City 11 days later.[20]

Mice are not partial to any one airline according to Robin Urbanski, a spokeswoman for United Airlines in Chicago. The crew found eight baby mice in a pillow case after United flight 897 arrived in Beijing, China from Washington, D.C. No party affiliation was noted.[21]

A Ptomaine Thanksgiving

For Thanksgiving, United Airlines wanted to make a goodwill gesture to its 3,000 union mechanics, baggage handlers, and other employees at Chicago's O'Hare Airport, but five employees needed medical attention for nausea, and others for vomiting, after eating a turkey dinner. The unions criticized United for giving million-dollar pay increases and bonuses to senior management after asking employees to take significant pay cuts to survive bankruptcy. The catered meals ended when employees found the turkey was not edible.[22]

TSA Screening Complaints Continue to Soar

If passengers are unanimous about one thing, it is that security screening is one of the biggest travel hassles. In 2003, Congress ordered the Transportation Security Administration to report its complaints. In September 2007, the Department of Transportation received 877 complaints about U.S. and foreign airlines, but TSA had 2,502 complaints about its service and baggage damage. TSA says it missed and underreported complaints when travelers were frustrated by busy phone lines and recordings, and e-mails were never properly handled.[23]

Michael Chertoff, head of Homeland Security, has not had uniform procedures at all airports. Some security screeners are government employees and some work for private contractors. Some are given proper training and some are not. There is confusion about liquids, plastic containers, quart-size plastic bags, and what is and is not carry on luggage. Screening lines are backed up because only two of six lanes are open. You can't always trust what the TSA website says because what counts most is how the policy is implemented when you are trying to board a plane.[24]

"Perhaps no other agency today so consistently and thoroughly reinforces the notion of government going through the motions without ingenuity or intelligence as the TSA does," writes *Newsweek's* Anna Quindlen. "Oasma bin Laden could get through the line if the name on his license was the same as that on his ticket and he wasn't packing Oil of Olay."[25]

Only the Federal Emergency Management Agency ranks below Homeland Security as the least-liked federal agency, according to the Associated Press. But a survey of 10,000 people by the American Customer Satisfaction Index, ranked Homeland Security, TSA's parent, at the bottom, replacing the IRS.[26]

A November 2007 report by the U.S. Government Accountability Office, the investigative arm of Congress, concluded that TSA needs to adapt more stringent security measures, and that screeners repeatedly missed bomb parts. GAO investigators conducted covert tests at TSA checkpoints in 19 airports in March, May and June 2007.[27]

International Problems, But China Is Doing It Right

In September 2007, the general manager of the new Beijing Capital International Airport said that passengers arriving for the 2008 Olympic Games will spend no more than three minutes going through customs and less than 10 minutes waiting for a security check. He said that 95 percent of all arriving international travelers will wait no more than 25 minutes before entering the process of check-in and border-checks. As an added bonus, the airport will provide free food for any passenger who is delayed for more than two hours, and free accommodations if flights are delayed for four hours because of the airlines' reasons. Another new service will be to send delayed luggage to passengers in Beijing free of charge within 24 hours. The Chinese government holds its people accountable and responsible. Michael Chertoff, U.S. airline management, the FAA, and members of Congress should take notice.

Sometimes rules are complicated for international flights and different whether leaving or returning to the U.S. Just ask Russian-American jazz musician Valery Ponomarev, who suffered a broken arm when he wanted to carry his trumpet on board an Air India flight from Paris to New York. The 63-year-old Ponomarev, who has lived in the U.S. for 35 years, kept his trumpet with him on a connecting flight before arriving at Charles de Gaulle Airport. In his protest, he obviously blew a couple of sour notes because four of Paris' finest gendarmes subdued him, broke his arm and held him in detention without treatment for six hours. Ultimately, the U.S. Embassy came to his rescue.[28]

Overzealous Italian military police forced a Caribbean steel band returning to London to leave a Ryanair flight because a passenger thought they were terrorists. The five musicians were on their way home after playing at a festival in Sardinia. One band member, who is blind and wore sunglasses, was led to his seat by his friends, where another read football scores to him. The five were the only Black people on the flight. They were stranded in Sardinia on New Year's Eve, and to get home had to first fly to Liverpool. They missed the bus to London, it was too late to book into a hotel, and the band was stranded in the rain, carrying their steel drums. The airline offered them £100 each and flight vouchers but the musicians say that doesn't cover the cost of their train tickets from Liverpool to London, and they want £800 for their distress and inconvenience. "I'm appalled by the way Ryanair has acted. It's a disgrace," said Jason Constantine, a band member. "It is not really about the money. It is the principle."[29]

Southwest Airlines' Crisis Plan Works

Since it began service in 1971, Southwest Airlines has never had a fatal accident. And after three decades of flying, its crisis plan was put to the test on March 5, 2000, when one of its Boeing 737-300 planes with 142 people on board, on flight 1455 from Las Vegas, skidded off the end of a rain-slicked runway after landing in Burbank. Authorities at the Burbank Airport and local police said the plane hit the runway traveling too fast, crashed through a perimeter fence, struck a car, and stopped on Hollywood Way next to a gas station. Airline and federal investigators said the cause of the incident had not been determined. In its statement, Southwest said: "It's not certain at this time why the aircraft was not able to stop."[30]

Southwest's public relations department was praised by *USA Today* for its actions and response. "How its crisis plan worked is a lesson for any company," wrote Marilyn Adams. While there were no fatalities, the crash triggered the airline's first crisis response in 29 years.[31]

- At the airline's Dallas headquarters, five senior executives set up a command center. They fielded 100 calls in the first hour.

- About three hours after the 6:11 p.m. accident, Southwest's CEO, Herb Kelleher, held a press conference.

- Meanwhile 50 employees were on a plane to Burbank.
- "Job descriptions went out the window," said Ginger Hardage, SWA's vice president of public relations. Joyce Rogge, vice president of marketing, headed an aid team that had been hand picked and trained in advance. The assistant team set up a command center at a hotel near the airport. The morning after the accident, they began calling passengers and offered medical care, counseling, and even groceries.
- SWA gave passengers travel vouchers with a letter of apology.

One of the few glitches in the crisis effort happened when a passenger called Southwest's 800 number, and the reservations agent had no idea where to direct the call.

Southwest's public relations team was tested again December 8, 2005, when flight 1248 from Baltimore landed in a snowstorm at Chicago's Midway Airport, broke through a fence at the end of the runway and into a highway intersection. A 6-year-old boy riding in a car with his parents was killed when the Boeing 737 slammed into the car. None of the five crew members or 95 passengers was seriously injured. It was the first Southwest crash that involved a fatality.

"Southwest's safety record had been a major selling point, a unique proposition," said Jonathan Bernstein, president of Bernstein Crisis Management. "Its reputation for safety, quirky-friendly service, and financial stability should help it move quickly past the tragedy in consumers' minds. Any company that creates a cushion of goodwill with all its stakeholders before a crisis will survive a crisis better than a company that hasn't done that in advance. And nobody has done a better job of that in the country than Southwest."

Three hours after the 7:14 p.m. crash at Midway, CEO Gary C. Kelly met with the media at Southwest's Dallas headquarters. He met with reporters again the next morning at 7:30 a.m. before leaving for Chicago with 100 other members of the airline's "Go Team." His first words were: "There are no words to adequately convey our grief and sorrow. ... The entire Southwest family is grieving this loss."

Bruce Hicks, general manager of Alliant Group in Houston says in the past airline officers rarely made a public appearance, let alone an apology. "The lawyers used to be concerned that if you showed any empathy that you somehow were admitting liability and would end up paying some legal cost for doing so," Hicks says. "But beginning in the 1980s, airline managers finally came to understand that ... you have to accept the liability when you run an airline."[32]

On January 27, 2007, another Southwest Airlines flight skidded off a runway at 1:30 p.m. and closed Spokane Airport for four hours. Flight 485 from Portland had landed and was taxiing to the gate when it slid off the runway while making a turn. No one was injured, but passengers in an Alaska Airlines flight which landed just behind the Southwest flight, were very concerned. "You could see the pilot's face," said Cynthia Dachtler, an Alaska passenger as she looked out the window. "We didn't realize at that second what had just happened." The Alaska pilot explained that after landing he immediately had to evade the Southwest plane as it skidded out of control. No one was injured. There was no public announcement or news release from Southwest's crisis or public relations team.[33]

On March 6, 2008, the Federal Aviation Agency fined Southwest $10.2 million, the largest fine ever, for using planes it believed were unsafe. The FAA said Southwest operated 46 Boeing 737s on 60,000 fights over a nine-month period, while failing to comply with a requirement to repeat inspections for structural cracks in the fuselage. The airline denied the accusations, admitted it was aware of missed inspections, and that it wanted to cooperate with the FAA. Two inspectors told the federal Office of Special Counsel, an independent agency that investigates such complaints from whistle-blowers, that FAA officials who were responsible, ignored safety violations at Southwest and leaked sensitive information to the airline. Their concerns were raised as early as 2003.[34] On March 12, the airline cancelled scores of flights and grounded 40 planes for inspection. SWA did notify the FAA, according to spokeswoman Laura Brown. Unlike its previous crisis responses, Southwest's public relations department did not return calls to *USA Today*, even regarding schedule information.[35]

No Crisis Plan for Dress Code

Southwest Airlines probably got far more exposure than it wanted from an incident involving Kyla Ebbert, a 23-year-old student at Mesa College, about how she was dressed. In July 2007, a male employee asked Ebbert to change her clothes or leave the plane she had already boarded for a flight from San Diego to Tucson. She was wearing a white denim miniskirt, high-heel sandals, and a turquoise summer sweater over a tank top, over a bra. She explained that she was taking a roundtrip the same day for a doctor's appointment and didn't have any other clothes. Temperatures in Tucson had topped 106 degrees all week. A flight attendant suggested she go to a gift shop and buy new clothes. She then offered to pull up the top of her sweater and pull down her skirt, and the compromise was accepted. During flight, she covered herself with a blanket.

The media had a field day when they heard about the incident. Ebbert appeared on numerous talk shows wearing the same outfit. Southwest received almost as much publicity for the "cover up" as it did in 1970, when it outfitted its flight attendants in go-go boots and hot pants. "My daughter is young, tall, blond and beautiful," says her mother, Michele Ebbert. "She looks like every other college girl in San Diego," she told Matt Lauer on the *Today Show.*

Dr. Phil read an apology on his show from CEO Gary C. Kelly, which Ebbert graciously accepted, but found laced with double-entendres. She returned two free airline tickets. "Southwest was insincere in its apology," said her attorney, Martin S. Reed of Anker, Reed, Humes, Schreiber & Cohen, Los Angeles. "Would they have used phrases such as 'the publicity caught us with our pants down' and 'this story has such great legs' if it was serious about righting this wrong?" However, the day before the *Dr. Phil* show, and Kelly's apology, Coleen Barrett, president of Southwest, spoke at Texas Christian University and defended the actions of its employee, and was further quoted as saying the airline won't likely apologize to Ebbert.

Ebbert, who works part-time at Hooters, was contacted by *Playboy* for a photo shoot. Before going public with the story two months after the incident, all Ebbert wanted was an apology from the airline. She now has her own website, www.kylaebbert.net.[36]

Sailing, Sailing ...

More people are taking cruises today than ever before – over 11 million in 2006. But all cruises are not like the television series' *Love Boat*. Between 1995 and 2006, more than 50 passengers died, fell, jumped overboard, or just disappeared. There have been reports of rape and assault. There have been shipboard fires and boiler explosions that have killed or injured passengers. Outbreaks of Norwalk Virus, also called Norovirus, and other illnesses, have ruined cruises for hundreds more. Engine and mechanical problems have forced ships to skip ports of call and create arrival delays, causing passengers to miss return home flight connections. Cruise ships have run aground, hit icebergs, and even sunk. Some ship passengers have been seriously injured, or died, on shore excursions.

There is little recourse for passengers because most ships fly foreign flags and are not subject to regulation. The Department of Transportation could easily create a database to list all incidents regarding cruise ships. Many of the top cruise lines have their headquarters in the U.S., but their ships are registered in another country. The thought of having such a website for consumers to check should be supported by the cruise lines, but would be fiercely opposed.

There are numerous blogs and websites on the Internet where passengers list the problems they have on a cruise. Almost every complaint you can imagine has been made by unhappy passengers: misleading advertising; misrepresentation of promotional items; poor or cold food; poor and rude service; dirty staterooms; cancelled excursions; itinerary and venue changes; food poisoning; thefts from staterooms; lack of supervision for children; dirty swimming pools; bait-and-switch tactics; no special attention for disabled passengers; being "nickel and dimed" for incidental items; lack of regular housekeeping; bed bugs on blankets; noisy, rowdy and drunk passengers; no followup on complaints; lost luggage; and lack of professional medical attention, equipment, and facilities.

The $25 billion-a-year cruise industry has had to deal with countless lawsuits, including 2,100 in South Florida alone in 2001. Most lawsuits are filed by a small group of lawyers in the Miami area who specialize in maritime law.[37]

Is There A Doctor On Board?

Most ships have a physician on board, but all may not be qualified in certain medical specialties. While a ship may have facilities for surgery, if someone has an emergency, the doctor may not be able to help. Take the cases of two 14-year-old girls who had appendicitis.

Laura Montero of Albion, Illinois was stricken on the Dawn Princess 250 miles off the Baja California coast in December 2007. The Princess Cruises' captain sent out a distress call. The U.S.S. Ronald Reagan responded and sent a helicopter to bring the young girl to its hospital facility for surgery. Lt. Cmdr. Gregory Leland, the pilot, lowered a litter basket to the cruise ship and then flew Laura to the Reagan. She was given excellent care by the U.S. Navy, later reunited with her mother, and the cruise ship stopped at its scheduled Mexican ports before returning to San Diego.[38]

Elizabeth Carlisle of Ann Arbor, Michigan was not as fortunate on Carnival Cruise Lines' Ecstasy in March 1997. The ship was two days out of Miami when she developed serious abdominal pain. The Ecstasy's physician, Dr. Mauro Neri, repeatedly advised the family that she was suffering only from flu. When her pain grew worse, in Cozumel, Mexico, the family flew home where her ruptured appendix was removed, and a subsequent infection left the teenager sterile.

The Carlisle's sued Carnival and lost in Miami-Dade Circuit Court, but won in 2003 in the Third District Court of Appeal. This was overturned by the Florida Supreme Court and now is being petitioned to the U.S. Supreme Court to challenge a series of cases that appear to immunize cruise lines from malpractice of their on-board physicians.

The fine print on the ticket the family bought has a disclaimer that the doctor is on board only for the convenience of passengers. "He is not and shall not be considered in any respect whatsoever as the employee, servant or agent of the carrier, and the carrier shall not be liable. ..." Dr. Neri, a resident of London, was an independent contractor with Carnival for $1,057 a week, even though he was introduced at a welcome party, wore an officer's uniform, and his name and photograph used in all promotional materials. The issue in court has divided judges regarding the responsibility of cruise lines, and whether the ship's doctor is an agent of the cruise line. "This is a very important question for millions of passengers," says Charles Lipcon, a Miami attorney. "Unless cruise lines are responsible for their doctors, there is basically no recourse for passengers."[39]

Crises With Independent Tour Operators

The rule of any crisis, or when there is negative or adverse media exposure, is to get closure as quickly as possible. Litigation only prolongs the crisis, and you never know how many customers you lose as a result of the story being told over, and over. All cruise lines offers shore excursions, but disclaim having any liability whatsoever for whatever happens on shore. Some ship passengers have died on shore excursions. One would have to question to what degree land tour operators are monitored, especially when a van or bus driver crashes, a small airplane or helicopter crashes, there is no emergency resuscitator on a scuba diving boat, or when a tour is not what it was promised to be. Land tour operators advertise their services to vacationers while they are on the ship, or the cruise line does it in advance on a website.

A bus carrying 16 American tourists on a side excursion to Chungara Lake near the border of Peru and Bolivia, crashed down a 300-foot embankment in northern Chile and killed 12 passengers. All of the victims were sailing on the Celebrity Cruises' Millennium from Valparaiso, Chile to Ft. Lauderdale, Florida. The independent excursion was not affiliated with Celebrity, the operator was not properly licensed, and the bus was in poor condition.[40]

Celebrity immediately responded and reported the incident to the U.S. Consulate in Santiago, U.S. Coast Guard, and Bahamian authorities. The accident occurred at approximately 4:30 p.m. local time, and the injured were taken to a local hospital in Arica, Chile. The cruise line obviously had a crisis plan in place that it followed:[41]

- A doctor, nurse and other staff members from the Millennium were sent to the hospital to assist the injured, family members, and local authorities.

- Celebrity notified all of the emergency contacts of the affected guests.

- A news release was immediately issued and posted on its website.

- Family members of the victims were flown by Celebrity to Chile.

- A statement was immediately issued by Don Hanrahan, president of Celebrity Cruises: "We continue to work with ... authorities to assist our injured guests and the family members of those who died in this tragic accident. Our deepest sympathies go out to all of our guests impacted by this terrible event, as well as their family members."

- Celebrity scheduled a press conference at 9 a.m. the following day at its headquarters in Miami. Speakers included Hanrahan and Dr. Mauricio Lynn, medical director of Trauma Resuscitation and Mass Casualty Intake Management at Jackson Memorial Hospital.

- Celebrity established two toll-free phone lines from both in and outside of North America for family members of guests sailing on the cruise.

- John Krousouloudis, Celebrity vice president for marine operations, led a special assistance team sent to the ship to help its guests and crew.

- Celebrity pledged to be actively involved in the investigation of the accident.

- Celebrity released additional information as it became available and posted information as well on its website, www.celebrity.com.

2002 A Bad Year For Virus

Passengers on many cruise lines in 2002 became sick with Norovirus, or Norwalk and Norwalk-like viruses which can cause diarrhea, stomach pain, and vomiting for 24 to 48 hours. The virus is spread through food and water, and close contact with infected people, or things they have touched, and afflicts 23 million Americans a year. During a several month period, some 1,000 passengers and crew on two voyages of Disney's Magic, and four voyages of Holland America's Amsterdam, contracted the virus.

According to Disney Cruise Line spokeswoman Marilyn Waters, the company offered a free cruise to passengers who became sick and to travelers who stayed in the same room as sick people. Holland America cancelled a sailing of the Amsterdam to sanitize the ship and to break a person-to-person cycle. Remote controls, clock radios, and even Bibles, were wiped down. Crew members replaced 2,500 pillows and dry-cleaned, steam-cleaned and disinfected every surface aboard the ship. On its last voyage before the intense cleaning, 58 passengers and 18 crew members developed symptoms and 87 of the 1,305 passengers left the ship at various ports in the Caribbean and were flown home.[42]

According to the Centers for Disease Control and Prevention, other ships were affected. The Oceana, operated by P&O Cruises of Great Britain, reported 114 passengers and three crew members became sick on only the ship's third voyage. Also plagued was Carnival Cruise Lines' Fascination.[43]

While most of the early virus cases happened on ships cruising the Caribbean, in 2006 there were five straight outbreaks of ships sailing from Seattle to Alaska, and the Pacific Northwest cruises became the hardest hit. Nine major vessels representing five cruise lines sail out of Seattle during the summer months, carrying some 740,000 or more passengers. As cruise line passengers increased from 9.22 million in 2002, to more than 11 million in 2005, the number of gastrointestinal illnesses increased. The average number of passengers per 100,000 afflicted between 2001 and 2004 was 42 in the Northwest, 17 in the Northeast and 29 for all other cruises.[44]

Fires, Power Failures and Pirates

One person was killed and 11 injured when a fire started by a careless smoker broke out at 3 a.m. on Carnival's Star Princess in the Caribbean. Some 100 staterooms were scorched and the blaze blackened dozens of exterior cabins. The ship carried 2,690 passengers and 1,123 crew members.[45] Near Bora Bora in French Polynesia, rescue teams evacuated 127 passengers on Windstar Cruises' Wind Star. No one was hurt and 17 of the 92 crew members stayed behind to put out the fire that started in the engine room.[46]

In July 2006, when the Crown Princess rolled and listed badly to its portside, passengers and crew were thrown to the deck, seawater flooded several upper decks, water gushed from the swimming pool, gym equipment and television sets were flipped over, and shattered glass was strewn across the decks. The new $500 million ship had just departed Port Canaveral, Florida on its way to New York with 3,100 passengers and 1,200 crew. The ship righted itself before returning to port. Princess Cruises, one of 12 brands of Carnival Corp., posted a letter on its website blaming human error for the tilt. Initially the incident was attributed to a steering problem. Some 240 people were hurt in the tilt and 116 treated in hospitals.[47]

Holland America had problems during the summer of 2002 when two of its ships lost power. The cruise line cancelled the Statendam's trip from British Columbia to Alaska after the vessel lost power, drifted for an hour, and had to be towed 20 miles back to Vancouver. The cruise line offered passengers a full refund plus future discounts ranging from 25 to 150 percent of the cruise fare.[48]

A week later, Holland America's Ryndam lost power at 1:30 a.m. on its way from Skagway, Alaska to Glacier Bay, and was at the mercy of the currents. The Ryndam previously had two consecutive sailings hit by contagious illnesses and the ship spent a week in port for intensive sanitation.[49]

In 2006, also on an Alaska cruise, the Norwegian Dream of Norwegian Cruise Lines, lost two of its four engines, was six hours late returning to Seattle, and stranded most of its passengers overnight because they missed their airline connections. The ship also skipped the port of Sitka, Alaska. Passengers on board who did not book their tickets through Norwegian had to buy new airline tickets.[50]

Modern day pirates are attacking both merchant and cruise ships off the coast of Somali. Between March and November 2005 more than 20 attempted hijackings and seizures were reported. At 5:30 a.m. on November 5, the Seabourn Spirit came under attack by two boats firing automatic weapons and rocket-propelled grenades at the ship. Miami-based Seabourn Cruises kept the 302 passengers safe in a public room and no one was injured. It was the first such attack on a luxury cruise liner.[51]

Antarctica – Crisis Plans A Must

Any cruise line sailing into the Antarctic must have a crisis plan in place. Tourism in the world's southernmost continent is booming and increased from 6,700 tourists in the 1992-1993 season to more than 29,500 in 2006. The frequency that ships are having accidents is raising concerns among tour operators and environmentalists.

November 22, 2007, the MS Explorer, the first cruise ship built for the Antarctic's conditions, hit submerged ice just south of the South Shetland Islands, took on water through a fist-sized hole in its hull, and sunk. All 154 passengers and crew members were rescued. The ship was built in 1969 and had made dozens of voyages to the North and South Poles. In 2004 it was purchased by G.A.P. Adventures, of Toronto, Ontario, Canada, which specializes in unique, small group, outdoor adventure travel.

Registered in Liberia, the ship had a double, ice-hardened hull, and its relatively small size allowed it to navigate among ice floes. "I'm perplexed that a hole that size caused that much damage," said Sven-Olaf Lindblad, whose father built the Explorer, and founded the company that became Lindblad Expeditions, a partner with the National Geographic Society. "It's very sad. I was hoping she'd be retired and become a museum somewhere."[52]

When the captain sent a mayday signal, three ships in the area rushed to the Explorer. The closest, Norwegian cruise ship MS Nordnorge, had 200 empty cabins and G.A.P. negotiated with the ship's owner to rescue everyone, and take them to nearby King George Island. The passengers were in lifeboats in six-foot swells for five hours before the Nordnorge arrived, and had everyone on board. G.A.P. arranged for the Chilean Air Force to fly passengers to Punta Arenas over the next couple of days.

Within hours after striking the submerged object, G.A.P. Adventures had its critical incident management team at work. The company immediately began posting updates on its website and a voice mail message, listing all of the details regarding the passengers, crew and ship. Phone hotlines were set up to handle calls from passengers' family, friends, and travel agents. Customer service representatives began phoning passengers' emergency contacts.

Since the passengers had only the clothing on their backs, in Punta Arenas the company gave each passenger a $200 voucher and made arrangements for a local department store to stay open after hours. While counseling was offered, not all passengers were aware of the service. The company mailed each passenger a $9,300 check as reimbursement for the trip and personal belongings lost with the ship, but some complained that this did not come close to covering the full cost involved. G.A.P. representatives in Punta Arenas did not have the authority to book seats on flights not in coach. While most passengers were thankful for the rescue effort, some complained about the evacuation, and overcrowding and broken engines on some lifeboats.

G.A.P. officials had differences with its insurance company on how passengers should be compensated for flights home and refunds. The company ultimately was forced to defer to the insurance carrier. "Had we been in charge, we would have handled things differently," says Susan Hayes, the company's vice president of marketing. G.A.P. has since worked to improve its emergency response procedures, including who should be called and when. It says its business remains bullish, with bookings up 41 percent, and more passengers than ever on wait lists.[53]

A check of its website of press releases and "in the news" clippings during the year has nothing regarding the Explorer's sinking, including even the information that had been posted on its website. Perhaps the home page says it best. The first paragraph is "What to expect from a G.A.P. Adventures Trip" and the last sentence is "Whatever happens, it's best to remember that it's all part of the experience."[54]

Earlier in the Antarctic cruising season, in January, 294 passengers on the Norwegian cruise ship Nordkapp had to be evacuated after the ship struck a rock at Deception Island.[55] A third incident happened December 29 when the Norwegian cruise ship MS Fram lost power during an electrical outage and drifted into a glacier wall. There were 300 passengers on board, no one was injured and there was slight damage to a starboard lifeboat and railing. The Fram was built in 2007 and designed for cruising in Arctic waters.[56]

Because the region's blinding sleet, fog, high winds, and treacherous seas make sailing treacherous for even the most rugged of ships, some experts fear catastrophic accidents and environmental damage. "If a ship like that [MS Explorer] can go down, it really should be a wake-up call about allowing vessels that are not ice-strengthened and do not have double hulls, to go down there at all," says Jim Barnes, executive director of The Antarctic and Southern Ocean Coalition.

While almost all of the tourist ships are small, Princess Cruises' Golden Princess with 2,425 passengers sailed the icy waters in 2006, and was the largest tourist vessel to operate in the area. A paper presented at a meeting of the Antarctic Treaty recommended barring large cruise ships, but the Secretariat has not done so. According to Julie Benson, spokeswoman for Princess, the California-based company has scheduled four more cruises for the Star Princess, a ship the same size as the Golden Princess. In response to the fact that Princess does not sail ice-strengthened ships, Benson said: "We don't believe that [ice-strengthening] is necessary because we cruise in the summer months when it's relatively ice free and our ships transit only in open water areas with very limited ice floes."[57]

The International Association of Antarctica Tour Operators has 99 members with a goal to promote safe and environmentally responsible travel. "Our concern is that companies outside the membership are not playing with the rest of the operators," says Denise Landau, executive director of the association.[58]

Listening and Anticipating = #1

Crystal Cruises is consistently ranked #1 in its category for cruise ships. The philosophy of Gregg L. Michel, its president, is to listen and anticipate. In 2007, for the 12th consecutive year, Crystal was voted the "World's Best Large Ship Cruise Line" by the readers of *Travel+Leisure* magazine.

Following 30 days on the Crystal Symphony, I departed the ship in May 2007 at Civitavecchia, the coastal port for Rome. All cruise ships have transportation from the port generally to a central station where tourists can take taxis to their hotels or trains to other cities. We heard rumors of a taxi driver strike in Rome, which was confirmed by the hostess on our bus. She immediately alleviated our concerns saying Crystal was taking us to another location where vans had been reserved to take us to our preferred locations.

In keeping with Crystal's exemplary customer service, the hostess said there would not be any charge for this service and all gratuities had been taken care of by Crystal. She further apologized for any inconvenience. During the next several days in Rome, I met other people who had been on Mediterranean cruises who had to find their own solution to the taxi strike. One couple said their cruise line dropped them at the central point without any warning of the strike. They felt they were fortunate to find a gypsy driver who took them to their hotel even thought they were charged 10 times the normal rate. Another couple was not as fortunate, and had to walk nearly two miles pulling their bags on wheels. Crystal did not want to see its passengers inconvenienced in anyway, much less stranded, and anticipated and did what had to be done. This is customer service.

Crystal asks passengers to complete a questionnaire at the end of each voyage. Michel reads a report summary of every cruise with a tabulation of the questionnaires and sometimes reads individual comments. He also reads every letter addressed to him from a guest, and although he does not necessarily respond to each personally, someone on his staff does. He is probably more hands-on and connected than many senior executives in the travel industry.

The Ultimate Texas Hold'em Game in the casino was implemented from an idea that originated from the questionnaires. A land program was developed in 2008 based on a letter from a guest. Another guest suggested in a letter that the spa and gym attendants continuously sanitize the fitness equipment and provide personal service with towels and water bottles, which was done.

As a further convenience to guests, Michel implemented early embarkation on Crystal ships with a complimentary lunch, and a service to check hand-carry luggage before guests' rooms are ready. Each year he hosts a President's Cruise and spends a few days visiting every World Cruise. He likes to meet with guests individually, and conducts a public question and answer forum open to all passengers. Crystal also conducts on-going research with guests through focus groups or quantitative studies.

Michel hosts an Awards Gala for his top producing travel agents each year. During the several days of seminars for agents, he schedules meeting times where the agents share their clients' positive and negative feedback. He also has been very aggressive in establishing and maintaining environmental "green" standards on all ships.

Responding to Problems Beyond Control

When you have a team prepared to respond crises can be resolved quickly even when not anticipated. This happened to Crystal on October 26, 2005 when the Crystal Serenity was headed for Barcelona, only to learn that Spanish fisherman were on strike and blockaded the harbor. To keep on schedule, Crystal hoped to go to Port Vendres, but the port could not accommodate the ship's needs. The Serenity anchored in Barcelona harbor during continuing negotiations between the government and fisherman, and after much deliberation, sailed to Gibraltar.

Guests scheduled to board in Barcelona were accommodated in hotels there for two nights, and then flown to Malaga, an hour from the port. Because of a political situation involving Gibraltar and Spain, there was no direct flight from Barcelona to Gibraltar. Passengers were given free hotel accommodations and meals, reimbursed for two days lost on the cruise, given $200 credit for a future cruise, and free Internet access for two days to contact family and friends.

Departing passengers were flown back to Barcelona and re-accommodated with complimentary rooms and meals, and transfers from the hotel to the airport. Guests who made their own air travel arrangements were given travel assistance. Travel agents with guests on board were faxed, and all passengers onboard, and in Barcelona, received communications throughout the two day ordeal. The cost to Crystal was more than $2 million.

Doing it right helps you be #1.

Are We Any Safer On Land?

Added to the spiraling cost of gasoline, the driving public is now worried about the safety of the nation's highways and bridges. Following the rush-hour collapse of the 40-year-old, I-35W bridge in Minneapolis on August 1, 2007 that killed 13 people, the American public was made aware of a deteriorating infrastructure that politicians have ignored for years. "Fully 27 percent of our 600,000 bridges have aged so much that their physical condition, or ability to withstand current traffic levels, is simply inadequate," said Sen. Patty Murray (D-Washington). "Some 78,000 are structurally deficient."[59]

At its current level of spending, $10.5 billion a year, only half of the structurally deficient or functionally obsolete bridges in need, would be replaced by 2024. To eliminate the backlog during the same 17-year-period would require spending $12.4 billion a year.[60] Some of the most classic bridges in the country are in need of extensive repair, and there most likely will be more I-35W bridge crises before the backlog is eliminated.

China made a commitment in 2007 to have more than 6,000 bridges it identified as damaged or dangerous to be fixed or rebuilt. Of China's 500,000 bridges, only 1.2 percent was found to be considered dangerous. From 2000 to 2005, the country spent $1.97 billion to repair some 7,000 bridges. It also put in place a maintenance system requiring all highway and toll road operation companies to employ bridge engineers to monitor the structures. "In the past, designing a bridge needed at least one year, but now it usually takes one month," says Xiao Rucheng, secretary-general of the Institute of Bridge and Structural Engineering and a professor at Tongji University in Shanghai. "Now you can even find bridge designers working overnight to finish the task. Many bridges [in China] were designed and built 20 years ago when designers did not predict the huge traffic flows today."[61] At the rate China is building new bridges it soon will have as many as the U.S., but almost none in danger.

Customer Care = Repeat Business

Deborah Gardner, CMP, a professional speaker and president of Compete Better Now!, Phoenix, Arizona, has been in the sales hospitality business for 22 years. In many of her workshops and programs she cites personal experiences. In July 2006, she was the very first guest at the Shamburg Renaissance Hotel in suburban Chicago. "From all of the world traveling I do, I rarely get sick. However, as I approach the front desk, wishing I was home in my own bed, the front desk clerks noticed I could hardly stand," she said.

"They quickly checked me in and asked if there was anything I needed. Once I was settled in my room, the housekeeper knocked on the door to know if I needed anything at all. She was told by the front desk I was not feeling well. Just 20 minutes later, room service arrived with a bowl of hot soup, crackers, a 7-Up, and a get well-card from the chef and staff," Gardner said. "I was so surprised. I also was so impressed with the trail of communication from the front desk to the housekeeper to room service to the chef regarding my situation and felt much better just because they took notice while serving me.

"Collaborating in your department, office, or team, by taking the initiative to own your responsibilities is huge, when servicing your customers," she said. "It's up to you to take charge on how the customers are serviced. Do you think I will return to that hotel when in the Chicago area again? You bet I will."[62]

Since so much of the success, and failure, of the companies in the hotel and hospitality industry depends on customer service, case histories, anecdotes and dos and don'ts will be covered in more detail in Chapter 14.

Summary Checklist

- The travel, tourism and hospitality industry is one of the largest in the world and one of the most unprepared to deal with crises.
- Peter de Jong of the Pacific Asia Travel Association said it best on page 151.
- Crises are just waiting to happen for airlines, cruise lines, hotels, restaurants and tourist destinations.
- Those responsible in Washington need to be held accountable for recommendations made by Inspectors General and others.
- The heads of Homeland Security and TSA need to adopt what their counterparts are doing in the rest of the world.
- Accepting responsibility and apologizing can quickly bring closure to a crisis and prevent exposure to tarnish the image and reputation of a company and organization. It also might save a lot of money spent for litigation.
- Silence is not golden in a crisis. Honesty works.
- Having a plan and team in place is invaluable. The team needs to rehearse and practice its roles so it will be ready as Southwest Airlines.

- The U.S. needs to look at what the rest of the world is doing with high speed rail, intercity travel and highway infrastructure.

Endnotes

[1] World Travel & Tourism Council; Global Travel & Tourism Summit 2008.

[2] *Crisis – It Won't Happen to Us!,* Pacific Asia Travel Association booklet, April 2003.

[3] Robert Crandall, "Charge More, Merge Less, Fly Better," op/ed, *The New York Times,* April 21, 2008.

[4] Rita Beamish, "NASA won't disclose air safety survey," Associated Press, October 24, 2007; "NASA mum on plane data that might scare you," CNN.com, October 24, 2007; "Airline Consumer Group Unangles NASA Air carrier Survey – Flying Public Deserves Answers," *PR Newswire* and *U.S. Newswire* for Coalition for an Airline Passenger's Bill of Rights, January 3, 2008; www.nasawatch.com/archives/207/11/airline_survey.html, November 2, 2007

[5] Alan Levin, "FAA: Dallas air-traffic controllers falsified safety reports," *USA Today,* April 24, 2008.

[6] "I Don't Like to Fly," *Newsweek,* National Affairs, May 20, 1996.

[7] "Flying Into Trouble," *Time,* March 31, 1997, pg. 53.

[8] Mary Schiavo, *Flying Blind, Flying Safe,* © 1997 Mary Schiavo with Sabra Chartrand, Avon Books; *Time,* March 31, 1997, pg. 56-57.

[9] Ibid., pg. 57.

[10] Ibid.

[11] Ibid.

[12] Stephen J. Hedges, "Did FAA cause a jet crash?," *U.S. News & World Report,* September 1, 1997, pg. 36.

[13] Randolph E. Schmid, "Planes still lack anti-fire devices for cargo holds," Associated Press, *The Philadelphia Inquirer,* August 18, 1997, pg. A2.

[14] Christopher Hitchens, "Airport Insecurity," *Vanity Fair,* June 1997, pgs. 58, 60, 62.

[15] "ValuJet changing name and business strategy," *The Press Democrat,* Santa Rosa, California, September 24, 1997, pg E1.

[16] Del Quentin Wilber, "Regulators Urged to Steer Airlines Toward Better Customer Service," *The Washington Post,* September 26, 2007.

[17] Air Transport Association, *Airline Handbook,* Chapter 2, and E-mails from Anastasia Kostoff-Mann, chairman/CEO, Corniche Travel Group, West Hollywood, California, May-June 2008.

[18] Anastasia Kostoff-Mann, *op.cit.*

[19] Robert Crandall, *op.cit.*

[20] Leisa Zigman, "Hidden Camera Video Shows Mice On Airplane," KSDK-TV News,

St. Louis, Missouri, July 11, 2006; "Mice on a plane – and that's no joke," *USA Today*, July 13, 2006; Michelle F. Simmons, American Airlines customer relations, e-mail to the author, July 19, 2006.

[21] Associated Press, "Stowaway mice," *The Seattle Times*, Seattle, Washington, January 10, 2008, pg. A2.

[22] Associated Press, "A bird of peace sickens workers," *The Seattle Times*, Seattle, Washington, November 24, 2007, pg. A2.

[23] Scott McCartney, "Complaints soar over TSA airport screenings," *The Wall Street Journal*, November 25, 2007.

[24] Scott McCartney, "TSA works to clear up carry-on confusion," *op.cit.*

[25] Anna Quindlen, "Taking Off Your Shoes," The Last Word, *Newsweek*, November 13, 2006, pg. 80.

[26] Eileen Sullivan, Associated Press, "Poll: TSA is as unpopular as the IRS," *The Seattle Times*, December 21, 2007.

[27] Spencer S. Hsu, "Airport screeners repeatedly miss bomb parts," *The Washington Post*, November 15, 2007.

[28] Jens F. Laurson and George A. Pieler, "Offend few, benefit many with common-sense discrimination," *Daily Herald*, Provo, Utah, December 7, 2006.

[29] "Caribbean steel band forced off plane after passenger feared they were terrorists," *Daily Mail*, London, England, September 13, 2007.

[30] Stan Wilson and Tony Frassrand, "Jetliner skids off runway into busy street," CNN.com, March 6, 2000.

[31] Marilyn Adams, "Southwest Passed First Crisis Test," *USA Today*, March 20, 2000.

[32] Dan Reed, "Southwest's 'goodwill' should keep fliers," *USA Today*, December 8, 2005.

[33] "Air traffic normal after Sunday slide off," *Spokesman Review*, Spokane, Washington, January 28, 2008.

[34] John Crawley, "FAA proposes record $10 mln fine for Southwest Air," Reuters, March 6, 2008; Vittorio Hernandez, "Southwest Airlines Violated FAA Safety Rules, Fined $10.2 Million," AHN, March 7, 2008; Alan Levin, "Inspectors: FAA officials gave Southwest a pass on safety checks," *USA Today*, March 9, 2008.

[35] Alan Levin, "Southwest grounds planes due to failed inspections," *USA Today*, March 12, 2008.

[36] Gerry Braun, "Southwest fashion police set no-fly zone," *Union*-Tribune, San Diego, September 5, 2007; "College Student's fashion Sense Gets Grounded on Runway," *The Chronicle of Higher Education*, September 6, 2007; David Schoetz, "Underdressed Passenger or Overreacting Airline?," ABC News, September 7, 2007; Mike Celizic, "Thrown off plane for outfit deemed too skimpy, Woman shows off threads Southwest almost grounded her for wearing," *Today Show*, MSNBC.com, September 11, 2007; Peter Pae, "Southwest Airlines seeks to minimize in-flight attire debate," *Los Angeles Times*,

September 16, 2007; "Southwest Airlines' Half Hearted Apology to Kyle Ebbert on the Dr. Phil Show," PR Web Press Release Newswire, September 16, 2007; "Legs in the Air," www.playboy.com.

[37] Amy Martinez, "Lawyers turn cruise lawsuits into industry," *The Miami Herald*

[38] Allison, Hoffman, "Navy Rescues Sick Girl On Cruise Ship," Associated Press, December 19, 2007.

[39] James J. Kilpatrick, "Case of the Sick Child at Sea," www.lipcon.com, Lipcon, Marguilies & Alsina, P.A.; "Cruise Ship Passenger Left Sterile After Doctor Ignorance, Carnival Cruise Lines, Carnival Ecstasy," www.cruisebruice.com, July 26, 2007.

[40] "Tour bus plummets into canyon, kills 12," CNN.com, March 22, 2006; Linda Garrison, "Cruise Passengers Killed in Bus Accident in Chile," About.com Guide to Cruises, March 23, 2006; www.expertclick.com.

[41] "Several Believed Killed Or Injured In Bus Accident," Press Room Details from Celebrity Cruises, www.celebritycruises.com, March 22, 2006.

[42] Mike Brannon, "Feel the Magic – in your stomach," Associated Press, *Arizona Daily Star*, Tucson, Arizona, December 1, 2002; "Tainted cruise ship to be sanitized," Associated Press, *Arizona Daily Star*, November 22, 2002; "Holland America to Cancel Sailing of MS Amsterdam Ship Will Be Out Of Service for Nov. 21 For One Sailing," Press Release, Holland America Line-Westours Inc., Seattle, Washington, November 19, 2002.

[43] "4th cruise ship reports people sick with virus," Associated Press, December 5, 2002; "CDC reports another sick ship," CNN.com, December 5. 2002.

[44] Vanessa Ho, "Some who cruise. it ... also lose it," *The Post-Intelligencer*, Seattle, Washington, July 15, 2006, pg. A1.

[45] Monique Hepburn, "Fire on cruise ship kills 1, injures 11," Associated Press, *The Seattle Times*, Seattle, Washington, March 24, 2006, pg. A10.

[46] Reuters, "Fire forces cruise liner rescue," CNN.com, December 3, 2002

[47] Travis Reed, "Dozens hurt when cruise ship tilts," Associated Press, July 19, 2006; "Cruise line blames human error for tilt," *USA Today*, July 26, 2006.

[48] "Tugboats rescue luxury boat," August 5, 2002, and "Holland America cancels cruise after power failure," August 6, 2002, *The Seattle Times*, Seattle, Washington.

[49] "Power outage briefly leaves Alaska cruise ship adrift," Associated Press, *The Post-Intelligencer*, Seattle, Washington, August 13, 2002.

[50] Candace Heckman, "Delayed cruise ship has passengers scrambling," *The Post-Intelligencer*, Seattle, Washington, August 12, 2005.

[51] "Cruise ship repels Somali pirates," BBC World News, November 5, 2005.

[52] Monte Reel," Antarctic liner sinks; all on tour rescued; ice punches hold in hull," *The Washington Post*, November 24, 2007; "154 Flee Sinking Cruise Ship In The Antarctic," *San Francisco Sentinel*, November 23, 2007; David Pett, "Disaster, response," *Financial Post*, April 1, 2008.

[53] Ibid.

[54] "Explorer News," www.gapadventurs.com, November 25, 2007; G.A.P. Adventures website, *op.cit.*

[55] Colin Woodard of *The Christian Science Monitor*, "Are polar cruises safe? Not all ships are equal," *The Seattle Times*, December 2, 2007, pg. L4.

[56] Bill Cormier, Associated Press, "Cruise ship strikes glacier in Antarctica," *The Seattle Times*, Seattle, Washington, December 30, 2007, pg. A11; Hurtigruten cruises, www.hurtigruten.com.

[57] Frederico Quilodran and Richard Jacobsen, Associated Press, "Boom in Antarctic tourism raises concerns," *The Seattle Times*, Seattle, Washington, November 27, 2007, pg. A12.

[58] Ibid.

[59] Minneapolis Star Tribune, August 1, 2007; "Just $1 Billion Approved to Fix Nation's Bridges," www.driversdrive.com, September 20, 2007.

[60] Robert S. Kirk and William J. Mallett, "Highway Bridges: Conditions and the Federal/State Role," *Congressional Research Service Report for Congress*, August 10, 2007.

[61] Xin Dingding," Thousands of unsafe bridges to be fixed," *China Daily*, August 14, 2007.

[62] E-mail and correspondence from Deborah Gardner, April-May 2008, www.competebetternow.com.

CHAPTER 9

WORKPLACE CRISES - MURDER, VIOLENCE, HARASSMENT AND DISCRIMINATION

The workplace can be a company's crisis nightmare. Murder. Violence. Sexual harassment. Discrimination. Bullying. And regardless how prepared a company or organization believes it is, many workplace crises will not be prevented.

Every company, organization and institution should have, at a minimum, a crisis management plan in place and ready to immediately respond in the event of violence in the workplace. Violence in workplaces is increasing at an alarming rate in the U.S. Now colleges and universities, and schools must be prepared for violence, often by students.

Some two million American workers are victims of workplace violence each year. It can strike anywhere and no one is immune. Workplace violence is violence, or the threat of violence, against workers and can occur at, or outside of the workplace. It can range from threats and verbal abuse to physical assaults and homicide. It is a growing concern for employers and employees nationwide.[1]

Additionally, the crisis plan must be all encompassing and include harassment and discrimination. Regardless how hard a company tries and how much money it spends on education and training programs, it will always be vulnerable.

Statistical gathering sources do not include all places of employment. The Bureau of Labor Statistics of the U.S. Department of Labor gathers information on work-related incidents. Fatal injuries were slightly down with 5,703 in 2006 compared to 5,734 in 2005. The good news was that workplace homicides decreased to 516 in 2006, the lowest annual total ever reported by the census, and a 50 percent drop from a high in 1994. However, this does not include some of the more dangerous occupations, such as driving a taxicab or working in a liquor store, gas station, fast food chain, or 24-hour convenience store.[2]

Robbery is the motive in most murders at food and drink establishments. Liquor stores, restaurants, gas stations and grocery stores that are open late at night and early in the morning are especially vulnerable because they deal in cash.[3]

When he was Secretary of the U.S. Department of Labor, Robert Reich issued guidelines to reduce violence and homicides for the health care and social services industry where he noted that two-thirds of workplace violence occurs. "Health care and social service workers often face aggressive patients, visit clients' homes in dangerous neighborhoods, encounter violent situations in hospital emergency rooms, or face other dangerous situations," Reich said. He added that guidelines will be developed for other industries, including the night retail industry.[4]

Some workers are at increased risk for workplace violence. Among them are workers who exchange money with the public; deliver passengers, goods, or services; or work alone or in small groups, during late night or early morning hours, in high-crime areas, or in community settings and homes where they have extensive contact with the public. This group includes health-care and social service workers such as visiting nurses, psychiatric evaluators and probation officers; gas and water utility employees; phone and cable TV installers; letter carriers; retail workers; and taxi drivers.[5]

Verbal Violence, Homicide Increasing

Verbal violence with threats, intimidation and harassment is now the single most common form of workplace violence, representing 41 percent according to the Society of Human Resource Management.[6]

Workplace homicide is now the fastest growing category of murder in the U.S. It is the leading cause of on-the-job death for women and the second leading cause for men. According to Workplace Violence Headquarters other physical violence includes work-related rapes, robberies, aggravated assaults with a gun or knife, and simple assaults such as fist-fights and unwelcomed fondling. The organization says more than six million employees are threatened, intimidated or harassed at work each year ranging from gender or racial slurs, and bullying, to actual threats of bodily harm. It believes the numbers are even higher because many companies do not report all incidents to the police.[7]

In an average week in the U.S., one employee is killed and at least 25 are seriously injured in violent assaults by current or former co-workers, according to a study by *USA Today*. The report said in nearly eight of 10 cases the killers left behind clear warning signs, but employers ignored, downplayed or misjudged the threat.

The report found that many companies fail to identify risks or teach managers how to defuse tensions that can lead to an attack. "We found threats were ignored," said Jeff Landreth, a senior vice president of Guardsmark, a New York security services company. He studied some 100 cases. Other experts say while companies are doing much to prevent attacks, they could be doing even more.[8]

Before companies began beefing up security and had higher levels of workplace violence, some even re-hired killers. In 1979, Randy Don Landin, a maintenance worker at Honeywell in Minnesota, strangled a co-worker to death. He was released from prison four years later and hired back by Honeywell to work in Minneapolis. However, after two confrontations at work he was transferred. In 1988, he left a death threat on the locker of Kathleen Nasser, a co-worker he allegedly stalked and threatened for weeks. Landin later killed her with a shotgun in her driveway.[9]

A firing is the most common cause for a workplace killing and occurred in 60 of 224 fatal accidents in the *USA Today* study. Next was a fight, disagreement or a disciplinary action for being late or for poor performance. Workplace killers are different from the typical murderer according to James Alan Fox, a criminologist at Northeastern University. According to his research, 73 percent of the killers are white compared with 45 percent of murderers in general, and more than half are over 35 while only about a quarter are 35 or older in the general population of murderers. Most are male.[10]

Domestic Violence Carries Over to the Workplace

One reason that homicide is now the leading cause of death for women in the workplace is that domestic violence is now in the workplace. According to the American Institute on Domestic Violence, in 2001 the health-related costs of rape, physical assault, stalking, and homicide by intimate partners exceeded $5.6 billion each year. More than 500,000 women are stalked, and 5.3 million women abused, by an intimate partner each year. Between 85 and 95 percent of all domestic violence victims are female.[11]

A 2005 survey reported by the National Coalition Against Domestic Violence found that 21 percent of full-time employed adults were victims of domestic violence.[12] Another study found that more than 75 percent of domestic violence perpetrators used workplace resources to express remorse or anger towards, check up on, pressure, or threaten their victim.[13] Responses by employers were disappointing. While 66 percent of corporate leaders identified domestic violence as a major social issue, more than 70 percent of U.S. workplaces have no formal program or policy that addresses workplace violence.[14]

Be Prepared to Assist Employees, Families

Workplace violence has created a new industry of consulting firms to help companies identify troubled workers and potential problems. Unfortunately, all too often, employers make a critical mistake by believing it can't happen to them.

Managers should be trained so they can identify "at risk" individuals. Consultants help companies and institutions know how to recognize potentially dangerous situations.

Human resources departments have employee assistance programs to provide support for employees following a crisis and also help "at risk" employees alleviate potential violence. Psychologists and therapists, specially trained in grief counseling, should be identified and ready to call to assist victims, families of victims, and fellow workers. Relationships need to be established not only with hospitals that can provide emergency care, but mortuaries as well in the event of a death.

While human resources can provide tremendous support toward healing the emotional psyche of employees during and after a crisis, the public relations team must deal with the damage done to the company's image and reputation.

Trends in Harassment and Discrimination

Harassment and discrimination of an employee because of race, sex, ethnicity, national origin, religion, color, age or disability is illegal. Before Congress passed Title VII of the Civil Rights Act of 1964, discrimination was widespread. The Age Discrimination in Employment Act of 1967 added age to protect individuals who are 40 years of age or older. Title I and Title V of the Americans with Disabilities Act of 1990 prohibit employment discrimination against qualified individuals with disabilities in the private sector as well as state and local governments. Sections 501 and 505 of the Rehabilitation Act of 1973 prohibit discrimination against qualified individuals with disabilities who work in the federal government and the Civil Rights Act of 1991 provides monetary damages in cases of intentional employment discrimination.

The U.S. Equal Employment Opportunity Commission (EEOC) enforces all of these laws and provides oversight and coordination of all federal equal employment opportunity regulations, practices and policies. For any company receiving federal money the Office of Federal Contract Compliance Programs (OFCCP) in the U.S. Department of Labor can be a source of help.

Because of openness in gay lifestyles, there has been an increase in the number of complaints against companies discriminating against male and female employees who are gay. The military has its own "don't ask, don't tell" policy which was introduced as a compromise measure in 1993 to allow all citizens, regardless of sexual orientation, to serve openly in the military. Passed by Congress and signed by President Bill Clinton, Pub.L. 103-160 (10 U.S.C. § 654) prohibits any homosexual or bisexual person from disclosing his or her sexual orientation, or from speaking about any homosexual relationships, while in the U.S. armed forces. The policy requires that as long as gays or bisexuals hide their sexual orientation, commanders are not allowed to investigate.

Typically an employee will report discrimination or harassment to a supervisor, to human resources, or the personnel office. If the employer does not take action to resolve the problem, the employee has a several options. Every state has an oversight agency responsible for harassment and the employee has the EEOC and OFCCP at the federal level. Litigation is another possibility.

"Race discrimination is the most filed allegation and consistently represents about 35 percent of all discrimination charges filed with the EEOC," says former chair Cari Dominguez, who also was a former assistant secretary of labor. She also was director of the OFFCP where she organized and directed the team that researched, wrote and implemented the Glass Ceiling Initiative in 1990. "There have been numerous high profiled race discrimination claims involving intimidation through the display of nooses, as well as racially motivated job assignments and placements.

"Gender discrimination claims, which also include sexual harassment and pregnancy discrimination, closely follow race at number two, of the most often filed type of charges," she adds. "The women's movement and the dramatic rise of women in the workplace have fueled the resolve to eradicate these prejudices from the employment scene. Sex harassment charges tend to get a lot of publicity, as we have seen through public stories such as those involving Isaiah Thomas, Bill O'Reilly and former New Jersey Governor Jim McGreevey. Often, these public allegations trigger other claimants to follow suit.

"The Glass Ceiling Initiative, launched by the Department of Labor in the late 1980s, and still in effect today, did a lot to remove attitudinal and artificial barriers from the workplace, allowing greater access and opportunities for all, including women and people of color," says Dominguez. "With shifting demographics and the graying of America, the EEOC has also seen the rise of other complaints. Age discrimination is one of he fastest growing claims, along with national origin, and religion, the latter spiking significantly following the 9/11 attacks. Muslims and Sikhs, in particular, felt a national backlash against them.

"The Americans with Disabilities Act, established to eliminate discrimination on the basis of disability, both physical and mental, has enhanced employment opportunities by removing physical barriers and making workplaces more accessible to people with disabilities. While the Act protects people with physical and mental disabilities, it doesn't protect alcoholics and drug addicts unless they are recovered and no longer use abuse substances.

"Discrimination and harassment speak to deep-seated prejudice and attitudinal biases which can cause a company serious public relations, marketing, and morale problems that ultimately translate to losses in profitability, good will, and human talent," says Dominguez. "Money spent on prevention and education is a sound investment. Protracted litigation is very costly and the image and reputation of a company can become irreparably damaged in newspaper headlines and on television."

She cited a number of ways a company can illegally discriminate against an employee including:[15]

- hiring and firing;
- compensation, assignment or classification;
- transfer, promotion, layoff, or recall;
- job advertisements;
- recruiting;
- testing;
- use of company facilities;
- training and apprenticeship programs;
- fringe benefits;
- pay, retirement plans, and disability leave; and,
- other terms and conditions of employment.

Bullying – A New Type of Harassment

The Workplace Bullying Institute says bullying is four times more prevalent than illegal and discriminatory harassment. According to a September 2007 survey conducted for the Institute by Zogby International, 37 percent of American workers, an estimated 54 million people, have been bullied at work. It affects 49 percent or 71.5 million American workers when witnesses are included. The survey of 7,740 online interviews reported than in 62 percent of the cases employers, when made aware of a bullying problem, did nothing and made the problem even worse. Perhaps one reason is that 72 percent of the bullies are bosses and 55 percent of the victims are rank-and-file workers.

Often the bully is the same gender or same race as the person being targeted and 31 percent of the time the bully enjoys civil rights protection, being a member of a protected group. Women are targeted by bullies more frequently than men (57 percent) and especially by other women (71 percent).

"This is a silent epidemic that won't change until employers recognize that it causes absenteeism and less productivity, and that affects their bottom line." said Drs. Gary and Ruth Namie, psychologists from Bellingham, Washington who specialize in this field. They note that bullying annually causes a turnover of 21-28 million workers and the additional cost of litigation.[16]

Pay Disparities Can Lead to Harassment Litigation

The Equal Pay Act of 1963 protects men and women who perform substantially equal work in the same establishment from sex-based wage discrimination. Nearly half a century later, this law is still abused and there are some companies doing business today who do not give women, and minorities as well, equal pay as their male counterparts doing the same job. Janet Conney sued the University of California at Los Angeles for sexual harassment and retaliation for complaining of discrimination and won.

In 1998 she had a position at UCLA where she researched, published and was mentored by senior colleagues. In February 2001 she was promoted to assistant clinical professor at a salary of $103,000. Then three of her male colleagues, including a supervisor, created a hostile work environment for her, being overly critical of her work, and making disparaging comments about her to others in the department, including suggestive comments to her about her body.

In July when UCLA did not receive grant funds in a timely manner, she was informed that they would not be able to give her the promotion. She was reassigned as a two-thirds-time employee with a reduced salary of $66,000, but maintained a full-time schedule. Her male co-workers were offered promotions and paid 50 to 100 percent more. In 2002 her contract was terminated, and following her complaints of sex discrimination, UCLA withheld her last paycheck and did not pay her for accrued vacation time.

Conney filed her complaint in California state court in 2003. On July 27, 2004, a California superior court jury awarded her $2.95 million in damages and found UCLA violated state laws by discriminating against her on the basis of her sex, and retaliated against her after she protested. The university contested the verdict, the California Supreme Court did not hear the appeal, and Conney received an award of $4.07 million. The story was widely covered on all of the major network and cable news channels.[17]

Too Much Hugging and Kissing

While there is good reason to be extremely concerned about sexual harassment, many school districts may be overreacting. The most recent is a trend throughout the country banning any form of public affection, including giving a good friend a hug.

One of the most ludicrous examples of "sexual harassment" was when six-year-old Johnathan Prevette was suspended for kissing a girl classmate in his first grade. The administrators of Southwest Elementary School in Lexington, North Carolina, considered this might be a "hostile political act." They were soundly ridiculed by the media worldwide for overreacting. The offending Prevette missed coloring, playtime and an ice cream party.[18]

Megan Coulter, a 13-year-old eighth grade student in Mascoutah, Illinois, was sent to detention for hugging friends goodbye for the weekend. She got hit with detention again a few weeks later for doing the same thing in a "no-hug" zone. "We're trying to educate our children in the very best way we know how, and that includes some training in socialization skills," said Sam McGowen, the superintendent of the Mascoutah Community Unit School District No. 19. Her parents, Melissa and Dean Coulter, met with school officials, presented their case and discussed the policy that led to detention. Coulter said McGowen was receptive and promised to look into revising the policy.[19]

In Prattville, Alabama, Madison Muir, a 12-year-old in the seventh grade, was sent home after giving a grieving friend a hug during a school break. Administrators at Pequot Lakes Middle School in Minnesota give students a two-hour detention if caught embracing three times a day or four times a week. Kyle, Texas officials say hugging causes children to be late for class and distracts from learning so they discipline huggers. A junior high school in Iowa City, Iowa banned hugging because girls would hug in groups and stop the flow of traffic.[20]

Victoria Sharts, principal of Percy Julian Middle School in Oak Park, Illinois, banned all hugging because "it creates bottle necks in the halls and makes children late for class." She said the hug ban is just one element of a comprehensive discipline and anti-bullying campaign.[21] High fives may be next.

Most of these administrators are reacting to a 1999 Supreme Court decision that found school districts liable for damages in cases of peer sexual harassment. The case was brought by the mother of a fifth grade student who was being repeatedly harassed by a fellow student, and the school district took no action. Justice Sandra Day O'Connor wrote the decision: "We stress that our conclusion here – that recipients may be liable for their deliberate indifference to known acts of peer sexual harassment – does not mean that recipients can avoid liability only by purging their schools of actionable peer harassment, or that administrators must engage in particular disciplinary action."[22]

Rob Horner, a University of Oregon professor who works with schools across the nation, has a dissenting view. "Schools need to define and actively teach what they do want to see in student behavior," says Horner. "To say 'no hugging' really blows it. That's exactly the sort of trap that, as soon as you say that, what is the first thing everyone is going to want to do?"[23]

School board members and principals and superintendents were admonished in an episode of ABC's *Boston Legal* on January 22, 2007. Their ears should have been ringing as the writers made a mockery of rules and restrictions on hugging.

Intimacy Also A Problem

Mark Everson left as president of the American Red Cross just six months after he took the job to rebuild its public image. The charity's board of governors took quick action after learning that "Mr. Everson engaged in a personal relationship with a subordinate employee" and "... the situation reflected poor judgment on [his] part and diminished his ability to lead the organization in the future." Everson, is 53, married with two children and a former corporate executive and commissioner of the Internal Revenue Service. He was the fifth leader of the Red Cross in just six years.[24]

Richard S. Levick, president and CEO of Levick Strategic Communications, Washington, D.C., compliments the Red Cross' board for its actions and what he considers several good strategic decisions. He is an attorney and his firm protects brands and reputations during the highest stakes global crises and litigation

1. They got it over with realizing they would have only a two-day news story. The first day announced Everson had been dismissed and the second day was for the media and public to analyze it.

2. By dismissing Everson during a time the organization did not need any more negative publicity, it sent a message internally and externally that it is setting a higher standard, which is what should be expected from people who run to disasters, not away from them.

3. The fact that he had not become entrenched in his job, and that the scandal broke within the first six months of his tenure was, ironically, a break for the board. It was easier to distance the organization from Everson.

4. Had the Red Cross known about the allegations and done nothing, they would have set up a ticking time bomb situation. What if the wife or girlfriend went public, and the media and public learned the organization had done nothing? They faced the issue head-on, chose the timing, and the message.

"Organizations and companies – even those whose reputations aren't as in flux as the Red Cross' – can learn a thing or two from how one of the world's most recognizable charities (and brands) handled this crisis," says Levick.[25]

A Slam Dunk Against The Knicks

Anucha Browne Sanders took Madison Square Garden and Isiah Thomas, coach of the New York Knicks, to court for sexual harassment and came away with $11.6 million in punitive damages. Browne Sanders, who was senior vice president of marketing and business operations, said she was showered with raises and bonuses for most of her five-year tenure, but fired in January 2006 in retaliation for telling the truth about Thomas. James Dolan, chairman of Madison Square Garden which owns the professional basketball team, insists she was fired after a series of marketing and budgeting failures, and that she had tried to subvert an internal investigation of her harassment claims against Thomas.

"I am extremely pleased that we have reached a settlement," Browne Sanders said. "The jury's verdict in this case sent a powerful and enduring message that harassment and retaliation at Madison Square Garden will not be tolerated. ... It has been a long journey, but I believe that justice has been done."

During the three-week trial, the jury of five men and three women heard Browne Sanders describe her ordeal with the Knicks. She exposed the club's tawdry side from its dysfunctional clubhouse to its star player's sexual exploits with an intern. Jeffrey Nix, a friend who was a plaintiff witness, said she complained that Thomas berated her with foul language. "What the f--- is your job? What are your job responsibilities, you f---ing ho?," Thomas told the former vice president in 2004 according to Nix's account.

In opening arguments in Manhattan federal court, her attorney, Anne Vladeck, said Browne Sanders was "a woman who was fired from her dream job because she dared to complain about sexual harassment" and after Thomas initially abused her, made "an about-face and repeatedly professed his love for her." Defense attorney Kathleen Bogas described her as "a liar who made up charges against Thomas to mask her incompetence."

Thomas, a former guard for the Detroit Pistons who in 1996 was voted one of the NBA's top 50 all-time players, told the jury that he wouldn't stand for a white man calling a Black woman a "bitch" but wouldn't be as angry if the same words came from the mouth of a Black man. When asked if he was bothered by a Black man calling a Black female, "bitch," he replied: "Not as much. I'm sorry to say, I do make a distinction. A white male calling a Black female a bitch is highly offensive."

He did acknowledge that in December 2005, he tried to kiss Browne Sanders on the cheek at a Knicks game and asked "No love today?" when she pulled away, according to court papers. But he disputed her allegations that he asked her to "go off site" with him for private time. His attorney described Browne Sanders, a former Northwestern basketball star, as a physically imposing woman who was savvy enough to navigate the trash-talking world of professional basketball. Thomas later denied ever calling her a "bitch" or "ho" or that he was ever interested in her romantically.

The jury ruled that Thomas was liable for sexual harassment and that Dolan, the team's owner and chairman, should pay the victim more than $11 million in damages for allowing her to work in a hostile environment. The jury was divided on punitive damages. As the two sides were prepared to return to the U.S. District Court they reached a settlement.

Fraser Seitel gave his "Best Dressed CEO Award" this year to Dolan, "the sports CEO with the resolute pigheadedness to demonstrate his own brand of sartorial splendor, whether or not it costs him millions. ... [he] showed up for his televised deposition in a grimy black T-shirt, rather than your traditional suit and tie. He proceeded to testify with a winning formula of arrogance, disdain, and condescension. Dolan's video ensemble and performance must have resonated with the jury who refused to award Browne Sanders the $9 million she asked for. Rather, they awarded her $11.6 million!"[26]

Worked to Death

For years some employees have complained that they were being worked to death. In Japan, it became a reality. Death from overwork, known in Japanese as "karoshi," has increased steadily since it was recognized in 1987 by the government. According to Japan's Ministry of Labor, for the year ending March 2007, the government acknowledged 147 cases of death from overwork out of 303 complaints.

Kiroko Uchino won a lawsuit against the Japanese government which initially had rejected her application for workers' compensation benefits she filed after the death of her husband, Kenichi. He was a middle manager in charge of quality control at a Toyota factory in Toyota City and died at the age of 30 after putting in long hours. He had worked more than 80 hours of overtime per month for six months before his death and in the month before he collapsed and died at work, he had put in 114 hours of overtime.[27]

Complaint Leads to Congressional Investigation

Halliburton Co. has been no stranger to members of Congress or anyone on Capitol Hill since it has become the favored and most financially rewarded military contractor supporting the Iraq war. It didn't need any additional negative media exposure, or to have its management appear yet again before a Congressional committee, but this is what happened when Jamie Leigh Jones of Conroe, Texas filed a federal lawsuit in May 2007 against the company, its former subsidiary, KBR Inc. and others. She claimed she was raped by co-workers while working for a Halliburton subsidiary in Baghdad in 2005.

Jones began working for KBR in Texas as an administrative assistant in 2004 when she was 19. She later transferred to Iraq with another Halliburton subsidiary. Her lawsuit claims she lived in coed barracks in the Green Zone, and after enduring harassment from some fellow workers, she was drugged and gang-raped July 29, 2005. In an interview with ABC News and *20/20*, she says the company then put her under guard, in a shipping container, and warned her that if she left Iraq for medical treatment she would no longer have a job. The lawsuit says the facility was under direct control of the U.S. government, KBR and Halliburton, collectively.

She said she was held in the shipping container with a bed, table and lamp, for at least 24 hours without food or water and KBR armed security guards would not let her leave. Jones borrowed a cellphone from a guard and called her father in Texas. He called Congressman Ted Poe (R-Texas), who contacted the State Department. Representatives from the U.S. Embassy in Baghdad went to the camp where Jones was held and rescued her from the container.

According to an ABC News interview, U.S. Army physicians showed Jones had been raped, but the rape kit disappeared after it was given to KBR security officers. Following reports by ABC and other national media that federal authorities did not prosecute the alleged suspects, and that the Houston office of the EEOC found Jones' allegations were "inadequate and did not effect an adequate remedy," Congress became involved. Rep. John Conyers (D-Michigan), chairman of the House Judiciary Committee, asked the Justice Department to give a full account of its investigation and to tell him whether it has jurisdiction to prosecute the alleged attackers under the Military Extraterritorial Jurisdiction Act.

The *Houston Chronicle* reported that not only did federal authorities not prosecute the alleged suspects, but that a Florida woman was also raped at the same living quarters in a separate 2005 incident. Sen. Bill Nelson (D-Florida) of the Senate Foreign Relations and Armed Services committees has demanded that the Justice Department provide a full accounting of the government's handling of the rape allegation by the Florida woman.

In an e-mail to all KBR employees, Bill Utt, chairman, president and CEO of KBR, disputed Jones' allegations. "There continues to be extensive media coverage regarding litigation involving a former KBR subsidiary employee, Ms. Jamie Jones. As transparency is a KBR core value, I want to share with you our perspective of the situation," he wrote.

"First and foremost, KBR in no way condones or tolerates any form of sexual harassment. The safety and security of all employees remains KBR's top priority. ... Any and all allegations related to inappropriate sexual behavior are taken seriously and are investigated immediately. In response to Ms. Jones' allegation, an investigative process was initiated in Ms. Jones' case and was subsequently taken over by government authorities in accordance with their procedures.

"While the allegations raised by Ms. Jones are serious, after a review of the case KBR noted inaccuracies in the accounts of the incident in question and disputes portions of Ms. Jones' version of the facts. We have expressed our position in detail to the EEOC and some of this information is now public."

"It is true that KBR expressed their position in detail to the EEOC," said Todd Kelly, Jones' Houston attorney. "I would love for the entire country to read that explanation of events with the same critical eye that they have viewed Jamie Jones."[28]

Jones, who now lives in California, established a nonprofit foundation, The Jamie Leigh Foundation, which is dedicated to helping U.S. citizens and legal residents who are victims of sexual harassment, rape and sexual abuse while working abroad for federal contractors, corporations, or government entities. "We believe that overseas contractors and corporations should act responsibly, and be held accountable to provide safe housing and a work environment free of sexual harassment, and limit the potential for abuse," she writes.

"We believe that U.S. civilians who perpetrate crime while working in foreign countries should be held accountable for their actions. The Jamie Leigh Foundation will assist victims through advocacy, education, referral and providing support. We work toward the day that no person shall face sexual abuse and harassment, and all persons, regardless of gender, will be able to work without fear, consternation, and safety concerns." The website at www.jamiesfoundation. org also has a link to the House of Representatives with her December 19, 2007 testimony before Congress.

Managers Need to Listen

Had Lockheed Martin management and supervisors in human resources listened to Charles N. Daniels the company may have avoided paying $2.5 million, the largest settlement with an individual in a racial-discrimination case handled by the EEOC.

"I have to believe it was strictly due to the color of my skin," said Daniels, an African-American. "I was born in an era where I was told things are going to get better. We still have a long way to go."

Between 1999 and 2001, Daniels, 45, said he was harassed almost daily while working for the world's largest military contractor. In South Carolina, he said he was told he could be lynched or buried in a roadside grave where his body would never be found. One co-worker told him, "We should do to Blacks what Hitler did to the Jews." Weekly Ku Klux Klan newsletters were distributed in an employee break room.

Threats and verbal attacks continued when he and a group of co-workers were transferred to Florida, and then Hawaii where they modified Navy P-3 patrol planes. At Whidbey Island, Florida, one co-worker told Daniels, a former air Force staff sergeant, that he and others could make a person disappear where he would never be found.

According to EEOC investigators, a Lockheed human resources director in court testimony said she investigated Daniels' complaints and confirmed that racial comments were made, but dismissed them as "Boys will be boys." Daniels said when he reported his complaint to human resources and no action was taken, he was then reassigned to work in Maine. When he asked not to be forced to relocate, he was terminated.

"Lockheed Martin pretty much told me, 'We're Lockheed Martin. We never lose,'" he said. "Hopefully things will change." Joe Stout, a spokesman for Lockheed said that the incidents reported by Daniels were "isolated" and did not reflect the company as a whole. Stout did not report what action was taken regarding continued employment, or remedial training, by the human resources people who cost Lockheed $2.5 million.[29]

A New Approach to Employee Relations

HCL Technologies, an outsourcer-company headquartered in Noida, India just outside of New Delhi, is setting a new example for the way employees are involved. Vineet Nayar became CEO in 2005 and his management philosophy is "Employees first, customers second" even when he talks to customers.

He established a 360-degree feedback with workers grading their bosses on performance. Nayar then took it a step further and HCL may be the only company in the world that posts the results on the company's intranet for everyone to see. Employees can see the scores of their supervisors. His objective was to hold managers accountable for their faults.

HCL is the fifth largest info-tech outsourcer in India and expects to add 10,000 more employees to its workforce of 45,600. The challenge of attracting and retaining workers has prompted many companies to increase perks and salaries, since there is little employee loyalty when it comes to paychecks.

Nayar's team rated him 3.6 out of 5 for how well he keeps projects running on schedule and this was among his lowest scores from the 81 managers who rated him. And everyone in the company has this information. He posted his own scores before asking his team to follow suit.

He also responds quickly and publicly to employee concerns, and posts on the intranet his responses to every question left by an employee. Nayar spends about seven hours each week, even on Sundays, responding to some 50 questions a week, and does not hand them off to a subordinate to answer.

Even though HCL's employees were the primary beneficiaries of Nayar's innovative management philosophy, some were initially skeptical. However, he has cut the company's 20.4 percent attrition rate, once one of the highest in the industry, three quarters in a row and posted a 42 percent rise in quarterly net income, and increased annual revenues 42 percent over the previous year to $1.5 billion.[30]

Summary Checklist

- No company, organization or institution is immune from a workplace crisis.
- Have plans in place for murder, other violence, harassment and discrimination.
- Look to outside consultants who are specialists in their fields to work with management and train and educate employees.
- Identify and know how to call when psychologists or specially-trained therapists are needed to assist families and co-workers of victims.
- Have relationships established with local hospitals, emergency response units and others who may be needed in a crisis.
- Continually preach the need for compliance and against any and all forms of harassment and discrimination. Leadership must start at the top.
- The value of a company's image and reputation and the public exposure of its "dirty laundry" must be considered with a trial.
- Educate employees regarding bullying.
- Attorneys' fees and the cost of a trial also must be considered as a reasonable solution to settling a complaint rather than with a lawsuit.
- When you know you have a problem deal with it immediately, as did the Red Cross.
- Be open to new and innovative ways to build employee morale and productivity.
- Be sure all employees are in an equal-work-equal-pay status.
- Insure that the company has an open door policy regarding any employee complaint and there will not be any type of retaliation whatsoever.

- Be sure to read Chapter 11 regarding crises in sports because there are additional case histories regarding harassment and discrimination.

Endnotes

[1] OSHA Fact Sheet, "Workplace Violence," Occupational Safety and Health Administration, U.S. Department of Labor, 2002.

[2] "National Census of Fatal Occupational Injuries In 2006," news release from Bureau of Labor Statistics, U.S. Department of Labor, August 9, 2007.

[3] Janet Zimmerman, Á Crime watch for restaurants," *USA Today*, July 10, 1997, pg. 3A.

[4] Associated Press, "Government seeks to reduce violence on job," *The Dallas Morning News*, March 1996.

[5] OSHA Fact Sheet, *op.cit.*

[6] "Workplace Violence Articles," The National Institute for the Prevention of Workplace Violence

[7] "Magnitude & Effect," "Aggressors & Victims," Workplace Violence Headquarters website.

[8] Stephanie Armour, "Managers not prepared for workplace violence," *USA Today*, July 15, 2004.

[9] Associated Press, "Freed killer charged in new slaying – ex-con accused of shooting co-worker," *Chicago Sun-Times*, July 24, 1988.

[10] Stephanie Armour, "Inside the minds of workplace killers," *USA Today*, July 15, 2004.

[11] American Institute on Domestic Violence, www.aidv-usa.com.

[12] *The Survey of Workplace Violence Prevention*, Bureau of Labor Statistics, October 2006; "Domestic Violence in the Workplace," National Coalition Against Domestic Violence, Washington, D.C.

[13] "Workplace Statistics," Corporate Alliance to End Partner Violence, 2007 and National Coalition Against Domestic Violence, *op.cit.*

[14] Anne O'Leary Kelly and Carol Reeves, "The Effects and Costs of Intimate Partner Violence for Work Organizations, *Journal of Interpersonal Violence*, Vol. 22, No. 3, pgs. 327-344; "The Facts on the Workplace and Domestic Violence Against Women," Family Violence Prevention Fund; National Coalition Against Domestic Violence, *op.cit.*

[15] Author interview and e-mails with Cari Dominguez, January and February 2008.

[16] The Workplace Bullying Institute, bullyinginstitute.org; workdoctor.com.

[17] *NBC Nightly News With Brian Williams*, January 17. 2007; "Former UCLA Prof. Receives $4 million in Sex Discrimination Case," Feminist Daily News Wire, March 16, 2007; "Janet Conney v. The Regents of the University of California, et al," Association of University Women, www.aauw.org.

[18] *Public Relations Tactics*, February 1997, pg. 1.

[19] Associated Press, "Parents, School Resolve Hugging Dispute," November 13, 2007; Sara Bonisteel, "Students Feel the Squeeze as Schools Ban Hugs," Fox News, November 8, 2007.

[20] Sara Bonisteel, *op.cit.*; Associated Press, "Kyle school bans hugging in halls," News 8 Austin, November 16, 2007.

[21] Mike Puccinelli, "Oak Pak School Bans Hugging," CBS 2 Chicago, September 28, 2007.

[22] Sara Bonisteel, *op.cit.*

[23] Associated Press, "Hugging Ban Sparks dispute at Oregon School," May 15, 2005.

[24] David Crary, "Red Cross loses another leader – President Ousted After 6 Months," Associated Press, November 28, 2007.

[25] Richard S. Levick, Esq., "Ripping Off the Band-Aid: From the People Who Run to Disasters, Not Away From Them," *Crisis Manager*, Bernstein Crisis Management, Inc., January 7, 2008 and "Levick Stop the Presses," www.levick.com/blog/.

[26] Associated Press, "Harassment case settled by Knicks," October 2, 2007; Agence France Presse, "Knicks' Isiah Thomas found guilty of sexual harassment," October 2, 2007; Larry Neumeister, Associated Press, "Deal Reached in NY Knicks' Sexual Harassment Case," BlackAmericaWeb.com, December 10, 2007; Thomas Zambito, "Isiah explains double standard on slurs in Garden trial," *New York Daily News*, September 18, 2007; Associated Press, "Sexual harassment trial begins vs. Knicks coach," ESPN, September 26, 2007; Kati Cornell, "Friend: Accuser Complained of Thomas' Behavior," *New York Post*, September 18, 2007; "Dolan Silent on Isiah," *New York Daily News*, October 4, 2007; Fraser P. Seitel, "2007 Sports PR Winners & Sinners," www.odwyerpr.com, December 17, 2007.

[27] Chisaki Watanabe, "Payment ordered in death blamed on overwork," Associated Press, Tokyo, December 1, 2007.

[28] Robert Crowe, "KBR e-mail disputes rape allegation," *Houston Chronicle*, December 14, 2007; Brian Ross, Justin Rood and Maddy Sauer, "Halliburton/KBR Employees: Company Covered Up Sex assault and Harassment," ABC News, December 13, 2007; Associated Press, December 19, 2007; Brian Ross, Maddy Sauer and Justin Rood, ABC News *20/20*, December 19, 2007.

[29] Mark Niesse, "Lockheed settles $2.5M racism suit," Associated Press, January 4, 2008.

[30] Jena McGregor, "The Employee Is Always Right," *Business Week*, November 19, 2007.

CHAPTER 10

EVEN THE GOVERNMENT MAKES MISTAKES

Working for the government means never having to say you're sorry.
– The Cosby Show, CBS, August 10, 1998

Regrettably, how true this is. In many countries throughout the world, government leaders and employees at local, regional and national levels are held accountable and responsible for their performance. Perhaps if this were a standard in the U.S., there would be fewer crises, an increase in trust with the public believing what it is told, and better customer service.

There have been a number of different polls on the subject of trust, and one of the most extensive was reported December 2005 at the World Economic Forum in Davos, Switzerland. Some 20,000 people were interviewed in 20 countries, and public trust in national governments and the United Nations fell the most during the previous two years and to its lowest level since tracking began in 2001. The most distrusted governments were Brazil, South Korea, Mexico, Canada, Spain, Argentina and the U.S. Trust remained positive in Great Britain, India, Italy, Indonesia and France. The Russian government is the only institution in any country polled to have consistently increased trust.[1]

Before the forum's poll, Porter/Novelli released numbers on a survey it commissioned that showed that 8 percent of the people believed the government to be a believable source of information. That means 92 percent of the American public do not believe what they hear from the government.[2] In a "whom do you trust?" national survey of 1,003 adults by the Pew Research Center for People and Press, only 6 percent trusted the federal government. City-county and state governments rated slightly better at 14 percent and 9 percent, respectively.[3] A *Time*/CNN poll found that 80 percent of Americans believe the government is hiding the truth about the existence of intelligent life on other planets.[4]

A 1998 book by scholars at Harvard's Kennedy School of Government reports a 30-year decline in public trust in government. The authors cite four contributing trends: changing values; fear of economic change; the expanding gap between political elites and most Americans; and the role of the mass media. Negative political ads on television and a more critical and intrusive media increase the public's cynicism and distrust.[5]

Government agencies and the military are at a disadvantage in a crisis because of a lack of credibility. The public must be convinced it is being told the truth. Because of this, crisis communicators in government need to place a priority on strategic communications planning. Unfortunately, all too often this is not possible because of the institutional culture. The typical public affairs office in a federal department or agency is headed by a political appointee, often with limited public relations experience or none at all. Few are experienced in long-term strategic planning and issues management. Many only know a political-campaign approach. This makes it difficult to win public support in a crisis when the opposition uses the most sophisticated, state-of-the-art communications techniques and retains the best available public relations professionals.

With more than 3,200 political firms and more "spin doctors" in Washington than lobbyists it is no wonder why there is such little trust. Or as Mortimer B. Zuckerman, editor-in-chief of *U.S. News & World Report*, wrote about Bill Clinton's former political consultant, Dick Morris: "He knows nothing. He thinks he knows everything. That clearly points to a career as a political consultant."[6]

At one time the only crises inside the beltway were those such as former House Ways & Means Chair Wilbur Mills (D-Arkansas) frolicking in the Tidal Basin Pool with the "Argentine firecracker," Fanne Fox; or former presidential hopeful and Sen. Gary Hart (D-Colorado), photographed with Donna Rice after challenging the media to try and catch him in an extra-marital affair.

Then there was Watergate and other crisis "gates." Politicians began behaving badly and some members of Congress had to resign because they were sentenced to prison. Some high level political appointees also resigned for a number of reasons. The public trust factor in the government further disintegrated when agencies charged with intelligence and security shredded information Congress wanted to make public. In other situations key undercover operatives were publicly outed. Then there are scores of crises involving state and local governments. Hollywood responded to a number of the crisis situations by turning them into scripts for dramatic shows, sitcoms and movies.

One major problem in the federal government is that there is little management or policy continuity. The White House appoints the officials who run the government at the various departments and agencies. These political appointees establish and manage administration policy. Career employees execute the policy. Many cabinet secretaries, assistant secretaries and agency administrators and directors leave before the end of the entire four-year term of the president. Few are in the same position for two terms. This means a constant change at the top. Few *Fortune* 500 companies could survive such disruption. For example, one administration could have a successful program in place and working, and a new administration with a change in policy may eliminate it, alter its focus or priority, or replace it with a new program.

Government leaders complain when they get "bad press." This happens when the people responsible for media and public relations are inexperienced because few government departments or agencies have established standards for this position. At local, state, regional and national levels, no one would hire a lawyer who had not passed the bar. The same would be true for an auditor or accountant who was not a Certified Public Accountant, an engineer who was not a Professional Engineer, an architect who was not a member of the American Institute of Architects, or a physician who was not licensed. When it comes to people put in charge of public relations, very few in government are members of a professional organization.

FEMA Tried to Fake It

The Federal Emergency Management Administration had been under ongoing public scrutiny due to the way it mishandled Hurricane Katrina in August 2005. So at the height of the 2007 fire disaster in California, FEMA staged a fake press conference to get out a message that the organization was responding far better in California than it did in New Orleans and the Gulf Coast. FEMA announced its October 23 press conference only 15 minutes before it was to begin, making it almost impossible for the media to be represented. Asking questions and posing as reporters were members of the FEMA public relations staff. There was a telephone conference line so reporters could listen but not ask questions.

Vice Admiral Harvey Johnson, deputy administrator at FEMA, stood at the podium and responded to softball questions asked by members of his staff who did not disclose who they were. Parts of the conference were televised live by cable-news channels.

While the staged scenario was going on in Washington, Homeland Security Secretary Michael Chertoff and FEMA Administrator David Paulison were on a flight to San Diego. The press conference that should have been held was right after they landed. But the questions asked would have been much tougher than, "Are you happy with FEMA's response so far?"

While he arrived as the briefing started and participated in the event, John "Pat" Philbin, FEMA's director of external affairs, said he did not "advise, authorize or approve" the news conference, and accepted responsibility for what became a media frenzy once the media learned all the facts about the staged briefing. Philbin, a veteran of 31 years of service as a public affairs officer in the U.S. Coast Guard, was in line to be named to the same position in the Office of National Intelligence. He had a Ph.D. in communications from the University of Maryland and wrote a description of what happened and sent it to *The New York Times* and *Washington Post* for publication as op-ed articles. He said he regretted what happened and called it a "bad decision." Aaron Walker, press secretary at the agency, resigned to join a public relations firm in Utah.

"I think it was one of the dumbest and most inappropriate things I've seen since I've been in government," said an angry Michael Chertoff. "I have made unambiguously clear, in Anglo-Saxon prose, that it is not to ever happen again, and there will be appropriate disciplinary action taken against those people who exhibited what I regard as extraordinarily poor judgment."

FEMA Administrator David Paulison, a former career firefighter in Miami/Dade until rising to become chief, called CNN to apologize, and called the briefing an "error in judgment." He also added that to prevent any recurrence, reporters will be given at least a one-hour warning before a press conference, and those calling in will be able to ask questions.[7]

Here is what Philbin sent to the media on November 7:

Setting the record straight about FEMA's press briefing

By John P. Philbin, former director of external affairs for FEMA

Wondering whether a government action is the result of conspiracy or mistake, the smart money bets on mistake. Their furor over FEMA's recent "phony" press briefing shows that many have become so reflexively cynical that they no longer even bother to ask. They simply assume conspiracies are afoot.

In this case, there was no conspiracy and no reason to hatch one. The California wildfire operations had gone reasonably well, especially FEMA's efforts. There was no bad news to hide and there were no hard questions to duck.

Here is what happened. There was pressure to inform the public quickly and the staff, exhausted from round-the-clock duty, dropped the ball on announcing the brief. I was busy with meetings and unaware prior to the briefing that reporters had been given inadequate time to arrive and the phone line was listen-only. The staff tried to salvage the event by asking the kind of questions they had been fielding that morning.

Mistakes were made by well-intended staff, and I made two. I did not ensure staff had made adequate preparations. And when I found out in the middle of the briefing, I did not intervene. Because I was in charge, I take responsibility for letting this hastily planned briefing go forward. However, neither I nor anyone else on the staff is guilty of any attempt to deceive.[8]

Even the FBI Needs to Pay Its Phone Bill

If you don't pay your phone bill, you get disconnected. This happened to the FBI, which owes tens of thousands of dollars to various telephone companies who finally cut off service because of nonpayment. An audit by the Inspector General at the U.S. Department of Justice revealed the unpaid bill to one telecom was $66,000.

Many of the phone lines were FBI wiretaps used to eavesdrop on suspected criminals. The audit showed that at least one case involved a wiretap used in a Foreign Intelligence Surveillance Act investigation. According to the FBI, wiretaps are used in the government's most sensitive and secret criminal operations.

More than half of nearly 1,000 bills used to pay for telephone surveillance in five unidentified FBI field offices were not paid on time according to IG Glenn Fine. The latest audit is a series of reports from Fine's office during the past seven years regarding the FBI's financial and inventory management problems that included a persistent failure to account for hundreds of guns and laptop computers.

"To tell it bluntly, it sounds as though the telecoms believe it when the FBI says the warrant is in the mail, but not when they say the check is in the mail," says Michael German, a former FBI agent and now national security policy counsel for the American Civil Liberties Union.[9]

Air Force Flies Nuclear-Armed B-52 Across U.S.

On August 29, 2007, the Air Force flew a B-52 armed with six nuclear-tipped cruise missiles from Minot, North Dakota to Barksdale, Louisiana, and no one noticed the mistake for more than a day. Following a six-week investigation that found widespread disregard for the rules handling nuclear weapons, the Air Force relieved four colonels of their command and disciplined more than 65 lower-ranking officers and airmen.

"This was an unacceptable mistake and a clear deviation from our exacting standards," said Michael W. Wynne, Secretary of the Air Force. "We hold ourselves accountable to the American people, and want to ensure proper corrective action has been taken." The nuclear warheads were supposed to have been removed before the flight.

Not everyone considered this an isolated event. Hans Kristensen of the Federation of American Scientists expressed skepticism.[10]

The Feds and the Hemingway Cats

You would think the people running the U.S. Department of Agriculture would have more important things to do that worry about the 47 six-toed cats that live on the grounds of the Ernest Hemingway Home and Museum in Key West, Florida.

The 1851 Spanish Colonial house where the author lived, wrote and entertained scores of celebrities has been a museum since 1964 and in 1968 was listed as a National Historic Landmark. Today it is a major tourist attraction with 400 to 600 daily visitors who photograph and pet the cats. All of the cats are named for Hemingway's wives, fictional characters, Hollywood friends and colleagues, including Truman Capote, Zane Grey, Charlie Chaplin, Sofia Loren, Emily Dickinson and Archibald MacLeish. All descendents of Snowball, his first polydactyl cat that was given to him by a ship's captain.

The Beltway Bureaucrats say because it is a museum and historic landmark, that it must have a federal animal welfare license in order to keep the cats. They make no distinction between the Hemingway cats and their larger lions, tigers and leopards in a circus or zoo, and contend the museum must have an animal exhibition license to keep the cats or it will be fined nearly $10,000 a day. "They're operating illegally," said USDA spokesman Jim Rogers. Museum officials say the cats are pets that live at the house. They already have spent nearly $200,000 to comply with federal animal regulations that require feeding them organic food, providing proper food storage, and a weekly visit by a veterinarian.

According to Michael Morawski, the museum's chief executive, the feds want even more restrictions, such as 12-to-15-foot-high wall similar to those found around golf driving ranges and ball fields. "When we told them that our National Historical Site designation precludes us from doing anything like that," said Morawski, "they responded, 'You'll have to round them up and put them in cages.'" The museum did install angled screens on top of the five-foot brick wall that surrounds the one-acre property, and installed a misting system around exits.

The disagreement began when Gwen Hawtof and Debra Schultz, two former members of the Florida Keys Society for the Prevention of Cruelty to Animals, complained that the Hemingway house-cat population was excessive, and there was a potential for cats to escape and be run over. Mostly the cats roam around the flowering gardens, fountains and louvered salons of the house and outbuildings, or curl up in kitty condos scattered throughout the gardens. They rarely left the property until 1999, when Schultz established a feral cat-feeding site a half block away and a few began disappearing and turning up at the animal shelter as strays. However, in 2005 there were 12 occasions when cats left the property, and two were killed by cars. According to Morawski, many of the cats are spayed or neutered but a few are allowed to breed to maintain the tradition and an optimal population.

Since the controversy became public, Hawtof and Schultz have unlisted telephone numbers and are no longer associated with the SPCA. The museum has gone to federal court asking for a ruling. The USDA has declined to say why they started an investigation after decades of neglect from Washington. And the feds plan to have Terry Curtis, a veterinarian and animal behaviorist from the University of Florida, observe the cats' mental state and physical condition. Locals call Curtis the "cat whispurrer."[11]

Who knows, maybe the Secretary of Agriculture is a dog lover?

Boycott the Olympics - The Soviets Will Leave Afghanistan

In 1980, White House lawyer Lloyd Cutler urged President Jimmy Carter to use the U.S. Olympic Team as a bargaining chip to force the Soviets to leave Afghanistan by threatening to boycott the Games in Moscow. It didn't work because Cutler and his staff had not done their homework. The decision and Carter's response were based on impulse and emotion, and carried out in a less-than-professional fashion.

Cutler's recommendation and Carter's actions nearly destroyed the modern Olympic movement. Some journalists compared the action to that of Roman Emperor Theodosius in 393 A.D., when he ended the Games after 1,200 years. The athletes, coaches and administrators wanted to go to Moscow. The White House brought tremendous pressure to bear on the sponsors not to fill their commitments and even threatened the tax-exempt status of the U.S. Olympic Committee.

The result – the Soviets were still in Afghanistan four years later when it and its Soviet bloc nations retaliated and boycotted the 1984 Olympic Games in Los Angeles.

The ignorance of the president's key advisers regarding the Olympic movement and protocol in international sports was exemplified two years earlier. In Athens in May 1978, the International Olympic Committee awarded Los Angeles the 1984 Games. To show the world that the nation was supporting Los Angeles, a signing ceremony was arranged at the White House on October 12, 1978, so President Carter could host Lord Killanin of Ireland, president of the International Olympic Committee, and show his personal support for Los Angeles.

Present for the event were the IOC's executive director, Monique Berlioux; Los Angeles Mayor Tom Bradley; John Argue, president of the Southern California Committee for the Olympic Games and one of the driving forces in bringing the Games to the City of the Angeles; John Ferraro, president of the City Council; Deputy Mayor Anton Calleia; Robert Kane, president, and Colonel F. Don Miller, executive director of the U.S. Olympic Committee.

Anton Calleia noted that the signing of the agreement between the city's organizing committee and the IOC ended months of intense negotiations in which Los Angeles had been perceived by the IOC as challenging its right "to own and run" the Olympics. For the first time, the agreement was not executed by the host city. The USOC provided the guarantee and became a partner with the non-profit organizing committee. The U.S. government was not a signatory to the document.

"Our hope was that being in the White House and with the president of the United States would build upon good will created in recent negotiations in Mexico City, and would serve to promote an air of mutual respect and cooperation," said Calleia. "We extracted some unprecedented concessions from the IOC. It was time for us to be gracious."

"When we arrived at the White House we were led into the Roosevelt Room, almost adjacent to the Oval Office," said John Argue. "In every other country in the world, when the head of the IOC arrives, the red carpet is rolled out. The president of the country is there to welcome him. Lord Killanin did not expect that kind of reception, but he did expect to meet Carter.

"Jack Watkins, a White House staffer, coordinated the activities. After a delay, Jody Powell came in and said: 'The president has no time to see you.' Carter, who was next door, was a no-show. The fact that our guests from Europe were stood up by the president without an adequate explanation or apology was a slap in the face to Lord Killanin and Democrat Mayor Tom Bradley. It was an almost impossible protocol *faux pas* to explain to our guests. It was truly an amateur performance. The president could have stuck his head in and told everyone that an emergency had arisen, then apologized for not being able to spend more time and left. What should have been a positive event turned out to be a disaster," said Argue.

Calleia believes that Powell could have been more diplomatic. "Powell could have told us, 'The president has become tied up on a matter of national security and apologizes' which would have been accepted by everyone," said Calleia. He further recalls that day marking the start of Israeli-Egyptian negotiations on a peace treaty based on Camp David accords in which Carter had had "hands-on" involvement. "After the contract signing, a former Bradley staffer then working for the president, Michael Pohl, took us on a tour of the White House," said Calleia. "In the basement we ran into Israeli Foreign Minister Moshe Dayan. It was rumored that U.S. Secretary of State Cyrus Vance and the Egyptian Foreign Minister Muhammad Ibrahim Kamal also were on hand. It is possible the president was personally involved in these negotiations. Whether he was or not, he could have taken a time out to greet Lord Killanin and the delegations from the U.S. and International Olympic Committees and Los Angeles. The fact remains that we were disappointed he didn't do a brief drop-in or send an apology. Lord Killanin handled the situation with poise and dignity."

In spite of the embarrassing and frustrating treatment at the White House and the subsequent boycott by the Soviets, the Los Angeles committee went on to stage the most successful and profitable of all Olympic Games. Years later, when Argue visited the Carter Presidential Museum and Library, he noted with interest that the boycott is nowhere in evidence. "Apparently the Carter curators are not proud of it," he said.[12]

As the world knows, 25 years later, the U.S. took over the role of the Soviets in Afghanistan.

Politics and Sports Don't Mix

Forcing the U.S. Olympians to stay home from Moscow in 1980 should have been a lesson to all politicians that sport and athletes cannot be held hostage, nor used as a weapon when diplomats fail to do their job. When politicians interfere in international politics, the first to get hurt, and hurt the most, are the athletes and their coaches. Then there are the administrators who get passed over for office or appointment to an important committee on an international sports federation.

And, there are the referees and officials from the U.S. who do not get assigned to games. All of this happened because of the 1980 Moscow boycott. And, most likely it will happen again.

The Bush Administration committed another serious diplomatic *faux pas* in 2006 when it announced Cuba would not be allowed to compete in the inaugural World Baseball Classic. Normally the State Department is responsible for embarrassing U.S. citizens worldwide; this time it was the Treasury Department. Cuba was one of 16 nations invited to compete in the prestigious tournament, and was scheduled to play Panama on March 8 in San Juan. Puerto Rico and the Netherlands were in the same pool, and the two top teams advanced to Orlando.

Since baseball became an Olympic sport in 1992, the Cubans have won three of the four gold medals. In the World Cup competition that began in 1938, Cuba has won 25 times, including 12 of the last 13 competitions. The country's national team has even held its own against Major League Baseball. In 1999, thanks to President Clinton, Cuba played two exhibition games against the Baltimore Orioles, splitting the series. Fidel Castro upstaged the White House when he said that any money won by the Cuban team would be donated to the victims of Hurricane Katrina. This embarrassing turn of events ensured Cuba's participation. Treasury backed down. To add insult to injury, the U.S. team never made it past the second round, while Cuba, placed in one of the toughest competition brackets, went to the finals, only to lose to Japan, 10-6.

Later in the year during election campaigning, a wannabe Senator from the state of Washington sought to bar Iran from the soccer World Cup. The Iranian team was scheduled to compete in Nuremberg, June 11 against Mexico. In an interview with Alicia Mundy of the Seattle Times bureau in Washington, D.C., Republican Mike McGavick was passionate, saying: "You cannot have this. Nuremberg is where the Nazis marched, where we held war-crimes trials, and that's where Iran's president will attend the game?"

During the Reagan Administration, the State Department had a senior position dedicated to international sports politics that liaised with our national governing bodies and Olympic committee. The job no longer exists, but is needed to help control outbursts by uninformed politicians who do not understand the politics of international sport.

Politicians and diplomats should heed the advice of Hispanic-American Philosopher George Santayana, who warned, "Those who cannot remember the past are condemned to repeat it."

Take A Lesson From EPA Philadelphia

Communicating is one of the simplest and best ways to keep what normally could be only an incident from turning into a crisis. Communicating is a must during any crisis mode. It also is essential in providing customer service. The Mid-Atlantic States regional office of the U.S. Environmental Protection Agency in Philadelphia is a model not only all governments should follow, but most businesses as well. The standards for communications that were established in the late 1990s by this office were even higher than those of EPA headquarters in Washington, D.C., and all other regional offices.

The outstanding customer service principles and the importance of personal communications skills are detailed in Chapter 14.

The press and media relations office in the Office of Communications and Government Relations adopted a new policy regarding when news releases would be distributed. As an oversight and enforcement agency, all EPA offices, in concert with the Department of Justice, had been issuing news releases regarding compliance and litigation at the close of business on a Friday, or before a holiday. Called a "hit-and-run" tactic, most public relations practitioners consider this not only unprofessional, but unethical. Unfortunately, this is a practice used by most government agencies so no one is available to answer difficult questions. The named-and-cited company is blindsided and not prepared to refute any allegations. If a publicly-held company disclosed important information with the same timeliness, it would be in violation of, and subject to, penalties by the Securities & Exchange Commission.

When the Justice Department lawyers strongly objected, a compromise was suggested that the home and cell telephone numbers of all attorneys involved be included in the news release, and they be available to answer any media calls. This created further outrage.

As a result, with the endorsement and approval of W. Michael McCabe, the regional administrator, a policy was adopted by the EPA press office in Philadelphia that the deadline for distribution of any such news release would be noon on a Friday or the day before a holiday, and that a copy would be sent as well to the public relations staff of the company cited in the news release. EPA headquarters and a few of its other regions subsequently adopted the policy.

Summary Checklist

- Never fake a press conference. Never have people pretend to be reporters if they are not.
- Always tell the truth. Never lie.
- Accept responsibility and be accountable.
- Apologize.
- Prioritize issues.
- Listen and anticipate.
- Do not mix sports and politics. Never, ever use sports as a vehicle for failed diplomacy.
- Communicate. Establish personal communications rules.
- Never use "hit and run" media techniques.
- Set standards at the highest professional levels.
- Remember the words and philosophy of Santayana: "Those who cannot remember the past are condemned to repeat it."

Endnotes

[1] Mark Adams, "Trust in Governments, Corporations and Global Institutions Continues to Decline," news release of World Economic Forum, Geneva, Switzerland, December 15, 2005.

[2] *Jack O'Dwyer's Newsletter*, August 7, 1996, pg. 2.

[3] ."Whom do you trust?" *The Washington Post*, May 4, 1997.

[4] "Public Still Alienated," *Government Executive*, August 1997, pg. 8

[5] Joseph S. Nye, Jr., Philip D. Zeilkow and David C. King, *Why People Don't Trust Government*, Harvard University Press, Cambridge, Massachusetts, 1998, and "Why Government Fell From Grace," *Government Executive*, January 1998, pg. 8.

[6] Mortimer B. Zuckerman, Editorial, "Famous Lost Words," *U.S. News & World Report*, January 13, 1997, pg. 68.

[7] "Another embarrassment for FEMA," *NBC Nightly News with Brian Williams*, October 26, 2007; Devlin Barrett, "Chertoff blisters FEMA over fake media event," *The Associated Press*, October 28, 2007; "FEMA PR Exec Loses Shot At DNI Post," *odwyerpr.com*, October 30, 2007; "FEMA Conference Shows PR Flaws, *odwyerpr.com*, November 19, 2007; Spencer s. Hsu, "FEMA leader apologizes for staged briefing," *The Washington Post*, October 27, 2007; "Just Who Was At That Fake FEMA Briefing?," *CBS News*, November 9, 2007; "FEMA Chiefs Should Take Blame," *odwyerpr.com*, November 1, 2007.

[8] "Philbin Tells Role In FEMA Mishap," *odwyerpr.com*, November 6, 2007.

[9] Lara Jakes Jordan, The Associated Press, "Unpaid phone bills halt FBI's wiretaps," *Detroit News*, January 11, 2008; "FBI's wiretaps cut off due to unpaid phone bills," *China Daily*, Beijing, January 11, 2008.

[10] Pauline Jelinck, The Associated Press, "Air Force Punishes 70 for nuclear mistake," *News & Observer*, Raleigh, North Carolina, January 18, 2008 and *The Seattle Times*, Seattle, Washington, January 20, 2008.

[11] Laura L. Myers, Reuters, "Claws out in Florida Keys over Hemingway cats," *Boston Globe*, July 17, 2007; Carol J. Williams, *Los Angeles Times*, "At Hemingway's home, a federal dispute over cats," *San Francisco Chronicle*, July 29, 2007; Karen Haymon Long, "Papa's Place: Ernest Hemingway Home And Museum," *The Tampa Tribune*, Tampa, Florida, August 19, 2007; "Feds Say Key West Hemingway Cats Illegal; USDA says Hemingway Museum Needs A License to 'Exhibit' Cats; Critics Call USDA Action 'Insane,'" CBS News, October 19, 2007.

[12] John Argue, Esq. and Anton Calleia, correspondence and telephone calls with Rene A. Henry, October 1997.

CHAPTER 11

FOUL! IS THIS ANYWAY TO PLAY THE GAME?

Sport, at any given level, has had its share of crises. One could write a book, or even volumes, about crises in the sports world. However, when there is a sports crisis, it receives more than a disproportionate share of media attention.

Every day a newspaper or broadcast journalist reports the story of a crisis somewhere involving a team or athlete. Many crises exacerbate and are headlines for days. O.J. Simpson. Barry Bonds. Major League Baseball. Marion Jones. Doping. Mike Tyson. Steroids. Michael Vick. Gambling. Cheating. Drugs. Lying. Murder. Sexual harassment. Discrimination. There have even been crises involving little league competition, the U.S. Olympic Committee and major colleges and universities. No one is immune from a crisis. Very few are prepared with a plan and know how to respond. And, if the crisis involves something of national interest, chances are that Congress will get involved, and there will be hearings with a media circus.

Sport bridges age, race, gender, nationality and religion. In some countries it even is a religion. Today it is one of the most powerful marketing and branding tools available. Companies worldwide recognize the extent to which sport pervades domestic and international lifestyles and use sport to promote, market and sell products, services and corporate images.

The earliest recorded crisis in sports involved the Olympic Games, which began in 776 B.C. The festivals were held every four years and continued following the subjugation of Greece by the Romans in 146 B.C. Nearly 300 Olympiads were held for 1,200 years until 393 A.D., when Roman Emperor Theodosius ended them because of rampant corruption. During the fifth century B.C., some cities rewarded their victorious athletes with prize money. There were cases where athletes accepted money from an opponent in exchange for conceding the victory, or just plainly taking "a fall."[1]

From Role Models and Heroes to Disgraced

Time and again, individuals who have become champions and among the very best in the world in their sport, have fallen from the pinnacle of honor to total disgrace. "Few aspects of American life influence young people more than sports and the stars who live in that dizzying sphere of highly paid men and women," says Joseph J. Honick, of GMA International, Bainbridge Island, Washington,, and a frequent author of commentaries. "So important are these people as financial assets that their teams invest heavily in public relations efforts to protect them when they get into difficulty with the law."[2]

O.J. Simpson was virtually sitting on top of the world. His amiable personality and natural charisma won him millions of dollars for numerous endorsements. He had been one of the greatest running backs in college and professional football, a Heisman Trophy winner, Associated Press' Athlete of the Year, elected to the NFL Pro Football "Hall of Fame," and was working as an actor, broadcaster and a spokesperson for a number of products.

Then in 1994 he was tried and after a lengthy and highly publicized trial, acquitted of the murder of his ex-wife, Nicole Brown Simpson, and her friend, Ronald Goldman. A California civil court found Simpson liable for their deaths and ordered him to pay the heirs $33.5 million. Following the trials, he lost his endorsements, acting and broadcasting roles. He continued to be in the news with minor legal problems, but made headlines again in September 2007 when he was charged with numerous felonies, and robbery and burglary with a firearm. After breaking bail terms, Judge Jackie Glass in Nevada's Clark County District Court doubled his bail to $250,000 and accused him of being "arrogant or ignorant or both."[3]

Michael Vick was another great college and professional football player who also had it all. He was the first overall pick and the first Black quarterback taken in the National Football League's 2001 draft. At 22, and in his first season, he was a candidate for Most Valuable Player and named to the first of his three Pro Bowls. In 2004 his $130 million contract made him the highest paid player at the time. Additionally, like Simpson, he also had income from numerous product endorsements.

Then in April 2007, extensive facilities for dog fighting were found on his 15-acre home near Smithfield, Virginia. Vick and three other men were convicted on federal felony charges for illegal interstate dog fighting. At first, he denied any involvement, but then apologized, accepted responsibility, and surrendered to U.S. Marshals three weeks before his sentencing. He was sentenced to serve 12-23 months at the U.S. Penitentiary at Leavenworth, Kansas followed by three years of supervised probation. Judge Henry E. Hudson publicly noted Vick's lack of cooperation in the early stages of the investigation, as well as his continued lying his drug use after conviction and while free on bond, and also ordered him to set aside $1 million to care for the confiscated dogs.

Vick was suspended indefinitely from the Atlanta Falcons and from playing in the NFL, and ordered to repay nearly $20 million in bonus money. Three banks filed multi-million suits to recover $5 million in loans, and he is liquidating multi-million dollar homes he owns in Virginia, Georgia and Florida. He still faces trials on separate state charges in Surry County, Virginia.[4]

Marion Jones was the fastest woman in the world and won three gold and two bronze medals at the 2000 Olympic Games in Sydney, Australia. She was considered to repeat for the U.S.A. in Beijing in 2008. On October 6, 2007, she pleaded guilty to two counts of lying to federal investigators and was sentenced to six months in prison. While she had steadfastly denied ever using any substance, following her public admission she apologized. "I have been dishonest. ... I have let [my family] down. I have let my country down, and I have let myself down. ... I hope you can find it in your hearts to forgive me," she said. "Her admission is long overdue and underscores the shame and dishonor that are inherent with cheating," said Peter Ueberroth, the president of the U.S. Olympic Committee.

Jones, who has a stadium named after her in Belize, returned all of the medals she won in Olympic and international competition, and will have to repay some $700,000 in prize money. "Jones will be remembered as one of the biggest frauds in sporting history," said Lamine Diack, president of the International Association of Athletics Federation, the world governing body for track and field. "If she had trusted her own natural gifts and allied them to self-sacrifice and hard work, I sincerely believe that she could have been an honest champion." The IAAF also erased all of her records from the date she admitted taking the drugs.[5]

Barry Bonds holds the Major League Baseball record for total home runs with 762 and most in a single season, 73 in 2001. He was honored seven times with Most Valuable Player awards, one of many records he set for the San Francisco Giants. However, if they are not erased from the record books they most likely will have asterisks. Bonds comes from a prominent baseball family. His father, Bobby, was a former major league all-star and he is the godson of Willie Mays, the legendary Hall of Fame outfielder who played for the Giants when they were in New York.

In 2003, Bonds came under investigation by a federal grand jury regarding the Bay Area Laboratory Co-operative (BALCO) drug scandal. In November 2007, he was indicted and charged with obstruction of justice and four counts of perjury and faces a maximum of 30 years in prison.[6]

In March 2006, Baseball Commissioner Allan H. "Bud" Selig appointed former Senate Majority Leader George Mitchell to investigate the use of anabolic steroids and other performance-enhancing drugs by professional baseball players. In December 2007, after 20 months of investigation, the Mitchell Report named 90 players, including Bonds, following some 700 interviews and 115,000 pages of documents. "We have the toughest testing program in American sports," Selig told members of Congress during a hearing. He also said he hoped to complete his review of the report by mid-February 2008. Almost all of the players named immediately denied use of any drugs.[7]

When Roger Clemens appeared before Congress and denied ever using steroids or drugs, the way the media reported the story, you would not have thought there was anything to write about in world news. Perhaps because Clemens wears the pinstripes of the New York Yankees, the *New York Daily News* ran 12½ pages about the hearing including both the front and back pages of the tabloid.

Accept Responsibility and Win

Anyone who has ever lived on a golf course knows the hazards associated with the location. I've not only had a number of windows broken by golfers, but some even came into my fenced yard to retrieve their ball. No one ever left me a note, accepted responsibility, or offered to pay for the damage.

Compare these "anonymous" golfers with the integrity and ethics of R.C. Slocum, the winningest coach in Texas A&M football history. Playing in a foursome with alumni and friends at the Crown Colony Club in Lufkin, Texas, he hooked not one, but two three-wood shots into the bay windows of a house located on the fairway. He soon made sure the owner knew it was his fault, and that he was going to pay for the damage.

"After what happened with my first three-wood shot, I couldn't believe I hooked my second shot and broke another window," Slocum said. It was the 18th hole, so immediately after we finished playing, I went to the house and rang the doorbell. When the owner answered, I explained what happened, and said I wanted to pay for the broken windows. She invited me in, we had a nice visit and I was told to always stop by anytime I was in Lufkin."

The lady, Jessie Jordan, was the widow of Leland Jordan, a pioneer in the Kuwait oil industry. Because of Slocum's honesty and the friendship that developed, she endowed the Leland and Jessie Jordan Institute for International Studies at Texas A&M. "She was a wonderful lady, well traveled, and very interesting," Slocum added. "When she made the gift during a luncheon in her honor, she had only one stipulation, and that was that Coach Slocum not be allowed to play on her golf course."

Leadership When Most Needed

Slocum's leadership and character was evident not just on the playing field. As the Aggies' head football coach, he never had a losing season in 14 years, and from 1989-2002 he compiled a record of 123-47-2, won four conference championships, three times was named Southwest Conference Coach of the Year, and reached 100 wins faster than any other active coach.

When Texas A&M named him head coach, Slocum inherited a program that twice had been on probation, was corrupt, and under severe sanctions from the National Collegiate Athletic Association. He was known for playing strictly by the rules. "I wouldn't trade winning a game or two for my reputation as a person," he said. "From day one, I'm going to do things the way I think they should be done. I can walk away and look myself in the mirror and say 'We did it the right way.'"

Tradition is one of the most important elements of Aggie culture. For 90 years, Texas A&M students built and burned a Bonfire on campus before the big game against the University of Texas. Disaster struck at 2:30 a.m. on November 18, 1999, when the 40-foot high stack of some 5,000 logs collapsed. Of the 58 students working to build the Bonfire, 12 were killed and 27 were injured. Slocum called a team meeting that morning and cancelled practice. He soon had the entire A&M football team on the site, working to assist rescue workers and manually removing the logs.

The administration of the university did not have a crisis management and communications plan in place, and Slocum knew the importance of having key spokespersons and everyone having the same message, especially with 50 satellite television trucks and some hundred journalists on campus. He brought the players and coaches together and told them to expect to be cornered by reporters for a quote. He named one player from the defensive team and one from the offensive team who would be trained and to whom all reporters would be directed. They would speak for all of the players, and Slocum would speak for the coaches, and the message would be controlled.

The university held a memorial service on the night the Bonfire would have burned. More than 100,000 mourners carried white candles to the site of the disaster and then marched to the football stadium. Slocum delivered a passionate speech to comfort the mourners and instill pride in the school. The next day the A&M football team defeated arch-rival Texas.

If I were asked to name role models for coaches, R.C. Slocum would be at the top of the list. Others who were part of his coaching team are like a "who's who" list in football and include the current A&M coach, Mike Sherman, former head coach of the Green Bay Packers; Bob Davie, former head coach of Notre Dame; Bob Toledo, who coached UCLA and now Tulane; Tommy Tuberville, University of Mississippi and now Auburn; Gary Kubiak, current Houston Texans head coach; Phil Bennett who coached Southern Methodist University; Mike Hankwitz, formerly at University of Arizona; Kevin Sumlin, currently at the University of Houston, and many others who have important assistant coaching positions in the National Football League and in colleges.

A New President, A New Athletic Director, A New Coach

In 2002, R.C. Slocum had two new bosses. In August, Robert Gates, who headed the CIA under President George H. W. Bush and later became Secretary of Defense for his son, was named president of Texas A&M. At the end of the season, Bill Byrne became athletic director, the same position he held at University of Nebraska. Gates and Byrne lured Dennis Franchione from the University of Alabama for $2 million a year. In 1998, Franchione left Texas Christian University to coach at Alabama and inherited a program sanctioned by the NCAA that banned playing in post-season bowl games for two years, reduced 21 scholarships over three years, and probation for five year. He turned the program around, and in 2002 Alabama officials rewarded him with a 10-year contract extension worth $15 million. After publicly stating he would not leave Alabama, Franchione resigned, accepted the A&M job, and never returned to Tuscaloosa. He told his players of his decision during a video teleconference.

During his five years at Texas A&M, Franchione posted a record of 32-28, only two winning seasons, a 19-21 record in the conference and one that was never ranked in the postseason national polls. During the 2004 season, Franchione started a secret e-mail newsletter to fans that included information regarding specific injuries, recruiting information, and his critical assessments of players. The recipients paid $1,000 a year and had to pledge that information in the newsletter would not be used for gambling. The newsletter became a public issue on September 27, 2007, when a reporter from the *San Antonio Express-News* gave a copy to Byrne.

The last issue of the newsletter, dated September 13, 2007, revealed that the $2 million-a-year coach earned a net profit of $37,806.32 from the newsletter. Several days later the coach apologized to the team, and his personal assistant, Mike McKenzie, who wrote the newsletter, was terminated.

Mike Sherman, who twice had served as Slocum's offensive line coach, was brought back to campus to take over the head coaching reins. Since 2002, Slocum's last year coaching, he has continued to serve A&M as a special advisor to the president of the university.

How Much Is Enough?

While college football exists only because there is an academic institution, the coaches make far more than the presidents, chancellors or internationally prominent and award-winning professors. The average coach's salary is more than $1 million compared to less than $400,000 for the chief administrator. Many coaches are being paid more than $2 and $3 million. They also receive additional income from media, shoe and apparel contracts and other outside sources. A Knight Commission Report of more than 2,000 faculty members at institutions' with the most visible athletic programs, said that salaries paid to head football and basketball coaches are excessive, and the financial needs of athletes get higher priority than academic needs.[8]

Some are even being paid not to coach. And some universities are paying coaches they fired who didn't perform as well as the new coaches who promise championships. Two weeks after firing Bob Davie as its head football coach, Notre Dame lured George O'Leary away from Georgia Tech. But on December 15, 2001, only five days after being hired and having never coached the Irish in even one game, O'Leary resigned when discrepancies were discovered on his resume. The year before, he had signed a new six-year contract at Georgia Tech for $1.1 million a year and Notre Dame was responsible for paying a $1.5 million buyout to hire him.[9]

Mike Price is another coach who never coached a game after being hired by Alabama. In December 2002, he left Washington State to replace Texas A&M-bound Dennis Franchione. In May 2003, Price's contract was rescinded after news reports of an incident in Pensacola, Florida. A story in *Sports Illustrated* said Price had been seen at a strip club "making it rain," yelling "Roll Tide, Roll!" and allegedly later checking into a hotel with at least one exotic dancer. Price filed a $20 million libel and defamation suit against the magazine and purportedly settled two years later for $12 million.[10]

Loyalty, Commitments and Ethics

So many college coaches today go to the highest bidder, even after signing long term contracts and telling their teams, administrators and fans that they have no intention of ever leaving. The presidents, chancellors and athletic directors who proselytize and encourage coaches to breach existing contracts are even guiltier than the rich-wannabe-richer coaches. If academia is supposed to be the bastion of ethics and integrity, then the leaders in higher education need to lead by example. In every situation you would expect the university seeking to hire a new coach would ask permission from the university where the coach is under contract before making any contact. However, this does not always happen.

In professional sports, if one team approaches the coach of another without permission, there are major penalties including heavy fines and potential loss of draft choices. Perhaps this is needed in intercollegiate sports as well. Quickly the words *ethics, integrity, loyalty, breach of contract* and *commitment* are disappearing from the higher education vocabulary.

A role model for loyalty is Joe Paterno who is nearing 60 years on the football staff at Penn State University. He is not paid mega millions like scores of his counterparts. His reported salary is only $512,664. As with other coaches, he does receive additional income from endorsements and personal appearances, but his total compensation would be modest compared to other coaches. When he was promoted from assistant to head coach in 1966 he was paid $20,000. Paterno has endowed his university with gifts of more than $4 million for faculty positions, scholarships and to support two building projects. The profits from the sale of Joe Paterno mugs, T-shirts and other products have gone to the university library. He and his wife also contribute time and money to other major fund-raising initiatives.

The Hall of Fame coach has a record of 373 wins, 124 losses and 3 ties. His loyalty to Penn State is so strong that he turned down offers to coach in the NFL with the Pittsburgh Steelers in 1969, and the New England Patriots in 1972. The latter included an ownership position.

After 20 years as head football coach at West Virginia University, Don Nehlen retired as college's 17th winningest football coach. The Mountaineers hired Rich

Rodriguez who was a walk-on when he was a student, and earned a scholarship playing for Nehlen. After seven successful seasons, on December 16, 2007, one year after signing a new seven-year contract and vowing his undying love to his team, the state and the university, without notice, he accepted a job at University of Michigan for more than $2 million a year. Reportedly, no one at Michigan asked permission to approach Rodriguez, nor did he ask permission of his superiors to contact Michigan.

WVU filed suit in Monongalia County Circuit Court for $4 million for breach of contract and a buyout clause in the contract. In January 2008, Rodriguez offered $1.5 million as a "gesture of good faith." The final amount will be determined in court. During the controversy, two signs proclaiming Grant Town, West Virginia, population of 1,000, as the hometown of Rich Rodriguez, were taken down.[11]

Less than a year earlier, Michigan hired West Virginia's head basketball coach, John Beilein, who had five years remaining on his contract. Beilein paid WVU $1.5 million for the penalty in his contract. A year earlier when another university sought to hire him, negotiations broke down over the buyout clause. His predecessor, Gale Catlett, who also played for and graduated from WVU, coached the Mountaineers for 24 years.[12]

Who Can You Trust?

Can you trust a basketball referee who cheats on his income tax? Or one who is a gambler and bets on games? People responsible for officiating the conduct of a sport should have the highest standards of ethics and integrity. The National Basketball Association was rocked with a scandal in 1997 when referees were taking first-class airline tickets given them by the league, downgrading them to cheaper fares, pocketing the difference, and not reporting the gain as income.

Then in 2007, a story by columnist Murray Weiss in the *New York Post* reported an FBI investigation into allegations of Tim Donaghy, a 13-year NBA referee, betting on games to control the point spread.[13] Donaghy placed tens of thousands of dollars in bets on games during the 2005-06 and 2006-07 seasons and had been approached by lower level mob associates to work on a gambling scheme.[14] Donaghy resigned from the league after officiating 772 regular season and 20 playoff games prior to reports of the FBI investigation.

He was one of the game referees between the Detroit Pistons and Indiana Pacers at the Palace of Auburn Hills in November 19, 2004 when Pacers' players went into the stands and fought with Pistons fans. On August 15, 2007, Donaghy pleaded guilty to two federal charges but could face more at the state level if it is determined that he deliberately miscalled individual games to control the point spread.[15]

In the airline ticket downgrading crisis, the referee's union contract allowed the officials to do just that as a way of supplementing their incomes, but the Internal Revenue Service required them to report the excess reimbursements as income on their tax returns. More than a dozen pleaded guilty, were fined several thousand dollars, put on probation, and ordered to pay back taxes on unreported income plus interest. Several were reinstated by NBA Commissioner David Stern. Henry Clinger "Hank" Armstrong of Virginia Beach, Virginia, Jesse Kersey of Williamsburg, Virginia, George T. Toliver of Harrisonburg, Virginia and Mike Mathis of Cleveland, Ohio lost their jobs.[16]

Bill Belichick and the Jets

When Bill Belichick got caught videotaping and stealing the signals of the New York Jets in the opening game of the season for the New England Patriots, it wasn't the first time he had a conflict with the Jets. In 1997 he was an assistant coach of New England when the Patriots lost Super Bowl XXXI to Green Bay 35-21. He followed head coach Bill Parcells to the Jets, and was to be named head coach two years later when Parcells stepped down. During the press conference to announce his promotion, Belichick told the media he had accepted an offer to return to New England as head coach. Parcells and the Jets claimed he was still under contract, and demanded compensation from the Patriots. NFL Commissioner Paul Tagliabue agreed and gave the Jets a first-round draft pick in 2000.[17]

Matt Estrella, New England video assistant, was caught just before halftime allegedly taping hand signals from the Jets' defensive coaches on the sideline, defying an edict from NFL Commissioner Roger Goodell who had warned teams before the season that the would not tolerate cheating. Several teams had suspected the Patriots of stealing signs. A former assistant coach under Belichick, Eric Mangini, was coaching with the Jets and his information was given to an NFL security official. It took Goodell only five days to react to the spying incident and most people felt his penalty was too light: $500,000 for Belichick, $250,000 for the team, and the loss of a first round draft pick. Coaches and management at other teams, fans and media felt Belichick should have been suspended for one or two games and more draft choices forfeited. Some felt the league should have overturned New England's 38-14 victory.

The following week, Belichick apologized to his players, and then with a written statement to the public. Controversy grew during the season as New England continued to win and the media began comparing the Patriots to the 1972 Miami Dolphins team that went undefeated in 17 games and won Super Bowl XLII. Don Shula, the Dolphins coach, said a perfect New England season would be tainted by what some called Spygate and there should be an asterisk in the record book. The New York Giants took care of that with a 17-14 win over the heavily favored Patriots in the Super Bowl.[18]

A New York Jets fan and season-ticket holder filed a $184 million class action lawsuit against Belichick and the New England Patriots. "They violated the integrity of the game," said Bruce Afran, lawyer for Carl Mayer of Princeton Township, New Jersey. "They were deceiving customers," said Mayer. "You can't deceive customers."[19]

During the season Belichick didn't make many friends. He was chosen "2007 PR Sinner of the Year in Sports" by Fraser P. Seitel in his annual awards. "Belichick is blessed with the best team in the NFL. ... [he] is arrogant, nasty, and unkept in physical appearance – dressing perpetually in a dirty grey hoodie. ... he could care less about public relations," writes Seitel.[20]

Then Sen. Arlen Specter (R-Pennsylvania), the ranking Republican on the Senate Judiciary Committee, learned that the league had destroyed the tapes, and he wanted answers from the NFL. Goodell, who should have known you never ignore a member of Congress, did not respond for a month until there was discussion of having hearings. Following threats of litigation by the NFL against church and other charitable groups for having Super Bowl fund raisers on large screens, Sen. Specter authored a bill that would exempt religious organizations that wish to show professional football games. Congressman Heath Shuler (D-North Carolina), a former Washington Redskins quarterback and evangelical Christian, plans to introduce similar legislation in the House of Representatives.[21] Following a meeting with Goodell, Sen. Specter confirmed that Belichick had been illegally taping opponents' defensive signals since 2000, including games in 2004 against the Pittsburgh Steelers.[22]

Diversity Training Is No Laughing Matter

When Kirk Reynolds was public relations director for the San Francisco 49ers professional football team he produced a 15-minute diversity and media training video that featured off-color racial humor, lesbian porn, a spoof of gay marriage and topless strippers.

The training film opens with Reynolds impersonating, and seated behind the desk of, San Francisco Mayor Gavin Newsom, and then goes on to insult virtually every diverse group in the city. San Franciscans were outraged when a copy was anonymously sent to the *San Francisco Chronicle* and turned into a team embarrassment. Team lawyer Ed Goines apologized saying, "The video is absolutely contradictory to the ideals and values of the San Francisco 49ers." However, many of the players defended Reynolds and the video. "I thought it was one of the funniest things I ever saw," said cornerback Mike Rumph.

John York and Denise DeBartolo York, the team owners, met with and apologized to community leaders. "The video was offensive in every manners," the Yorks said. "We regret that anyone from our organization would produce such senseless, inexcusable behavior. ... Policies are being put in place to ensure that nothing like this every happens again."

Investigative reporters uncovered the fact that a similar film had been produced by Reynolds in 2003, and that the 49ers had time to prevent a public relations disaster. After John York saw a piece of the new video, it took five months before he took disciplinary action against Reynolds. Then the video was kept quiet until Reynolds could find another job. A "Deep Throat" within the 49ers organization mailed copies to the newspaper, mayor's office and threatened to send it to the NFL.

The importance the team placed on diversity training was exposed when the organization planned a training meeting, but did not inform the players until after football practice. The team assembled for the meeting, but midway through the session, half of them left when a union representative told them they weren't obligated to stay because practice and meeting time is limited to six hours.[23]

It's All In A Name ... Or Is It?

The capital of the State of Washington is Olympia which was incorporated in 1859. The newspaper in the city, *The Olympian,* began publishing daily in 1889. The Olympic National Forest is located on the Olympic Peninsula and was established as a forest reserve in 1897. Mount Olympus, the highest peak of Washington's Olympic Mountains, was named in 1788.

The U.S. Olympic Committee was not formally founded until 1921, and the first of the modern Olympic games held in Athens, Greece in 1896. The USOC is a non-profit organization chartered by the U.S. government and given certain priorities under the Amateur Sports Act of 1978, now called the Ted Stevens

Olympic and Amateur Sports Act. Sen. Ted Stevens (R-Alaska) was one of the sponsors of the bill.

The federal charter gives the USOC exclusive jurisdiction over all matters related to the U.S. participation in the Olympic Games, Paralympic Games and the Pan American Games as well as the exclusive rights for the five Olympic rings, and various words including Olympic, Olympiad, Citius Altius Fortius and even Pan American, which at the time was already being used by Pan American World Airways and the Pan American Health Organization. The Act was amended in 1998 giving the USOC even broader powers over its trademarks and imagery. Excluded were persons or companies who used any of the words before September 21, 1950, and the use of the word "Olympic" refers to a geographic region and not to any Olympic activity, and where the goods or services are marketed west of the Cascade Mountain range in Washington, and operations, sales and marketing outside of this area are not substantial.

In 2007, the USOC sent a strong letter to Jason Bausher, an Eagle Scout, graduate of Yale and an Olympic National Park ranger who authored a tourist guide book, *Best of the Olympic Peninsula*. Bausher, who lives in a 10' x 12' trailer in Quinault, Grays Harbor, had applied for a trademark for his book and this raised a red flag at the USOC, that then warned him he could face a lawsuit unless he withdrew the trademark application. "If you go after everyone [on the peninsula] using the word 'Olympics' in commerce, the economy of the Olympic Peninsula would collapse," Bausher told the *Colorado Springs Gazette*. "There's no double-entendre or trading on the good name of the Olympic movement." He also said they wanted to restrict him from where the book could be sold and promoted, and believes the USOC should have backed off when it determined his book was geographic in every way, and not treading on the Olympic Games.

Then the owners of Olympic Cellars Winery in Port Angeles and Sequim went public about selling wine on the Internet and to customers east of the Cascade Mountains. "In no way are we trying to impede the ability of this company to sell their wine locally and within Western Washington," said Darryl Seibel, a spokesman for the USOC. Kathy Charlton said her winery had been using the Olympic name since 1992 and in 1999 had received permission from the USOC to use the website name www.olympiccellars.com.

According to the Washington Secretary of State there are more than 1,000 corporations with Olympic in the name, and even more with Olympia and Olympian. Throughout the state, stories appeared in local daily and weekly newspapers and on websites about what Washingtonians considered bully tactics by the USOC. This prompted an editorial in *The Seattle Times* titled "Olympian Stupidity," which said, "The U.S. Olympic Committee ought to take care not to alienate a good part of Washington state, which will be a neighbor to its 2010 Winter Games in Vancouver, B.C."

Getting straight answers from the USOC is difficult when Jim Scherr, the CEO, does not respond to correspondence and ignores requests. He obviously is unaware of the fact that everyone who contacts him is a potential donor to the USOC, which spends millions of dollars for direct-mail fund-raising. Col. F. Don Miller was executive director of the USOC from 1969-1985 and twice saved it from extinction. He answered and personally signed every letter sent him including those from job seekers, potential vendors and even adversaries. Scherr needs to learn from his successful predecessors. On the other hand, Rana Dershowtiz, the interim general counsel, was prompt and thorough in responding to every question presented. "The USOC is not currently suing ANY companies on the Olympic Peninsula with regard to the use of the word Olympic," she wrote. "We are, however, in contact with several companies to determine whether they fell in to the geographic exemption ...." She also noted that had Bausher applied for a copyright for his book, rather than a trademark, the USOC would not have raised an objection.

While there are two sides to every story, the USOC needs do to a great deal more explaining and apologizing to the media and general public in Washington. An aggressive marketing public relations program properly presented could result in increased donations.[24]

A Roller Coaster of Turmoil and Crises

For years the U.S. Olympic Committee had stable leadership and dedicated employees and volunteers. Col. F. Don Miller, spent more than half of his life in the Olympic movement, coached the U.S. boxing team at the 1951 Pan-American Games, and oversaw the organization's move from New York City to Colorado Springs, and the building of a training center. After he retired as executive director, he headed the U.S. Olympic Foundation until his death in 1996.

George Miller, a retired Air Force general, succeeded him in 1985 but resigned two years later because of conflicts with Robert Helmick, the USOC's elected president. Baaron Pittenger, who joined the USOC in 1977, and had been the assistant executive director since 1981, took over on an interim basis for a year. Following a search in 1988, Dr. Harvey Schiller, who had been active in the USOC, was named the new executive director. When he quit just 18 days later, Pittenger was again brought back to lead the organization on an interim basis.

In 1989, the USOC went after Schiller again. He left his job as commissioner of the Southeastern Conference to return to Colorado Springs. During his tenure, there were reports he lobbied to become commissioner of Major League Baseball and he was reprimanded for using his position to obtain free ski passes and equipment. U.S. Skiing, the governing body for Alpine and Nordic skiing, publicly called for the resignations of Schiller and Robert Helmick.[25]

Schiller left in 1994 to become president of Turner Sports. John F. Krimsky, Jr., who joined the USOC in 1986, to head marketing and fund-raising, took over as interim head for a year. Krimsky resigned in 1999 to rejoin Schiller at YankeeNets, a joint venture of the New York Yankees and New Jersey Nets. In October 2005, following a tip from the New York Internet Crimes Against Children Task Force, police raided Krimsky's home in Sherman, Connecticut and arrested him after they identified 329 digital photos on his computers showing nude girls and boys, ranging in age from 5 to 15, either posing, or involved in different sexual acts. In December 2007, he pleaded not guilty in Danbury Superior Court to four counts of child pornography. All of the headlines and stories associated him with the USOC.[26]

Next in line was Dick Schultz, who was hired in 1995 under a cloud of conflict of interest charges when he left his job as athletic director at the University of Virginia. He had been executive director of the NCAA, and he retired from the USOC in 1999. In 2000, Norm Blake, a former CEO of Promus Hotels and USF&G, was hired after a study concluded the organization should be run more like a business. He was fired after only nine months. Scott Blackmun, the general counsel, acted as interim director for a year, but he and the USOC could not come to terms to make it permanent.

The next USOC head was Lloyd Ward who had been chairman and CEO of Maytag Corporation for 15 months, and only the second Black executive at the time to head a major U.S. corporation. His resignation was attributed to differences with Maytag's board of directors.[27] Ward headed the USOC from October 2001 until March 2003, when he resigned ending three months of turmoil and being investigated for possible conflicts of interest. Ward, the first Black to head the USOC, was accused of trying to direct Olympic business to a company with ties to his brother; a major sponsor threatened to pull back $10 million; the ethics compliance officer quit as did the president, Marty Mankamyer; and, Senators Ben Nighthorse Campbell (D-Colorado), a former Olympian, and Ted Stevens (R-Alaska) said they might have found evidence of fraud. Ward was reprimanded and stripped of an $184,000 bonus. Senator Campbell said if Ward and his right-hand man, chief operating officer Fred Wohlschlaeger, a former Maytag executive, resign that Congress likely would not pursue allegations of mismanagement and fraud.[28]

During Ward's tenure, Sandy Baldwin, the first woman president of the USOC, resigned in May 2002 following a series of media reports that academic information in her official biography was inaccurate.[29]

While the USOC was going through these years of turmoil, embarrassment and public scrutiny, it also had to face two other major crises that involved president Robert Helmick and Alfredo LaMont, director of international relations. At the time, Helmick was considered the most powerful American in the Olympic movement. He resigned both his USOC post as well as a lifetime member of the International Olympic Committee. As head of the USOC, he controlled a $75 million annual budget and a federation of 41 national governing bodies of sport. An attorney from Des Moines, Iowa he once was considered a successor to Juan Antonio Samaranch to head the IOC.

In 1990, he set new ethical standards for the USOC's volunteers, officers, directors and paid staff. The organization's bylaws say that an officer shall not participate in any evaluation or transaction in which he has a financial interest and that the organization's properties, services, opportunities, authority and influence are not to be used for private benefit. One year later he came under the scrutiny of Mike Dodd, an investigative reporter for *USA Today*. On September 5, 1991, Dodd reported potential conflicts of interest because Helmick was paid $275,000 by clients doing business involving Olympic sports, including Turner Broadcasting regarding rights for the 1991 Pan American Games in Cuba, and from two different clients to use his influence to have golf and bowling to be Olympic sports.[30]

Two days later Helmick met with the USOC executive committee, denied any wrongdoing, and said that he would terminate and refrain from any business perceived as a conflict of interest. He also disclosed two other business deals that amounted to $150,000. Stories about conflicts continued in *USA Today* until his resignation September 17. "Everything the president of the USOC does, even tangentially, should be disclosed, because it could be deemed a conflict or an appearance of conflict," said William E. Simon, former secretary of the treasury and USOC president from 1981 to 1985.[31]

In March 2000, Alfredo LaMont, former director of international relations for the USOC, pleaded guilty to felony tax charges in 1997 and 1998 in connection with Salt Lake City's tainted bid for the 2002 Winter Olympic Games, and a failed effort by Rome for the 2004 Summer Games. He was forced to resign from the USOC in January 1999. "Originally I was to provide the bid committee with information and advice on how Salt Lake City might defeat other U.S. cities which were vying for selection by my employer, the USOC, LaMont said in a written document statement to the court.

"After Salt Lake City was selected to be the U.S. candidate city, I provided information and assistance to influence the votes of IOC members to ensure that Salt Lake City was selected as the site of the Winter Olympic Games," said LaMont. "These agreements were secret, and not to be disclosed by anyone, including to my employer, to the public, or to the Internal Revenue Service." Using the alias Antonio Aguilar, he received more than $48,000 from Salt Lake City and $40,000 from Rome. The money was sent to an unidentified individual in Mexico City and then sent to LaMont.

LaMont cooperated with the federal prosecutors and testified against Tom Welch and Dave Johnson, president and vice president respectively of the Salt Lake City bid committee. Eventually Mitt Romney rescued the city's tarnished image, restored confidence in Olympic sponsors and made the 2002 Winter Games a success. The criminal fraud case against Welch and Johnson was later dismissed. It was discovered that the bid committee had spent nearly $1 million for gifts, scholarships, cash and gratuities for IOC members and their relatives. Nine of the 114 members of the IOC resigned or were expelled for accepting bribes.[32]

The Games Began, The Scandals Continued

As Yogi Berra used to say, "It ain't over 'til it's over," the scandals continued when the competition began at the Salt Lake Games. When Yelena Berezhnaya and Anton Sikharulidze of Russia were awarded the gold medal for figure skating pairs, there was immediate suspicion of the judges. The Russians had won the short program over Jamie Salé and Scott Pelletier of Canada who were the crowd's favorites. In free skating, the Russians made a minor, but obvious, technical error while Salé and Pelletier had a flawless performance. The media and fans were in shock and outraged when the judges named the Russians the winners in pairs skating for the 11th consecutive time dating back to 1960.

Judges from Russia, the People's Republic of China, Poland, Ukraine and France placed the Russians first, while judges from the U.S., Canada, Germany and Japan chose the Canadians. Suspicion almost immediately turned to the French judge, Marie-Reine Le Gougne. Christine Brennan of *USA Today* then exposed a deal that had been made between the French and Russian judges and wrote that the decision ruined "one of the great performances in Olympic history." Didier Gailhaguet, France's Olympic team leader and head of its skating federation, pressured Le Gougne into voting the way she did to get an advantage for a French couple competing in ice dancing several days later.

In an unprecedented move, the International Olympic Committee upgraded Salé and Pelletier to a gold and allowed Berezhnaya and Sikharulidze to keep their gold medals. The International Skating Union suspended LeGougne and Gailhaguet for three years, and barred both from the 2006 Winter Olympics in Turin, Italy. On July 31, 2002, Russian organized crime boss Alimzhan Tokhtakhounov was arrested in Venice on U.S. charges that he masterminded the fix.[33]

An IOC general assembly was held during the Winter Games and after all of the problems involving ethics and conflicts of interest, the more than 100 members present solidly rejected a recommendation by the organization's executive board to adopt conflict of interest rules. The members complained that the new rules, which would have required everyone to list potential conflicts with the ethics committee, were too broad and required too much paperwork. IOC President Jacques Rogge of Belgium boasted of a modernized IOC that embraces transparency, democracy and reform but did not mention ethics.[34]

Political Correctness, Or Is It?

In August 2005, the National Collegiate Athletic Association, the governing body for all intercollegiate sports, forbid colleges and universities to use American Indian mascots, nicknames or imagery for any NCAA championship competition. Some 20 institutions, but not all schools with Indian-related nicknames were affected, such as several schools using the name Warrior but with no Indian symbols.[35]

The University of Illinois "Fighting Illini" lost Chief Illiniwek, but several colleges fought back with lawsuits. The NCAA allowed Utah and Central Michigan, which derived their names from the local Utes and Chippewas, to continue use of their nicknames because of support from those tribes. The Florida State Seminoles and alumni and friends were outraged, and this resulted in support from politicians. "NCAA officials insulted the school and Seminole Indians by calling the nickname 'hostile' and 'abusive,'" said Florida Governor Jeb Bush. Congressman Tom Feeney (R-Florida) said he would have the House Judiciary Committee look into amending antitrust laws that favor the NCAA.[36]

In the first challenge to its policy, the NCAA granted a waiver to Florida State because the Seminole Tribe of Florida said it was an "honor" to be associated with FSU. This means the NCAA does not consider "hostile" or "abusive" when before FSU football games, a student dressed in Indian regalia as Chief Osceola, gallops on a painted horse to midfield, and throws a flaming spear into the ground while the fans do the tomahawk chop.[37]

The State of North Dakota won an injunction against the NCAA to allow the University of North Dakota to continue using the nickname "Fighting Sioux." Schools with generic names such as Redmen, Indians, Braves and Savages had to change. Exceptions were made to those colleges that had approval to use the names of local tribes. In some cases, there not only were no local Native Americans to support the schools, there were none that even complained.

Allowing Florida State to be exempt did not sit well with all Native Americans. "It appears the NCAA couldn't take the heat or pressure, and didn't see the hostility that this would generate," said David Narcomey, a member of the general counsel of the Seminole Nation of Oklahoma. "NCAA sports are wonderful, the NCAA not so wonderful," writes Jeff Zillgitt in *USA Today*. "The organization has an uncanny and flabbergasting habit of turning decisions into public relations nightmares. ... Another bungled move by the NCAA, an organization that fancies itself as a group of thinkers, but oftentimes is shortsighted and reactionary."[38]

While Florida State's mascot and imagery were considered acceptable, William & Mary was cited because there were two small feathers in the W&M logo. Years before the NCAA edict, the college, which was founded in 1693, had changed its nickname from Indians to Tribe and no longer had a mascot dressed as an Indian. In the 17th and 18th centuries, William & Mary had a school that taught Native Americans from local tribes, including the one of Pocahontas. Local tribal leaders said they had no problem with the new nickname. However, the NCAA said the two feathers had to go. "While the college's rationale for the use of the nickname and imagery is not inherently hostile or abuse, and the college may not intend to malign Native Americans, the continued use of such Native American references creates an environment over which an institution may not have full control," said

NCAA's executive committee. "Fans, opponents and others can and will exhibit behaviors that indeed are hostile or abusive to Native Americans."[39]

Bob Williams, managing director of public and media relations for the NCAA, takes exception to the action being called politically correct. "The policy was adopted to ensure NCAA championships provide an environment for our student athletes and fans that is free from racial stereotyping of Native Americans," he says. Discussion of the subject began in 2001, and was prompted by three events: the executive committee's detailed review of the Confederate Battle Flag issue; a request from St. Cloud State University president Roy Saigo to consider a resolution saying that the NCAA does not condone the use of Native American mascots, logos and imagery; and a U.S. Commission on Civil Rights statement on the use of Native American images and nicknames in sports. The issue was referred to the organization's Minority Opportunity and Interest Committee and the Subcommittee on Gender and Diversity Issues.[40]

The NCAA's directive was an unfunded mandate. The cost of designing a new logo and then implementing changes for signage, uniforms, stationery, wearing apparel and all can be very expensive. A logo design can cost from $25,000 to $100,000. The implementation is another significant cost. Unlike universities with major football programs, many of the impacted colleges also have limited resources – Carthage College, Chowan College, Indiana University of Pennsylvania, McMurry University, Midwestern State University, Newberry College, Northeastern State University and Southeastern Oklahoma State University.

According to Williams, consideration was given to the cost to member institutions and several who made the decision to comply were given extra time to make the change to their facilities and uniforms to coincide with their normal schedule of replacement.

People for the Ethical Treatment of Animals (PETA) has not yet complained to the NCAA about the use of live mascots at college games, the organization did request that that the nickname "Gamecocks" be stopped because it represented dog fighting. Lisa Wathne, captive exotic animal specialist at PETA, says requests to date have been made directly to specific schools. "The pranks played by opposing teams, which often focus on and cause harm to school mascots, is certainly one of the reasons PETA opposes the use of live animals as mascots," she says.[41] The NCAA will have a major problem on is hands if PETA and The Humane Society launch a campaign to stop the use of live animal mascots.

In 1999, the NCAA gave CBS Sports the exclusive right to televise the men's basketball tournament through 2014 for $6 billion. The organization could well afford to set aside just $1 million to help the institutions affected by the Native American initiative offset their costs. In 2006, Congressman Bill Thomas (R-California), then chair of the powerful House Ways & Means Committee, questioned the tax-exempt status of the organization. "From the standpoint of a federal taxpayer, why should the federal government subsidize the athletic activities of educational institutions when that subsidy is being used to help pay for escalating coaches' salaries, costly chartered travel and state-of-the-art athletic facilities?" he asked.[42]

Until the 1960s, the NCAA would not allow Historically Black Colleges and Universities to compete in its Division I, II or III national basketball championships. History was made in 1966 when Texas Western (now University of Texas at El Paso) started five Black players in the championship game against Kentucky. Coach Don Haskins did not play any of his five white players and rotated two Black reserves to defeat favored Kentucky 72-65.

Silent When It Is Challenged

In 1993 the NCAA's Committee On Infractions sanctioned Texas A&M because an overzealous booster had paid nine football players for work they didn't perform. An investigative reporter for *The Dallas Morning News* first reported the players were absent from their summer job. The university did its own investigation and voluntarily submitted a 1,227 page report to the NCAA. The Aggies were banned from television and a postseason bowl in 1994, and placed on probation until 2004. The NCAA also said Texas A&M was guilty of lack of institutional control, and had not properly communicated the importance of compliance, to which the administration took exception.

The author, who then was executive director of university relations convened a group of 12 nationally recognized public relations leaders to review and comment on the university's programs and initiatives in support of NCAA compliance objectives. The panel was chaired by, and discussion of the group totally controlled, by Harold Burson, founder and chairman of Burson-Marsteller, the world's largest public relations firm. Each panel member considered compliance a matter of broad public policy extending well-beyond Texas A&M and its immediate problems.

The members of the panel were Sarah Hardesty Bray, then vice president for external affairs, Council of Advancement and Support of Education, now senior editor, *Chronicle of Higher Education*; Robert S. Condron, associate director of public information and media relations, U.S. Olympic Committee; Clifford Dektar, past president of the Los Angeles chapter of the Public Relations Society of America; Gail Stoorza-Gill, chairman and CEO of Stoorza, Zeigaus and Metzger, Inc., San Diego, the nation's largest female-owned public relations agency; Dr. Walter Harrison, then vice president for university relations at the University of Michigan, now president of the University of Hartford and past chair of the NCAA's executive committee; Charles F. Lennon, Jr., executive director of the University of Notre Dame Alumni Association; John Martin Meek, president and CEO of HMI Inc., Washington, D.C., and, Dr. Michael Mulnix, executive director of university relations and assistant professor of journalism, University of Nebraska-Lincoln; Margaret Nathan, president and COO of Stern, Nathan & Perryman, Dallas; Charles R. Richardson, national chair of the Educational and Cultural Organizations Section of PRSA and director of media relations, Hardin-Simmons University, Abilene, Texas; Don Smith, president of the New York Sports Commission and adjunct professor of marketing at New York University; Bob Steiner, vice president of California Sports, Inglewood, California and former sports information director at University of California at Berkeley; Frederick G. Thompson, president of Kerr Kelly Thompson, Greenwich, Connecticut and adjunct professor of communications at New York University; Hon. Chase Untermeyer, director of public affairs at Compaq Computer Corporation, Houston, and former assistant to President George H. W. Bush for president personnel; and Kellen Winslow, Esq., attorney of Schook, Hardy & Bacon, Kansas City, Missouri, and sports broadcast commentator.

The panel heard presentations regarding how Texas A&M's institutional control and communication of compliance from Rene A. Henry, executive director of university relations; Tedi Ellison, director of athletic compliance; Frank Shannon, executive director of the 12th Man Foundation, the alumni support group; and Randy Matson, executive director of A&M's Association of Former Students. Information was shared from panel members on how compliance was communicated at Notre Dame, Michigan and Nebraska.

It was the unanimous view of the panel that:

1. Texas A&M University, as demonstrated by its compliance communications program – an initiative supported at the university's highest administrative

level – is and has been, at least for the past six years, making a good faith effort to meet all NCAA compliance requirements.

2. The Texas A&M program, as presently constituted, is an appropriate and effective program both in concept and implementation. Doing more – new programs, greater commitment of human and/or monetary resources, etc. – would provide no greater guarantee against the act of a single determined individual intent on a violation of compliance regulations.

The panel also concluded and recommended that a significant group of nationally visible athletic-oriented colleges convene a meeting to review their present compliance programs and reach some agreement on what they think constitutes a good faith compliance communications program. The findings of this meeting would form the basis of a meeting that would include participation by NCAA committees overseeing compliance, enforcement and infractions with appropriate representatives from the member institutions.

The purpose was to develop clear-cut compliance and enforcement guidelines that would be more comprehensible to and enforceable by colleges and to bring to the general public a greater awareness of NCAA compliance/enforcement/infractions objectives.

Two members of the media attended the meeting of the panel. The NCAA was invited and never responded, even to decline the invitation. Burson sent personal letters, with a copy of his report and recommendations, to Dr. Judith E. N. Albino, president of the University of Colorado System and then president of the NCAA; and to all members of the NCAA national office, president's commission, executive committee, administrative committee, infractions committee and communications committee. Not one person had the courtesy to so much as even acknowledge his letter or the report. It was comparable to a complete boycott and rejection of the committee's actions. The media applauded Texas A&M and said it was vindicated and had done everything possible for compliance.

When the NCAA publicly announced the penalties against Texas A&M, it released its story to the media after 5 p.m. on Friday, September 10, the night before the Aggies were to play the University of Oklahoma in Norman. With its "hit and run" tactic, no one at the NCAA was available to talk with the media about a garbled eight-page news release that had contradictory statements. The author, who spent Friday evening returning media calls, suggested the media ask the chairman of the NCAA's committee on infractions why there was such a rush to make the announcement and wouldn't it have been more professional to do so on Monday morning. David Swank, dean of the Oklahoma law school and a former acting president of the university, chaired the NCAA committee that made the announcement. A favored and undefeated Aggie team, stunned and devastated by the news, lost the next day to the Sooners.

The NCAA also needs to be more careful in what it says in its reports sanctioning member universities. Ray Keller, a booster of the University of Alabama, claimed the NCAA defamed him when it imposed penalties on the Crimson Tide in 2002, and was awarded $5 million by a jury for mental anguish, economic loss and damage to his reputation. In its report, Keller and others were referred to as "rogue boosters," "parasites" and "pariahs." The NCAA didn't use any names in announcing the penalties, but their names appeared in news accounts and the university sent Keller a letter barring him from its athletic program.[43]

The Ethics of Breaching Contracts

Colleges and universities once were considered the bastions of ethics, integrity, loyalty and commitment. Regrettably, too many presidents and chancellors today no longer embody or practice these qualities when it comes to intercollegiate sports.

Every year football and basketball coaches are proselytized and enticed to breach their contracts at one institution so they can hopefully produce a championship season at another. It is greed and to win at all cost.

When given a new and extended contract with a raise or bonus, the coach always responds with rhetoric such as "this is my home, my team, my fans, and I will be here forever." The saga continues like a soap opera until the coach breaches his or her contract to steal away in the middle of the night for even more money at another university.

The president of any university seeking a new coach should properly ask permission from that individual's current employer before any discussion. However, with the advent in "amateur sports" of agents as intermediaries, the recruiting effort becomes blurred and asking permission is all too often ignored.

When any decision is made regarding a head football or basketball coach almost always the president or chancellor is involved. Often a coach is fired for not winning and the school is responsible for not only the salary on the remaining number of years on the contract, but one as well for the new coach, plus any buyout penalties. Colleges are getting smarter when they give long-term contracts and bonuses to coaches and now include buyouts as some guarantee of longevity.

Even if they want to, few coaches are at a college for 20 or more years. Even the most loyal are often forced out because alumni and fans want more. The epitome of loyalty and commitment is Joe Paterno who has been at Penn State as an assistant or head coach for nearly 60 years.

There also have been crises where a coach was lured from one school at considerable expense and ended up never coaching a game for his or her new team. The crises included lying on a résumé or outrageous public behavior embarrassing to the university. Costs have gotten out of hand. Four of every five major college sports programs need subsidies that include student fees and other subsidies in order to balance the budget. What kind of message is this sending to the American public?

In professional sports, if one team wanted to hire someone employed by another team, without asking permission, there would be penalties. Even with permission, the losing team generally is awarded cash or draft picks or both as compensation. In business if one company steals an executive from another it most likely ends up being resolved with a lawsuit with damages being awarded. Unfortunately, colleges and universities have an unwritten rule that you do not file suit against another institution in higher education.

Since it is increasingly obvious that the CEOs in higher education will not self regulate, the National Collegiate Athletic Association, the governing body for college sports, needs to get involved and establish guidelines. If College A wants the head football coach at College B, then not only should it pay a bonus penalty but perhaps give up "x" number of scholarships to College B for the term of the coach's contract.

The NCAA's Committee on Infractions is quick to penalize an institution for any of a myriad of rules larger than the New York City telephone book. However, the coach can then leave, go to another university leaving one in shambles with fewer scholarships, probation and other sanctions. Why shouldn't the penalties follow the offending coach? In the real world of business the penalties would follow an executive. Why not in intercollegiate sports?

Where is Professor Kingsfield when we need him? (Professor Charles Kingsfield was played by the legendary John Houseman in "The Paper Chase," and taught contract law at Harvard.)

Summary Checklist

- A star athlete, coach, or anyone involved in sports who become involved in a crisis will receive far greater media attention in a crisis than the average person.
- Accept responsibility, admit a mistake and apologize as soon as possible.
- Deal with a crisis when you know about it. Never delay.
- Be clear with the message sent. The USOC's public relations response to the media and public in Washington came off as a bully and arrogant. The CEO sets the example and needs to respond to all letters, e-mails, faxes and phone calls.
- When there is information to be delivered, get it out and get it all out. If an editor asks a question regarding something you know to be true, give the correct answer. Chances are the editor has the information confirmed and wants to know if you are telling the truth or lying.
- A good investigative editor may sandbag you by withholding some information and printing a story quoting you and then come back several days later with a followup story that exacerbates the crisis.
- If stung by a hit-and-run media tactic, be sure the media knows, and answer questions with questions directed back to the organization that made the announcement.
- Think of the consequences when adopting any initiative requiring change.

Endnotes

[1] C. Robert Paul, Jr., "History of the Ancient Olympic Games 776 B.C.-193 A.D., Part 1," *The Olympic Games*, revised March 1984, U.S. Olympic Committee, Colorado Springs, Colorado, pgs. 1-3.

[2] Joseph J. Honick, "Sports Hypocrisy, PR Hypes, Who's Hot and Who's Not," o'dwyerpr. com, December 20, 2007.

[3] Linda Deutsch, The Associated Press; Wikipedia.com.

[4] Associated Press, November 20, 2007; Wikipedia.com; CNN.

[5] Amy Shipley, "Jones Pleads Guilty, Admits Using Steroids," *The Washington Post*, October 6, 2007; A.J. Perez, "Saddened Jones pleads guilty in doping case," *USA Today*, October 6, 2007; "Jones used steroids for two years before 2000 Games," ESPN.com news services, October 5, 2007; "Marion Jones Admits Using Steroids," NPR, October 5, 2007; Jerome Pugmire, "IAAF erases Marion Jones' results dating to September 2000 for dop-

ing," Associated Press, November 23, 2007.

[6] Paul Elias, "Federal grand jury indicts Barry Bonds," *USA Today,* November 16, 2007; "Barry Bonds indicted on perjury, obstruction charges," ESPN.com news services, November 19, 2007; Wikipedia.com.

[7] Bill Shaikin, "Mitchell report is complete," *Los Angeles Times,* December 12, 2007; Associated Press, "Selig defends drug testing program," MSNBC, December 18, 2007; Associated Press, "Selig hopes to complete review of Mitchell report by spring," *USA Today,* January 17, 2008.

[8] Steve Wieberg and Jodi Upton, "College football coaches calling lucrative plays," *USA Today,* December 4, 2007; "Faculty Perceptions of Intercollegiate Athletics," Knight Commission on Intercollegiate Athletics, October 15, 2007.

[9] Tim Coyne, Associated Press, "Notre Dame hires Georgia Tech's head coach," December 9, 2001, SI.com; *op.cit.,* "O'Leary out at Notre Dame after one week," December 14, 2001; *op.cit.,* "O'Leary resigns at Notre Dame," December 15, 2001.

[10] Jim Moore, "Mike Price never figured his date with Destiny would end like this," *Seattle Post-Intelligencer,* May 5, 2003; Alicia A. Caldwell, "Publisher settles defamation suit by ex-WSU coach Price," Associated Press, October 10, 2005.

[11] Thayer Evans and Pete Thamel, "Michigan Hires Rodriguez as Coach," *The New York Times,* December 17, 2008; Associated Press, "Grant Town removes signs proclaiming it WVU coach's hometown," December 18, 2007; Bob Hertzel, "WVU has lost more than Rod," *Times West Virginian,* Fairmont, West Virginia, December 28, 2007; Pam Ramsey, Associated Press, "WVU sues Rodriguez, seeks $4 million contract buyout," *USA Today,* December 28, 2007; Associated Press, "Rodriguez will pay what court orders," *Charleston Gazette,* Charleston, West Virginia, January 29, 2008; Associated Press, "Rodriguez files response to suit," February 2, 2008;

[12] "Michigan Buying Beilein from West Virginia," CBS Sportsline, April 2, 2007; Associated Press, "Beilein settles buyout with West Virginia for $1.5 million."

[13] Murray Weiss, "NBA In A Fix," *New York Post,* July 20, 2007.

[14] Adrian Wojnarowski, "Questionable calls," Yahoo!, July 20, 2007.

[15] Jack McCallum, "Game-Fixing and Dogfighting Rock Pro Sports" and "Stern Action Required," *Sports Illustrated,* July 30, 2007 and October 29, 2007; Wikipedia.com.

[16] Lynn M. Waltz, "Ref To Blow Whistle On Colleagues," *The Virginian-Pilot,* Norfolk, Virginia, July 31, 1997; Harry Minium and Lynn M. Waltz, "NBA Referee From Beach Pleads Guilty to Tax Evasion," *The Virginian-Pilot,* Norfolk, Virginia, September 5, 1997; Leigh Montville, "Called for Traveling," *Sports Illustrated,* April 20, 1998.

[17] Bob George, "How exactly will history judge Parcells?" BosSports.net, January 13, 2006; Christine Brennan, "Cheating no shock, given its history," *USA Today.*

[18] Rich Cimini, "Eric Mangini exposes Bill Belichick's spy games," *New York Daily News,* December 10, 2007; John Clayton, "NFL penalty for Belichick, Patriots is far too light,"

ESPN.com, September 13, 2007; Greg Doyel, "Belichick's legacy rests on 'if,'" CBS Sports.com, September 13, 2007; Greg Bishop, "NFL fumbled handling of New England tapes," *The New York Times*, December 16, 2007; "Shula: Patriots are 'tainted,'" Seattle Times News Services, *The Seattle Times,* Seattle, Washington, November 7, 2007;Mike Reiss, "A sorry state," *Boston Globe*, Boston, Massachusetts, September 13, 2007; Wikipedia.com.; Greg Bishop and Pete Thamel, "Spygate Revisited," *The New York Times,* February 2, 2008.

[19] "Jets ticket holder files $184 million suit against Pats, Belichick," CBSSports.com, September 28, 2007.

[20] Fraser P. Seitel, "PR Sinner of the Year," odwyerpr.com, December 17, 2007.

[21] Jacqueline L. Salmon, "NFL stand may not have a prayer," *The Washington Post,* February 8, 2008.

[22] Laurie Kellman, Associated Press, "Specter: Belichick Was taping Since 2000," ABC News, February 13, 2008.

[23] Phillip Matieer and Drew Ross, "49ers' personal foul," *San Francisco Chronicle*, June 1, 2005; Vanessa Hua, "Video with porn, racism typical for locker-room culture," *San Francisco Chronicle*, June 2, 2005; Kevin Lynch, "49ers players defend video as owners apologize for it," *San Francisco Chronicle*, June 2, 2005; Phillip Matier and Andrew Ross, "York could have avoided humiliating team over video," *San Francisco Chronicle,* June 2, 2005; Joan Ryan, "49ers diversity tape gives insight into team's values," SFGate.com, June 5, 2005; Phillip Matier and Andrew Ross, "Training video prequel: 49ers apologize anew," *San Francisco Chronicle,* June 8, 2005; Kevin Lynch, "Diversity Training: Yet another snag," *San Francisco Chronicle*, June 10, 2005; Ilene Leichuk, "49ers can't say 'sorry' enough," *San Francisco Chronicle*, June15, 2005.

[24] Bill Vogrin, "For USOC, protecting its brand is no game," *The Gazette*, Colorado Springs, Colorado, September 24, 2007; Curt Woodward, Associated Press, "Just whose Olympics are they, anyway?", *The Seattle Times*, August 12, 2007; Joel Connelly, "Olympic bosses need To Take A Time Out," *Post-Intelligencer,* Seattle, Washington, June 13, 2007; Melissa Allison, "Panel gets a bit huffy over Olympic winery," *The Seattle Times*, January 11, 2008; "Local company faces down USOC," *Kitsap Business Journal*, April 4, 2001; "USOC Drops the Hammer on Pottery Olympics!", *The Source Weekly*, Bend, Oregon, August 8, 2006; Associated Press, "Bush Campaign Refused to Pull Olympic Ad," August 26, 2004; Editorial, "Olympian Stupidity," *The Seattle Times*, January 15, 2008; www.olympicmounainschool.com/olympic.htm; "U.S. Olympic Committee picks on Washington winery," *Wine Press Northwest*, January 2, 2008; Letters and e-mails with Jason Bausher and Rana Dershowitz, interim general counsel, U.S. Olympic Committee.

[25] Mike Dodd and Rachel Shuster, "Olympic officials face new heat,:" and Greg Boeck and Mike Dodd, "USOC's Schiller denies ski pass charge," and Mike Dodd, "U.S. Skiing points finger at USOC," *USA Today*, September 18, 1992, Pgs. 1A, 1C, 3C.

[26] Brian Gomez, "Former USOC marketing chief arrested on child porn charges," *The Gazette*, Colorado Springs, Colorado, December 5, 2007; Dan Mangan, "Ex-Yank Exec In Perv Bust," *New York Post*, December 6, 2007; John Pirro, "Southbury child porn suspect an ex-Olympic fundraiser," *News Times*, Danbury, Connecticut, December 6, 2007; Associated Press, "Ex-USOC Exec Faces Child Porn Charges," sports.aol, December 6, 2007; Associated Press, "Former USOC marketing chief faces child pornography charges," *International Herald Tribune*, Paris, France, December 7, 2007.

[27] David Barboza, "Maytag's Chief Executive Resigns, Citing Differences," *The New York Times*, November 10, 2000.

[28] "FLASH!! Lloyd Ward Resigns as Executive Director of the USOC," *Swimming World Magazine*, March 1, 2003; Richard Sandomir, "Olympics; USOC Moving Away From Interim Replacement," *The New York Times*, March 7, 2003; Vicki Michaelis, "USOC resembling 'Keystone Kops,'" *USA Today*, January 24, 2003; Vicki Michaelis, "Senator wants Ward cohort out for 'clean slate' at USOC," *USA Today*, March 2, 2003.

[29] "U.S. Olympic chief resigns in resume scandal," CNN.com, May 24, 2002; Mike Moran, "USOC Accepts Resignation of President Sandy Baldwin," news release, U.S. Olympic Committee, May 24, 2002.

[30] Mike Dodd and Rachel Shuster, "Helmick says clients were OK; critics disagree," *USA Today*, September 5, 1991, pg. 2C.

[31] Ibid.

[32] Jere Longman, "U.S.O.C. Official Quits Over Tie to Utah Group," *The New York Times*, January 15, 1999; Hans Camporreales and Lisa Riley Roche, "Ex-USOC official to plead guilty," *Deseret News*, Salt Lake City, March 14, 2000; Knight Ridder/Tribune News Service, "LaMont in limbo after court ruling in bid scandal," *The Gazette*, Colorado Springs, Colorado, November 19, 2001; Lisa Riley Roche, "Prosecutors went after 3 others before Welch, Johnson," *Deseret Morning News*, Salt Lake City, December 6, 2003; "S.L. bid scandal leads to Olympic reforms," *Deseret News* archives, Salt Lake City.

[33] "French Olympic Figure Skating Judge Admits She Was Pressured," MSNBC, rense.com, February 14, 2002; Rene A. Henry, "Politics and Bad Decisions In Olympics Will Never End," *Arizona Daily Star*, Tucson, Arizona, February 18, 2002; Christine Brennan, "No defense for bad judgment," *USA Today;* "A Duo Deprived," editorial, *The New York Times*, February 13, 2002; Associated Press, "French judge seeks hearing," SI.com, February 17, 2002; Steve Wilstein, Associated Press, "French Skate Chief Accused," February 19, 2002;

[34] Amy Shipley and Tracee Hamilton, "IOC Rejects Proposal," *The Washington Post*, February 5, 2002.

[35] Seth Perlman, Associated Press, "NCAA bans Indian mascots during postseason," *USA Today*, August 5, 2005.

[36] "Gov. Bush: NCAA insults Seminoles," *USA Today*, August 9, 2005; Steve Wieberg and Eddie Timanus, "Schools consider appeals to NCAA," *USA Today*, August 10, 2005.

[37] Steve Wieberg, "NCAA allowing Florida State to use its Seminole mascot," *USA Today*, August 23, 2005.

[38] Thomas O'Toole and Steve Wieberg, "Other schools set to appeal Indian names," *USA Today*, August 23, 2005; Jeff Zillgitt, "Excuses, inconsistencies mar NCAA mascot ruling," *USA Today*, August 24, 2005.

[39] Bob Williams, managing director of public and media relations, National Collegiate Athletic Association, "State by NCAA Senior Vice President for Governance and Membership Bernard Franklin on the College of William & Mary Review," May 16, 2006.

[40] E-mail to the author from Bob Williams, managing director of public and media information, National Collegiate Athletic Association, Indianapolis, Indiana, March 2008.

[41] E-mail to the author from Lisa Wathne, captive exotic animal specialist, People for the Ethical Treatment of Animals, February 2008.

[42] Associated Press, "Congress questions NCAA's tax-exempt status," October 4, 2006.

[43] Alan Clemons, "Nine women, 5 men on jury in Keller trial," *The Huntsville Times*, Huntsville, Alabama, October 24, 2007; "Alabama Football Booster Ray Keller Wins Judgment Against NCAA," PRNewswire, November 29, 2007.

CHAPTER 12

INSTITUTIONAL ARROGANCE IN THE IVORY TOWER?

A college or university campus is like a small city and is equally as vulnerable to a multitude of crises. Higher education has always had its own unique institutional culture, and is now affected by a new set of emerging social, economic and cultural demands and expectations. As a result, it is subject to a number of specific crises of its own.

Following are just a few of the different crises colleges and universities have experienced. All are true stories. Most could have been avoided. All were widely covered in the media.

- A co-ed files a date rape complaint. The administration stonewalls the media, does an internal investigation, and keeps everything confidential. The victim and her parents disagree with the college's actions and decide to hold a press conference. The president, who is an attorney, says "no comment." The young woman becomes the cover story of national news magazine and then goes on the speaker's circuit further embarrassing the college.

- A nationally prominent football coach at a major university dies while having sex with a prostitute at a downtown hotel. It is a page one story.

- The parents of a high school senior tell the university that its admissions officer, a man, made improper sexual advances to their son, and offered to trade sex for financial aid and his admission as a freshman. Attorneys tell the president to say nothing and pay off the family. The parents are furious because the admissions officer is not fired, but only transferred to another campus office. Further investigation finds that others in the department sought sexual favors from prospective students, and even a mother, in return for admission and scholarships.

- The president of a college comes home earlier than expected and finds his wife having sex with a member of his board. The board asks the president to move out and let his soon-to-be-ex-wife temporarily live in the university's house.

- A television network plans a story on the millions of dollars of debt by college students, a great deal of which is in default, and sends a news team to the campus to investigate. The alumni office and athletic department have affinity bankcards they market to students which generate substantial income for the university. The producer believes that colleges profit while putting students in debt or bankruptcy before graduation.

- The chancellor is again arrested for drunk driving. The joke around town is that if you want an appointment to see him, you better meet in the back seat of a police car, because he is spending more time there than his office.

- A superstar journalism professor is charged with plagiarism after it is documented by an investigative reporter. The leadership of the faculty pressures the president to take no action because they believe in time it will be forgotten. It is not forgotten.

- A building is named for a donor whose land gift was valued at $14 million. A reporter finds that the land is appraised at less than $1 million, and carried on the county's tax roles for considerably less. State approval was given for the building based on the gift's land value. The state demands the president find other funds. The president suggests raising student fees which further angers legislators. The roof literally and figuratively falls in on the building. It collapses during construction.

- During a banquet honoring student athletes, an assistant athletic director publicly insults the local newspaper publisher because a reporter did not run his news release. The publisher immediately leaves. The president has to intervene before an apology is made.

- A professor seeks $100,000 for one of his pet research projects. The director of development does get $50,000 for the professor who is so upset that he refuses to thank the donor. The philanthropist cancels a $1 million gift to the university. The professor is neither reprimanded nor disciplined.

- A fraternity party, with pledges dressed as slaves, receives unexpected media coverage because of racist overtones. The dean of students says the matter will be handled internally and confidentially. Leaks to the media reveal that the penalty given the fraternity was not as severe as critics had hoped. This angers a Black state legislator. The student newspaper responds with an editorial telling the legislator to stay out of university affairs and runs it with a racist political cartoon. This provokes the legislature's Black Caucus, which calls for the president's resignation. The governor demands an apology from the student newspaper, but the dean of journalism and the adviser support the students and refuse. In the end, the president's office apologizes for the actions and naiveté of its students and future journalists.

- The college has an unwritten policy to conceal purchases of liquor by having the retailer provide receipts labeled "soft drinks and ice." The district attorney issues grand jury subpoenas to a number of university leaders, including deans, vice presidents and the executive assistant to the president. All are indicted and plead guilty, no contest, or are convicted. The continuing story reads like a daytime soap opera and tarnishes the ethics and integrity of the university. The cover-up is always worse than the original crime.

- One of the state's leading sportswriters calls a university attorney at his home on a weekend to inquire about a lawsuit involving an athlete. The attorney chastises the sportswriter for bothering him. The journalist apologizes and says: "The hearing is scheduled tomorrow and I want to be sure I have the correct information." The attorney rudely responds: "When did you ever care about having anything accurate." The journalist's wife is an alumnae and the writer had always been a friend to the school. The attorney refuses to apologize and the general counsel supports him, seeing nothing wrong with his arrogant and rude actions. The head of university relations, a coach and the athletic director make the apologies.

- An animal rights group plans to demonstrate over the use of laboratory animals on campus. The dean of the medical school has T-shirts printed and plans his own "get in your face" demonstration. The head of university relations has to seek help from the president to avoid the confrontation and a crisis.

And other stories could go on, and on, and on.

Why So Many Crises?

The institutional culture of higher education is unlike any other – for-profit, non-profit, government or even the military. It is a complex structure of turfs where people joke that "politics are so vicious because the stakes are so low." Compared to other businesses and organizations, those involved in higher education tend to be more insular and involved only within their own academic family or specialty. Another problem is that academicians, who usually have no management training or management experience, generally run the colleges and universities rather than businessmen.

Many faculty members have only their own experience in higher education, first as an undergraduate student, then graduate school, working for a Ph.D., a graduate assistant, and then on the tenure track. They have not spent one day of their life outside of academia. This structure makes most higher education institutions extremely vulnerable to crises.

Professor Carole Gorney of Lehigh University points out that colleges and universities are vulnerable to a staggering number of potential crises. "Higher education institutions have to deal with crime and violence, fires, power outages and natural disasters," she says. "Like corporations, they are accountable for endowment investments, employee relations and managing funds. The science laboratories have the same potential for creating environmental accidents or generating activist criticism as any chemical plant.

"Every organization at some time is going to face criticism, opposition and unexpected events. But such situations become true crises only when they are mismanaged," Gorney adds. "For a plan to be successful, it should cover every aspect of an institution's operation. Categorize potential crises and list specific anticipated problems within each category."[1]

Some of the reasons there are so many crises in higher education can be attributed to the following:

- CEOs in academia are less inclined to prepare in advance for crises than their counterparts in corporate America.
- The institutional culture of higher education with its tenure, work ethic and *laissez faire* attitude compared to for-profit and non-profit organizations and governments.
- A strong lack of executive leadership.
- Individuals with the wrong disciplines – fundraisers, lawyers, academicians – being selected to head advancement and public relations. Or in cases where the individual is highly qualified, that person does not receive total support from the president or chancellor when dealing with others in the academic family.

- When lawyers are the CEOs, many do not know how to win in the court of public opinion and are reluctant to bring in outside help, even alumni.
- The head of public relations not having direct access and communication with the president.
- Reacting passively, not at all, or having a "no comment" syndrome.
- Unmitigated arrogance.

"College and universities have become all things to all people," says Stephen M. Reed, associate vice president for external relations in the office of the president at California State University, Monterey Bay. "We have increased our costs by adding new academic programs without jettisoning those which are either duplicated or not longer have any student interest. We have added 'public' programs and institutes with little thought of their fiscal consequences or financial sustainability or the entitlement expectations from both internal and external stockholders.

"As the institution operates further away from its core competency, the crisis risk profiles increases like a lit fuse burning towards a stick of dynamite. Regardless of our stated mission, we are, always and forever will be only in the business of public service. We try to be entrepreneurial, we try to be proprietary, but we are not in the business of business. We are in the business of providing public service," Reed says.[2]

The fact that presidents and chancellors place so little value on having strong leadership in public relations could well be one major reason so many crises happen in higher education. In fact, higher education changed the name of the function from public relations to university relations. Because of the financial pressures and spiraling costs, recent trends have been to hire fund-raisers to be the top advancement or public relations executive at a college or university.

Most fund-raisers do their jobs well, but many are limited in their experience to only this field. They know how to bring in money but have no training or experience whatsoever in the broad spectrum of public relations disciplines, especially crisis management. One important fact that has been overlooked at many public institutions is that the single most important revenue source is the state legislature, where support can best be initiated through public relations and public affairs.

Keep Alumni and Development Apart From Public Relations

Placing alumni, public relations, public affairs and development all under one leader is another common practice. This can be a disaster if the person heading the three very different departments is not experienced in the disciplines required for each.

Having a completely separate and independent alumni organization provides many benefits for an institution. An alumni office independent of the institution may not be subject to certain Freedom of Information Act requests. It also can make payment for items that cannot be purchased by a public university. Alumni can be an extremely powerful and friendly constituency when not controlled by the university.

Another problem for higher education is the way the educational practice division of executive search firms and university search committees look at qualifications for the person to head public relations. A mistake is to believe that a journalist is the answer. Few journalists have ever created and implemented a comprehensive public relations campaign, and most are skilled in only one of the media areas – television, radio, newspapers or magazines. The executive recruiters and campus committees also place more emphasis on candidates having a Ph.D. or master's degree rather than experience in the "real world" or being members of or recognized by the Public Relations Society of America, such as being accredited or elected to the College of Fellows. Preference also is given to those whose only experience has been in higher education rather than people experienced in diverse fields who they consider "alien" to higher education.

When seeking the head of advancement or public relations for a college or university, the president and his search committee would be far better served going to the corporate division and its public relations search specialist at an executive search firm, and not the educational practice division.

"Campuses have understood for years the importance of having strong development offices. They have learned more recently the value of good admissions officers, who by necessity, have become marketing experts," writes Jerrold K. Footlick, a former editor at *Newsweek* for 20 years and now a professor at Queens College in New York. "Yet fewer institutions have grasped the importance of building a powerful public affairs office that is staffed with skilled, experienced, and well-remunerated professionals who can tell an institution's story in the best ways, and protect it in times of crises. If the public affairs office is staffed with junior people earning junior incomes, the quality of their work will probably be commensurate with their standing."[3]

An individual's ability to pick up a $100,000 gift or write a brilliant speech or op/ed is not going to prepare an institution to prevent or manage a crisis.

Issues Facing Higher Education

Higher education is facing a score of issues that could turn into crises. The people responsible for communicating the story of higher education need to be concerned with these issues, as well in rebuilding and rewinning the public's trust. Some may be misperceptions, but it is how the public perceives the issue that must be considered with a solution professionally communicated.

The rising cost of tuition - For years, the cost of a college education has been rising faster than inflation. From 1979-1993, tuition increased at public colleges and universities 211 percent and at private institutions 242 percent, while the consumer price index rose only 75.4 percent. Between 1985-1995, tuition and room and board rose 82 percent at public schools, and 91 percent at private colleges. In 2007, the price of a college education again rose faster than inflation, 6.6 percent for public and 6.3 for private colleges and universities. This has caused an increase in debt for students and their parents. In the mid-90s, nonfederal loans accounted for 6 percent of student aid, but rose to 24 percent by 2007.[4]

Harvard is doing something about it. In December 2007, it announced relief for middle-income families. Tuition, room and board at Harvard costs more than $45,000, but students from families earning less than $60,000 are accepted free. Now families earning between $60,000 and $120,000 will pay a percentage of their income, rising to 10 percent, and those between $120,000 and $180,000, will pay just 10 percent of their incomes. The annual cost to Harvard is estimated at more than $20 million, which is negligible based on its endowment of $35 billion.[5] Since Harvard's announcement, Yale and others have followed suit. With its endowment of more than $23 billion, Yale is cutting its tuition in half to $23,000 for families earning less than $200,000. Stanford followed, and families earning less than $100,000 will not pay tuition, and for those with incomes under $60,000, room and board will be excluded. William & Mary introduced a scholarship program for Virginia families earning $40,000 a year or less, to have 100% of needs met, without loans. As a result, Pell eligible students increased 20 percent in two years.

Unless the well-endowed colleges and universities do something, Congress will do it for them. Sen. Charles Grassley (R-Iowa) and ranking Republican on the Finance Committee, wrote 136 institutions with endowments of $500 million or more requesting detailed information on their endowments and financial aid. More than 75 have endowments in excess of $1 billion. Some advocates are proposing that the schools with the most money commit at least 5 percent of their endowment to financial aid for those who cannot afford tuition, fees, room and board.[6]

The length of time it takes to get a degree. Four years is no longer the norm. Some students cannot get courses when needed to graduate on time because the university can't provide all of the prerequisites or sequence classes in a timely manner. This goes back to light faculty work loads or some not teaching at all. Some students opt to take the minimum course load to seek higher grade point averages. With increased tuition costs, others need to work at full or part-time jobs to pay for their education expenses. Colleges need to give a guarantee to incoming freshmen and transfer students that they can graduate on time.

Violence and crime. On April 16, 2007 Seung-Hui Cho killed 32 people and wounded many more on the campus of Virginia Tech in Blacksburg, Virginia before committing suicide. This was the deadliest school shooting in U.S. history and was given world-wide media coverage. The tragedy drew criticism of U.S. laws and culture, and sparked intense debate about gun violence, gun laws, gaps in the U.S. for treating mental health, and many other issues. A state-appointed body criticized Tech administrators for failing to take action that might have reduced the number of casualties. Others have posted opinions on websites and blogs as to whether or not the crisis was preventable.[7]

There are approximately 16 million students enrolled in 4,200 colleges and universities. From 1995 to 2002, college students between the ages of 18 and 24, were victims of approximately 479,000 crimes of violence annually. The crimes included rape/sexual assault, robbery, and aggravated and simple assault. Additionally there were homicides.[8]

This is one area where new state and federal standards apply to higher education. Unfortunately not all crimes are reported or get into the system, so these statistics could well be understated. To avoid any negative publicity, some institutions deliberately did not report crimes that happened on city streets running through the campus, or that took place in fraternity or sorority houses. Administrators say the federal reporting requirements were too vague, but in 2000, under a revised law, any institution that falsely reports faces a $25,000 penalty for each wrong figure. Incidents of alleged homicides, rapes, assaults, arson, hate crimes, burglaries, liquor law violations and drug arrests must be reported and posted on the website of the U.S. Department of Education.[9]

In 1997, the General Accounting Office of Congress found that 23 of 25 colleges it audited did not properly report their crime statistics, especially those involving rape and assault. Some of the more flagrant were the University of Florida which excluded 35 rape cases from 1996-1998; the University of Pennsylvania reported 18 armed robberies in 1996, but excluded more than 200 robberies that took place on city sidewalks and streets that cut through its Philadelphia campus; and Minnesota State University-Moorhead reported one sexual assault in 1994-1995, but the local rape crisis center said there were 35. Mount St. Clare College in Clinton, Iowa was fined $25,000 for a history of deception and the college's administrators said they interpreted reporting requirements different than federal bureaucrats. "Bigger schools did things worse than we did. They were not fined," said Wylie Piller III, the college's general counsel.[10]

"Colleges manipulate their statistics," says the late Ben Clery, president of Security on Campus Inc., King of Prussia, Pennsylvania, a watchdog group and probably the nation's leading voice on college safety. "One loophole colleges use is to channel student-on-student crimes, like drug dealing and rape, into campus judicial systems meant to handle matters like plagiarism. Clery's sister was murdered by a fellow student in her dorm room at Lehigh University.[11]

Today campus safety has become a priority at almost every college and university. Higher education administrators have installed new lighting and emergency phone call boxes; increased private security; require all students, faculty and employees to have visible photo identification; and installed card key locks for dormitories and buildings, and even laboratories and rooms within buildings.

The University of Washington says that preventing violence is everyone's responsibility. The university has a free 50-minute briefing session open to students, faculty and staff, and provides a security guard to accompany anyone to any location within the campus community. A phone number is available to report threats, seek advice or counseling, and to request additional security guard assistance.[12]

While many institutions are making every effort to improve campus emergency communications, one administrator believes much more can be done. "We are not putting wireless public address systems into classrooms, labs, academic or other campus buildings, the recreation center, gymnasium or athletic fields," he says. "We cannot, in fact, make an emergency announcement to the entire campus community as one would expect. The emphasis has been placed on e-mails and text messaging because we believe those cutting edge tools are the only viable solutions. The simple, economical system is the solution. If you have a hammer, everything starts looking like a nail."

The workload of professors. A number of state legislatures are looking into faculty workloads. Many professors teach only one course. Others are in purely administrative or research positions and do not teach at all. Years ago, the education editor at one of the nation's leading newspapers, speaking at a conference on higher education, said that if every professor just taught one course there would be no teaching shortage crisis. The hours a professor works is an issue that has faced higher education since the 1980s, but this story has not been communicated by academia to the general public.

In certain professional disciplines, some universities are relying on part-time, adjunct professors who are superstars in their fields of public relations, journalism, or any of the entertainment arts and may not even have a master's degree, much less a Ph.D. They are able to provide their students with the most professional instruction and keep administrative costs at a minimum.

The increased use of teaching assistants. Many professors delegate classroom teaching to graduate assistants who are not fluent in English, and certainly not as competent in the subject. Television networks have done investigative stories taking cameras into classrooms to let the viewing audience decide if you can understand what they say.

Tenure – a lifetime job. This is becoming a very contentious issue in higher education. The average working person and taxpayer cannot relate to anyone who is given a lifetime employment contract after a probationary period of six or seven years. This is the albatross for the public relations communicators. Until a professor is granted tenure, s/he is considered to have a tenure-track appointment and evaluated on teaching ability, or research, publishing, and service to the department. At larger universities, research often is considered as important, or even more important, than teaching. The only way a tenured professor can be terminated is for gross misconduct or incompetence, but because of potential litigation, most institutions will just wait for the individual to retire.

Teaching versus research. Where are college and universities placing their emphasis? On teaching students or research being conducted by faculty? Universities aggressively promote their Nobel prize laureates, Pulitzer prize winners and top name faculty members in recruiting brochures. However, at many research institutions, chances of a student actually seeing one in a classroom are slim to none. Too many of these star professors generate grants and contracts, and stay in their research laboratories or in the field, but no where near a classroom or the minds of the undergraduate students. Institutions could win public favor if these outstanding faculty members would just give several lectures a year to students, or bring exceptional undergraduate students into their laboratories as assistants. MIT is making an exception and one colleague reports that his son had four guest lectures from one star professor, another is actually teaching in one of his classes, and he went ice skating with another. This is not the norm but should be.

Undergraduate education versus graduate and professional programs. The liberal arts colleges place an emphasis on undergraduate education. In the larger research-oriented universities, all too often the emphasis is placed on graduate programs and professional degrees, at the expense of the students seeking their bachelor's degrees.

Controlling student behavior. Binge drinking and drugs have become a societal problem, and the reason for periodic student deaths. Hazing is another problem, and like alcohol and drugs, illegal but one difficult to control at most institutions.

Pressure and interference from outside sources. This is becoming an increasing problem at most universities. Some legislators, where the public institution is receiving minimal public support, want to micromanage and dictate policy. Alumni and friends who are major donors threaten to withdraw gifts if demands are not made, and often will cancel multimillion dollar gifts when refused. Other special interest organizations protest research or programs at the institution.

Lawrence H. Summers was forced out as president of Harvard in 2006 after an uproar over his suggestion that one reason women are underrepresented in science is "issues on intrinsic aptitude." The new law school at University of California Irvine had a crisis before it even opened. Conservatives criticized the selection of Erwin Chemerinsky, a professor at University of Southern California and a nationally known expert on constitutional law, who holds liberal views, to be the first dean. The offer was revoked, there was outrage in academic and legal circles, and he eventually was hired.[13]

On March 13, 2006, a Black woman falsely accused three members of Duke University's lacrosse team of raping her at a party. There was immediate local outrage. It went national when Rev. Jesse Jackson and Rev. Al Sharpton began speaking out and went to Durham to meet with local Black community leaders. Richard Brodhead, president of Duke, forced the lacrosse coach to resign and cancelled the remainder of the season. A year later North Carolina Attorney General Roy Cooper dropped all charges, declared the three players innocent and said they were victims of a tragic rush to accuse. Mike Nifong, the Durham

County District Attorney and the initial prosecutor, was running for reelection and was re-elected. In June 2007, he was disbarred for "dishonesty, fraud, deceit and misrepresentation" and found guilty of criminal contempt. Brodhead eventually apologized for his handling of the allegations. At first Duke was criticized for not condemning a culture of white elitism that tolerated such abuse, and when the truth was revealed, administrators were accused of being blinded by liberal political correctness.[14]

An example of never knowing when a crisis is going to end, on February 22, 2008, 38 members of the 2006 Duke lacrosse team filed suit in federal court and held a media event at the National Press Club in Washington, D.C. Named as defendants were the university, Brodhead and more than a dozen Duke officials, as well as the city of Durham, its city manager and various police officers. The lawsuit described team critics and protesters as an "angry mob" and the players were "reviled almost daily in local and national press" according Chuck Cooper, attorney for the players.[15]

Overcharging the government for research and charging non-authorized items. For every dollar the federal government spends with a university to support basic and applied research, the school can charge an overhead expense. A number of prestigious research institutions were exposed in the 1990s by Martin Anderson in his book *Imposters in the Temple*. The institutions compounded the problem by stonewalling the media about overhead charges. Federal auditors found Stanford University was the worst offender by adding 74 cents for every dollar it received in federal funds. Others named in the corruption scandal included University of California at Berkeley, University of Chicago, California Institute of Technology, Carnegie-Mellon, Columbia, Cornell, Dartmouth, Duke, Emory, Harvard Medical School, University of Hawaii, Johns Hopkins, MIT, University of Pennsylvania, Pittsburgh, Rutgers, Southern California, Washington and Yale.

Overhead charges are to cover the cost of lights, janitorial services, water and other utilities in the laboratories where the projects were being conducted. However, some charges made for overhead included flowers, a piano, antique chairs, a new shower curtain and bathroom window shades, and wedding reception for the president's house; salary and benefits for the president's chef; the president's golf club membership, opera tickets and a trip to the Caribbean with his wife; a dozen engraved crystal decanters; a chauffeur for the president and his wife; depreciation on a yacht; administrative costs of running a commercial for-profit shopping center; construction costs of a new alumni club; expenses for terminating employees; and even legal expenses to lobby Congress and defend against scientific fraud.[16] Higher education has not agreed on a definition of overhead rate and neither has the federal government, so overhead rates can range from 30 to as high as 90 percent.

Administrative waste and inefficiency. Higher education largely operates without oversight. It is self-governing, self-regulating and largely unregulated. This must be addressed on a continuing basis. Administration and staff positions have been increased significantly more than faculty. Anytime there is a story to be told about saving money, the public should be told. Tuition generally covers only about one-third of the actual cost of a student's education, so the more students a college has, the more money it loses.

Conflicts of interest. Perception is important, and university presidents, chancellors, deans and faculty members will come under scrutiny when they sit on the boards of directors of outside organizations or have outside income-producing interests.

Athletics. The least impropriety involving an athletic program, even if it is an honest mistake, is ammunition for headlines and a page one story. Media exposure given to athletic scandals has a disproportionate influence on the public image of higher education. There are violations involving compliance with the NCAA. Then there are misdemeanors and felonies involving athletes. Sometimes even coaches create scandals. Sport at most universities today is big business. A quick look at the athletic department budgets and one might think you were reviewing the financial statement of a *Fortune 500* company. The cost of running sports programs at major institutions is spiraling completely out of control and needs to be brought back to reality.

In 2007, the average earnings of the 120 major college football coaches was $1 million plus a myriad of benefits, perks, and bonuses. Four coaches made $3 million or more, a dozen $2 million and another 50 $1 million. Joe Paterno, one of the winningest coaches ever in college football, is paid $512,664 by Penn State University. Twice he not only has turned down lucrative professional offers, but he and his wife have endowed the university more than $4 million. I wonder how much the $1 million plus coaches and their agents are giving back to their respective schools.

By contrast, *The Chronicle of Higher Education* reported the median salary for 162 presidents and chancellors of public research universities and systems was $397,000. University officials respond saying the high salaries are an investment in that generates revenues through increased ticket sales and prices, television rights fees, marketing revenues, donations, and even applications for admission. However, the NCAA reports that four of every five major college sports programs need subsidies that include student fees and other subsidies in order to balance the budget.

If the same rules are applied to all, there will be a level playing field, and costs can be reduced for all across-the-board. The ultimate responsibility lies with the CEOs and the boards of regents and governors to whom they report. All must start being held accountable.

What kind of message is this sending to the American public? Many public colleges and universities who once called themselves "state supported" now, because of decreasing funds, use the term "state assisted." Some who received less than 15 percent public support from their legislature now even say they are just "state located."

The NCAA has been gutless when it comes to limiting spending on sports. For example, why does a college football team need to have two or three times more uniformed players than a professional NFL team? Or larger coaching staffs? There is no justifiable answer. The number of players on a team should be limited and scholarships appropriately reduced over a three-year period. You don't need a course in Econ 101 to know that with fewer players, fewer coaches and support staff that training, travel and per diem, and all costs would be slashed. A level playing field can be created but only if the presidents and chancellors who run the NCAA do their jobs.

The NCAA and its leadership and members forget that intercollegiate sports exist for one reason only: because there is an academic institution. The institution of higher learning does not exist so there can be football, basketball and other sports team. In response to the overpaid coaches and the cost of athletic programs, some presidents will offer the excuse that the funds are paid by alumni and friends. If this is the case, let those so-called "philanthropists" endow scholarships to young people who otherwise might not be able to afford a college education, and who might just be the next Nobel prize laureate, break through scientist, or even a governor, or president of the U.S.

What a different world it would be if coaches were given bonuses not for winning, but for molding character of individuals and insuring the scholar athletes graduate with degrees. And hold these same coaches to conduct standards, with salary deduction penalties, if thugs are recruited who might win games, but end up being arrested and disgrace the institution. Taking the money out of winning would result in fewer recruiting violations, more honest athletic programs and less negative publicity for the institutions.

Sport Can Be An Important Tool to Sell Higher Education

Sport can be a powerful and dynamic marketing communications tool if the campaign using this tool is strategically planned and professional executed. It also can be one of the most cost-effective ways of not just telling, but selling the story of higher education. Sport bridges age, race and gender gaps. It delivers the message with impact to important publics that cannot be reached through traditional higher education information distribution channels. The opportunities exist at all levels from NCAA Division I through Division III programs and junior and community colleges.

In 1991, after more than half of the states in the U.S. slashed the budgets of public colleges and universities, the Texas Legislature warned academia to prepare for across-the-board cuts of 10 percent. In the face of such devastating reductions, higher education had become a favorite target for the media. There was no grass roots public support to refute any of the typical charges regarding faculty workloads, rising tuition costs, tenure, use of teaching assistants, and scandals in athletics.

Dr. William Mobley, then president of Texas A&M, took a leadership position to create a campaign and organize a coalition effort to rebuild public trust, and head off the proposed cuts by the legislature. Just as consumer products companies use research to determine the message and media to use, focus group research was conducted in Dallas, Houston and San Antonio, followed by a statewide public opinion poll to define the issues, and create the message the public wanted to hear.

Sport was the vehicle chosen to reach a major segment of the public that was not a constituent group of higher education – the audience that pollsters call the Bubba factor. After an aggressive 18-month campaign, instead of the mandated 10 percent budget cut, the Texas Legislature actually increased spending nearly 7 percent, which represented a swing of 17 percent and more than $1.5 billion.

Texas A&M prepared the campaign that was used by the other colleges and universities in the state. Radio and television sports were produced for use on football, basketball and other sports telecasts and broadcasts. Print ads and feature stories were created for game programs. Coaches were part of a speakers bureau and were given paragraphs to insert in their remarks at booster clubs.

Through a Committee on Education, the former Southwest Conference launched a successful statewide program that even included donated billboards.

Unfortunately, millions of dollars of free advertising time go to waste every year during football season and the NCAA "March Madness" basketball tournament. If the NCAA, various conferences, and colleges and universities wanted to win public financial support for higher education, they lost. Take any random number of television commercials produced by the institutions, switch the names and no one would know the difference. Most appear to be produced only to give alumni bragging rights with no central message. They generally always have a bell tower, show students walking across campus, and then with professors in a laboratory. Not one really told the American public how they benefit from what higher education is doing with their tax dollars.

Department Crisis Plans Are Important

One crisis plan and team will generally not be sufficient in higher education. There should be sub-plans coordinated with the university's plans, especially where there is a medical school, veterinary school or agriculture school. And at most universities, the athletic department needs its own crisis team to "what if" and develop its own plan. While the lead will still be university relations and the institution's top public relations professional, the sports information director and the athletic director must be prepared to deal with crises in their areas.

Here are just a few examples of crises that can happen in athletic departments:

- An athlete dies of a heart attack or stroke during practice in any number of sports, including football, soccer and basketball.
- Even worse, the death occurs during a game.
- Several athletes are arrested for a gang rape.
- An athlete is arrested for shoplifting (or any other crime) in another city during an away game. This is worse when more than one are involved.
- A coach is arrested for a DUI.
- A score of athletes violate the university's honor code or cheat on an examination.
- A fan dies in the stands at a football or basketball game or other event.
- A band member or someone participating during a halftime ceremony at midfield has a seizure or stroke and the game is being nationally televised.

- A coach or member of the administration has an extra-marital affair with a member of the staff or a student athlete. Even worse, the woman becomes pregnant.
- A van, bus or vehicle has a serious accident while a team is traveling to or from a road event. One or more student athletes are killed and several others are taken to various hospitals in the area.
- A coach dies having sex with a prostitute in a downtown hotel.
- A violation of NCAA rules for any number of reasons.

The athletic director, sports information director and all coaches need to have emergency telephone contact numbers for everyone that needs to be notified. This can be a plasticized wallet card with direct dial office, home, and cell phone numbers, as well as people in university relations who need to be called.

Higher Education Can Take A Lesson from West Virginia University

Colleges and universities could take a lesson from West Virginia University regarding the message that needs to be communicated to the general public. David C. Hardesty, Jr., when he was president of West Virginia University, said that that research indicates that the state gets a return of $10 on every $1 invested in WVU. He also pointed out to the legislators and the people of the state many other good things the university is doing: university physicians provide $50 million of charity care each year; law students give 11,000 hours of free legal services; students give 100,000 hours of community service; 3,600 new and experienced miners are trained in safety each year through the Mining Extension Service; 30,000 children participate in summer reading programs; state farmers are increasing sales $1 million a year by participating in university programs; the university trained 17,500 volunteer firefighters from around the state and U.S. last year.

And, the university's math department earned $739,000 of national grant money to support math education in Appalachian middle schools; 97,000 people subscribe to WVU's small-community water resource publications; more than 340 companies are involved in energy saving research projects; and 100 new histories of West Virginia war veterans are now recorded in the archives of the Library of Congress.

The citizens of West Virginia truly benefit from their flagship university in Morgantown. If the presidents of other universities started letting taxpayers in their states know how they directly benefited, chances are legislators in their state capitols would start increasing, not decreasing support for higher education.

Private institutions are affected as well. When money is needed, the colleges and universities go to the public for support. With federal programs being cut or reprioritized, competition for all available funds is extremely competitive. Just as Hardesty and WVU have done, others should let their state's taxpayers and legislators know why an investment in education is one of the best investments that can be made for the economy and well-being of the state.[17]

Summary Checklist

- "What if ..." all of the possible issues that could be considered a crisis.
- Anticipate, plan/prepare and respond.
- Develop a campaign to tell the story to the general public in the simplest of terms.
- Conduct focus group research and public opinion polls to understand the concern of the taxpayers as well as the legislators. Take key words to use in the campaign message.
- Consider using sport as one element among the diverse benefits American colleges and universities generate to win and build public trust.
- If there is a crisis never try to conceal it or keep it internal. Sooner or later a good investigative reporter will have the story and things will be even worse when it is made public.
- When someone leaks a crisis to the media often it is the only way justice can be sought. It would have been far better to have been open and transparent.
- Have the most qualified and experience public relations professional responsible. Reporting should be directly to the president.
- Separate crisis plans and teams are needed in most athletic departments as well as at universities with medical, veterinary and agricultural schools.
- The general counsel's office needs to meet with university relations and the crisis team at least annually to understand the importance of communicating.
- Any employee or department receiving a media request needs to immediately respond and inform university relations.
- In a crisis, get the story out and close the case as quickly as possible.

- Do not overact to pressure from whatever source. Always do what is right.
- Remember a no response can often be worse than a "no comment."
- Because an academic society can be very insular at times, listen to outside help before, during and after a crisis.
- Organize an advisory team of outstanding public relations professionals who are alumni with a vested interest in the institution and use their talent, experience and knowledge.
- Most of all, have a crisis management and communications plan and sub-plans in place.

Endnotes

[1] Carol Gorney, "Crisis Management – How to plan ahead for potential crises," *AS&U*, January 1990, pg. 20a.

[2] E-mails, correspondence and discussion with Stephen M. Reed, associate vice president for external affairs, office of the president, California State University, Monterey Bay, Seaside, California, February-March 2008.

[3] Jerrold K. Footlick, "Doing the Right Things," *Case Currents*, Council for Advancement and Support of Education, May 1997, pgs. 31, 34.

[4] "Financial Facts," *U.S. News & World Report*, September 8, 1997, pg. 77; Associated Press, "Cost of Tuition, Room, board Jumps Again at U.S. Colleges," *San Francisco Chronicle*, September 25, 1997, pg. A3; Associated Press, "Cost of college rises faster than inflation, student aid," *The Seattle Times*, October 23, 2007.

[5] Jessica Helley, "Harvard aid plan offers tuition discounts," CNNMoney.com, December 27, 2007.

[6] Amy Rolph, "Congress wants rich schools like UW to give students a break," *Seattle Post-Intelligencer*, Seattle, Washington, March 3, 2008.

[7] Widipedia.org, "Virginia Tech massacre."

[8] Joetta L. Carr, Ph.D., Western Michigan University, "Campus violence White Paper," American College Health Association, Baltimore, Maryland, February 2005.

[9] Donna Leinwand, "Campus crime underreported," *USA Today*, October 4, 2000, pg. 1.

[10] Ibid.

[11] "Campus Crime: Hear No Evil, See No Evil, Report No Evil," *Philadelphia Magazine*, March 1998, pgs. 51, 160; securityoncampus.org.

[12] "Safe Campus," www.washington.edu.

[13] David G. Savage, "Where religion, ideology and the Web cross," *The Los Angeles Times*, February 17, 2008.

[14] Aaron Beard, "Judge Finds Duke Prosecutor in Contempt," Associated Press, August

31, 2007; David G. Savage, *op.cit.*

[15] Anne Blythe and Barbara Barrett, "38-player lacrosse suit gets fanfare," *The News & Obseerver*, Raleigh, North Carolina, February 22, 2008.

[16] Martin Anderson, *Imposters in the Temple*, Hoover Institution Press, Stanford, California, 1996.

[17] Rene A. Henry, "Higher Education Can Take A Lesson From WVU," Huntington News Net, May 7, 2006.

CHAPTER 13

THE AGGIE PIGS
AND PRESIDENT BUSH

Stink at Pig Farm and Bush Library

COLLEGE STATION, Texas – Residents of a rural area near Texas A&M University are raising a fuss over the relocation of a pig farm being displaced by construction of the George Bush Presidential Library.

School officials plan to move the Texas A&M Swine Center from a corner of the 90-acre (36-hectares) library site a few miles west to a place known as Brushy Community.

"The bottom line is, Brushy Community residents don't want the pigs out there," said Tam Garland, an A&M veterinarian whose home would be about 300 yards from the pig center. "Whether it's five pigs or 500 pigs, we don't want them. You can't keep a pig from stinking."

– *International Herald Tribune*, Paris, France, September 21, 1994[1]

With that breaking news story a crisis that Texas A&M University could have avoided went international.

The next day the story was on television throughout the world. CNN International broadcast a feature that showed former President and Mrs. Bush breaking ground for the his presidential library. The story cut to pigs wallowing in a pig pen and finished with a strong quote from Reverend Cedric Rouse, minister of the African-American Clayton Baptist Church and president of the residents' association. Rouse called the university's actions "environmental racism." Until this time, the story was reported only occasionally by the local media, the student newspaper, and sporadically by the Dallas and Houston newspapers.

The story began in 1993 when the university announced plans to build a new Animal Science, Teaching, Research and Extension Complex on a 582-acre site

8.5 miles from the center of the campus. The new facility was to have a beef cattle center, a sheep and goat, animal euthenics and nutrition, and physiology centers. The land was purchased in 1989 and a beef cattle center opened in 1993.

Expensive homes and ranches, owned predominantly by members of the A&M faculty and administration were on one side of the center. Across the highway was an established community of Black families, the Brushy Community. This was founded by a group of Black pioneers who moved from Clayton, North Carolina after the Civil War. The Clayton Baptist Church was named for the pioneers' former hometown southeast of Raleigh. Most of the Blacks were hourly-wage employees working for the university in foodservice, maintenance, groundskeeping, and other similar jobs.

A Reputation As A Good Member of the Community

For decades, Texas A&M and the community had good relations. Few people challenged A&M because of its dominant position. There really was no serious controversy between the community and the university until the decision to have pigs at the new animal center. When George Bush decided to locate his presidential library at A&M, the swine center was in the middle of the 90-acre site. Something had to give.

The first signs of any conflict came when the university was closed for 1993 Christmas holidays. Required public announcements were published in the local paper on Christmas Eve and Christmas Day.

In early spring 1994, Dr. Charles Lee, then deputy vice chancellor of agriculture and life sciences, asked the author, then executive director of university relations at Texas A&M, for help. He wanted to contain the situation, was looking for advice how to handle the problem, and wanted to head off a crisis. The position of the administration was made clear by Dr. E. Dean Gage, who was the university's interim president: "We are going to do the right thing. We are not going to force a pig farm on the community. The people that live there are not just community residents, they are employees and members of the Texas A&M family. If we have to find another location, we will. Let's get closure on this as quickly as possible."[2]

A 180 Degree Turn

Before the dispute could be resolved, the board of regents named Ray Bowen the new president. He was a 1958 graduate of A&M who had been acting president at Oklahoma State. Bowen took over as president in June 1994 and named

Dr. Jerry Gaston, a sociology professor, as interim vice president of finance and administration. Working in tandem, the two took a hard line against the people in the community. This violated all principles of both community relations and employee relations. An incident rapidly escalated into a full blown crisis.

Tension increased at the meetings between the community and A&M. Faculty members joined with the Black community to form a coalition. The university held all meetings on campus during business hours. This meant that Blacks from the Brushy Community had to take off from work without pay. The more the community leaders pushed for fairness, the harder the line the university took. Bowen and Gaston clearly drew a line in the sand. Anticipating a major international crisis about to explode, on December 12, 1994, the author prepared a detailed situation analysis for A&M's leadership.

SITUATION AND ISSUES ANALYSIS

Subject: Animal Science Teaching Research Education Center/Swine Center

Background: During the spring of 1994 the primary issue was to reduce the number of pigs on the site to alleviate any problems related to air and water pollution. This was done by locating half of the animals to a new site in McGregor.

The issue today is that the community does not want any pigs at all near its community, and wants a new location for the Swine Center.

Key Issues: There is a community of nearly 200 families surrounding the proposed center. Half of the families are poor African-Americans. All are against the relocation of any pigs to the new Animal Science Center.

The accusation of "environmental racism" against Texas A&M.

Adversaries could use the George Bush Presidential Library Center as the primary media focus with the Texas A&M University administration accountable and responsible.

SPECIFIC ISSUES:

Planning

University: Extensive planning and study over a number of years with impact statements.

Downsized plan at an additional cost of $600,000.

Community: "Planners talked to only four families, none of whom were Black."

60% of prevailing winds will affect 100 Black families and four churches (two of which are African-American and one Asian-American).

"The research, impact analysis and site selection were not properly or professionally done."

The community has proposed alternative sites.

"The university has circumvented the law by downsizing, and using a loophole to avoid reporting to the state natural resources authority."

"With less than 1,000 pigs there is no authority for air and water quality. A&M is free to do whatever it wants with no controls."

"This violates the basic principles of good urban planning – placing livestock in a residential area."

"This is nothing more than environmental racism."

"The architectural firm should be held liable for doing an improper impact study and analysis."

[Author note: Quotes are comments made by members of the Brushy Community affected by the new center.]

Technology

University: State-of-the-art technology.

Facilities are designed for twice the number of pigs and capacity of waste.

Odor and pollution of air and water will be controlled.

Center will be an environmental showplace for everyone to see.

University will guarantee the technology that there will be no odors or pollution.

All odors will be monitored. The swine industry now spends $25-30 million each year on technology.

Community: "Any lagoon will leak. Data from Iowa points out Texas A&M has not done its research."

"The system proposed is primitive. The technology is inferior and would not be allowed by EPA."

"Livestock animal waste is the #1 ground polluter in the U.S."

"During heavy rains, lagoons can overflow and contaminate ground water and the Brazos River."

"Current water table is at 70' in sand with a high hydraulic absorption capacity."

"Spreading lagoon waste as fertilizer will only take the pig smell from a small, confined area, and spread it over a larger, broad area."

"Regardless of what is done, pigs still will smell."

Community Relations

University: The university wants to be a good citizen. It is listening to what people in the community want.

Community: "There is constant conflict between 'town and gown.' The university has terrible community relations. Texas A&M is very arrogant, especially its attorneys." Faculty cited examples of where they had worked where there were excellent town and gown relationships (i.e. Illinois). "A&M needs to respond to community needs."

"We cannot trust the university to keep its word. A new administration may reverse what had been promised by a previous administration. The recent indictments and convictions prove that 'Aggies do lie, cheat and steal.' You can no longer trust anyone at Texas A&M."

"When the university allowed the Ku Klux Klan to have a campus rally, it turned off a lot of Blacks in the Bryan-College Station community."

Construction

University: State-of-the-art construction technology will be used.

Community: "Every building the university builds is flawed and needs immediate attention. Major items are excluded or overlooked." Community leaders cited several buildings (medical school, new vet medicine building, and architecture) that have been recently opened as having major construction flaws.

Maintenance

University: Any problems will be immediately corrected.

Community: "Maintenance is a low priority at Texas A&M." Professors from the community cited classrooms where 20% of the seats are broken and students have to sit in aisles or on the floor, with complaints having been made for as long as three years.

"University employees and faculty know that maintenance is an inherent problem at A&M."

Real Estate Values

University: The university undertook a study and found that there had been no appreciable loss of real estate property values.

Community: "Location of any pigs near a residential community will destroy property values."

"People are taking losses already with the knowledge that pigs will be located near the community."

"People cannot afford to move and live anywhere else."

Emotional Impact

University: Decisions have to be made with students as a priority.

The facility is important to the livestock industry in Texas.

The university has spent an additional $600,000 to accommodate the needs of the community.

Community: "The Black families do not have air conditioning. Unlike rich, white folks, we cannot shut our windows, and turn on air conditioning, to shut out the pig smell."

"If the smell is no problem, then why not leave the facility where it is. If it is a problem, why is the smell OK for 100 Black families and not the Bushes?"

"The social activities of the Black community take place outdoors both at the churches and individual homes. This would not be possible with odors from the pigs."

"Most Black families cannot afford dryers and hang clothes to dry on clothes-lines. Are these people expected to go to work with their clothes smelling with the stench of pigs?"

"Who is more important? The 100 Black families, and the Brushy Community, or A&M students?"

"You can't `spring clean' with hog smell coming through a house."

"We want Texas A&M to be the best university in the country – providing the best education and teaching possible for the students and our children, who will be future students. We support A&M, but A&M needs to support us."

"A&M has handled this wrong from the very beginning. I am tired of bad press. This will only create more bad press, and it is my university. The university is behaving wrong. Listen to the folks."

"We are too poor to try to fight A&M and its staff of attorneys."

"We want an answer soon, so we know if we have to start fund-raisers and benefits to get money to pay our attorneys."

"If you are concerned and listening, do what we ask."

"The worry of having a pig farm is our neighborhood is killing us – blood pressure, nerves, and worry about those of us with asthma and respiratory diseases."

Executive Summary

University: The university has studied this problem for a number of years and believes it has made a valid decision regarding the location of the new animal science center and, in particular, the swine center. It believes this is in the best interests of everyone involved. In recent months when serious concerns have been raised by the community, the university has listened to the community. It first downsized the facility at considerable expense, and found a site in McGregor to accommodate half of the swine. Now, the university is listening to complaints from the community that it does not want any pigs located on the site of the proposed swine center. The university wants to be a good citizen and neighbor, and is considering its options.

Community: The community believes that the university is making it the victim because the pigs have to be moved from their present location to make room for the new Bush Presidential Library Center. The families are concerned about air and ground water pollution, the impact on their environment, and lifestyle, and how this could destroy the value of their homes and property. State-of-the-art technology, and the additional cost to the university, are not considerations.

Media Relations Evaluation

For public and media reaction, the community will focus on the Bush Library and the Bush family, as much as it will on the university for creating this problem. The controversy will become a significant race issue.

If this happens, the controversy becomes a media crisis, and the story will be one of national and even international magnitude. A possible storyline could be about "the lives of 100 Black families being destroyed because of the Bush Library."

During the Saturday (December 10) meeting, the community indicated it would wait for a response from the university before taking further action. If the issue escalates, the media interest will do so accordingly. The issues involved with this controversy are exactly what 60 Minutes, Hard Copy, 20/20, Eye-to-Eye and other television news magazines are looking for, as well as all national newspapers and magazines.

With a quick response, this controversy could be contained without embarrassment to President Bush and his family, and any further embarrassment or tarnish on the image of Texas A&M.

Recommendation

1. The university should issue a press release and statement this week that would:
    * thank the community for making known its concerns;
    * assure the community that all concerns are being reviewed and considered;
    * announce that all work on the new center and the Bush Library is being temporarily suspended; and,
    * put construction on hold until the university has plans for an alternate site that is acceptable to the Brushy Community as well as the neighbors in the new community.

2. President Bowen should meet with the community Tuesday evening, December 20 and assure them that he is personally involved and outline the process that will be taking place.

3. If a decision is made to still locate a downsized swine center on the proposed site, then a "what if?" analysis must be prepared and discussed.

Rene A. Henry
December 12, 1994

This was not what the Aggie administration wanted to hear. President Bowen no longer wanted the author's advice regarding this crisis. The author warned about timing since the university was going to close for the Christmas holiday season, which would have been a perfect time for the opposition to mount a campaign. Most university officials would not be available to defend their position.

The administration did compromise by holding a meeting on December 20 with the community residents in the animal science center in the community. The morning of the meeting, the story was statewide. The headline in the *Houston Chronicle* was, "Rural residents turn up noses at A&M pig farm ... Bush Library forcing swine center to move."[3] The *Houston Post* headlined, "Community wants no `stinking' pigs."[4] "Disgruntled over swine ... Some residents are angry with A&M's plans to move pig farm because of new Bush library" was the headline in *The Dallas Morning News*.[5] All ran an Associated Press story that led with: "COLLEGE STATION, Texas – Residents of a rural area near Texas A&M University are raising a stink over the relocation of a pig farm being displaced by construction of the George Bush Presidential Library."[6] The next day the story was all over the world. Then things quieted while the community, and the college, tried to find a solution.[7]

University Revises Original Plans

During this time, the university modified the design of the complex to relocate the Swine and Dairy Products Centers, established a water quality management plan with the Texas State Soil and Water Conservation Board, and established other practices to assure surface and groundwater protection, and air quality.[8] When asked about residents' complaints about the stench of manure, Dr. John Beverly, deputy vice chancellor and associate dean insisted: "There's not going to be a problem."[9] The university proposed to keep 50 to 75 pigs at the center for teaching and research purposes. However, according to Dr. Albert Schaffer, a professor emeritus of sociology and community resident, if the pigs were allowed to breed, there could be 700 to 800 pigs there at any one time.[10]

The conflict involved more than just the swine. Apart from the smells and flies, residents were concerned about contaminated ground water, contaminated aquifers and illness that could be caused by the high level of nitrates, phosphates, other chemicals, and viruses and other micro-organisms. "We are very concerned over losing control of our lives and very existence, and having to cope with an obnoxious environment," said Schaffer. "It these matters come to pass, investments in our homes are virtually worthless."[11]

In June 1995, the university moved ahead with construction. The residents established Residents Opposed to Pigs and Livestock, and filed a lawsuit in federal court in Houston in August. Dr. Ruth Schaffer, Albert's wife, and also a professor emeriti of sociology at A&M, expressed her concern over the safety of drinking water. "No one with a well less than 100 feet deep should be drinking out of it at this time," she said.[12] This was amplified by Jim Mazzullo, a geology professor at A&M and also a community resident, who said studies done by a firm contracted by the university revealed the site is "unstable." Mazzullo said: "The report speaks for itself. …[The site] is underlaid by unstable clay, and has a very shallow water table that makes it incredibly susceptible to contamination by animal waste … and the problem is exacerbated because so many people depend on wells in the area."[13]

The geology professor believed one of the proposed university safety measures was essentially flawed. He said that an underground plastic liner to contain wastes and other materials with potential health hazards "will not remain impermeable, and will leak water quickly" because "the type of clay is expansive, and will swell and shrink with the weather. ... There's just no way to engineer around the clay."[14]

Possible Critters in the Water

According to the U.S. Environmental Protection Agency, nationwide livestock waste impairs river waters to a greater extent than storm sewers and run-off, combined sewer outflows or industrial sources. About 150 diseases can be contracted from drinking water contaminated by animal wastes.

Health safety concerned the fear that cryptosporidia, a parasite organism that is passed in animal feces, will filter into the water system. Catherine Wade, a technician in Texas A&M's College of Veterinary Medicine pathbiology department said that cryptosporidia is a parasite only smaller than a human red blood cell. "The parasite usually causes diarrhea for about two weeks when humans and animals are infected. The body, unable to develop resistance to the parasite, continually loses fluid and minerals."[15]

Problems with pigs anywhere near residential communities has been well documented by the media. CBS television featured problems with pigs in North Carolina where there are more pigs than people. The state's pig population of 8.5 million exceeds the state's 7.2 million people. Television cameras showed farms located in predominantly Black communities, and how some 30 percent of the ground water wells near hog farms had become contaminated. Morley Safer of *60 Minutes* said: "A good neighbor never stinks up his community with feces and urine." But this is exactly what happened in 1995 when a rain-swollen lagoon adjacent to one of the farms spilled 22 million gallons of hog feces and urine over the North Carolina countryside.[16]

Pig Problems Not Isolated In College Station

With increased consumption of pork, which is now a $30 billion industry in the U.S., livestock farms are creating controversy wherever they are located. Colorado farmer Galen Travis says it is not just the smell of reeking hog manure that concerns him, but that deep lagoons where hog waste is stored could seep through the dry soil and pollute the Oglala Aquifer, the underground lake that provides drinking and irrigation water to much of the western Great Plains. Voters in North Carolina, Kansas, Nebraska and Oklahoma are opposing new hog farms and restricting those now in operation.[17]

In January 1996, in the face of pending litigation, Texas A&M began construction on the $5.5 million complex. Even the local newspaper suggested the university delay construction until a court decision was handed down. Here are excerpts from the editorial board's opinion piece:

> *Our View*
> *A&M should wait a bit*
>
> "*Despite court-ordered mediation with unhappy residents of the Brushy Community, Texas A&M University officials have vowed to continue construction of the early phases of an animal science complex that will house sheep and goats and, for periods of three or four months at a time, swine.*
>
> "*What's the rush? U.S. District Judge Ewing Werlein, Jr. has asked lawyers ... to come up with a compromise by the end of the month. By continuing its construction ... A&M officials are saying there can be only one solution: their's.*
>
> "*...If the judge rules against A&M, that work – and expense – will be for naught. The prudent and neighborly thing would be to wait for the judge's ruling, whatever it might be.*
>
> "*The big fear is that government projects take on lives of their own. Once started, they are hard to stop. ... A delay of a few weeks will push the completion of the animal center back, but so would an adverse ruling from Judge Werlein.*"[18]

Residents Call on Governor Bush for Help

In January 1996, Judge Werlein did not grant an injunction requested by the residents, but warned the university not to build facilities for animals. He then ordered the two parties into mediation scheduled for March. In February, the Schaffers called on Texas Governor George W. Bush for help, since he appoints the regents who approve of such projects. "Unless the governor takes some kind of action," said Al Schaffer, "his father's presidential library will be tarnished with the image of environmental racism." He added that his organization has been patiently working with the A&M administration for nearly two years. "They talk about being good community citizens, but their actions contradict their press releases. The university has been trying to bully this center through its final stages. They have not backed off once from their original plans. Their arrogant attitude has been 'what is good for Aggies is good for the world.'"[19]

Governor Bush referred to matter to Mary Nan West, a South Texas rancher and chairman of A&M's board of regents, and Fred McClure, a Dallas business-man and member of the board of regents.

Chairman/rancher West, a strong advocate for the animal center, said that she and her regents did not plan to discuss the issue with the governor. "I don't see why it should be discussed between the governor and the board of regents," she said. "'It's not up to the governor or the legislature to tell any university what to build where. I don't know what the big hullabaloo is. I certainly believe the administrators (at A&M), and they tell me they have complied with all the environmental rules and regulations."[20]

"The whole question of moving the complex has been under discussion since the early 1980s," McClure said. "It is not something that was just decided when the president decided to place his library here."[21] The land for the center was purchased in 1989.[22] The decision to build the Bush Presidential Library complex on the site of the existing pig farm was May 3, 1991.[23]

If It Walks Like A Duck, Talks Like A Duck ...

The university's spokesperson, Jim Ashlock, responded by calling Schaffer's com-ments a misrepresentation of the issue to the governor. "They say we are building a 'pig and livestock farm.' It is not a pig and livestock farm. It is not a farm. It is an educational center."[24]

Public sentiment had turned against the university. In an editorial in the student newspaper, Elaine Mejia, a senior political science major wrote, "Texas A&M world class university with world class problems. ... Despite the fact that legal ac-tion and mediation are pending, administration officials have proceeded with their plans to violate the most basic of land use principles – when possible, it is best to avoid using the same area of land for two competing functions. When land is being used to sustain the lives of American citizens, no corporation, government, person or university should be allowed to contaminate it, particularly when there are other options available." After citing many of the statements made by both sides, the Aggie student described cases of environmental racism and environmen-tal justice. She then wrote, "A&M's choosing to locate the center in the Brushy Creek area is nothing unique. Rather, A&M is added to a national list of suspect organizations that may have chosen locations based on the characteristics of their residents – in this case, low-income and African-American. ... Historically, there has been a disparity in enforcement of environmental regulations as well."[25]

Community Leaders Have Their Say

Community leaders began to speak out. In a letter to the editor of the local newspaper, *The Eagle*, Cora Rogers wrote: "It saddens me and it hurts to know that A&M would want to treat human beings like animals. They think more of their animals than they do about humans. ... Our lives and health are at stake. ... A&M can find another place that is not in a residential community ... that will not pollute the air and water and keep A&M's name out of lawsuits and media. A&M officials have built a reputation of not keeping their word. ... We have put our roots here. ... Some people here have worked 20-25 years and have finally retired to what? The hollering of animals at night when we try to sleep, the smell and the flies, bad water or contaminated water, diseases and more health problems to add to what we already have, fires, stress to deal with all of this, and death. Thank you A&M. If hell is anything like this, then I welcome hell."[26]

Another resident, Ruby Ellis, said "We've worked all our lives for what we have. I'm thankful for A&M. It gave us work. But now it looks like they're trying to take our lives." Etta Ruth Williams, whose grandfather was one of the Black pioneers who first settled the community, added, "We won't be able to go outside. We were here before A&M was here, and now it looks like they want to take over our homes. Like most of her neighbors, Williams spent most of her working life at the university in menial jobs. Her mother worked in the campus laundry."[27]

En Fin ... An Agreement?

When court-ordered mediation on March 2-3, 1996, and 23 hours of negotiation, failed to resolve the dispute, a hearing date was set for March 29 in U.S. District Court in Houston. Only minutes before the hearing was to begin, with principals to the litigation and witnesses in the courtroom, the two sides had a preliminary verbal agreement in Judge Werlein's chambers. Two years after the incident-now-turned-crisis began, when the two sides first met on March 29, 1994, the university and community agreed:

* A&M would post a $5 million performance bond to pay for any damage to its neighbors.
* A&M would pay the community $600,000 for legal and other expenses.
* The center will have an average of 1,000 and no more than 1,300 animals of all types would be housed on the site at one time. This is a reduction from 1,687 A&M planned before the agreement.

* No more than 10 pigs would live at the facility full time and 10 sows and their piglets would be there no more than 70 days at a time.
* Some of the manure produced by animals will be removed to another site for composting.
* The residents will have a council to monitor operation of the center to make sure it does not harm the surrounding area.
* A&M agreed not to try and buy more land around the center for agriculture purposes but could for something such as a library.[28]

In May, the general outlines of the settlement was approved by the university's board of regents but the two sides still had a few details to work out.[29] Things got no better during the torrid and humid Brazos summer. By August the organization representing the community, Residents Opposed to Pigs and Livestock, accused the university of trying to renege on the agreement. Reverend Cedric Rouse said A&M reneged on some areas and refused to accept other sections written by A&M attorneys and agriculture specialists.[30]

A Breakdown. Agreement? No!

Negotiations continued until September, when Delmar Cain, the school's new general counsel, asked the Residents Opposed to Pigs and Livestock to indemnify the university against all future lawsuits from the residents, and all people living within two miles of the center. At this time the differences between the residents' attorney, Bob Hager of Dallas, Texas, and the university had narrowed, and were close to being resolved. Hager said that it would be impossible, if not illegal, for indemnification and requested a court date from Judge Werlein.[31]

Rouse said A&M now intends to build a poultry center and a center for exotic animals at the site, and to exclude non-university-owned animals from the count. Dr. Al Schaffer said A&M officials now are interested in condemning land near the complex sometime in the future because the agreement had a 15-year moratorium on land purchases in the area. All charges were denied by A&M's assistant general counsel, Bill Helwig.

Another major hangup was over providing names of members of the ROPL organization. According to Mrs. Schaffer, Judge Werlein specifically told the university that the community should not provide a list of names until the settlement is signed, and then the list would be given not to A&M, but to the Texas Attorney General. She said that A&M was misleading the public by claiming it is ready to sign an agreement and blame the community for not giving it names of members. Lawyer Helwig disagreed saying the judge told the community they would have to submit names before they could expect A&M to finalize the agreement.[32]

Speaking for the community, the Schaffers said many members were afraid of retaliation by the university if their names were on a list provided before any settlement. Both also said pressure had been exerted on some faculty members, and they too were concerned about vengeful retaliation by the administration.

With the situation still not resolved, construction on the new animal science center was completed in May 1997. The community called on the U.S. Environmental Protection Agency for help under both the Clean Water Act and the Civil Rights Act, for environmental justice, since federal funds were used in a racially discriminatory way. The university, now with its third general counsel since the dispute began, had committed even more public funds by retaining an outside law firm.

Several times during this conflict A&M had an opportunity to end the crisis. "The university could have had a very favorable settlement at the end of the mediation in March 1996," says Albert Schaffer. "We were worn down. Our attorneys were pressuring us to settle. Then we would have been willing to allow 1,600 animals at the center and take a relatively small sum of money. A&M offered $144,000."[33] The "agreement" reached less than a month later in Judge Werlein's chambers was a maximum of 1,000 animals and A&M would pay the community $600,000.

"We also are concerned about the center's deterioration over time, since A&M has a poor record of maintaining facilities, especially agriculture," writes Schaffer. "We also believe that A&M will use eminent domain to expand the facility if we lose the lawsuit. They will build a large swine center for 1,500 or more animals and move the dairy cattle to the area. Moving it from the site opens that area for development."[34]

One publication appropriately summed up the crisis by writing, "Texas A&M University is facing an unusually messy lawsuit – one involving race, George Bush, land use, and animal waste."[35]

A Saga That Continues

On August 12, Roliff H. Purrington, Jr., partner in the Austin, Texas law firm of Mayor, Day, Caldwell & Keeton, wrote attorneys for the plaintiff and cited a number of concessions and expenditures the university had made, including $366,000 to acquire a closed composting system, adding odor and pathogen monitoring systems, and that since the last mediation efforts that more than $600,000 had been spent on upgrades and environmental controls at the facility.[36]

Noting that "we have no authority to make any settlement offers to ROPL," Purrington added that "We would, however, recommend something roughly along the following lines to our client: one time cash payments of $2,000 to members of ROPL located north of Highway 60 and along the south side of Highway 60 east of the facility, e.g. those African American residents whom we believe reside in the 'true' Brushy Community, not those ROPL members along Kemp Road or in the other subdivisions to the east, for instance, where the Schaffers live." Purrington added that the university would expect full releases for any and all claims and dismissal of the current lawsuit with prejudice and in return "TAMU would agree to release ROPL members, particularly Dr. Tam Garland and Drs. Al and Ruth Schaffer from what we believe are, at best, negligent and, at worst, intentional misrepresentations throughout the community and in the press in connection with the nature of the ASTREC facility."[37]

Nearly 18 months after the two sides reached an agreement in his chambers, Judge Werlein, who was appointed to the bench was by George H. W. Bush on November 20, 1991,[38] dismissed large portions of the lawsuit. On September 11, less than two months before the Bush Presidential Library was scheduled for formal grand opening events, he cited immunity for Texas A&M under the Eleventh Amendment that generally bars suits against an unconsenting state since a judgment against the university would interfere with the fiscal autonomy of the state.[39]

"After two years in court, to dismiss it was a big shock to us," said Ruth Schaffer. Judge Werlein left intact only the group's claims alleging emotional distress, nuisance and, trespassing. Residents Opposed to Pigs and Livestock subsequently filed a similar state district court action in Brazos County that is nearly identical to the federal lawsuit.[40]

Aggie spokesman Ashlock said that the university decided to move the swine facility although other animals, including some farrowing sows, will still be located at the center. The A&M attorneys asked Judge Werlein for a summary judgment in the federal case while State District Judge Carolyn Ruffino instructed both parties to file a status report by December 29, 1997.[41]

The problem, which was nearly resolved only months after it became an incident in the spring of 1994, will have taken nearly four years and a cost to taxpayers estimated at several million dollars, as well as millions more in embarrassment and loss of reputation for A&M.

According to the office of the general counsel, at any one time there are about 30 lawsuits involving the university. In addition to the Brushy Community, this included the following:[42]

* A $25 million suit by former freshman and member of the Corps of Cadets, Travis Alton, accusing four top officials of ignoring hazing problems in the now-disbanded Fish Drill Team that led to his being assaulted.

* A dispute with computer scientist Dhiraj Pradhan, who has tenure and holds an endowed chair and is the ninth-highest paid A&M employee with a salary of $181,767, who was suspended in August 1997. The university charges the professor took $100,000 intended for research and Pradhan claims his troubles are caused by opposition to post-tenure review.

* Doug Donahue, a former cook in foodservices, claims he was fired because he called attention to food theft and time card fraud in the department. A&M claims he was a disruptive influence at work. Two former foodservice managers were paid out of court settlements in their litigation against the university: Lloyd Smith, former director of the operation, $118,750, and George Nedbalek, business manager, $95,000

* Matt Carroll, a graduate student in architecture and former commander of the Corps of Cadets, is taking his case to the U.S. Supreme Court. He claims he lost his job as project manager for an A&M project because he refused to sign timesheets that didn't accurately reflect the hours worked by the students employed. He views the episode as a violation of the Aggie Code of Honor, which states: "Aggies do not lie, cheat or steal or tolerate those who do."

Bowen, Gaston and Ashlock responded that the university is an "easy target" for lawsuits. "There's no way an organization as complicated and as people-oriented as this one is not going to have some disputes," said Gaston. "That's the way it's going to be."

Meanwhile, diagonally across the state from College Station, in the Texas Panhandle, hog producers are looking to make the Lone Star the hog capital of the world. In fact, Amarillo Republican State Senator Teel Bivin said, "I see no reason why this area should not produce 75 percent of the world's pork." The northernmost 23 counties of Texas had 52,000 pigs on farms in 1992, some 279,000 by 1996 and an estimated 1.352 million in the year 2000. One magazine wrote:

"Banned temporarily from locating in Kentucky and exiled by voter referenda in 18 counties in Kansas, the pork industry is moving whole hog to the Lone Star State. Nippon Meat Packers, with 1996 revenues of $4.9 billion; Murphy Family Farms, the country's largest pork producer; Premium Standard Farms, Va., Inc., a Spanish company; and Seaboard Farms, all now have pork production facilities in Texas and are looking to expand them further to get into the export market to meet demand in Japan, Mexico, Canada and the Pacific Rim.[43]

The A&M crisis damaged both the university's community relations and employee relations efforts. One must ask a number of questions in reviewing this case. Why did a crisis like this happen in the first place? If there was a misunderstanding, could it have been resolved with compassion? Several times, Texas A&M had an opportunity to end the conflict, to cut short its financial losses and not lose face. Was it institutional arrogance? Was it ego? Was it a holdover militaristic attitude when A&M was an all-male, all-white military school? Was it a refusal to admit a mistake? Only the leadership at Texas A&M can answer those questions.

Summary Checklist

- Consider whether this was or was not a classic case of academic institutional arrogance.

- What could have become a "no crisis" or one contained just in the local town of the university became internationally embarrassing. The crisis should have lasted only days, not four years.

- The actions of the university violated all rules of community relations and employee relations.

- Much of the discussion and negotiation could have been done behind the scenes rather than in the media.

- In situations like this there will be experts giving opinions. In this crisis, the university's own experts, siding with the community, criticized and had opinions other than those the administration was quoting.

- Never change the playing field or rules in the middle of a game.

- In almost every crisis prepare a "Situation and Issues Analysis" looking constructively at all issues and developing pros and cons. This is an excellent model to follow.

- Use the new facility as a means of rebuilding goodwill destroyed during the four years of contentiousness.

Endnotes

[1] *International Herald Tribune*, September 21, 1994, Paris, France, pg. 3.

[2] Letter from Dr. E. Dean Gage, College Station, Texas, March 26, 1997.

[3] *Houston Chronicle*, December 20, 1994, section A, pg. 25.

[4] *The Houston Post*, December 20, 1994, pg. A-21.

[5] *The Dallas Morning News*, December 20, 1994, pg. 23A.

[6] Ibid.

[7] Tara Wilkinson, "Brushy Creek residents fight research complex," *The Battalion*, Texas A&M University, College Station, Texas, July 11, 1995, pg. 1.

[8] News release, Office of University Relations, Texas A&M University, College Station, Texas, August 16, 1995.

[9] Associated Press, "A&M, neighborhood head for court," *The Dallas Morning News*, February 12, 1996, pg. 22A.

[10] Chip Lambert and Jim Wyss, "A&M pig center causing controversy," *The Eagle*, Bryan, Texas, pg. 1.

[11] Letter from Dr. Albert Schaffer, College Station, Texas, May 22, 1997.

[12] Tara Wilkinson, *The Battalion, op.cit.*, pg. 6.

[13] Chip Lambert and Jim Wyss, *The Eagle, op.cit.*, pg. A8.

[14] Ibid.

[15] Tara Wilkinson, *The Battalion, op.cit.*, pg. 6.

[16] *60 Minutes*, CBS, December 22, 1996 and July 6, 1997.

[17] John Greenwald, "Hogging the Table ... Corporate pig factories are supplanting traditional farms – and critics are raising a stink about it," *Time*, March 18, 1996, pg. 76.

[18] Eagle Editorial Board, "A&M should wait a bit," *The Eagle*, Bryan, Texas, February 4, 1996, pg. A11.

[19] Keely Coughlan, "Gov. Bush to Brushy Creek's rescue?," *The Eagle*, Bryan, Texas, pg. A9.

[20] Keely Coughlan, "Gov. Bush refers Brushy Creek query to two A&M regents," *The Eagle*, Bryan, Texas, February 21, 1996, pgs. A1, A4.

[21] Ibid.

[22] Letter from Dr. Albert Schaffer, *op.cit.*.

[23] Keely Coughlan, "Gov. Bush to Brushy Creek's rescue?", *The Eagle*, Bryan, Texas, February 14, 1996, pg. A9.

[24] Ibid.

[25] Elaine Mejia, "Brushy Creek reeks of questionable treatment," *The Battalion*, Texas A&M University, College Station, Texas, February 27, 1996.

[26] *The Eagle*, Bryan, Texas, February 26, 1996, editorial page.

[27] Richard Stewart, "A&M stirs community's ill will with `arrogant' expansion march," *Houston Chronicle*, February 11, 1996, pg. E1.

[28] Associated Press, "A&M, neighbors reach accord," *The Dallas Morning News*, March 30, 1996, pg. 24A.

[29] Keely Coughlan, "Regents OK Brushy Creek pact ... A&M, residents still discussing details of livestock center," *The Eagle*, Bryan, Texas, May 25, 1996, pg. 1.

[30] Keely Coughlan, "Brushy dispute smolders ... A&M denies claims that it reneged on deal," *The Eagle*, August 6, 1996, pg. 1.

[31] Letter from Dr. Albert Schaffer, *op. cit.*.

[32] Keely Coughlan, "Brushy dispute smolders ... A&M denies claims that it reneged on deal," *The Eagle*, August 6, 1996, pg. A10.

[33] Letter from Dr. Albert Schaffer, *op.cit.*

[34] Ibid.

[35] Rachanee Srisavasdi, "A Community Sues as Texas A&M Tried to Move 1,000 Animals to the Neighborhood," *The Chronicle of Higher Education*, December 6, 1996, pg. A50.

[36] Letter of August 12, 1997 from Roliff H. Purrington, Jr., Austin, Texas to Robert E. Hager of Nichols, Jackson, Dillard, Hager & Smith, Dallas, Texas.

[37] Ibid.

[38] Senate Judiciary Committee, February 20, 1998.

[39] RESIDENTS OPPOSING PIGS AND LIVESTOCK, Plaintiffs, v. TEXAS A&M UNIVERSITY, RAY M. BOWEN, ITS PRESIDENT AND THE BOARD OF RE-GENTS OF TEXAS A & M UNIVERSITY, NAN WEST, JOHN H. LINDSEY, MI-CHAEL O'CONNOR, ROBERT H. ALLEN, ALLISON BRISCO, DON POWELL, GUADALUPE L. RANGEL AND ROYCE E. WISENBAKER Defendants, Civil Action NO. H-95-4113, United States District Court for the Southern District of Texas, Houston Division, *Memorandum and Order*, Ewing Werlein, Jr., United States District Judge, September 11, 1997.

[40] "Ruling is blow to A&M livestock complex foes," *The Dallas Morning News*, November 13, 1997.

[41] Ibid.

[42] John Kirsch, "A&M target of lawsuits," *The Eagle*, Bryan, Texas, February 8, 1988, pgs. A1, A5, A8.

[43] Robert Bryce, "Making Bacon in the Panhandle," *The Texas Observer*, October 10, 1997, pgs. 8-13.

CHAPTER 14

THE IMPORTANCE
OF CUSTOMER SERVICE

*A customer is the most important visitor on our premises. He is not
dependent on us. We are dependent on him. He is not an interrupter of
our work, but the purpose of it. He is not an outsider to our business.*
– Gandhi

Well done is better than well said. – Benjamin Franklin

There is no magic to customer service. It is basically just good old fashioned
common sense. It is how you want to be treated when you are spending money
for a product or service. Treat everyone the way you would want to be treated,
only better. Nonprofit and government organizations also need customer service.
Magazines, including *Business Week*, rate the top 25 companies for customer
service and annually most of the same names are always on the list.

Time and again crises have been created, as well as exacerbated, by poor or
non-existent customer service. Something as simple as not returning a phone call,
or not responding to a letter, e-mail or fax, can create a crisis. That is why it is
important to return every call and answer every letter, e-mail and fax. Consider
what happened to one of the country's major homebuilders when a secretary
didn't get back to a new home buyer, or make her boss aware of the situation. The
customer was concerned her dishwasher wasn't working when she was planning
an important dinner party on Saturday. She stayed home all day Thursday, waiting for a repairman who never arrived, and in spite of repeated calls to the builder
on Friday, the same happened. She had a multitude of errands to run Saturday.

The secretary considered the woman a chronic complainer, and just didn't like
her. When the home owner called at 4:45 Friday afternoon, the secretary ignored

her, and went home. During the new home owner's dinner party, the conversation got around to how the builder was handling repairs, and how badly this one woman had been treated. Before the evening was over, all of the guests discussed problems with their houses that needed fixing. An attorney was one of the dinner guests and suggested a class-action law suit. The next day the entire new home community was mobilized, and by the time the secretary's boss got to work on Monday morning, a class-action suit had been filed asking for sales rescissions.

Not only did the home builder have to correct probably many more items than otherwise may have been needed, but a cash settlement and costly attorney's fees impacted quarterly earnings, tarnished its good reputation because of negative media exposure, and sparked action for class-action suits by homeowners in other subdivisions. What makes this crisis even worse is the fact that the homebuilder was one of the first to establish a customer relations department, and was well respected by its customers and fellow builders. However, when employees don't follow company policy, even the best programs can fail.

When you think of customer service, one person who makes excellent points is Lou Holtz, a champion football coach, television analyst and a motivational speaker. Here is what he says about "what our customers mean to us."[1]

- Customers are the most important people in our business.
- Customers do not depend on us, we depend on them.
- Customers never interrupt our work, they are our work.
- Customers do us a favor when they call; we don't do them favors by letting them in.
- Customers are part of our business, not outsiders.
- Customers are flesh-and-blood human beings, not cold statistics.
- Customers bring us their wants; we fulfill them.
- Customers are not to be argued with.
- Customers deserve courteous attention.
- Customers are the lifeblood of this, and every other business.
- Customers are who we are when we're not working (So let's treat them the way we want to be treated ourselves!).

The Boss Sets the Example

Leadership for customer service starts at the very top. Harry S Truman said it best: "The buck stops here." But you also have to let every employee in the organization know the importance of customer service, and empower all employees to act in the best interests of the organization. That is the philosophy of Carl Sewell, who built his Cadillac automobile dealer agency in Dallas into #1 in the world. He wants to turn a one-time car buyer into a lifetime customer. He instills in his employees that the customer is always right, even if she or he is wrong. Several of his commandments include:[2]

- Underpromise, overdeliver.
- Whatever the customer asks, the answer is always "yes."
- No complaints? Something's wrong.

However, not everyone agrees that the customer is always right. Deborah Gardner, president of Compete Better Now!, Phoenix, Arizona, and who speaks professionally on customer service, says, "Customers may think they are right, but in their heart they know they are not always right. It's just a matter of a competitive stance of trying to push your buttons to see what they can get away with. I know, I'm a customer too."

She also advises her sales audiences to think about all of the time, effort, and money that go into converting prospects into customers. "Once they become your customers, do you think your customers are satisfied? Customer satisfaction doesn't always mean customer loyalty," Gardner says. "These days, even if your customers appear completely satisfied with your product or service, 40 to 50 percent of them will leave you and start doing business with your competition. Today, satisfying the needs of your customers by providing fast, efficient service is no longer enough. You must move beyond customer satisfaction and engage your customers in memorable experiences that are consistent with your brand promise."[3]

No CEO did a better job than the late Lord Taylor. He headed Taylor Woodrow, a British conglomerate involved in everything from building nuclear power plants and the English Channel tunnel, to housing developments in the U.K., U.S., Canada and Spain. Following a social function where a friend confronted him about a problem, he sent an edict to all employees that he be sent any customer complaint. Failure to do so would result in immediate termination, whether the employee was a secretary or a division president. Because of his hands-on management style, and empowering his employees to resolve customer problems, within months complaints virtually disappeared.

AMICA, a 100-year-old insurance company headquartered in Providence, Rhode Island believes loyal employees create loyal customers. Some 25 percent of its employees have been with the company for 20 or more years.[4]

Take Customer Service to the Bottom Line

"Consumers who have a positive experience naturally spend more time and money in a store or shopping online," said Glenda McNeal, senior vice president, Retail and Emerging Industries, American Express Merchant Services. "Excellent service is of the greatest importance as retailers work to retain and build their customer base."[5]

Just as good customer service will build a business, and often allow a company to charge more for its products and services than the competition, bad customer service affects profits. Several years ago, McDonald's learned that rude employees cost the company an average of $60,000 in lost sales at each restaurant. This amounted to an annual corporate loss of $750 million.[6]

In one Shoe comic strip, the creator had one character saying, "My boss said that I'm rude, have a bad attitude, and lousy people skills," and the response was, "So that's how you got promoted to customer service!"[7]

New York City fired the head of its customer service office for an essay he posted on the Internet. Fletcher Vredenburgh said he was responsible for handling complaints from "griping, often whining, often stupid New Yorkers."[8]

Some 80 percent of adults polled in a 2007 Harris Interactive poll vowed never to buy from the same company after a negative experience, up from 68 percent in 2006. Pushed to the point of absolute frustration with customer reps online and by phone, 28 percent said they cursed and 19 percent admitted to shouting. The poll showed regional differences, with 83 percent of Westerners saying they will never do business again with the offending company. Southerners are least likely to swear, but 12 percent fantasized about picketing or defacing the company's headquarters. The biggest swearers were 34 percent of the people in the Midwest. In the Northeast, the respondents were unlikely to get emotional, file a complaint, or give a bad review, but just take their business elsewhere.[9]

A poll of 2,013 adults several years earlier by the Public Agenda, a New York based nonprofit organization, said a lack of respect and courtesy in the U.S. is a serious problem, and 61 percent said it only keeps getting worse. The organization reported that poor customer service had become so rampant that it caused nearly 50 percent of those surveyed to walk out of a store.[10]

Modern technology has virtually destroyed the personal touch of customer service. The average American business executive spends some 60 hours a year on hold according to a survey in 1998 by the firm Accountemps. The daily total of 17 minutes was up two minutes over a previous survey in 1993, and you can imagine what it would be today. Many companies have caller ID and sophisticated software that lets them know in nanoseconds whether they are talking with a Bill Gates or a store clerk. "For me, the most frustrating thing is that you can never get a person if you have some question you want to ask," says Dale Myers, a Philadelphia advertising saleswoman.[11]

Modern technology also has made it possible for the consumer to be heard. Angry consumers who cannot get satisfaction from a company now post their complaints on blogs or websites such as The Consumerist (www.consumerist.com) where they can share their problem with hundreds of thousands, or even millions of potential customers. Some have videotaped their problems to post on You Tube (www.youtube.com).

In its cover story on customer service, *Business Week* magazine wrote that 2007 will be the year fed-up consumers finally dropped the hammer. In a story titled "Consumer Vigilantes," the subhead was most appropriate: "Memo to Corporate America: Hell now hath no fury like a customer scorned." The magazine cited numerous case histories of how consumers fought back from actual near violence to get attention in an office, to posting on the web shortcut telephone numbers to quickly reach a live person at a call center.[12]

Dr. Leonard L. Berry, one of the gurus of customer service, is a professor of marketing at Texas A&M University and the author of *On Great Service* and *Discovering the Soul of Service*. He lists the following as the top 10 customer service complaints:[13]

1. True lies. Blatant dishonesty including selling unneeded services or quoting fake, low estimates.

2. Red Alert. Companies that assume customers are stupid and treat them accordingly.

3. Broken Promises. Service providers who do not show up on time or provide poor service.

4. I Just Work Here. Employees who are not empowered to resolve the problem.

5. The Big Wait. A line made long because too few checkout lanes are open.

6. Automatic Pilot. Impersonal, going-through-the-motions non-service.

7. Suffering In Silence. Employees who don't bother to tell customers how a problem will be resolved.

8. Don't Ask. Employees who seem put out by requests for help.

9. Lights On, No One Home. Clueless employees who can't answer simple questions.

10. Misplaced Priorities. Workers who conduct personal business while the customer waits.

Respond to Every Letter, E-Mail, Fax and Phone Call

Joan Short is president of WorldWide Golf & Travel, Inc., a travel agency in Newport Beach , California. Firms like hers are the lifeblood of cruise lines and tour operators. Most of Short's clients want, and are willing to pay for, exceptional service. They look to her for guidance, and not the Internet for the best discount price. She booked one of her clients in the penthouse suite on Celebrity Cruises' luxury Azamara Journey, a ship that has only 355 staterooms. When her client returned from what was described as a "cruise out of Hell," she wrote Celebrity's president, Daniel J. Hanrahan, detailing the problems and letting him know it was the first time in her 16 years in the business that this had happened.

Hanrahan never had the wherewithal to respond to Short. The job was assigned to an "executive representative," a Beverly Boys-Brown, who eventually did contact her. Short asked that an apology be sent to her client. Then another "executive representative" sent a letter to her client with a $700 certificate for his next cruise on the Azamara. "It was not much of a letter, and my client has vowed never to again sail on the Azamara," said Short. "He asked that I mail the certificate back to the president which I did."

The author e-mailed customer service at Celebrity Cruises and Lyan Sierra-Caro in public relations at publicly-held Royal Caribbean International, which owns Celebrity, asking for the company's response to this case history. No one from public relations responded, but Faye Miles, another "executive representative," sent an apologetic e-mail. Royal Caribbean makes it impossible to respond to any "executive representative." None have personal e-mails, which is rare for any "executive" so empowered and in authority, but only a generic e-mail address that is always answered by another and different "executive representative."

The failure to communicate will cost Royal Caribbean, and all of its brands, untold revenues in the future from Short, and her clients, friends, and contacts in the business.

Too Many Complaints? Fire the Customers!

During the summer of 2007, and at the same time that Sprint Nextel Corp. launched an advertising campaign to attract new customers, the company disconnected more than 1,000 customers for complaining too much. "These customers were calling customer service lines to a degree that we felt was excessive," says Roni Singleton, public relations manager of corporate communications. "In some cases they were calling hundreds of times a month for a period of six to 12 months on the same issues even after we felt those issues had been resolved.

In December, the company named Daniel R. Hesse as CEO and he believed customer service was going to be one of his biggest challenges. In his very first operations meeting with senior management he saw that this subject was not even on the agenda. It now is the first issue discussed. Since merging in 2005, Sprint Nextel has ranked last among the country's five major wireless carriers in annual customer service surveys by J.D. Power & Associates.[14]

Listening and Gate Guardians

Jim Cabela, vice chairman of the board of Cabela's Incorporated, Sidney, Nebraska, takes several hours each week to read and respond to letters and e-mails sent to him by customers. His senior managers do likewise. This is probably why the company has become the world's foremost outfitter, and is always ranked among the top for customer service. He also has taken ideas suggested by customers and profitably incorporated them into the business.

"Customer service is definitely the backbone of our business – a backbone that bends but won't break," says Cabela. "Superior service gives you an edge keeping your customers. Having a superior product is also very important, but without the superior service to back it up, your customers will go someplace else where they can get the same product and that little something extra.

"Exceed your customers' expectations. This goes back to the idea of excellent customer service, but it also goes beyond that," Cabela says. "Consumers have grown to expect quality customer service, and to be successful, you must reach beyond those expectations."[15]

Listening is essential to customer service because listening is essential to communicating, negotiating, resolving conflicts, and avoiding crises. Listening ranks as one of Stephen R. Covey's *7 Habits of Highly Effective People.* Unfortunately, too many in American management no longer listen or respond to customers, shareholders, suppliers, or employees.

One successful executive who does listen is Mark Cuban. He was a teenage entrepreneur, his first job was as a bartender, and then he founded a dot.com and computer technology companies. He now owns the Dallas Mavericks professional basketball team, as well as a film and television production company, and a chain of movie theaters. He answers every e-mail sent to him whether it is from a fan, adversary or someone trying to sell him something. Maybe that's why he's worth $2.8 billion.

AT&T once had one of the best customer service operations in the U.S. If you wrote Robert Allen, when he was the CEO, you would get a response from his corporate headquarters in Basking Ridge, New Jersey. If the issue was considered serious enough, his office would follow it up with a personal telephone call. But today, Stanley T. Sigman, president and CEO of wireless at AT&T, does not respond to mail from customers. The response comes from someone saying, "I am in the office of the president." But what can you believe when the woman responding is three time zones away in California from Sigman's office is Atlanta? Who's kidding who about being physically located in the office of the president? Why not just tell the truth?

Don't expect anyone in management at American Airlines to respond, even if you write Ralph Richardi, senior vice president of customer service. All you will get back is a one-way, do not respond e-mail from someone in customer service. You can never respond to or reach that same person again. According to Steve Larnes, who says he is in the executive office of American Airlines, his department answers any correspondence sent to management. "Our managers are too busy with more important things than to respond to letters from customers," he told this author.

For someone setting the example of a CEO who doesn't want to listen, the epitome would be Torstein Hagen, chairman and CEO of Viking River Cruises. According to an unsigned, anonymous e-mail from Viking, "... at this time, and in perpetuity, he [Hagen] will not accept direct contact from passengers or solicitors." Perpetuity can be a long time. Another travel industry executive, Bill Kerby, CEO of Maupintour, Weston, Florida, ignores any correspondence sent to him.

All of these "non-responders" should copy the practice of Mark Cuban and one day they too might be worth $2.8 billion.

At Amazon.com it is impossible to get the name of the head of customer service, or for that matter, any officer. "… there isn't one question you've listed that is answerable," wrote Craig Berman, who leads global public relations for the company, when asked for the name. "For numerous reasons, we do not disclose contact information for employees. We have very convenient mechanisms on the website for customers to contact Amazon with questions." However, the company's phone numbers are generic, the e-mails are generic and if you ask a question the company chooses not to answer you can wait in perpetuity for a response.

The people hired to help the boss sometimes can be a serious problem. Gate guardians who keep a wall around the CEO, and want to know everything about the caller, have been responsible for crises. The field of public relations is all about communications. However, when a journalist wanted to talk to Ray Kotcher, senior partner and CEO of Ketchum, and chair of the Council of Public Relations Firms, he was told by the gate guardian that Kotcher does not take "unscheduled phone calls."[16] When was the last time you "scheduled" a phone call to speak to someone?

Gate guards cost Landor Associates, an internationally prominent design and brand-consulting firm based in San Francisco, the opportunity to do a prestigious and lucrative corporate identity and logo program for the George Bush Presidential Library & Museum. The head of university relations at Texas A&M University in College Station, where the presidential library is located, was putting together a short list of firms to be considered for the project. Both the switchboard operator and an overly officious secretary at Landor guarded management so well that the individual calling to request a capabilities statement and client list could never speak to anyone in authority. The caller gave his name, title and affiliation and what he wanted but could not disclose the fact that the program was for the Bush Library. The director of the library was given complete information packages on several recommended firms. No information on Landor Associates' qualifications and experience was in the package. Today, almost all of the information requested can be accessed on the Internet.

The palace gate guards need to listen to the caller. Donald Keough, former president of Coca-Cola and now chairman of the board of Allen & Company Incorporated, a New York investment banking firm, related the following story in an interview with *Leaders* magazine: "I was calling one of my associates at Coca-Cola – it's a big headquarters, big place. I called up and said, 'This is Don Keough, I'd like to speak to (name of individual).' The secretary on the other end of the line said, 'Who is this?' I replied, 'Don Keough.' And she asked, 'How do you spell that?' I said K-e-o-u-g-h. And then she wanted to know 'What business are you in?' I told her 'I work for The Coca-Cola Company.' She said she would try to get her boss to call me back at some later date." He didn't say how much longer the secretary continued to work for Coca-Cola.

There is one gate guardian whose face I would have loved to have seen when I had a perfect reply. I called her boss, the chairman of a major *Fortune* 100 company and a major philanthropist, and said: "Hello, this is Rene Henry. Is (name) available?" She replied, "Does he know you, Mr. Henry?" I said, "Yes, for about 25 years. We're friends and he also was a former client."

That wasn't sufficient for this secretary. "Who do you work for, Mr. Henry?" At the time, I was immersed in the 1988 George Herbert Walker Bush presidential campaign, so I just answered, "The Vice President." Her voice was so cold it would have frozen water if I had a glass in my hand, when she curtly said, "the vice president of what?" I couldn't resist, and almost laughing, understated, "The United States of America." There was absolute silence. Within five seconds my friend was on the phone, "Rene, how are you?"

When management consultant and author Tom Peters called 13 firms to pose a basic question or to file a complaint, his research turned up everything from great service to being disconnected. He called Yoplait and wanted to know the yogurt maker's stance on bovine growth hormones, and the operator refused to transfer the call. At Ben & Jerry's the same question brought a swift transfer to the public relations department, and an eight-minute discussion on why the ice cream maker shuns the additive. He called IBM to request an annual report and information regarding the annual meeting. He was transferred to stockholder relations, and an enthusiastic operator gave way to a disinterested voice recording. The information he wanted arrived two weeks after the annual meeting.[17]

When Peters called General Motors to ask why it was taking automakers so long to develop electric cars, his request to speak with CEO Jack Smith was denied. He was transferred to the library, then to a non-working number, then cut off. When he called Nordstrom and asked to speak to the CEO about a problem in the shoe department, just one transfer later CEO Bruce Nordstrom was on the line. He listened patiently and promised to fix the problem.[18]

Sometimes it is fun to give the gate guardians some of their own medicine. Management in corporate America and their gate guardians could learn much from Jim Cabela.

Excelling In Service

One organization that is consistently rated for being among the very best in customer service is The Ritz-Carlton Hotel Company. The hotel chain has received all of the major awards that the hospitality industry and leading consumer organizations can bestow. It is the first, and only hotel company, honored twice by the Department of Commerce with the Malcolm Baldrige National Quality Award. Ritz-Carlton and customer service are synonymous

The Ritz-Carlton Credo: The Ritz-Carlton Hotel is a place where the genuine care and comfort of our guests is our highest mission. We pledge to provide the finest personal service and facilities for our guests who will always enjoy a warm, relaxed, yet refined ambiance. The Ritz-Carlton experience enlivens the senses, instills well-being and fulfills even the unexpressed wishes and needs of our guests.

The company's motto is: "We are ladies and gentlemen serving ladies and gentlemen." Three steps of service to be practiced by all employees are:

1. A warm and sincere greeting. Use the guest's name.

2. Anticipation and fulfillment of each guest's needs.

3. Fond farewell. Give a warm goodbye and use the guest's name.

All employees successfully complete training certification to ensure they understand how to perform to the hotel's standards in their position. Each employee will understand their work area and the hotels goals as established in each strategic plan. They also will know the needs of their internal and external customers (guests and employees) so that the hotel may deliver the products and services they expect. Employees treat other employees as customers and practice teamwork and lateral service to create a positive work environment.

The hotel has empowered its employees to know that any employee who receives a customer complaint, "owns" the complaint. Employees are empowered to resolve the problem and to prevent a repeat occurrence. Customer service basics at Ritz-Carlton are instant guest pacification will be ensured by all; react quickly to immediately correct the problem; follow-up with a telephone call within 20 minutes to verify the problem has been resolved to the customer's satisfaction; do everything you possibly can to never lose a guest.

Employees use guest preference pads to record specific needs. Guest incident action forms are used to record and communicate every incident of guest dissatisfaction. Uncompromising levels of cleanliness are the responsibility of every employee. The hotel has employees escort guests, rather than pointing out directions to another area of the hotel, and to be a Ritz-Carlton ambassador in, and outside of the workplace, always talking positively.

The hotel chain says to "smile – we are on stage," and to always maintain positive eye contact and use the proper vocabulary with guests. Words include "good morning," "certainly," "I'll be happy to" and "my pleasure." It also insists on proper telephone etiquette, to answer within three rings with a "smile," and when necessary ask the caller "may I place you on hold?" Do not screen calls and eliminate call transfers when possible.

Most of all, it says, "protecting the assets of a Ritz-Carlton Hotel is the responsibility of every employee."[19]

Satisfaction Guaranteed

In October 1989 Hampton Hotels offered the hospitality industry's first 100 percent satisfaction guarantee, that states if for any reason guests are not completely satisfied with their stay, they will not be expected to pay. On their first day, employees must complete training on the 100 percent satisfaction guarantee and sign a training completion certificate. All Hampton Inns must participate in the program.

Hampton says its research shows that hotel employees take much more pride in their hotel and in their work, knowing that their hotel stands behind its product and service, and guarantees complete satisfaction to every guest. The hotel trains its employees to care about good service and teaches them the five secrets of customer loyalty:[20]

- I'll take care of that for you.
- Take responsibility.
- We want your business.
- Thank you for thinking of us. Thank you for your business.
- Consider it done.

Some years ago I stayed at the Hampton Inn in Wheeling, West Virginia and was awakened early in error by a wake-up call I did not request. After the hotel's standard, complimentary breakfast, I went to check out and was told there was no charge. I insisted on paying something, but the desk clerk said absolutely not.

"Our goal is to provide the best accommodations and service in the lodging industry today," said Edward T. Hitchman III, the general manager. Why doesn't the entire hospitality industry should adopt this guarantee?

Cabela's also has a 100 percent satisfaction guarantee. One loyal customer who has spent more than $12,000 over 20 years, returned a pair of hunting boots he bought four years earlier. There was no tread on the soles, and it was obvious the boots had been worn many times during the four years. The customer complained they just didn't fit right, and Cabela's gave him the benefit of the doubt that his boots just did not feel right for four years, so he was given his choice of a replacement pair or refund.[21]

Avery Comarow, writes in *U.S. News & World Report* about his father going to Sears with a 30-year-old Craftsman mechanical screwdriver. In keeping with the company's no-questions-asked pledge since 1929 to replace any unsatisfactory Craftsman hand tool, he was given a new screwdriver. A number of companies provide customers with lifetime guarantees of their products. L. L. Bean, a company that consistently ranks very high on customer service lists, will provide a replacement, refund, or a charge credit. Le Creuset guarantees its cookware for 101 years. Briggs & Riley will replace a piece of luggage with a reconditioned one if it cannot be fixed.[22]

Even the Government Has Customer Service

Federal, state and local governments all talk about customer service but few practice what they preach. At some government offices, customer service is an oxymoron. Today, public demands for quality service are at an all-time high, trust in government is eroding, and the public's willingness to pay for services through taxes and fees is dropping.[23]

Quality of service from a government department or agency will vary from office to office, and also from administration to administration. In 1992, when Marvin Runyon was named the 70th Postmaster General, he inherited an organization that suffered from media critics, late night comedians and increased violence among its workforce. He placed an emphasis on customer service, and to head communications, he hired Larry Speakes, the White House press secretary under President Ronald Reagan from 1981-1987. "To me, communications is the most important thing you do in business. If you can't communicate with your employees, your customers, your suppliers – then you're not going to do a good job," Runyon said.

During his six years heading the U.S. Postal Service, he reduced staff by 46,000, rejuvenated marketing, instilled a sprit of pride and competitiveness and converted the post office into a thriving business with three successive years of billion-dollar-plus profits.[24] In 2001, Jack Potter, a career postal employee, was named the 72nd Postmaster General. Management at USPS no longer communicates the way Runyon's team did, and customer service today all too often is non-existent. Internet blogs suggest Congress remove "service" from the USPS name and the slogan "we deliver, we deliver" is false advertising.

EPA Philadelphia - A Role Model for Governments

The mid-Atlantic States regional office of the U.S. Environmental Protection Agency in Philadelphia is a role model all government agencies should try to copy. The importance of personal communications skills and customer service is exemplified by the region's established policies.

"Our surveys of Congressional offices and state agencies consistently showed that prompt replies to call and mail were much preferred to more "perfect" replies that took days or longer. Why? The survey results, and my 35 years of government experience, tell me that people value a caring attitude at least as much as the specific information provided in response to their inquires," says Lawrence Teller, the region's senior communications advisor. "Even better is knowing what people are concerned about, and letting them know what EPA knows, even before they ask. The Internet and related technologies provide the means to service this 'right to know' approach."

The office was the first EPA region that established a sizeable cash award to recognize the outstanding customer service performer each year. Here are just a few practices established by the region's office of communications and government relations that serve as a model for everyone:

- Respond to all phone calls before, and no later than the end of the next business day, and preferably the same day. If the individual called cannot personally respond, then an associate should follow through.

- Respond to all letters, faxes and e-mails within 72 hours. E-mails should be responded to preferably within 24 hours. Give an interim reply when there is a good reason that a complete answer is going to be delayed.

- The voice mailbox should be updated weekly and always when on travel. Many employees updated their voice mailbox daily.

- When on travel or vacation, an "out of office" response should be left for e-mails, and preferably with someone as an emergency contact.

Teller, who spearheaded customer service not only for the region, but as the lead for all EPA regions, says additional principles of the organization's customer service include several later adopted by EPA's customer service steering committee as EPA's Six Principles of Customer Service:

- Be helpful! Listen to your customers.
- Respond to all phone calls by the end of the next business day.
- Respond to all correspondence within 10 business days. (Headquarters and the other regions would not adopt the 72-hour policy of the Philadelphia region).
- Make clear, timely, accurate information accessible.
- Work collaboratively with partners to improve all products and services.
- Involve customers and use their ideas.

Telephone Etiquette and Customer Service

A voice on the telephone often is the first impression a future customer, stakeholder, or potential client has of a company or organization. The tone, pleasantness, and politeness of the individuals in their telephone communications are responsible for the image the company projects to the public.

No company wants the reputation of being arrogant, rude, or uncaring, yet many do, because of the way employees handle telephone calls. CEOs need to asses the way calls are handled in their own organizations. Some organizations even block public access by not listing telephone, fax or e-mail addresses on the letterhead of some corporate executives. This practice only heightens problems and speaks volumes about the company's attitude towards customer service.

Here are tips for good telephone etiquette:

- Return all phone calls promptly.
- For whatever reason, if a call cannot be returned, have an associate respond.
- For voice mail, your greeting should include your name, the day and whether or not you are in town that day. If you plan to be out of town, let the caller know when you will return or refer to an associate with an extension number. Voice messages should be changed daily and at a minimum once a week.
- Never have another person place a call for you.
- Be sure all employees understand the organization's policy.

- Don't screen any phone calls. The only possible exception might be the most senior executive. Employees who work for tax-payer-supported organizations should take all calls without question.

- Always be courteous and say "please" and "thank you."

- If you're calling someone, give the secretary or receptionist your name. If you're not known to the individual you're calling, also give your title and the name of your organization.

- Identify yourself by name when you answer the phone. In large organizations it's also a good idea to identify your department.

- If it is late in the day, and calls can't be returned because you are in a meeting, have an associate or secretary return the call, and let the caller know when you will be able to return the call. If the call is important, give the caller your home number or ask the caller for his or her home number.

- It is important to let the caller know when you can return a call. An extended meeting may prevent a call from being returned one day, but let the caller know if you will be in meetings the next day or even going out of town.

- News media representatives work on tight deadlines. All media calls should be returned promptly, or immediately referred to the public relations office for response.

- Keep a log of all incoming and outgoing phone calls with day, date, and time. Then you know exactly when someone called you or when you called someone else. Some go an additional step and note the subject of the call.

- Take accurate and complete messages with the name of the caller, company, time, date the message was received, action to be taken, and the name of the person taking the message.

- If you are not certain how a name is spelled, politely ask the caller to spell it for you.

Summary Checklist

- Return every call and answer every letter, e-mail and fax.

- If the responsibility is delegated, still have the person to whom the first communication was directed respond and say what is happening.

- If you personally cannot respond, ask a secretary, assistant or someone else.

- Never lie or ask an employee to lie, saying "I work in the office of the president" when the person is miles away and may have never even met the CEO.
- Listen.
- Establish customer service principles for your organization.

Endnotes

[1] Lou Holtz, *Winning Every Day*, HarperBusiness, A division of HarperCollins Publisher, New York, N.Y., 1998.

[2] Carl Sewell and Paul B. Brown, *Customers For Life*, Pocket Books, a division of Simon & Schuster Inc., New York, N.Y., 1990.

[3] E-mails with Deborah Gardner, April-May 2008, and www.competebetternow.com.

[4] "The Customer Service Champs," *Business Week*, March 3, 2008, pg. 049.

[5] Kathy Grannis and Scott Krugman, News Release, NRF Foundation, Washington, D.C., January 17, 2008.

[6] Associated Press, "Rude employees cost McDonald's millions," July 11, 2001.

[7] Chris Cassatt, *Shoe*, December 29, 2007.

[8] Associated Press, "Call this customer service? Hey, it's New York," December 30, 2002.

[9] Sonal Rupani, "I hear America griping," *Business Week*, March 5, 2007.

[10] Matt Crenson, Associated Press, "We're rude, we're crude – hey, like it or lump it," April 3, 2002.

[11] William Bunch, "Call it customer disservice," *Philadelphia Daily News*, Philadelphia, Pennsylvania, August 8, 2001.

[12] Jena McGregor, "Customer Service Champs," "Rebel With A Stalled Cause," and "Consumer Vigilantes," *Business Week*, March 3, 2008, pgs. 037-052.

[13] Ibid.

[14] Reuters, "Sprint ditches customers who complain too much," July 9, 2007; Associated Press, "Sprint disconnects customers who complain too much," *USA Today*, July 9, 2007; E-mail to author from Roni Singleton, public relations manager corporate communications, Sprint Nextel, Atlanta, Georgia, July 10, 2007; Rene A. Henry, "The Customer Service Oxymoron," odwyerpr.com, July 11, 2007; Spencer E. Ante, "Sprint's Wake-Up Call," *Business Week*, March 3, 2008, pg. 054.

[15] David Cabela, *Cabela's – World's Foremost Outfitter – A History*, Paul S. Eriksson, publisher, Forest Dale, Vermont, 2001.

[16] "PR Group Heads Duck Questions," odwyerpr.com, January 15, 2008.

[17] Ellen Neuborne, *USA Today*, Section B, Pg. 1, May 10, 1994.

[18] Ibid.

[19] www.ritzcarlton.com

[20] "100% Satisfaction Guarantee Workbook," Hampton Inn/Hampton Inn & Suites.

[21] David Cabela, *op.cit.*, pg. 19.

[22] Avery Comarow, "Broken? No problem," *U.S. News & World Report*, January 11, 1999, pg. 68.

[23] Tod Newcombe, "Customer Service, Government Style," *Government Technology*, October 31, 2007.

[24] "Marvelous Marvin Moves the Mail," *The Strategist*, Public Relations Society of America.

CHAPTER 15

CLOSING THE BOOK

As soon as the crisis is over, call a meeting of the crisis team and review every aspect of the crisis and the crisis plan. A number of questions need to be asked:

- Could the crisis have been avoided?
- If yes, how could it have been avoided?
- What needs to be done to prevent it from happening again?
- Was the crisis plan followed?
- If not, what was not followed, and why not?
- What weaknesses can be strengthened?
- Were there any surprises?
- What changes, if any, need to be made to the plan?

What has been done to communicate with employees, stakeholders and vendors?

What needs to be done to reestablish or rebuild the image and reputation of the company, organization, institution, or individual?

Next, the team needs to meet with the CEO and other selected members of senior management. Learn from the crisis. Following the meetings, the crisis plan should be updated or revised accordingly. There should be discussion whether or not additional individuals should be added to the crisis team, or to replace any existing members.

While the crisis may be over, the memory of the crisis can remain for decades, especially if victims are involved. Depending on the nature of the crisis, be prepared for it to be the subject of a television drama, feature motion picture, or movie for television. It also could be a book, a chapter in a book, or cited time and again in various electronic media.

How to deal with continued exposure needs to be discussed not only with the crisis team, but the public relations team. The team needs to review the mission statement and strategic plan and specific public relations and communications activity plans. Amendments may be needed, and the public relations plan may need to be reprioritized in the wake of the crisis. Consider having a research organization conduct focus groups or a public opinion poll to determine the seriousness of any damage to brand image or corporate reputation.

As a followup, stay in contact with all involved publics. This will vary whether it is a for-profit company, a college or university, a nonprofit organization or an individual. Be sure to let the important media that reported on the crisis know what steps have been taken to prevent such a crisis from happening again.

And remember the Chinese proverb that in every crisis there is an opportunity.

INDEX

1984 Olympic Games, 206
9/11, 2, 5, 10, 31, 90, 152, 154, 186

ABC, 47, 75, 107, 107-109, 155, 189, 192, 193
Abrams, Floyd, 107
Academy of Motion Picture Arts and Sciences, 14
accepting responsibility, 20, 26, 54, 86, 176, 210, 216, 238
Accountemps, 287
acid rain, 14
acrylamide, 89, 90
Acts of Mother Nature, 11
Adams, Marilyn, 162
Adelphia, 115
Adelphia Communications, 16
administrative waste, 255
advocacy research, 44, 49
AEP, 15
Afran, Bruce, 223
African-American Clayton Baptist Church, 263
Ailes, Roger, 46
airlines, 7, 151-161, 176
Airline Deregulation Act, 153, 157
Air India, 161
Air Transport Association, 157
Al-Qaeda, 11
Alaska Airlines, 164
Albino, Judith E. N., 235
Alinsky, Saul D., 26, 45
Allegheny River, 128
Allen, Robert, 290
Allen & Company, 291
Alliant Group, 163
Alsop, Ronald J., 21, 23
Alta Dena Dairy, 108
Alton, Travis, 279
always tell the truth, 19, 26, 63, 86, 210
Amateur Sports Act of 1978, 224
Amazon.com, 291
Americans With Disabilities Act of 1990, 13, 184, 186
American Academy of Achievement, 97
American Academy of Orthopaedic Surgeons, 85
American Airlines, 153, 159, 290
American Bar Association, 122
American Chemistry Council, 95, 96
American Civil Liberties Union, 203

American College of Surgeons, 74
American Electric Power, 14
American Express, 286
American Lawyer, 75, 76
American Motors Corporation, 131
American Red Cross, 189
American Society of Newspaper Editors, 122
AMICA, 286
Anderson, Martin, 254
Anderson, Warren, 56
Animal Liberation Front (ALF), 11
Anker, Reed, Humes, Schreiber & Cohen, 165
Antarctic, 170, 172
anthrax, 13, 14, 31
anti-development activists, 11
anticipate, 18
AOL/Time Warner, 115
Aramony, William, 74
Argue, John, 206
Arledge, Roone, 109
Armstrong, Henry Clinger "Hank", 222
asbestos-related liabilities, 9
asbestos contamination, 9
Ashland Oil Company, 127-143
Ashlock, Jim, 274, 278
Associated Press, 105, 106, 122, 153, 161, 214, 271
AT&T, 115, 116, 121, 290
ATA, 157, 158
Atlanta Falcons, 215
Auburn University, 218
Azamara Journey, 288

B-roll, 38, 100
Babyak, Edward, 140
background, 58
Baer, William, 75
Baktis, Marina, 82
BALCO, 216
Baldwin, Alec, 83
Baldwin, Sandy, 228
Barnes, Jim, 172
Barnett, Susan, 108
Barrett, Coleen, 165
Battelle Institute, 134, 136, 139, 153
battery-powered radios, 51

Bausher, Jason, 225
Bay Area Laboratory Co-operative (BALCO), 216
Beatrice Foods, 8
Beilein, John, 221
Belichick, Bill, 222
Bell, Justice Roger, 111
Bell South, 115, 121
Bennett, Phil, 218
Benson, Julie, 172
Ben & Jerry's, 292
Berezhnaya, Yelena, 229
Berkey, Edgar, 138
Berlioux, Monique, 206
Berman, Craig, 291
Bernstein, Jonathan, 22, 32, 35, 64, 87, 89, 163
Bernstein Crisis Management, 22, 32, 35, 87, 89, 163
Berra, Yogi, 68, 229
Berry, Leonard L., 287
Beverly, John, 271
be flexible, 40, 51, 61
be in control, 53, 61
Bhopal, 5, 56, 95
Biomet, 84
Bivin, Teel, 279
Black, Clint, 82
Black's Law Dictionary, 105
Blackmun, Scott, 227
Blackwell Sanders Peper Martin, 118
Blair, Tony, 15
Blake, Norm, 227
Block, Philip, 137
Blunt, Roy, 122
Bogas, Kathleen, 191
Bollinger, Lee, 119, 120
Bonds, Barry, 213, 215
Bon Vivant, 7
Borovoy, Roger, 70
Boston Legal, 8, 189
Bowen, Ray, 264
Boys-Brown, Beverly, 288
BPetrolium, 15
Bradley, Mayor Tom, 206, 207
Braniff Airlines, 159
Braun, Jeff, 24, 42
Bray, Sarah Hardesty, 233
Brennan, Christine, 230
Brennan, Tim, 82
Bressler, Richard, 75
Brest, Paul, 70
Bridge, Bobbe J., 71
Bridgestone, 5, 85-88
briefing book, 37, 38, 48
Briggs & Riley, 295
Brill, Steven, 75
Brinkley, Christie, 83, 84
British Petroleum, 15
Brockovich, Erin, 9
Brodeur, Nicole, 92
Brodhead, Richard, 253
Bronx District Attorney's office, 91
Brookhaven National Laboratory, 83
Brown, Laura, 164
Browne, John, 15
Brushy Community, 263-266, 268, 270, 273, 278-279
bullying, 181, 182, 187, 189, 196

Burma, 12, 151
Burnett, Carol, 109, 110
Burson, Harold, 233, 235
Burson-Marsteller, 2, 31, 233, 235
Bush, George H. W., 46, 64, 68, 155, 218, 234, 278, 292
Bush, George W., 68, 90, 156, 273
Bush, Jeb, 231
Bush Presidential Library, 269, 274, 278
Business Wire, 40
Byrne, Bill, 218

Cabela, Jim, 289, 292
Cabela's Incorporated, 289, 292
Cable & Wireless, 116
Cain, Delmar, 276
California Institute of Technology, 254
California Sports, 234
California State University, Monterey Bay, 247
Calleia, Anton, 206
calling tree, 35, 36, 48
Campbell, Ben Nighthorse, 228
Campbell, Chad, 110
Cannon, Howard, 157
Capital Cities-ABC, 107
Carey, Jim, 70
Caribbean Broadcasting Union, 120
Caribbean News Agency, 121
Carlisle, Elizabeth, 166
Carnegie-Mellon University, 131, 254
Carnival Cruise Lines, 166, 169
Carson, Rachel, 14
Carter, Jimmy, 157, 205
Carter Ledyard & Milburn LLP., 23, 113
Carthage College, 232
Caryle, Thomas, 63
Casey, Robert P., 128
Castro, Fidel, 208
Catlett, Gale, 221
CBS News, 109
CBS Sports, 232
celebrity, 81, 101
Celebrity Cruises, 167, 168, 288
Celeste, Richard, 130
cellphone, 42, 43, 49, 53, 58, 193
Centers for Disease Control and Prevention, 169
Center for Corporate Response Ability, 141
Center for Risk Communication, 47
Central Michigan, 230
Chaffee, John, 137
challenge and opportunity, 6
Chambers, Tom, 71
Chandler, Ken, 75
Charlton, Kathy, 225
Chavez, Cesar, 3
Chavez, Hugo, 57, 98
Chekroun, Vanessa, 82
Chemerinsky, Erwin, 253
chemical industry, 95
Chemical Manufacturers Association, 95
Chemical Safety and Hazard Investigation Board, 96
Cheney, Dick, 9
Chertoff, Michael, 160, 161, 202
Chicago Bears, 93
Chicago Mercantile Exchange, 82
China, 5, 11, 12, 93, 94, 160, 161, 175, 230

Cho, Seung-Hui, 250
Chowan College, 232
Churchil, Sir Winston, 19
CIA, 31, 218
Cingular, 121
Citibank, 20
Citigroup, 20, 21
Citius Altius Fortius, 225
Civil Action, A, 8
Civil Rights Act of 1964, 13, 184
Civil Rights Act of 1991, 184
CJR, 112-123
Clarke, Darren, 110
Clarke, Heather, 110
Clayton Baptist Church, 263, 264
Clemens, Roger, 216
Clery, Ben, 251
Clinton, Bill, 60, 64, 68, 76, 185, 200
clipping service, 22
close the problem, 7
closing the book, 141, 301
Coalition for an Airline Passenger's Bill of Rights, 153
Coca-Cola, 23, 291, 292
Cogan, Phil, 96
College of Fellows, 248
College of William & Mary, The, 2, 69, 76, 77, 231, 249
Columbia Journalism Review, 3, 112, 123
Columbia University, 118, 119, 254
Columbine, 5
Columbus, Ohio, 14, 134
Comarow, Avery, 295
Comcast, 115
command center, 39, 40, 43, 49, 51, 53, 162, 163
CommCore Consulting Group, 53
common sense, 1, 3, 32, 81, 88, 283
communicate, 3, 18, 26, 36, 77, 100, 143, 289, 293, 295, 301
Compaq Computer Corporation, 234
compassion, 24, 26, 54, 61, 85, 107, 280
Compete Better Now!, 175, 285
compressed video, 54
Condron, Robert S., 234
conflicts of interest, 71, 92, 227, 228, 230, 255
Conney, Janet, 187
Constantine, Jason, 162
Consumerist, The, 287
consumer confidence, 31
consumer confidence index, 31
Conyers, John, 193
Cooper, Chuck, 254
Cooper, Roy, 253
coordinate with others, 86
Copeland, Kenneth, 93
Corcoran, William M., 9
Cornell, 254
Corniche Travel Group, 157
corporate America, 16, 57, 108, 246, 287, 292
correct misinformation, 22, 26
Cosgrove, Peter, 56
Coulter, Megan, 188
Council for Advancement and Support of Education, 233
Council of Public Relations Firms, 291
court of public opinion, 9, 21, 24, 69, 73, 81, 86, 133, 143, 247
Court TV, 75, 76
Covello, Vincent T., 47

Covey, Stephen R., 25, 290
Cox, 115
Cox, James, 64
Craftsman, 295
Crandall, Robert, 153, 159
credentials, 40
credibility, 18, 20, 24, 25, 52-54, 63, 65, 73, 200
crisis
    definition, 5
    five generic, 10
    managing, 51, 61
    prevent, 18
    resolve, 7
crisis book, 48
crisis management, 1-7, 10, 16, 18, 22, 32-35, 48, 69, 70, 78, 131, 141, 181, 217, 247, 261
crisis manual, 48
crisis plan, 2, 10, 16, 22, 31, 32, 34, 35, 44, 45, 51, 53, 76, 162, 164, 168, 170, 181, 258, 260, 301
crisis team, 2, 12, 18, 31, 33, 36-41, 48, 51, 143, 258, 260, 301, 302
    activities, 41
Cronkite, Walter, 46
Crucial Communication Group, LLC, 24, 42
cruise line, 17, 151, 166-170, 173, 176
Crystal Cruises, 173
Crystal Serenity, 174
CSI, 8
Cuban, Mark, 290
Cunningham, Brent, 114
customer service, 2, 7, 33, 151, 152, 156-158, 171, 173, 176, 199, 209, 283-291, 293, 295, 297, 299
Cutler, Lloyd, 205
Cyclone Nargis, 11

D.C. sniper, the, 5
Dachtler, Cynthia, 164
Daily Show, The, 7
Dale, Lynn, 108
Dallas Mavericks, 290
Daniels, Charles N., 194
Dartmouth University, 254
Dateline NBC, 106
date rape, 243
Davie, Bob, 218, 219
Dawn Princess, 166
Dayan, Moshe, 207
dealing with an angry public, 25, 43
DeCristofaro, Anthony, 74
deep background, 58
DeFrancesco, John, 52
DeGeneres, Ellen, 82
Dektar, Clifford, 234
DeLay, Tom, 57, 122
Department of Homeland Security, 10, 42
DePuy Orthopaedics, 84
Dershowtiz, Rana, 226
Detroit Pistons, 191, 221
de Jong, Peter, 151, 176
de Rossi, Portia, 82
Diack, Lamine, 215
Diet Pepsi, 38
Dilenschneider Group, The, 52, 113
discrimination, 12, 13, 35, 36, 181, 184, 185, 186, 187, 188, 194, 196, 197, 213

Discrimination in Employment Act of 1967, 13, 184
Disney, 9, 75
Disney/Touchstone, 8
Disney's Magic, 169
Disney Cruise Line, 169
Ditka, Mike, 93
Dodd, Mike, 228
Dolan, James, 190
Dollar, Creflo, 93
domestic violence, 183
Dominguez, Cari, 185, 186
don't restrict access, 65
don't withhold information, 65
Donaghy, Tim, 221
Donaldson, Sam, 47, 109
Doonesbury, 8
Dow Jones, 107
Dr. Phil show, 165
Duke lacrosse team, 254
Duke University, 253, 254
DuPont, 15
Durst, Douglas, 69

E-coli, 5, 17, 94, 99, 100
Earp, Naomi Churchill, 13
Earth First, 11
Earth Liberation Front (ELF), 11
Eastern Airlines, 159
Ebbers, Bernard, 16
Ebbert, Kyla, 164
Ebbert, Michele, 165
Eckert, Robert, 94
eco-sabotage, 11
eco-terrorism, 11
Edelman Public Relations, 52, 58, 63, 101
EEOC, 12-13, 35, 184-186, 193-195
Eisner, Michael, 116
Electronic Freedom of Information Act, 60
Ellis, Ruby, 275
Ellison, Tedi, 234
Emmert, Mark A., 92
Emory University, 254
Enron, 5, 16, 60, 71
environmental pollution, 14
EPA, 8, 9, 15, 61, 95, 130, 134, 136, 139, 209, 272, 277, 296, 297
Episodic Public Relations, 65
Equal Employment Opportunity Commission, 12-13, 35, 184-186, 193-195
Equal Pay Act of 1963, 187
Erbitux, 17
Eric Mower and Associates, 32, 33
Erin Brockovich, 9
establishing credibility, 18, 24
Estrella, Matt, 222
ethics, 3, 71, 78, 91, 106, 107, 112, 123, 216, 220, 221, 227, 230, 236, 245
Evans Group, 100
Everson, Mark, 189
expectations, 26, 243, 247, 289
Exxon, 14, 142, 143
Exxon Valdez, 5, 142, 143

FAA, 152, 154-156, 159, 161, 164
fact sheet, 19, 37, 53

Fairchild/Oppel in Dallas, 55
Fairhurst, Mary E., 71
Fastow, Andrew, 16
FBI, 11, 31, 203, 221
FDA, 17, 38, 89, 100
Federal Aviation Agency, 152, 154-156, 159, 161, 164
Federal Bureau of Investigation. *See* FBI
Federal Communications Commission, 76
Federal Emergency Management Agency (FEMA), 12, 161, 201, 202
Federal Trade Commission, 75
Federation of American Scientists, 204
Feeney, Tom, 231
FEMA, 12, 161, 201, 202
Ferraro, John, 206
Field, Patrick, 43
fight back, 105, 111, 123
Fine, Glenn, 203
Fineman, Michael, 88, 97, 99
Fineman PR, 88, 97-99, 98
Fink, James, 63
Fink, Keith, 82
Firestone, 5, 85, 86, 87
Firestone, Harvey, 85
First Amendment, 23, 70, 77, 105, 107, 109, 113, 119
Fisher, D. Michael, 137
Fitzgerald, Judge Judith, 9
Fitzpatrick, Kathy R., 73
Fitzwater, Marlin, 19, 64
five generic crisis, 48
Fleishman-Hillard, 87
Florida Keys Society for the Prevention of Cruelty to Animals, 205
flying mice, 159
focus-group research, 44
Foerster, Tom, 131, 141
FOIA, 59-61, 153, 248
Food Lion, 107, 108, 109
Footlick, Jerrold K., 248
Ford, 5, 85, 86, 87
Ford, Henry, 85
Ford Explorer, 85, 87
Forman, Jo, 83
Forrest, Carol, 96
Foundation, Bill, 83
Fox, Fanne, 200
Fox, James Alan, 183
Fox, Michael J., 77, 97
Franchione, Dennis, 218, 219
Franken, Al, 70
Franklin, Benjamin, 283
Freedom of Information Act, 59-61, 153, 248
Fukushima, Glen, 88
Funess, Richard, 108
Furyk, Jim, 110

G+A Communications, 75
G.A.P. Adventures, 171, 172
Gage, E. Dean, 264
Gailhaguet, Didier, 230
Gallo, Greg, 75
Gandhi, 283
Gannett Company, Inc., 112, 116, 121
GAO, 161, 250
Gardner, Deborah, 175, 285

Garland, Tam, 263, 278
Gaston, Jerry, 265
Gates, Robert, 218
gate guardians, 77, 289, 291, 292
GCI Kamer-Singer, 55
GE, 75
gender discrimination, 185
General Accounting Office, 161, 250
General Electric, 75
General Motors, 106, 292
George Bush Presidential Library, 263, 265, 271, 291
Georgia Tech, 219
German, Michael, 203
Gilman, Andrew, 53
Giraudoux, Jean, 70
Giuliani, Rudolph, 90, 98
Glass, Jackie, 214
Glass Ceiling Initiative, 185
GMA International, 214
Goines, Ed, 224
going postal, 13
Goldman, Ronald, 214
Goltz, Paul M., 135
Goodell, Roger, 222
Goodwin, Richard N., 114
Google, 23, 115
Gore, Al, 14
Gorney, Carole, 246
Government v. Rohn, 117
Grassley, Charles, 93, 249
Grasso, Richard, 98
Gray's Anatomy, 8
greed, 16, 26
Greenfield, Meg, 65
Greenpeace, 15, 16
Green Bay Packers, 218, 222
Griffin, Michael, 153
groundwater contamination, 84
Grove, Andrew, 70
GT&T, 114-116
Gumble, Bryant, 47
Guo, David, 138
Guyana Telephone & Telegraph (GT&T), 114-116

Hagen, Torstein, 290
Hager, Bob, 276
Hailey, Arthur, 10
Haje, Peter, 76
Hall, Jim, 156
Hall, John R., 55, 127, 129, 132, 133, 143
Halliburton, 9, 192, 193
Hall of Fame Assistance Trust Fund, 93
Hamilton, Joe, 109
Hampton Hotels, 294
Hampton Inns, 294
Hanni, Kate, 153
Hanrahan, Don, 168
Hardage, Ginger, 163
Hardesty, Jr., David C., 259
Hardin-Simmons University, 234
Harned, Patricia, 71
Harper. Charles, 56
HarperCollins, 90
Harris, Tom, 58
Harrison, Walter, 234

Harris Interactive, 24, 286
Hart, Gary, 200
Hartman, Lisa, 82
Harvard Law School, 43
Harvard University, 25, 131, 200, 237, 249, 253, 254
Harvey, Paul, 71
Haskins, Don, 233
have a plan, 18
Hawtof, Gwen, 205
HCL, 195, 196
HCL Technologies, 195
Helmick, Robert, 226, 227, 228
Hemingway cats, 204
Hemolytic Uremic Syndrome, 99
Henry, Rene A., 118, 120, 234, 292
Henry VI, 63
Henry VII, 63
Hesse, Daniel R., 289
Heyward, Andrew, 109
Hicks, Bruce, 163
higher education, 1, 2, 6, 34, 220, 237, 243-252, 255, 257-260
Hill & Knowlton, 25, 64
Hilton, Claude, 75
Hilton, Paris, 84
Hilton Hotels, 84, 116
Hinson, David, 155
Hirsch, Alan, 75
Historically Black Colleges and Universities, 233
Hitchman III, Edward T., 295
HMI Inc., 234
Hoffman-LaRoche, 95
Holdings, Zimmer, 84
Holland America, 169, 170
Holland America's Amsterdam, 169
Holtz, Lou, 284
Homeland Security, 10, 42, 90, 160, 161, 176, 202
Honeywell, 183
Honick, Joseph J., 214
Hooker Chemical and Plastics, 95
Horner, Rob, 189
hospitality industry, 151, 175, 176, 293, 294, 295
Hotel, Wheels, Moneychangers, 10
hotels, 84, 116, 151, 173, 174, 176, 293
Houseman, John, 237
Houston Texans, 218
Hoyt, Michael, 113, 114, 118
Hudson, Henry E., 215
human resources, 1, 13, 33, 34, 36, 41, 184, 185, 194, 195
Hunter, Mark, 112, 115, 116, 117
Huntington, West Virginia, 132
Hurricanes
    Charley, 12
    Frances, 12
    Ivan, 12
    Jeanne, 12
    Katrina, 12, 57, 201, 208

"I'm sorry", 54, 61, 85
IAAF, 215
IBM, 292
Illinois Bell System, 51
image, 5, 10, 14, 15, 42, 54, 69, 77, 97, 99, 105, 112, 113, 123, 134, 176, 184, 186, 189, 196, 213, 229, 255, 270, 273, 297, 301, 302

ImClone Systems, 17
implied consent, 22, 76, 77
Incident, The, 10
India, 11, 56, 95, 195, 199
Indiana Pacers, 221
Indiana University of Pennsylvania, 232
Indian Ocean, 11
Indonesia, 11, 151, 199
Innovative Communication Corporation, 112, 113, 121
Intel, 70
Internal Revenue Service, 91, 189, 222, 229
International Association of Antarctica Tour Operators, 172
International Association of Athletics Federation, 215
International Olympic Committee, 206, 207, 228, 230
Internet, 7, 8, 18, 21, 22, 23, 37, 39, 42, 48, 54, 56, 76, 77, 84, 85, 90, 97, 112, 113, 115, 118, 121, 122, 166, 174, 225, 227, 286, 288, 291, 296
Internet lies, 56
investor relations, 33, 34, 36, 41
InVision Technologies, 156
IOC, 206, 228, 229, 230
IR Magazine, 21
ITT, 112

J.D. Power & Associates, 289
Jackson, Jesse, 253
Jacobs, Martin, 129, 130, 141
Jacobson, Howard A., 118
Jay, John, 91
Jay, Stewart, 70
Jereski, Laura, 107
Joe, Linda, 88
Johnson, Dave, 229
Johnson, Harvey, 201
Johnson, James J., 70
Johnson, James M., 71
Johnson, Lyndon B., 59
Johnson, Scott, 137
Johnson & Johnson, 7, 21, 141
Johns Hopkins, 254
Jones, Jamie Leigh, 192
Jones, Marion, 213, 215
Jordan, Jessie, 217
Jordan, Leland, 217
JPMorgan Chase, 21

Kamal, Muhammad Ibrahim, 207
Kamer, Larry, 55
Kane, Robert, 206
Kapcio, Peter, 33
karoshi, 192
Katonah, New York, 91
Katonah Village Improvement Society, 91
Katrina, 5, 12, 57, 201, 208
KBR, 192, 193, 194
Kean, Bill, 20
Kelleher, Herb, 162
Keller, Ray, 236
Kelly, Charles, 140
Kelly, Gary C., 163, 165
Kelly, Todd, 194
Kennedy, John F., 46, 114
Kennedy, Ted, 47
Keough, Donald, 291, 292
Kerby, Bill, 290

Kerik, Bernard, 90
Kersey, Jesse, 222
Ketchum, 291
Killanin, Lord, 206, 207
Kimmel, Jimmy, 7
Kingsfield, Professor Charles, 237
Kirtley, Jane, 108
Kissinger, Henry, 109, 110
Knight Commission, 219
Kokes, John, 92
Koppel, Ted, 47, 155
Kostoff Mann, Anastasia, 157, 158
Kotcher, Ray, 291
Kountze, Tower, 118
Kozlowski, Dennis, 16
Krimsky, Jr., John F., 227
Kristensen, Hans, 204
Kubiak, Gary, 218
Kupka, Steven M., 118
Ku Klux Klan, 194, 267

L. L. Bean, 295
Lacy, Dan, 128, 129, 143
Laden, Oasma bin, 161
LaMont, Alfredo, 228, 229
Lampe, John, 86
Landau, Denise, 172
Landesberg, Lydia, 91
Landin, Randy Don, 183
Landor Associates, 291
Larnes, Steve, 290
Lauer, Matt, 165
Lautenberg, Sen. Frank, 137
lawyer, 1, 22, 24, 52, 54, 55, 60, 61, 63, 65, 66, 69, 72, 75, 77, 78, 85, 88, 91, 113, 117, 129, 131, 132, 133, 135, 151, 163, 166, 201, 205, 209, 223, 224, 246, 247, 273
Law & Order, 8, 91
Lay, Kenneth, 16
Lazier, Bruce, 132
Lee, Charles, 264
Leffall, Jr., LaSalle D., 74
Lehigh University, 246, 251
Leland, Lt. Cmdr. Gregory, 166
Lennon, Jr., Charles F., 234
Leno, Jay, 7
Letterman, David, 7
Levick, Richard S., 190
Levick Strategic Communications, 190
Levy, Ron, 65, 67, 68
Lewin, Nat, 108
Lewinsky, Monica, 76
Le Creuset, 295
Le Gougne, Marie-Reine, 230
Libby, Montana, 8, 9
libel, 23, 105, 106, 107, 108, 111, 113, 123, 220
Liberty Cable TV, 115
Likens, Peter, 42, 43
Limbaugh, Rush, 97
Lindblad Expeditions, 171
Lindsey, Joe B., 138
Lipcon, Charles, 167
listening, 7, 24, 25, 26, 27, 98, 114, 142, 157, 173, 194, 201, 261, 267, 268, 269, 289, 290, 291, 292, 297, 299
Little, Arthur D., 88
Lockheed Martin, 194, 195

Lockyer, Bill, 89
Long, Louise, 92
Lopez, Steve, 84
Los Angeles Department of Animal Services, 83
Love Canal, 95
Luedtke, Thomas S., 153
Luellen, Charles J., 128, 133
Lukaszewski, James, 63, 72, 73
Lukaszewski Group, The, 63
Luken, Tom, 136
Lutz, William, 57
lying, 16, 19, 20, 38, 71, 76, 78, 91, 153, 213, 215, 237, 238
Lynn, Mauricio, 168

"Mad Cow" disease, 5
Maderia, Rebecca, 38
Madison, Steve, 88
Madison Square Garden, 190
Madsen, Barbara, 71
Madwoman of Chaillot, The, 70
Major League Baseball, 208, 213, 215, 227
Malcolm Baldrige National Quality Award, 293
Mangini, Eric, 222
Mankamyer, Marty, 228
Mankowski, Tina, 92
Manning, Selvage & Lee, 108
Mapp, Kenneth, 117
Marks, Cheryl, 82
Mathis, Mike, 222
Matson, Randy, 234
Mattel, 94
Maupintour, 290
Mayor, Day, Caldwell & Keeton, 277
Mayo Clinic, 85
Maytag Corporation, 227
Mazzullo, Jim, 271
McCabe, W. Michael, 209
McClure, Fred, 274
McCurry, Mike, 76
McDonald's, 89, 111, 112, 123, 286
McGavick, Mike, 208
McGowen, Sam, 188
McGreevey, Jim, 185
McGrory, Brian, 55
MCI, 115, 116
McKenzie, Mike, 219
McMurry University, 232
McNeal, Glenda, 286
media center, 53
Meek, John Martin, 234
Meet the Press, 156
Mejia, Elaine, 274
Merrill Lynch, 20
Meyer, Joyce, 93
Meyers, Gerald, 131, 142
Miami Dolphins, 223
Michel, Gregg L., 173
Micronesia, 151
Middlesworth, Mike, 117
Midwestern State University, 232
Mike Hankwitz, 218
Miler, Brad, 153
Miles, Faye, 288
Milkman, Sam, 89
Miller, F. Don, 206, 226

Miller, George, 226
Mills, Wilbur, 200
Minnesota State University-Moorhead, 251
MIT, 43, 55, 253, 254
Mitchell, George, 216
Mitsubishi Motors Corp., 87
MMAR Group, 107
Mobley, William, 257
Mohawk Indians, 88
Monicagate, 5
monitoring service, 22
Monongahela River, 127, 131, 134
Montero, Laura, 166
Morawski, Michael, 204
More, Sir Thomas, 63, 77
Morris, Dave, 111
Morris, Dick, 200
Mothers Against Drunk Driving, 97
Mount Olympus, 224
Mount St. Clare College, 251
movie, 7, 8, 9, 10, 200, 290, 301
MS Explorer, 170, 172
MS Fram, 172
Mt. Holyoke, 13
Muir, Madison, 188
Mulnix, Michael, 234
murder, 14, 91, 181, 182, 183, 196, 213, 214
Murdoch, Rupert, 90, 116
Murphy Family Farms, 280
Murrah Federal Building, 59
Murray, Patty, 175
Mutts & Moms, 82, 83
Myanmar, 11, 12, 151
Myers, Dale, 287

N.Y. Times v. Sullivan, 105
Nacchio, Joe, 16
Nakayama, Granta, 15
Namie, Gary and Ruth, 187
Narcomey, David, 231
NASA, 153
Nasser, Kathleen, 183
Nathan, Margaret, 234
National, 159
National Basketball Association, 221
National Bureau of Standards, 135
National Coalition Against Domestic Violence, 183
National Crime Victimization Survey, 13
National Enquirer, 109, 110
National Football League, 74, 93, 214, 215, 218, 220, 223,
    224, 256
National Law Firm Marketing Association, 53
National Museum of American History, 96
National Press Club, 109, 254
National Public Radio, 56
National Transportation Safety Agency, 87
National Transportation Safety Board, 156
natural disasters, 6, 11, 12, 151, 246
Nayar, Vineet, 195
NBA, 191, 221, 222
NBC, 47, 75, 106
NCAA, National Collegiate Athletic Association, 217, 218,
    227, 255, 259
    "hit and run" publicity tactics, 235
    Committee on Infractions, 233-236

ethics and breaching of contracts, 236-237
leadership, 256
March Madness, 258
political correctness initiatives, 230-233
selling education, 258
spending, 256
Nedbalek, George, 279
Nehlen, Don, 220
Nelson, Bill, 193
Neri, Mauro, 166
never lie, 19, 54, 63, 86, 210, 299
Newberry College, 232
Newhart, Bob, 159
Newsom, Gavin, 224
News Corp., 90, 115
news media won't comment, 75
New England Patriots, 220, 222, 223
New Jersey Nets, 227
New Orleans, 12, 57, 201
New York Giants, 223
New York Institute for Law and Society, The, 88
New York Internet Crimes Against Children Task Force, 227
New York Jets, 222, 223
New York Knicks, 190, 191
New York Stock Exchange, 98
New York University, 234
New York Yankees, 216, 227
NFL, 93, 214, 215, 220, 222, 223, 224, 256
Nichol, Gene R., 76
Nicolazzo, Richard, 86
Nicolazzo & Associates, 86
Nifong, Mike, 253
Nightline, 155
Nike, 8, 23
Nippon Meat Packers, 280
no-response, 22
Nordstrom, 292
Nordstrom, Bruce, 292
Norovirus, 17, 165, 168
North, David S., 117
Northeastern State University, 232
Northeastern University, 183
Northwestern University, 58
Norwalk Virus, 165, 168
Norwegian Cruise Lines, 170, 171, 172
Notre Dame University, 218, 219, 234
not responding, 77, 283
no comment, 18, 52, 54, 63, 64, 73, 75, 76, 78, 243, 247, 261
no response, 76, 78, 113, 118, 261

O'Brien, Conan, 7
O'Connor, Sandra Day, 189
O'Donnell & Associates, 135
O'Leary, George, 219
O'Neal, Stanley, 20
O'Reilly, Bill, 185
Obama, Senator Barak, 94
Occupational Safety and Health Administration, 13, 95
Odwalla, 98, 99, 100
off-the-record, 57, 58, 61
Office of Federal Contract Compliance Programs, 185
Office of Management and Budget, 9
Ohio River, 55, 128, 131, 135, 137, 138
Oklahoma Natural Gas, 59

Olympiad, 213, 225
Olympic Cellars Winery, 225
Olympic National Forest, 224
Olympic Peninsula, 224, 225, 226
on-the-record, 57, 58, 61
Ono, Masatoshi, 85
Operation Doggy Drop, 83
Opinion Research Corp., 63
Oppel, Pete, 55
opposition research, 44, 49
organize the team, 33
Oscar, 10, 14, 114
overcharging the government, 254
Overkamp, Sunshine Janda, 74
Overload, 10
overtalk, 19, 26, 86
Owens, Susan, 71
Oxley, Michael G., 60

P&O Cruises, 169
Pacific Asia Travel Association, 151, 176
Pacific Gas and Electric Company, 9
Pacific Lighting, 10
Pakistan, 11
Pan American Health Organization, 159, 225
Pan American World Airways, 225
Papantonio, Mike, 15
Parcells, Bill, 222
passion, 24, 154
Paterno, Joe, 220, 237, 255
Paulison, David, 202
Pelletier, Scott, 229
Peña, Frederico, 155
Penn State University, 220, 237, 255
Pension Benefit Guaranty Corp., 159
People Express, 159
People for the Ethical Treatment of Animals, 97, 232
Pepsi, 5, 38
PepsiCo's Frito-Lay Inc., 89
Peroleos Mexicanos (Pemex), 95
Persian Gulf Desert Storm, 23, 65
PETA, 97, 232
Peters, Tom, 292
Peterson, Douglas, 20
Pew Research Center for People and Press, 199
PG&E, 9
Philbin, John "Pat", 202
Philip Morris, 98, 107, 108
phone-sex operator, 3, 112, 113, 114, 115, 116, 121, 122
Piedmont Airlines, 159
pig farm, 263, 264, 269, 270, 271, 274
Piller III, Wylie, 251
Pittenger, Baaron, 226
Pittsburgh Steelers, 220, 223
plan, the, 16, 31, 32, 34, 35, 36, 37, 48, 101, 134, 301
Pocahontas, 231
Poe, Ted, 193
Pohl, Michael, 207
politics and sports, 207
Ponomarev, Valery, 161
Porter/Novelli, 19, 43, 199
Portland Marathon, 92
postal service, 14, 89, 296
Potter, Jack, 296
Powell, Colin, 19, 23, 65, 77

Powell, Jody, 206
Powell, Michael K., 76
Powers, Robert, 15
Pradhan, Dhiraj, 279
pregnancy discrimination, 185
Prescott, Ball & Turben, 132
Preston, Paul, 111
Prevette, Johnathan, 188
Price, Mike, 219
Primetime Live, 47, 108
Prince, Charles, 20
Princess Cruises, 166, 170, 172
Prior, Cornelius, 116
Procter & Gamble Co., 89, 90
Promus Hotels and USF&G, 227
Prosser, Jeffrey J., 112, 114, 115, 117, 120, 121, 122
Prosser-ICC Foundation, 122
provably true, 106
PR Blunders of the Year, 88, 97
PR Newswire, 40
PR Reporter, 58
PSA Airlines, 159
public-opinion polls, 44
public's perception
    changing, 95
Public Agenda, 286
public figures, 106, 109
Public Relations Society of America, 234, 248
public relations team, 37, 40, 64, 163, 164, 184, 302
Purrington, Jr., Roliff H., 277
Puryear, Kay, 90

Queens College, 248
Quindlen, Anna, 161
Quinnipiac University, 73
Quinn Emanuel Urquhart, Oliver & Hedges, LLP, 88
Qwest, 16, 115

R.J. Reynolds, 56
radio, 7, 22, 39, 46, 48, 51, 57, 71, 75, 76, 89, 133, 248, 257
Rather, Dan, 46, 47
Reagan, Ronald, 68, 295
Red Cross, 132, 189, 190, 196
Reed, Martin S., 165
Reed, Stephen M., 247
Regan Books, 90
Rehabilitation Act of 1973, 184
Reich, Robert, 182
Reinwald, General, 56
remorse, 24, 26, 61, 85, 183
Reporters Committee for Freedom of the Press, 108
reputation, 5, 9, 10, 21, 23, 24, 25, 27, 33, 53, 54, 63, 64, 67, 69, 73, 74, 77, 99, 105, 106, 107, 110, 111, 116, 122, 123, 159, 163, 176, 184, 186, 190, 196, 217, 236, 264, 275, 279, 284, 297, 301, 302
Residents Opposed to Pigs and Livestock, 271, 276, 278
respond immediately, 18, 26
Reynolds, Catherine R., 96
Reynolds, Kirk, 223
Rice, Donna, 200
Richardi, Ralph, 290
Richardson, Bill, 83, 84
Richardson, Charles R., 234
Richter, Konstantin, 116, 117
Rigas, John, 16

risk management, 6
Ritz-Carlton Hotels, 293, 294
Roberts, Julia, 10
Roberts, Oral, 93
Roberts, Richard, 93
Robertson, Pat, 57, 98
Rodriguez, Rich, 220, 221
Rogers, Cora, 275
Rogers, Jim, 204
Rogers, Will, 54
Rogge, Jacques, 230
Rogge, Joyce, 163
Rohn, Lee, 116, 117
Roll Call, 122
Roman Emperor Theodosius, 205, 213
Romney, Mitt, 229
ROPL, 271, 276, 278
Rosen, Marc, 83
Rosen-Obst Productions, 83
Rosenthal, Irv, 96
Rouse, Cedric, 263, 276
Royal Caribbean International, 288
Ruffino, Carolyn, 278
Rules for Radicals, 26, 45
Rumph, Mike, 224
Rumsfeld, Donald, 57, 68
Runyon, Marvin, 14, 295
Russell, Mark, 7
Rutgers, 254
Rutgers University-Camden, 57
Ryanair, 162
Ryder Cup, 110

Saigo, Roy, 232
Salé, Jamie, 229
Salinger, Pierre, 46
Salt Lake City, 229
Salvation Army, 132
Samaranch, Juan Antonio, 228
Sanders, Anucha Browne, 190
Sanders, Richard B., 71
Sanders, Sir Ronald Michael, 122
Santayana, George, 1, 142, 208
San Diego State University, 24
San Francisco 49ers, 223, 224
San Francisco Giants, 215
Sarbanes, Paul, 60
Sarbanes-Oxley, 60, 71
Sartor Resartus, 63
satellite, 38, 39, 54, 100, 115, 217
Saturday Night Live, 7
Sawyer, Diane, 108
Schaffer, Al and Ruth, 271, 278
Scherr, Jim, 226
Schiavo, Mary, 154
Schiller, Harvey, 227
Schneider, Roy, 117
Schook, Hardy & Bacon, 234
Schrum, Roger, 134
Schultz, Debra, 205
Schultz, Dick, 227
Schwarzkopf, Norman, 23, 65
Scientology, 76
Scovel, Calvin, 156
Seaboard Farms, 280

Seabourn Cruises, 170
Seattle Marathon, 91, 92
Seattle Marathon Association, 92
Secretary of Homeland Security, 90
Securities and Exchange Commission, 60
Seibel, Darryl, 225
Seif, James, 136
Seitel, Fraser P., 55, 191, 223
Seiz, Allen, 135
Selig, Allan H. "Bud", 216
Seminole Nation of Oklahoma, 231
Seminole Tribe of Florida, 231
Senate Finance Committee, 93
Sewell, Carl, 285
sexual harassment, 12, 13, 181, 185, 187, 188, 189, 190, 191,
    193, 194, 213
    hugging, 188, 189
    kissing, 188
sexual harassment and discrimination, 12, 26
Shakespeare, 63, 68, 77
Shannon, Frank, 234
Shapiro, Steve, 83
Shark, 8
Sharon, Prime Minister Ariel, 98
Sharpton, Al, 253
Sharts, Victoria, 189
Sheraton Hotels, 116
Sherman, Mike, 218, 219
Sherry, Don, 59
Short, Joan, 288
Shula, Don, 223
Shuler, Heath, 223
Sierra-Caro, Lyan, 288
Sierra Club, 96
Sigman, Stanley T., 290
Sikharulidze, Anton, 229
silence is golden, 63
Simmons, Michelle F., 159
Simon, William E., 229
Simpson, Alan K., 107
Simpson, Nicole Brown, 214
Simpson, O.J., 91, 213, 214
Singerman, Martin, 75
Singleton, Roni, 289
Skilling, Jeffrey, 16
Skinner, Larry, 136
Skinner Tank Co., 136
Slade, Margo, 52
Slocum, R.C., 216, 218
Small, Lawrence M., 96
Smilnyak, Norman, 140
Smith, Don, 234
Smith, Jack, 292
Smith, Judy, 64
Smith, Lloyd, 279
Smith, Paul, 89
Smithsonian Institution, 96
Smith & Nephew, 84
Smith College, 13
Society of Human Resource Management, 182
Society of Professional Journalists, 106, 122
soundbite, 22, 37, 46
Southeastern Conference, 227
Southeastern Oklahoma State University, 232
Southern California Gas Co., 10

Southern Methodist University, 218
Southwest Airlines, 162, 164, 176
Southwest Conference, 217, 258
SPCA, 205
Speakes, Larry, 295
Specter, Arlen, 223
spokesperson, 18, 19, 21, 22, 25, 26, 32, 37, 44, 45, 46, 49,
    51, 52, 53, 56, 57, 64, 85, 92, 96, 100, 143, 156, 214, 217,
    274
Sporkin, Stanley, 69, 70
Sprint, 121, 289
Sri Lanka, 11
St. Cloud State University, 232
St. Croix Source, The, 117
St. John III, Burton, 59
St. Regis Mohawk Indians, 88
St. Thomas Source, The, 117
Standing for Truth Against Radiation, 83
Stanford University Law School, 70
STAR, 83
State Farm Insurance, 87
State of Washington, 20, 70, 78, 123, 208, 224
Steel, Helen, 111
Steiner, Bob, 234
Stern, David, 222
Stern, Nathan & Perryman, 234
Stevens, Ted, 225, 228
Stewart, Jon, 7
Stewart, Martha, 17, 91
Stewart, Neil, 21
Stewart, Shelley, 16
Stone, Robert J., 52, 113
stonewall, 18, 19, 43, 54, 69, 85, 98, 123, 132, 134, 137, 143,
    155, 243, 254
Stoorza, Zeigaus and Metzger, Inc., 234
Stoorza-Gill, Gail, 234
stop rumors, 22, 26
Stout, Joe, 195
streaming video, 54
Stryker, Johnson & Johnson, 84
student behavior, 189, 253
stupid things, 81
subprime mortgages, 5
Suckenik, Harold, 69
Sullivan, Timothy J., 2, 69
Sulzberger, Arthur O., 75
Sulzberger, Jr., Arthur, 75
Sumlin, Kevin, 218
Summers, Lawrence H., 253
Susan G. Komen Race for the Cure, 92
Susskind, Lawrence, 25, 43
Sven-Olaf Lindblad, 171
Swank, David, 236
Swartz, Mark, 16
Swayze, Patrick, 82
Swoboda, Frank, 76
sympathy, 24, 54, 61, 73

Tagliabue, Paul, 222
Taliban, 11
Talmud, 63
Taylor, Lord, 285
Taylor Woodrow, 285
teaching assistants, 252, 257
Ted Stevens Olympic and Amateur Sports Act, 224

telephone etiquette, 294, 297
television, 7, 8, 10, 18, 22, 23, 25, 38, 39, 42, 43, 46, 47, 48,
    53, 57, 65, 75, 76, 81, 82, 85, 93, 107, 109, 112, 132, 133,
    142, 155, 159, 165, 169, 186, 200, 217, 233, 244, 248, 252,
    256, 257, 258, 263, 269, 272, 284, 290, 301
Teller, Lawrence, 296
tell the truth, 19, 22, 26, 54, 63, 71, 86, 139, 210, 290
tenure, 190, 227, 228, 246, 252, 257, 279
terrorism, 10, 11, 26, 151
Texaco, 5
Texas A&M Swine Center, 263
Texas A&M University, 60, 61, 216-219, 233-235, 257, 263,
    264, 265, 266, 267, 268, 270-274, 277, 278, 280, 287, 291
Texas Christian University, 165, 218
Texas Open Records Act, 60
Texas Western College, 233
Thailand, 11
The Dubliner, 110
Thomas, Bill, 233
Thomas, Isiah, 185, 190, 191
Thompson, Frederick G., 2, 234
Thompson, Kerr Kelly, 234
Thompson, Richard, 83
Three-Mile Island, 5
Time Warner, 75, 76
Title I, 184
Title V, 184
Title VII, 13, 184
Today Show, 47, 165
Tokyo Chamber of Commerce and Industry, 87
Toledo, Bob, 218
Toliver, George T., 222
Toms, David, 110
tourism, 2, 151, 170, 176
tour operators, 151, 167, 170, 288
Toyota, 192
Transportation Security Administration, 160
Travel, 174
travel, 2, 69, 74, 151, 152, 157, 158, 160, 163, 171, 172, 173,
    174, 176, 177, 233, 256, 288, 290, 296, 297
Trudeau, Gary, 8
Truman, Harry S, 285
Trump, Donald, 88
TSA, 160, 161, 176
Tuberville, Tommy, 218
tuition, 249, 250, 255, 257
Tulane University, 218
Turner, Ed, 52
Turner, Tab, 85
TWA, 5, 159
Tyco International, 16, 60
Tylenol, 5, 7, 21, 141
Tyson, Mike, 213

U.S.S. Ronald Reagan, 166
U.S. Agency for International Development, 61
U.S. Army Corps of Engineers, 51
U.S. Commission on Civil Rights, 232
U.S. Department of Education, 250
U.S. Department of Justice, 31, 84, 140, 203, 209
U.S. Department of Labor, 13, 181, 182, 185
U.S. Department of Transportation, 41, 153, 154, 160, 165
U.S. Environmental Protection Agency, 8, 9, 15, 41, 42, 61,
    95, 130, 134, 136-139, 209, 272, 277, 296, 297
U.S. Food and Drug Administration, 7, 17, 38, 99

U.S. Government Accountability Office, 161
U.S. Olympic Committee, 205, 206, 213, 215, 224, 226, 234
U.S. Olympic Foundation, 226
U.S. Olympic Team, 205
U.S. Patent and Trademark Office, 91
U.S. Postal Service, 59, 88, 89, 296
U.S. Skiing, 227
U.S. State Department, 37
U. S. Supreme Court, 115
Uchino, Kiroko, 192
UCLA, 187, 188, 218
Ueberroth, Peter, 215
undergraduate education, 253
UNESCO, 121
Union Carbide, 56, 95
United Airlines, 160
United Farm Workers, 3
United Nations, 14, 199
United Way of America, 74, 75
University of Alabama, 218, 236
University of Arizona, 42, 218
University of California at Berkeley, 234, 254
University of California at Los Angeles, 187, 188, 218
University of California Irvine, 253
University of Chicago, 254
University of Colorado System, 235
University of Florida, 205, 251
University of Hartford, 234
University of Hawaii, 254
University of Houston, 218
University of Illinois, 230
University of Maryland, 202
University of Michigan, 221, 234
University of Mississippi, 218
University of Nebraska, 218, 234
University of North Dakota, 231
University of Oklahoma, 235
University of Oregon, 189
University of Pennsylvania, 251
University of Pittsburgh, 135, 138, 254
University of Southern California, 253, 254
University of Texas at El Paso, 233
University of Virginia, 227
University of Washington, 70, 91, 92, 251, 254
Untermeyer, Chase, 234
Urbanski, Robin, 160
USA Today, 97, 98, 108, 111, 131, 162, 164, 182, 183, 228,
    230, 231
USDA, 204, 205
USOC, 206, 224, 225, 226, 227, 228, 229, 238
utility company, 17
Utt, Bill, 193
UW Medical Center, 91, 92

Valdez, Alaska, 14
ValuJet, 5, 155, 156
Vance, Cyrus, 207
Vancouver, 170, 226
Vassar, 13
Verizon, 115, 116, 121
Vest, Charles, 55
Vick, Michael, 213, 214
Viking River Cruises, 290
Vincent, Ross, 96
Viniski, Janet, 134

violence, 13, 17, 88, 151, 181, 182, 183, 184, 196, 246, 250, 251, 287, 295
violence in the workplace, 13, 26, 36, 58, 181
Virginia Tech, 5, 250
Virgin Islands Telephone Company (Vitelco), 112, 116
Virgin Island Daily News, 112, 114, 121
Vitelco, 112, 116
Vladeck, Anne, 191
VNR, 38, 48
Vredenburgh, Fletcher, 286

W. R. Grace, 8, 9
Waco, 5
Wade, Catherine, 272
Waksal, Samuel D., 17
Walker, Aaron, 202
Walsh, John J., 23, 113, 118
Ward, Lloyd, 227
Washington, D.C., 13, 14, 31, 69, 83, 96, 109, 160, 190, 208, 209, 234, 254
Washington Post, The, 70, 76, 111
Washington State, 100, 219, 226
Washington State Supreme Court, 71
Watergate, 5, 58, 200
Waters, Marilyn, 169
Watkins, Jack, 206
Weatherup, Craig, 38
Webb, Millie, 97
Weiss, Murray, 221
Welch, Tom, 229
Wellesley College, 13
Wendy's International Inc., 89
Werlein, Jr., Ewing, 107, 273, 275, 278
West, Mary Nan, 274
Westchester County, 91
Western Airlines, 159
West Virginia University, 220, 221, 259
what if…, 18
Wheeler, Tim, 65
Wheeling, West Virginia, 129, 133, 135, 138, 294
when not to fight back, 111
whistleblower, 23

White House, 9, 19, 31, 46, 64, 76, 109, 156, 157, 201, 205, 206, 207, 208, 295
Whitman, Christine Todd, 8
Williams, Bob, 232
Williams, Etta Ruth, 275
Will Rogers, 61
Wilms, Sandra J., 77
Windstar Cruises, 169
Winslow, Kellen, 234
Winter Olympic Games, 229
Wiseman, W. Tom, 132
Wiz, The, 65
WMMR-FM, 89
Wohlschlaeger, Fred, 228
Woods, Elin Nordegren, 110
Woods, Tiger, 110
workload of professors, 252
workplace crises, 181
workplace violence, 13, 181, 182, 183, 184
Work Product Doctrine, 72
WorldCom, 5, 16, 60
WorldWide Golf & Travel, Inc., 288
World Baseball Classic, 208
World Economic Forum, 199
World Trade Organization, 121
Wright, Richard N., 135
WVU, 221, 259, 260
Wynne, Michael W., 204

Yahoo, 115
Yale, 131, 136, 225, 249, 254
YankeeNets, 227
Yoplait, 292
York, Denise DeBartolo, 224
York, John, 224
YouTube.com, 97, 287

Zillgitt, Jeff, 231
Zogby International, 187
Zonolite, 8, 9
Zuckerman, Mortimer B., 200